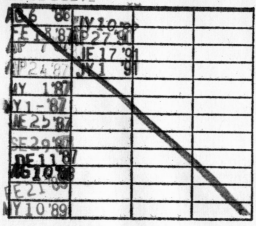

VICE-PRESIDENTIAL POWER

Advice and
Influence in the
VICE- White House
PRESIDENTIAL
POWER

Paul C. Light

THE JOHNS HOPKINS UNIVERSITY PRESS

Baltimore and London

The Johns Hopkins University Press, Baltimore, Maryland 21218

The Johns Hopkins Press Ltd., London

Library of Congress Cataloging in Publication Data
Light, Paul Charles.
  Vice-presidential power.

  Includes bibliographical references and index.
  1. Vice-Presidents— United States. I. Title.
JK609.5.L53   1983   353.03′18   83-48050
ISBN 0-8018-3058-3

Contents

Acknowledgments

A number of individuals helped on this book. I owe thanks to all. First, thanks must go to the various staff members who gave their time for interviews. All cooperated fully and added greatly to this book. I remain convinced that interviews are the best tool for identifying patterns of advice and influence in the White House. Second, the University of Virginia provided both research support and time away from my teaching to complete this book, while the Brookings Institution provided guest quarters whenever I journeyed to Washington. Third, among the many colleagues who offered insight or encouragement on the project were Stephen Wayne, Fred Greenstein, Austin Ranney, James Reichley, Walter Beach, Richard Fenno, Jameson Doig, John Kessel, Charles Jones, and Thomas Cronin. James Young and the White Burkett Miller Center at the University of Virginia also provided intellectual support. Fourth, I am indebted to the political science departments at the University of Iowa, University of Houston, University of Rochester, University of Pennsylvania, and Georgetown University for their combined criticism and suggestions on very early presentations of this work. The opportunity to present my hypotheses to these vigorous faculties proved extremely valuable in refining my work. Finally, thanks should go to a small group of friends who offered their patience as the project moved toward completion: Jeanne Hammer, Paul McWhinney, Mark Light, Lane Marshall Light, Stephen Wayne, Cheryl Beil, and last, but certainly not least, my friend and companion Margo Hauck. Thanks also go to my editor at Johns Hopkins, Henry Tom, who offered support at just the right time, and has shown faith in my work from the very beginning. Sharon Pamepinto and Brian Klunk gave considerable aid as my research assistants.

Because of all this help, the book is much better than it might have been. Despite all the advice and influence, however, I take full responsibility for the book.

VICE-PRESIDENTIAL POWER

1.

Introduction

> Twenty years ago, I wouldn't have advised my worst
> enemy to take the Vice-Presidency. It was God's way of
> punishing bad campaigners, a sort of political purga-
> tory for the also-rans. Now, you'd be crazy not to take
> the job.
>
> — Reagan aide

The past two decades have witnessed two major changes in the American
Vice-Presidency. First, Vice-Presidents have finally joined that small group
of White House aides who act as senior advisers to the President. After two
hundred years as errand-boys, political hitmen, professional mourners, and
incidental White House commissioners, Vice-Presidents can now lay claim
to regular access to the President and the opportunity to give advice on
major decisions. Though Vice-Presidents suffer the same wins and losses as
other senior advisers, they have finally gained the resources for a continuing
advisory role.

Second, if Vice-Presidents now have the staff and the access for an advisory
role, at least one, Walter Mondale, was highly successful in shaping administration policy. Mondale was able to persuade Jimmy Carter on a wide range
of policy decisions—from the appointment of several cabinet officers
(Califano, Bergland) to the rescue effort for the Vietnamese boat people,
from the establishment of the Department of Education to the restoration of
budget cuts in the social services, from the veto of a defense appropriations
bill to a mediator's role in the Camp David peace process.

That is not to say future Vice-Presidents will remain players in national
policy. Vice-Presidents, like all senior advisers and cabinet members, serve
at the President's pleasure. If the next President does not want an activist
Vice-President and does not want to spend time in conference with his
running mate, there is no law or constitutional provision that can compel

1

him to do so. If the next President wants his Vice-President kept in silence at the Old Executive Office Building, occupied as a figurehead director of some minor presidential task force or commission, there is no formal statute to stop him from doing so. If the Vice-President wants a strong advisory role, he is very much the President's instrument, subject to changes in presidential temperament and support. Moreover, if the President fails to give the proper internal signals, the Vice-President is also subject to the moods of the White House staff, few of whom will cede territory to a former (and possibly future) political rival. All in all, as Humphrey once stated, "It's like being naked in the middle of a blizzard with no one to even offer you a match to keep you warm—that's the Vice Presidency" (in *Time*, 14 Nov. 1969).

That said, contemporary Vice-Presidents are not without their own weapons in the battle for policy influence and power—not the least of which are the precedents set by Mondale, Rockefeller, and Ford. Vice-Presidents now have institutionalized access to many of the resources necessary for an advisory role. With increases in staff support, Vice-Presidents have more time and energy to devote to advisory activities. With greater sources of information, Vice-Presidents are better equipped to compete for the President's attention. With the West Wing office and regularized meetings with the President, Vice-Presidents have greater proximity to major policy decisions. Finally, given the increasing White House workload and changing political environment, Presidents now have greater incentives for using their Vice-Presidents in substantive roles. As one Reagan aide argued: "We've been through a ten-year evolution in the Vice-Presidency and there's no turning back. No President can afford to waste an officer who controls that many people and has such a potentially different perspective on national issues." Though the President's goals for using the Vice-President will vary, the basic conditions for a continuing advisory role have been met.

Having this new advisory role does not ensure actual influence over final policy outcomes. Observers must distinguish between the Vice-President's act of *giving* advice and the President's act of *taking* advice. A Vice-President may be able to voice his opinions, but nothing compels the President to accept the recommendations. Though the advisory role is a step toward influence, merely expressing ideas is not sufficient for influence. Both Rockefeller and Mondale were senior advisers to the President, but only Mondale had influence. Thus, this book is interested in two separate questions: *First,* how did Vice-Presidents finally gain an advisory role in the White House policy process? *Second,* why was Mondale more influential in that role than Rockefeller, Ford, Agnew, Humphrey, or Johnson? The first question can tell us a great deal about how institutions evolve and expand within the Executive Office of the President, while the second question can tell us more about patterns of influence and persuasion within the presidential policy process.

WHY STUDY THE VICE-PRESIDENCY?

Although questions of advisory roles and policy influence are interesting and important, why study the Vice-Presidency for answers?

A first answer is simply that the Vice-Presidency is important. In answering questions about advice and influence, we may learn something about an increasingly important office. Whether or not the office is the *best* solution to the problem of emergency succession, it is the *only* solution we are likely to have in the near future. Though Arthur Schlesinger, Jr., has found many faults with the office—prompting him to ask if the Vice-Presidency is "really necessary" (1974)—it remains the first route for emergency succession. We may argue about potential alternatives and vice-presidential nominating systems, but in the realm of real world politics, the office remains firmly fixed in the presidential system.

Moreover, whatever the checkered history of the office, it has become a primary recruiting ground for potential candidates. Like the Senate, the Vice-Presidency is now an incubator of presidential nominees. Of the past twelve presidential candidates, six were former Vice-Presidents. And, though no Vice-President has been elected to the Presidency immediately following his term as second-in-command since Martin Van Buren, the office currently offers greater visibility and access to party leaders than any other national or state office save the Presidency itself. This recruitment pattern is not likely to change in the coming decades. As one Ford aide surmised: "We've entered a long period of one-term Presidents, in which case the Vice-Presidency will become more valuable to the political pros. People seem to be getting tired of Presidents faster, but don't seem to blame Vice-Presidents for any of the problems." Vice-Presidents emerge with all the advantages of other candidates, without the liability of a record. Even with Mondale's extensive activity within the Carter administration, for instance, one observer argued that "there is not one single program in the Carter Presidency that the public could identify as Mondale's. He had plenty of impact, but can't be linked to any of the disasters. No one will blame Fritz for high inflation, even though he had something to do with it." Thus, it should be of some interest to see just what kind of training these potential candidates are now receiving in the Vice-Presidency.

A second reason for studying the office is that there has been a great deal of change in the past decade. The Vice-Presidency now offers a rare opportunity for studying institutional development in the modern Presidency. Ten years ago, Schlesinger wrote that "history has shown the American Vice Presidency to be a job of spectacular and, I believe, incurable frustration" (1974, p. 478). The Rockefeller and Mondale (and perhaps Bush) experiences show Schlesinger to be wrong. Even with his problems, Mondale's Vice-Presidency was different from those of the past. Mondale had the access, information, and support to play a strong advisory role in the

Carter administration. Though Mondale had his share of defeats, he never faced the "deep freeze" that so many past Vice-Presidents suffered. Rockefeller's frustration under Ford came less from the absence of resources than from his defeat in major battles to win control of domestic policy—a battle that never could have been fought in previous administrations and probably should not have been fought by Rockefeller. Yet, even with his eventual defeat and removal from the Republican ticket, Rockefeller won the initial contests. He was able to appoint his staff to key posts on the Domestic Council and was able to generate several major policy proposals. And, as one Rockefeller aide suggested, his ultimate defeat came from "his unwillingness to mop up after he won control of the Domestic Council. He should have cleaned out the council of the Nixon and Ford people and consolidated his victory." Whether Rockefeller could have won such a fight is doubtful. However, unlike his predecessors, Rockefeller was not fighting for airplanes or White House mess privileges for his staff or access to the President. Like Mondale, Rockefeller was operating at a different level from previous Vice-Presidents. He was fighting for *influence,* not just the opportunity to speak. There is little doubt that Rockefeller was frustrated in his effort to shape the Ford agenda. However, his defeat came less from the fact that he was Vice-President and far more from the lack of resources, opportunities, and strategies that all advisers need for influence.

This highlights a third reason for studying the office: Vice-Presidents are enough like other presidential advisers to shed some light on more general patterns of advice and influence within the policy process. Which resources are important for policy impact? Which strategies increase influence? What kinds of cycles affect the advisory process? The study of the Vice-Presidency should help answer some of these questions. There are, of course, several important differences between Vice-Presidents and other advisers. Vice-Presidents are rarely hired for their loyalty, long service, or even expertise. They are usually selected to balance the presidential ticket, to compensate for presidential weakness in specific areas of the country or specific regions on the ideological spectrum. Indeed, according to Nixon aides, Agnew was selected primarily because he was the least threatening of all the vice-presidential candidates. As one aide guessed: "Nixon had to pick someone to run with. Why not Agnew?" Once selected and elected, Vice-Presidents cannot be fired. Unlike cabinet members and White House aides, Vice-Presidents sign on for the duration. Moreover, the Vice-President's effort to build internal influence may be seen as a threat not just to staff territory, but to the President himself. And if the Vice-President is a defeated rival, his speeches may return to haunt him in office, as with Bush's statements about "voodoo economics."

Yet, there are many similarities that make generalization possible. Like cabinet members and other White House aides, Vice-Presidents are almost totally dependent on the President for their support. Like cabinet members and White House staffers, Vice-Presidents must function on the basis of ever-changing customs and practices, with no constitutional mandate in the policy process. Like that of other senior advisers, vice-presidential influence varies at different times and across different policy areas during the term. And though cabinet members and White House aides generally have greater advantages in terms of departmental troops or administrative authority, their ability to influence the national agenda is very much a problem of persuasion, not of formal prerogatives. Cabinet members can make end runs around the President, but like Rockefeller in his effort to win passage of the Energy Independence Authority, they are likely to be cut down by the President or the White House staff. Moreover, like that of cabinet members and the President's staff, vice-presidential impact rests in large measure on the President's personal style. The President's view of the office, his sensitivity to territorial threats, his policy goals, his management style, his willingness to listen to alternatives, even his ability to forgive past campaign insults, all affect the Vice-President's advice and influence (see Fenno, 1959). Finally, like other advisers, the Vice-President's relationship with the President is conditioned by the external political environment. The vice-presidential role is shaped by changing incentives—weakening national parties, lengthening primary campaigns, shifting policy issues and coalitions. Thus, in terms of their dependence on the President, their reliance on evolving roles, their need for an open White House decision-making system, and their responsiveness to changing political incentives, Vice-Presidents are very much like any other advisers who must use persuasion to shape the President's agenda.

VICE-PRESIDENTIAL POWER

If the Vice-Presidency can help us understand advice and influence, what features of the office and occupant should we study? Formal authority or influence networks? Constitutional prerogatives or policy cycles? Advisory skills or historical precedents? Unfortunately, the Constitution and formal prerogatives can tell us little about recent changes in the office. The Constitution only mentions the Vice-Presidency four times: twice with regard to succession, once with regard to presiding over the Senate, once with regard to the term of office. Not much for explaining advice and influence. Though the Constitution tells us why Vice-Presidents are so dependent on the President for support, we need a much more dynamic view of the office if we are to explain the past two decades of change.

One place to start is with Richard Neustadt's (1960) notion of presidential power. For Neustadt, the President's formal prerogatives guarantee little more than a "clerkship" in the Oval Office. As Neustadt argues: "A President, these days, is an invaluable clerk. His services are in demand all over Washington. His influence, however, is a very different matter. Laws and customs tell us little about leadership in fact" (1960, p. 7). The President's status and authority do "give him great advantages in dealing with the men he would persuade. Each 'power' is a vantage point for him in the degree that other men have use for his authority" (1960, p. 27). However, in what remains the most frequently quoted paragraph in Neustadt's book, "The power to persuade is the power to bargain."

> Status and authority yield bargaining advantages. But in a government of "separated institutions sharing power," they yield them to all sides. With the array of vantage points at his disposal, a President may be far more persuasive than his logic or charm could make him. But outcomes are not guaranteed by his advantages. There remain the counter pressures those whom he would influence can bring to bear on him from vantage points at their disposal. Command has limited utility; persuasion becomes give-and-take. It is well that the White House holds the vantage points it does. In such a business any President may need them all — and more (1960, pp. 28-29).

For Neustadt, the President's power to persuade rests on three sources: (1) the vantage points of the office, (2) the President's public prestige, and (3) the President's Washington reputation.

The central question here is whether Neustadt's model applies to the President's own staff, particularly the Vice-President. Neustadt argues that it does, noting that "like our governmental structure as a whole, the executive establishment consists of separated institutions sharing power. The President heads one of these; cabinet officers, agency administrators, and military commanders head others. Below the department level, virtually independent bureau chiefs head many more" (1960, p. 30). What about the White House staff and the Vice-President? Do Presidents have to persuade the staff? Again, Neustadt answers yes: "Some aides will have more vantage points than a selective memory. . . . Any aide who demonstrates to others that he has the President's consistent confidence and a consistent part in presidential business will acquire so much business on his own account that he becomes in some sense independent of his chief. Nothing in the Constitution keeps a well-placed aide from converting status into power of his own, usable in some degrees even against the President" (1960, p. 32). The President must engage in bargaining with virtually all of the players involved in the day-to-day business of government, creating a system that even demands bargaining with the Vice-President.

Yet, some advisers have more internal vantage points, higher prestige, and stronger reputations than others. Power is not equally distributed either inside or outside the White House. The Office of Policy Development and the Office of Management and Budget now have more leverage over domestic policy than other agencies or actors, while the National Security Council and secretary of state control foreign affairs. Though the Council of Economic Advisers, Congressional Relations Office, press secretary, and a number of lesser agencies all share some input on domestic and foreign policy, few have the same store of vantage points (e.g., legislative clearance in OMB), public prestige and visibility (e.g., the President's "inner circle"), or reputation for influence (e.g., Stockman or Regan) as their more powerful competitors. Presumably, less powerful actors have to rely more on persuasion than OMB, the Domestic Council, or the national security adviser. The fewer the vantage points, the lower the prestige, and the weaker the reputation, the more the need for persuasion. Unfortunately, until the 1970s, Vice-Presidents had few vantage points, little prestige, and a poor reputation. They generally entered office with more obstacles to advice and influence than opportunities.

Vice-Presidential Vantage Points

Vantage points are defined as anything an adviser can use to persuade the President. Vantage points rest on an adviser's formal authority or institutional position. They also rest on access to the Oval Office, control of internal resources, and connections to outside constituents. Though vantage points do not create automatic influence, they can be used in the policy process. Perquisites, allies, information, staffs, administrative support, private meetings with the President, can all be applied in the bargaining effort. For Vice-Presidents, there are three kinds of vantage points inside the White House: (1) constitutional, (2) statutory, and (3) institutional.

As noted earlier, the *Constitution* gives the Vice-President only passing notice. Article I, Section 3, states that "The Vice President of the United States shall be President of the Senate, but shall have no Vote, unless they be equally divided." Article II, Section 1, states that the President and Vice-President will hold their offices for four-year terms, etc., and "In Case of the Removal of the President from Office or of his Death, Resignation, or Inability to discharge the Powers and Duties of the said Office, the Same shall devolve on the Vice President." Though there has been some historical dispute over just what the word "Same" meant—the fixtures of the Oval Office or the powers—there is clear agreement that the Constitution gives the Vice-President very few prerogatives. The Vice-President is also mentioned in two Amendments: the Twelfth, requiring the President and Vice-President to run as a team, and the Twenty-fifth, establishing new procedures for determining presidential fitness.

In theory, the Vice-President's position as the only constitutional officer with both legislative and executive roots could be a source of power. In reality, as Gerald Ford wrote only weeks before Nixon's resignation: "The Vice President is a Constitutional hybrid. Alone among federal officials he stands with one foot in the legislative branch and the other in the executive. The Vice President straddles the Constitutional chasm which circumscribes and checks all others. He belongs to both the President and to the Congress, even more so under the Twenty-Fifth Amendment, yet he shares power with neither" (1974, p. 63). The problem is that the legislative branch has never accepted the Vice-President as anything but an interloper. Though Vice-Presidents have unlimited access to the Senate floor, they cannot vote except in the case of ties and do not participate in debates. They do provide information to the White House on legislative problems and share their Senate office with the President's liaison team. However, as we will note in Chapter 2, most vice-presidential lobbying is seen as a breach of Senate protocol. As Senate Majority Leader Mike Mansfield told then-Vice-President Ford in 1973, "Here, presiding officers are to be seen and not heard, unlike the House where the Speaker's gavel is like a thunderclap."

Two hundred years of federal *statutes* do not yield much in the form of vice-presidential vantage points either. As of 1982, the *Federal Code* showed just two formal assignments: (1) membership on the National Security Council and (2) membership on the Smithsonian Board of Regents. When Carter disbanded Nixon's Domestic Council in 1977, the Vice-President lost statutory input on domestic policy. Of the two remaining duties, only the National Security Council assignment can be seen as a vantage point. It serves as a source of information on foreign policy, while giving the Vice-President formal opportunities to participate in decision making. Nixon, for instance, attended 217 National Security Council meetings during his eight-year term as Vice-President, averaging two meetings a month. Though there is no evidence that Nixon used those meetings to win Eisenhower's support for specific policies, the Vice-President is better prepared to advise and influence with more information. The NSC assignment is likely to be more of a vantage point in White House management systems where decisions are made in large, regularized meetings. It is less likely to be a vantage point in free-flowing systems where decisions are made in small, ad hoc gatherings. Regardless of the setting, Vice-Presidents have no formal authority in the role. They cannot call NSC meetings except in the case of presidential disability and preside only at the President's pleasure. And even when emergencies arise, as during Reagan's recovery following the March 1981 assassination attempt, Vice-Presidents generally avoid any hint of usurping the President's power.

Vice-Presidents have been more successful in building vantage points from their *institutional* staff. Before the 1970s, however, Vice-Presidents had to rely on their minor task forces and commissions for staff support. Though the Vice-President's commissioner duties have decreased over the past twenty years, they were once a source of some advantage. Johnson, for instance, used his chairmanship of the Aeronautics and Space Council (not to be confused with NASA) for hiring staff. Since neither Johnson nor Humphrey had any staff guaranteed on the executive payroll, they were often forced to borrow personal staff on detail from departments or agencies. Commissions became an alternative route for expanding the Vice-President's staff. Humphrey used his chairmanships of a number of task forces for precisely that reason. As one Humphrey assistant said, "Those task forces became the only way to develop a substantive staff, especially with Johnson's paranoia. When Humphrey took over youth employment, he used his staff to help develop issues for the future. When Johnson withdrew from the 1968 campaign, Humphrey was able to pull his campaign team together pretty quickly by calling them in off the commissions." A Mondale aide echoed the conclusion: "Humphrey and Johnson weren't fools. They both knew that the only way to keep their staffs with them was to put them on somebody else's payroll. You don't spend all those years building a Senate staff only to lose them when you're elected Vice-President. You place them anywhere you can. That's exactly what we did in 1976, only by then we were able to come out in the open. We had the money in the budget to hire our own people."

Under Ford, Rockefeller, and Mondale, the Vice-President's institutional support expanded dramatically. From a vice-presidential staff of twenty in 1960, the office grew to seventy by 1974. Vice-Presidents gained new sources of information and expertise, hiring senior advisers for their independent use. Because Vice-Presidents had more money for staff, they were able to recruit more policy specialists. Moreover, as the staff grew, Vice-Presidents were able to build an administrative and political core in the office. No longer did the Vice-President's top policy staff have to double as campaign workers or administrators. The rise of the specialized staff provided some leverage in the White House. As Presidents became more conscious of the need to trim their own staffs, the Vice-President's office became more inviting as a source of at least some support. Further, as Vice-Presidents gained independent staff sources of information and expertise, there was less need to spend their time and energy just fighting for access to the President's paper.

With Rockefeller's appointment as Vice-President, these institutional vantage points increased significantly. In a series of early maneuvers, Rockefeller was able to convince Ford to give the Domestic Council to the Vice-President. As we will see later, the decision cost Rockefeller a great deal of political capital and generated an internal backlash. However, at least in the first six months of Rockefeller's term, the Domestic Council served as a major administrative vantage point. In appointing Rockefeller as vice-chairman of the Domestic Council, Ford placed his Vice-President at the fulcrum of domestic policy making, giving him a number of policy-making responsibilities. Had the Domestic Council been allowed to fulfill its mandate, Rockefeller would have been considerably more influential in the Ford White House.

Ultimately, Vice-Presidents have no vantage points which give them final authority. As a Rockefeller aide noted: "The Vice-President must acknowledge the fact that he has limited influence. So long as a President lives, the Vice-President has no power to decide any policy." Accordingly, this aide concluded that "Rockefeller doesn't get an 'A' for his service. He was a rebellious student. Couldn't get himself in a mold for the Vice-Presidency. From the day he arrived, he wanted the power to decide. The history of his life made it impossible for him to accept the role of no decisions." Thus, even with Rockefeller's vantage point at the Domestic Council, an aide offered the following example of isolation: "We learned about the budget ceiling in the 1976 State of the Union address at the last minute. We weren't consulted about what became the most important domestic policy decision of the term. We weren't even advised and we were supposed to be the instrument of domestic policy. The staff system skirted us. Jim Lynn (OMB director) simply went in and persuaded the President without us. It may have been a good decision, but it should have come through us." Nor do Vice-Presidents have any line authority. They cannot veto bills, issue executive orders, command troops, or transmit legislation. They have no formal power to make any decision on any policies, whether issues of pressing national need or their own travel schedule. It would be a mistake, however, to assume that Vice-Presidents have no vantage points for influence whatsoever. Despite the popular image of Vice-Presidents as ceremonial fixtures on the Presidency, they have been able to develop a new set of vantage points as a starting point for an advisory role and internal persuasion.

Public Prestige

As national political figures, however abused, Vice-Presidents have some public prestige. They are given the trappings of office and an attractive flag and seal, and are accorded some dignity when they travel — though Agnew was often forced to fly in what his staff called "Air Force Thirteen," a military transport without windows. They are generally welcome at Washington social gatherings and can be valuable on the midterm campaign trail. As one Johnson aide argued: "You and I may know what the Vice-Presidency is all about, but the public doesn't. They see the Vice-President as a reasonably important figure, someone who takes the oath of office right after the President." As Ford noted in 1974: "It is true that I am now surrounded everywhere by a clutch of Secret Service agents, reporters and cameramen, and assorted well-wishers. When I travel I am greeted by bands playing 'Hail, Columbia' and introduced to audiences with great solemnity instead of just as 'my good friend Jerry Ford.'" As Ford concluded: "Personally I prefer my old style of solo flying, and fondly look back on the solitude of a commercial airline seat. But I'm told a Vice President has no choice on the prestige bit" (1974, p. 63).

There is, of course, a difference between the official trappings of the office of Vice-President and any direct public support of the occupant. Vice-Presidents have elegant offices and a new full-eagle seal—redesigned at Nelson Rockefeller's personal expense—but there is some doubt about the depth and value of their political capital. Gallup rarely asks the public for their approval rating of the Vice-President's job performance. The Center for Political Studies at the University of Michigan, the source of most scholarly data on national elections, does not ask its respondents for their "likes" and "dislikes" about the vice-presidential candidates. We rarely study the impact of Vice-Presidents on presidential approval, though Agnew certainly affected Nixon's ratings in 1973. Nor do the national media pay much attention to Vice-Presidents. Even in the election campaign the average number of stories in the *New York Times* about presidential candidates outweighs the number of stories about the vice-presidential nominees by ninety-eight to nine (see Goldstein, 1982).

Presidential candidates, however, have given considerable attention to vice-presidential popularity, particularly in the context of their own campaigns. Donald Graham reports that "Richard Nixon, sure of his own nomination, commissioned polls to see which vice presidential nominee would help him most in the election. He found that more people would vote for Nixon without a vice presidential nominee than would vote for Nixon-Reagan, Nixon-Lindsay, or Nixon-Rockefeller" (1974, p. 44). That was hardly the kind of data that could help Spiro Agnew once in office. Other presidential candidates have seen their running mates as more important. Kennedy viewed Johnson as a key factor in building Southern support (though there is still some question whether Kennedy actually expected Johnson to accept the nomination), while Carter viewed Mondale as a significant force in the Northeast and Midwest. Both presidential nominees saw their ticket balancing as an important step in rebuilding party support after long campaigns. In theory at least, the closer the final electoral margin, the more the Vice-President will be perceived as a contributing factor in the victory. But even here, the Vice-President generates little independent political capital. As one Humphrey aide argued: "Once the election is over, the Vice-President's usefulness is over. He's like the second stage of a rocket. He's damn important going into orbit, but he's always thrown off to burn up in the atmosphere."

Even though we do not measure vice-presidential approval, and even though Presidents have short memories about their Vice-President's help in the election, there are several potent sources of public prestige that can be converted into vice-presidential prestige. Perhaps the most important source of public support is the Vice-President's status as a front-runner for the presidential nomination. Under the Twenty-second Amendment, Presidents can serve but two consecutive terms, elevating the Vice-President's attractiveness as a nominee. In an April 1973 Gallup poll, for instance, Agnew was the first choice for the Republican nomination, leading Reagan 35 percent to 20 percent. As Donald Graham notes: "Even in an August Gallup survey, conducted before the Vice President resigned, but after word that he was under investigation had leaked out, Agnew still attracted the support of 22 percent of all Republicans for the 1976 presidential nod. As soon as he was chosen to succeed Agnew, Jerry Ford began the most meteoric rise in the history of American politics. Almost overnight, Ford became his party's leading candidate for President, according to the Louis Harris survey" (1974, p. 42). In October, a Gallup poll without Ford's name showed Reagan the favorite choice among Republicans, leading Rockefeller 29 percent to 19 percent. In November, a Harris poll with Ford's name showed the new Vice-President now at the top, leading Reagan 25 percent to 20 percent, with Rockefeller now at 9 percent. As Graham concludes, as soon as Ford "went from a responsible, important job as House Minority Leader to one with no responsibility and only conditional importance, a quarter of the Republicans in the country suddenly decided that he was the party's best hope" (1974, p. 43). Early polls in Mondale's own campaign for the Presidency suggested that his service under Carter was a mixed blessing. In a December 1982 reading, pollster David Garth found that 25 percent of the public was "more likely" to support Mondale because of his vice-presidential background, while 15 percent was "less likely."

Reputation

According to Neustadt, a President's reputation is based on the anticipated reactions of other policy makers in Congress or the executive branch. For each President, "The people he would persuade must be convinced in their own minds that he has skill and will enough to *use* his advantages. Their judgement of him is a factor in his influence with them" (1960, p. 44). For Vice-Presidents, reputation rests on the past history of their office, as well as on the current image of the incumbent. Here, my interest is just in the past problems of the office.

For any Vice-President, the first obstacle to advice and influence is the poor reputation of the office. Whether in the Washington community or the nation as a whole, the Vice-Presidency carries a long history of bad jokes and poor occupants. According to one Mondale aide:

> One of the first steps to success is to get people to stop joking about the Vice-Presidency. The number of quotes by past Vice-Presidents on how bad the office is can overwhelm you. "The office isn't worth a warm pitcher of spit." "You are in a kind of coffin." My personal favorite is by Thomas Marshall. He used to say that the Vice-President is in a kind of cataleptic state; he can't speak, he can't

move, suffers no pain, and "yet is conscious of everything that is going on about him." The first step is just to get people to recognize that Vice-Presidents can be something beyond the past, more than just "the spare tire on the automobile of government."

Originally, the Vice-Presidency showed more promise. The first two Vice-Presidents, Adams and Jefferson, actually set a precedent for prestige, if not outright influence. Adams was considered one of George Washington's closest advisers and was included in cabinet meetings. He used his tie-breaking vote twenty-nine times in the Senate, his first tie breaker coming on legislation which would have restricted the President's removal power. More important, Washington issued clear signals that his Vice-President was to be consulted during presidential absences from Washington. However, as President, Adams came to view the office with some disdain, offering the following tongue-in-cheek advice upon receiving Vice-President Jefferson's refusal to accept a diplomatic mission abroad:

> The Vice-President, in our Constitution, is too high a personage to be sent on diplomatic errands, even in the character of an ambassador. . . . It must be a pitiful country . . . in which the second man in the nation will accept a place upon a footing with the *corps diplomatic.* . . . The nation must hold itself very cheap, that can choose a man one day to hold its second office, and the next send him to Europe, to dance attendance at levees and drawing rooms, among the common major-generals, simple bishops, earls, and barons, but especially among the common trash of ambassadors, envoys, and ministers plenipotentiary (C.F. Adams, 1850-56, vol. 2, p. 98).

Though Adams and Jefferson both succeeded to the Presidency immediately following their terms as Vice-President, neither had much to say in support of the second office. At the beginning of his term as Vice-President, for instance, Adams had expressed confusion about his duties, telling the Senate, "I feel great difficulty in how to act. I am possessed of two separate powers; the one is *esse* and the other is *posse*. I am Vice-President. In this I am nothing, but I may be everything. But I am president also of the Senate. When the President comes into the Senate, what shall I be?" (vol. 1, p. 460). Four years later, Adams had resolved his confusion, writing his wife that "my country in its wisdom contrived for me the most insignificant office that ever the invention of man contrived or his imagination conceived; . . . I can do neither good nor evil" (vol. 1, p. 289). Before the Twelfth Amendment was adopted in 1804, Vice-Presidents achieved the second office only by failure in reaching the first. When Jefferson, a Democratic-Republican, became Vice-President under Adams, a Federalist, there was little opportunity for an advisory role. Nor did either desire such a role. Jefferson felt that any direct involvement in the day-to-day Presidency was beneath the constitutional position of his office, while Adams disagreed with most of his Vice-President's ideas. Speaking of Jefferson during the campaign, Adams noted, "I am almost tempted to wish he may be chosen Vice-President. . . . For there, if he could do no good, he could do no harm."

Despite their respective opinions of the office, the Vice-Presidency survived these first administrations in good fashion. The Vice-Presidents were of good quality and performed well under difficult and uncertain conditions. However, with the ratification of the Twelfth Amendment, Vice-Presidents lost their political independence and became little more than fixtures on the President's ticket. Whereas Adams and Jefferson had been national figures in their own right, Vice-Presidents were now selected for political utility. Whatever the merits of the change, the prestige of the Vice-Presidency plummeted. Excepting Martin Van Buren, the new generation of Vice-Presidents had little national standing, was not included in the President's cabinet meetings, and had no executive responsibilities. The Senate role became an embarrassment, and Vice-Presidents lost whatever influence they once held on the credentials of disputed electors. The Vice-Presidency also lost its position as a recruiting ground for the Presidency. That role belonged to the secretary of state. The Vice-Presidency continued its decline over the next hundred years. If great men were not elected President, great men were not elected Vice-President. It remained for Franklin Roosevelt to usher in the first of two phases in the modern Vice-Presidency.

Phase one came with the inauguration of Henry Wallace in 1940 as Roosevelt's second Vice-President. Roosevelt's first Vice-President, John Nance Garner, had been dropped from the ticket after his bitter public criticism of the New Deal. Although Garner once had been a regular participant in cabinet meetings and had had private access to the President, his political views became increasingly incompatible with Roosevelt's. By the end of Garner's second term, he was unwelcome at cabinet meetings — prompting Interior Secretary Ickes to write that he found Garner's "old, red, wizened face" a "disgusting sight" (Young 1972, p. 172).

As Vice-President, Wallace brought two new functions to the office, both with Roosevelt's encouragement. Wallace's first new role was as spokesman for the Roosevelt administration. No previous Vice-President had traveled a fraction as much as Wallace. He was a vocal supporter of Roosevelt's effort to arm the U.S. for war and an outspoken critic of isolationism. Unfortunately, Wallace also became an advocate of friendship with the Soviet Union, a position popular in the midst of the war against fascism but unpopular once Germany was defeated. Wallace's enthusiasm during this first era of détente cost him his renomination in 1944. In a foreshadowing of McCarthyism, conservative Democrats demanded Wallace's removal from the presidential ticket. Wallace's second new role was as chairman of the Economic Defense Board, the first policy assignment in vice-presidential history. Roosevelt established the board in July 1941 to purchase strategic materials in preparation for war. Once war was declared, the agency was renamed the Board of Economic Welfare (BEW) and quickly became one of the most powerful wartime units. Wallace was not merely the figurehead chairman of a meaningless commission. He commanded a staff of three thousand and had the power to make final decisions. It was a major, substantive role that elevated the Vice-President to the President's wartime inner circle.

Yet, as Rockefeller learned thirty years later, major policy assignments often expose staff members to intense bureaucratic infighting. Wallace's decisions frequently meant public sacrifice and rationing, which in turn undermined the BEW. Moreover, in typical Roosevelt fashion, Wallace was not the only staffer involved in the strategic materials effort. The BEW shared overlapping responsibilities with the Reconstruction Finance Corporation (RFC) and Jesse Jones, Roosevelt's skilled secretary of commerce. Roosevelt had delegated the assignment to two agencies hoping that at least one would succeed. Unfortunately, Wallace and Jones had sharply different political philosophies. Wallace favored quick action regardless of price, while Jones supported caution and minimum cost. Wallace eventually charged that the RFC was dragging its feet in the war effort and asked Roosevelt for an executive order instructing the RFC to purchase any materials deemed necessary by the BEW. That order was issued on 13 April 1942. However, Wallace stepped up his campaign against Jones in 1943, creating a highly visible public conflict. Charges and countercharges were traded through the spring, leading to a final confrontation with FDR. Roosevelt wrote Jones and Wallace that "in the midst of waging a war so critical to our national security and to the future of all civilization, there is not sufficient time to investigate and determine where the truth lies" (Young 1972, p. 193). Roosevelt then abolished the BEW and Wallace's chairmanship, removed Jones from control of any RFC international economic programs, and established the Office of Economic Warfare in the vacuum. Though Jones lost some of his territory, the decisions cost Wallace all of his line responsibilities and returned the Vice-Presidency to ceremonial duties. Wallace continued his spokesman activities, but did not occupy any substantive positions for the rest of his term.

Wallace was the first of a new generation of Vice-Presidents, but did little to improve the reputation of the office. If anything, Wallace heightened suspicions of any substantive role for Vice-Presidents. The Wallace Vice-Presidency did set a precedent for an expanded role, but did not bring Vice-Presidents any permanent advisory duties. Indeed, Wallace's successor, Harry Truman, is often cited as the prime example of how Vice-Presidents are not kept informed on major national policy. Despite Wallace's precedent, Truman was not told about the atomic bomb, and eventually concluded that he was the worst-prepared Vice-President since Andrew Johnson. That is not to argue that Wallace was merely an increment on the past. Wallace was able to attach a new political function to the office—the spokesman role—and was able to push the Vice-Presidency past simple duties. Though Wallace failed to keep his BEW assignment, he was able to move the office forward. However, in terms of influence, Wallace did not improve the Vice-

President's position. His penchant for bureaucratic infighting actually undermined the influence potential for future Vice-Presidents. According to
one Rockefeller aide:

> Rockefeller had spent quite a bit of time talking to Wallace in the 1940s. They
> used to play tennis up at Pocantico Hills, New York, and Wallace would bash
> the tennis balls in frustration. The problem with Wallace was that the ex-
> periment failed. He reached up, but was pushed back. Rockefeller should
> have remembered the lesson when he was trying to take control of the Domestic
> Council, but he thought he'd be different. The fact is that nobody ever re-
> members the Vice-President's success, only the failure. They don't remember
> that Wallace did a hell of a job on the economic welfare board. They only re-
> member that he was dumped from the ticket.

Phase two of the modern Vice-Presidency came during the 1970s and is the
subject of this book. Recent Vice-Presidents have had better access to information and much stronger institutional support. They have been more
active in substantive policy and have taken on more important assignments.
Their staffs have grown, their public image has improved, and they now
have regularized access to the President. Although recent Vice-Presidents
have been given greater responsibilities, their reputations for influence
remain low. Vice-Presidents are still not expected to have any policy impact and must often spend more resources fighting their poor image than
gaining influence. As one Mondale aide noted: "Old myths die hard in
Washington. The press can't get it through their thick heads that the Vice-
Presidency has changed. There are too many clichés that sound good."
That view was confirmed when the *National Journal,* a widely read weekly
review of policy and politics, began an otherwise positive first report on
Bush with a quote from B. W. Bellamy's *Table Rules for Little Folks:*

> I must not speak a single word,
> For children must be seen not heard.

The Power to Persuade

The Vice-President's vantage points, public prestige, and reputation have
all improved somewhat over the past twenty years, but still remain low
when compared to those of other White House aides. Vice-Presidents now
have formal access to information and expertise, as well as to the President.
Public prestige has increased as the Vice-Presidency has regained its original
role as a springboard to the Presidency. Even reputation has grown somewhat in the aftermath of Mondale's Vice-Presidency. Of the changes, the
increase in the Vice-President's institutional and advisory vantage points is
most important. Though the growth in staff and now-regularized meetings
with the President do not guarantee influence, they do provide greater
opportunities for persuasion. Yet, unlike other actors who depend on status

or authority for policy influence, Vice-Presidents must still rely on their persuasive skills. Once they gain the chance to apply those skills in one-on-one meetings with the President, Vice-Presidents have greater input on substantive issues. More than those of any other players inside the White House, the Vice-President's advice and influence are conditioned by the President. As Mondale argued in 1979:

> My political influence is of a different nature. It's personal to the President. I am not a substitute or deputy President. I understand that. I don't have that kind of separate independence and I understand that. It's one of the aspects of the vice presidency. The President's name is Carter, not Mondale; I understand that. But, in a different way, I may have more influence in government than I ever had in the Senate because of my role with the President. In other words, I can be heard on all these issues; I know what the information is; I'm able to be heard on any matter I want to be heard on. And that is a different form of influence and independence from being a totally independent political person like a Senator (*National Journal*, 11 Mar. 1979).

In many respects, a Vice-President's advisory role and influence rest on the ability to adapt to limited vantage points, prestige, and reputation. As one aide argued: "You'd be better off comparing Vice-Presidents to basketball guards, not centers. When a guard has to go up against a center, he's got to be faster and smarter. He doesn't have any height advantage and can't slam-dunk the ball, but he can still shoot. The Vice-President isn't a center inside the White House and can't go one-on-one with most other advisers." Thus, Rockefeller and Mondale faced initial obstacles that were very different from other advisers. They entered office with few of the natural resources of the senior staff. They had no automatic access to the President and had no position in the paper loop. They had time-consuming responsibilities on councils and board, but little proximity to the President. They had to gain access first.

A PREVIEW OF FINDINGS

By now, it should be clear what this book is *not* about. This is not a history of the American Vice-Presidency, though I look at the institutionalization of the advisory role over the past twenty years. Nor is this a history of the last ten Vice-Presidencies. Nor will I look at the problems of presidential succession. Finally, this is not a study of how Presidents might best use their Vice-Presidents. I am not particularly interested in Mondale as an ideal "model" of the new Vice-Presidency. What this study *is* about is advice and influence. How did Vice-Presidents finally achieve an advisory role and why was Mondale more successful in shaping policy than his predecessors? The first asks about institutional changes that remain in the Vice-Presidency today, while the second looks at how individual advisers—whether Vice-

Presidents, OMB directors, or NSC advisers—affect the course of White House policy.

The first step in answering such questions is to define advice and influence. As a Humphrey aide suggested: "Everybody says Mondale had a lot of influence. But you have to distinguish input and influence. Input is the opportunity to have your say. It's now a basic right in the Vice-Presidency thanks to Rockefeller and Mondale. Influence is the ability to sway the President, to affect specific decisions." Thus, advice centers on an actor's view of what *should or should not be done.* Johnson advised Kennedy not to attend the Vienna summit with Khrushchev; Humphrey advised Johnson not to order the bombing of North Vietnam; Rockefeller advised Ford not to impose a spending ceiling on domestic policy; Mondale advised Carter not to rescind the fifty-dollar tax rebate; Bush advised Reagan to reduce the 1983 tax cut. In all five cases, however, advice did not equal influence. Each President made a final decision counter to the Vice-President's advice. Influence thereby rests on the impact of advice on actual decisions and involves an adviser's ability to *change outcomes from what they would have been.* Johnson would have been seen as influential had he stopped Kennedy from going to Vienna, had he delayed the summit, or had he changed the agenda for the meetings. Bush would have been seen as influential had he persuaded Reagan to drop the third year of the cut, had he delayed the third-year cut (which Reagan accepted in initial congressional negotiations), or had he reduced the amount of the cut.

Unlike more traditional definitions, where influence exists when A makes B do something B would not have done, this definition includes a broader range of White House activity. First, it allows for variations in influence by policy area—domestic, foreign, economic—and by stages of the presidential policy process—agenda setting, decision making, implementation. An adviser may have very little influence over domestic agenda setting, but considerable influence over economic implementation. Second, it allows for influence arising from what Matthew Crenson (1971) calls "non-decision-making," or the suppression of ideas. Mondale's control of the Carter agenda-setting operation, for example, provided an opportunity to elevate or understate issues and alternatives. Third, this definition allows for influence arising from inaction. Doing nothing can be quite effective in killing a proposal, particularly when active participation is essential for success. As Mondale acknowledged after leaving office, "I certainly didn't go out and cheerlead where I felt strongly against a position" (*Boston Globe,* 25 Feb. 1983). Finally, this definition allows for influence by degrees. Partial influence is still influence. Here, influence is not a zero-sum game where one adviser's gain is always another's loss. Because an administration involves hundreds of decisions, influence will vary across time and across issues.

Before Vice-Presidents can have influence, of course, they must first give advice. If Vice-Presidents are *behaving* like advisers, can we assume they *are* advisers? All advisers share a characteristic modus operandi. There is little difference between "adviser-like" activity and the real thing. If the Vice-President has advisory resources, has weekly meetings with the President, is in the paper loop, is involved in meetings when decisions are made, has a West Wing office, has the President's support, etc., then the Vice-President is behaving very much like other advisers. If the Vice-President keeps his staff isolated from the White House, spends a great deal of time on the road, avoids the West Wing, skips private meetings with the President, does not attend NSC or Cabinet gatherings, etc., then the Vice-President is not behaving like other advisers. Obviously, there are activities that Vice-Presidents have avoided because of their particular political status—Mondale did not like to speak up in large forums, preferring a more discreet setting. Yet, though each adviser may develop a slightly different approach, there are certain things that all advisers do—e.g., attend meetings, exchange opinions, meet with the President, use the paper loop—and certain things that all advisers need—e.g., time, energy, information, expertise, proximity. This is a study of Vice-Presidents as advisers, not advisers who just happen to be Vice-Presidents. However, all advisers—whether Vice-Presidents or OMB Directors, or chiefs of staff—share certain characteristics. One goal of this book is to build a theory of influence that is generalizable to all advisers, not just Vice-Presidents.

Once we know that advice has been given, there are several methods for measuring influence. A first approach is to compare the Vice-President's policy agenda with the President's program. If Mondale supported a new Department of Education and that policy was adopted, we might say that he had influence. If Mondale opposed the 1980 budget cuts and Carter moved ahead anyway, we would say that he lacked influence. By comparing Mondale's agenda with final outcomes, we can make a very rough estimate of the areas where the Vice-President did and did not have influence.

A second method for measuring influence is simply to ask the key players if the Vice-President had policy impact. This book is based primarily on just such questions asked of Mondale, Rockefeller, Ford, Agnew, Humphrey, and Johnson vice-presidential staff members, as well as companion groups of Carter, Ford, Nixon, Johnson, and Kennedy presidential aides. In all, over one hundred staff members were interviewed for this study. Most of these interviews concentrated on the three most recently completed Vice-Presidencies: Mondale, Rockefeller, and Ford. Of the 20 or so top Mondale aides, 18 were interviewed; of the top 20 Rockefeller aides, 16 were interviewed; and of the top 20 Ford vice-presidential aides, 15 were interviewed. In order to check these responses, sizable groups of top presidential aides were also interviewed. All totaled, 12 Carter, 14 Ford, and 10 Nixon aides were interviewed about their respective Vice-Presidents. Much smaller

groups of Reagan, Bush, Johnson, and Humphrey staff members were interviewed. Finally, apart from these 107 staff interviews, 11 representatives of
the Washington media were also interviewed. All of these respondents—staff
and media—were asked detailed questions about the nature of vice-presidential advice and influence, but because all were given assurances of confidentiality, no quotes will be attributed to specific sources.

Since presidential and vice-presidential aides have been known to tailor
history to fit their vested interests and since they sometimes have trouble
remembering the past, a third method for estimating influence is to look for
"tracks" surrounding specific decisions. According to one media observer:

> You can find Mondale's tracks all over domestic and foreign policy. Every ad-
> ministration has three or four or five people who participate in all the major
> decisions. The political dynamics of the White House require some narrowing
> of the number of people on any one decision. These four or five people are the
> ones who have clout—they leave the routine duties for the staff. For Carter, the
> inner circle basically included Jordan, Eizenstat, Powell, Brzezinski, and Mon-
> dale. Sometimes, Mondale would drop out, but Eizenstat would represent his
> opinions.

In searching for tracks of influence, we must first pinpoint the time when
the final decisions were made. To conclude that the Vice-President had
some measure of influence, we must answer several questions: Was the Vice-
President physically present in major policy meetings? Did he meet privately with the President shortly before the major meetings occurred? If the
Vice-President was absent, were members of his staff present in the meetings?
Did the Vice-President shape the decision earlier in the process? Clearly,
for influence to exist, the Vice-President must be involved *before* the decisions are made.

If we had tapes of all policy meetings in the Oval Office, we might not
have to rely on this kind of inference. Unfortunately, given that we have
few verbatim records from policy meetings in the Nixon, Ford, and Carter
administrations (though we now know that Roosevelt, Kennedy, and Johnson
all taped Oval Office meetings, joining the six thousand hours of tape from
the Nixon Presidency), we must estimate influence from agendas, interviews,
and tracks. Though we must exercise caution with such methods, they give
us an opportunity to draw some initial conclusions about advice and influence in the White House. I also draw occasional solace from the following
quote from an aide who finally answered the "how can we tell if he had
influence" question:

> There used to be a story that went around about this lawyer who was defending
> a man on trial for biting another man's ear off. This attorney had the key prose-
> cution witness on the stand and asked if the witness had actually seen the de-
> fendant bite the ear off. "No," replied the witness, "I didn't actually see it."

"Well," the attorney continued, "how can you accuse my client of this crime?" The witness calmly replied, "Because I saw him spit the ear out." I don't remember too many times that I saw Mondale persuade the President, but I sure saw him spit the ear out a lot.

The Plan of the Book

This book is divided into two separate sections. Part I centers on the question of advice and should be read as a study of the Vice-Presidency as an advisory institution: how did the Vice-Presidency take a place alongside the Office of Management and Budget, Council of Economic Advisers, National Security Council, and Office of Policy Development (formerly the Domestic Policy Staff) as a source of policy advice? Part II centers on the question of influence and should be read as a study of one adviser's influence over White House policy: How did Mondale emerge as one of the top players inside the Carter White House?

Part I starts with a discussion of the vice-presidential job description. In the past, Vice-Presidents have had three major functions: ceremonial, political, and policy. In Chapter 2, I look at how these jobs have changed and expanded over the past twenty years. The ceremonial function, for instance, has become less important, while both the political and policy functions have become more valuable. I look at different approaches to the advisory role—hidden-hand and advocate—and offer a comparison of the past ten Vice-Presidents.

Part I continues with an examination of the institutional Vice-Presidency. From a relatively small unit located on Capitol Hill in the 1950s, the Vice-President's office has become the fifth largest agency in the White House and is now located in both the West Wing and the Old Executive Building. In Chapter 3, I look at the process of change and argue that the Vice-President's office is an important source of advisory support. I offer a look inside the Vice-President's office with an analysis of what the office does and does not do.

Part I also examines presidential and vice-presidential goals as a factor in the job description. I assume that all White House activity is purposive; that all players have goals. At the very least, advice and influence rest on what the President wants the Vice-President to do. In Chapter 4, however, I argue that advice and influence also reflect what the Vice-President and the assorted staffs want the Vice-President to do. I look at differences in goals between these competing groups as one source of advice and influence. Chapter 4 concludes with a discussion of the new political and policy incentives that make the Vice-President's advisory role more valuable to the White House.

Part I ends with an effort to build a theory of Vice-Presidents as advisers. What are the resources needed for an advisory role? What kinds of conflict are involved in the vice-presidential job description? In Chapter 5, I examine six resources that are necessary for an advisory role: time, energy, information, expertise, proximity, and, most importantly, the President's willingness to listen. Without these resources, Vice-Presidents cannot act as advisers. I also argue that the Vice-President's job description is often incompatible with an ongoing advisory role — Vice-Presidents cannot perform the political and policy functions simultaneously.

Part II begins with a detailed history of the Rockefeller and Mondale Vice-Presidencies. Both were senior advisers, but only Mondale was consistently influential. In Chapter 6, I look at these two Vice-Presidents as case studies of influence. What were Rockefeller's major influence problems? What were Mondale's major advantages? How do the different staffs view the problems of influence? For Rockefeller, major disadvantages came from the long delay in confirmation, the acceptance of line assignments, his ties to Republican liberals, high visibility, the restrictive policy agenda, the absence of allies on the White House staff, and Ford himself. For Mondale, major advantages came from the merging of the campaign staffs, avoidance of line assignments, his ties to Democratic liberals, low visibility, an expansive policy agenda, allies on the White House staff, and Carter himself. Chapter 6 concludes with some comparisons between the two Vice-Presidencies.

Part II continues with an effort to build a theory of vice-presidential influence. In Chapter 7, I examine three resources that are necessary for influence: internal capital, the Vice-President's persuasive skills, and, most importantly, the President's persuadability. Chapter 7 continues with an analysis of the opportunities for vice-presidential influence, concentrating on the importance of policy vacuums in shaping impact. Chapter 7 ends with a look at different strategies of influence — offensive and defensive styles, coalition building, priority setting, and bargaining. This discussion also examines the nature of hidden-hand influence as a primary strategy of White House policy impact.

This book concludes with a discussion of the Bush Vice-Presidency. What do the models of advice and influence predict about Bush? How have Bush's goals shaped his influence to date? What are his strategies for influence? Looking at Bush, we can ask whether the advisory role still exists in the Vice-Presidency and whether any of Mondale's strategies have proved useful for his successor. Chapter 8 concludes with an examination of the Vice-President's role in the policy process. Can Vice-Presidents, or any advisers, disagree with the President? Can Vice-Presidents, or other advisers, perform an important role simply by being one of many generalists? As one Rockefeller aide concluded: "In the final analysis, the best thing the Vice-President can do is give it to the President right between the eyes. Let the

President know what the people really think—or at least what the Vice-President thinks they really think. That's really the only thing that is in short supply in the White House. There are lots of people to tell the President what to do, but not very many who will tell him that he's full of bull."

PART ONE

Advice

2.

The Vice-Presidential Job Description

You've got two choices. You can say to the Vice-President, "Have fun, have a good four years, go up to the Senate and play around, take some trips, enjoy that nice EOB office, have a good time at the new residence." Your Vice-President will do it and have no other choice, but pretty soon, he'll get restless and end up doing more harm than good. Or, you can say, "Here are some specific things I want you to do. I want you to stop by for lunch at least once a week and attend all the meetings you want. I want you to stay in political shape, take some of the heat, and help me cut the time on some of these projects." Not only will the Vice-President feel better, he'll probably end up helping you a great deal.

— Ford presidential aide

Despite two decades of change in the Vice-Presidency, the job description is cast and recast with each successive occupant. As one Carter aide noted: "If you came across a newspaper ad looking for a U.S. Vice-President, it would probably read 'WANTED: RESPONSIBLE PERSON TO DO WHATEVER SUPERVISOR WANTS, SOME TRAVEL, MUST BE WILLING TO RELOCATE, SALARY $75K, HOURS FLEXIBLE, ROOM FOR ADVANCEMENT, SOME EXPERIENCE HELPFUL BUT NOT NECESSARY.'" The past twenty years have produced significant additions to the vice-presidential job description, but Vice-Presidents remain without formal responsibilities. Subject to the President's approval, Vice-Presidents can pick and choose among a wide array of activities—from campaigning to lobbying to advising—but are not required to do anything. The job remains whatever the President and Vice-President make it.

Yet, if Vice-Presidents want some level of impact on policy, there are some activities that help and some that hurt. *Ceremonial* duties focus on the Vice-President as a delegate or commissioner, but add little to the opportunity for advice and influence. Though ceremonial duties offer pomp and perquisites, they absorb considerable resources that might be used in an advisory role. *Political* duties rest on the Vice-President as a public liaison officer, spokesman, campaigner, or lobbyist, but also cost time and energy. Though political duties offer few additional openings for advice and influence, they do help build the Vice-President's internal capital. *Policy* duties center on the Vice-President as a line assistant or senior adviser, and offer the greatest potential for advice and influence. However, policy duties also expose the Vice-President to the greatest internal conflict and demand the largest commitment of internal resources.

THE CEREMONIAL VICE-PRESIDENCY

At one time in recent history, ceremony was the only duty in the vice-presidential job description. According to one Johnson aide: "We were damn lucky to get the chance to travel to funerals and to handle the Space Council. That's all we had to keep busy. Johnson always kept thinking about programs, but had no chance to present them to Kennedy. If we hadn't been able to take some trips, I think Johnson would have gone off the edge. As it was, he was damn close anyway." The ceremonial Vice-Presidency involves a number of activities—from symbolic chairmanships to official mourning—but has little policy impact. Most of the ceremonial duties can be collapsed into two central roles: the Vice-President as a delegate and the Vice-President as a White House commissioner.

Delegate

The delegate role rests on the Vice-President's activity as a surrogate for the President and involves considerable foreign travel. Because foreign travel is under the presidential banner, the delegate role often uses the Vice-President as a simple extension of the White House, a kind of "international pawn" in the words of one aide. For ease of understanding, most domestic travel is viewed as political while most foreign travel is viewed as ceremonial.

By definition, delegate activity offers little freedom to maneuver. As one Humphrey aide noted: "We did a lot of traveling for the President, but were never allowed to negotiate anything. We were in a country as the President's representative *without* portfolio. When we went to Vietnam, we were there as Johnson's eyes and ears, without any kind of authority. When we talked, we talked for Lyndon Johnson, not Hubert Humphrey, and had to get every syllable cleared with the White House." Yet, Humphrey believed that the travel was important. As an aide noted: "The job permitted Humphrey to travel around the world and meet heads of state. Traveling made the job more tolerable. Humphrey was concerned about his background in foreign policy anyway and was convinced the travel was important for learning. Something about an audience with the pope or de Gaulle seasoned him."

The classic example of the delegate function is the state funeral. Rockefeller made two major foreign trips as Vice-President, one for the funeral of Chiang Kai-shek and one for the funeral of King Faisal of Saudi Arabia. "It wasn't as if we had anything to do but look sad either," a Rockefeller aide remarked. "What else were we supposed to do? Sit down and negotiate a new Middle East peace? How about a solution to the OPEC oil crisis?" Ford also acted as a delegate during his Vice-Presidency, but according to one aide: "Kissinger didn't want anyone running around like a loose cannon on his ship of state. Kissinger was very firm on not having Vice-Presidents spending too much time abroad. Even though they didn't say much, someone might get the wrong impression from a burp." That is not to argue that funerals are empty of substantive content. As one Mondale assistant said: "Mondale was not a professional mourner. The one funeral he attended was Tito's and that involved one-on-one meetings with foreign officials trying to warn the Soviets to keep their hands off Yugoslavia." In this case, Mondale was acting as both a delegate and a policy-maker, attending Tito's funeral as a surrogate for Carter, while communicating with other international actors. Bush performed a similar role in his trip to Brezhnev's funeral in 1982 and during his trip to Europe in early 1983.

Past Vice-Presidents have varied in the amount of their delegate activity. According to one count, Nixon made seven foreign trips as Vice-President, Johnson ten, Humphrey twelve, Agnew seven, Ford one, Rockefeller six, and Mondale fourteen (Goldstein 1982, p. 159). Vice-Presidents have used these trips for different purposes. During one trip to Africa, for instance, Agnew was able to squeeze in thirteen rounds of golf. Among recent Vice-Presidents, Johnson performed the foreign function with unusual vigor. According to one historian:

> During the thirty-five months he was vice-president, Lyndon embarked on a new "tour" on the average of every three months, visited dozens of foreign countries, conferred with the leaders of each, shook God alone knows how many hundreds of thousands, maybe millions of hands of varied colors, hooted and hollered, even in the Taj Mahal, got out of official cars and walked among and shook hands of the multitudes, and acted for all the world as if he were running for reelection to the Senate in Texas. When he was in India, John Kenneth Galbraith, then ambassador there, had to find him a translator. "I told him, 'If Lyndon forgets and asks for votes, leave that out'" (Miller 1980, p. 281).

However, despite the ambitious travel schedule, Johnson had few substantive responsibilities. Unlike Mondale, who worked on an Egypt-Israel peace plan during a 1977 trip to the Middle East, Johnson was rarely alone in private meetings with other leaders. He would communicate messages from Kennedy, but acted mainly as a goodwill ambassador, a kind of living symbol of Kennedy's concern.

Not all of Johnson's foreign travel was delegate activity. In his first visit to Southeast Asia, Johnson did negotiate with Ngo Dinh Diem, then chief of state in South Vietnam. According to George Reedy, Johnson's press secretary: "The basic purpose of the trip was to convince Diem that he simply had to institute some social and fiscal reforms if he were to survive. Diem was an absolute autocrat, and he'd been holed up in his palace for so many years that he'd gotten quite far from his people. I don't believe he himself realized how shaky his position was" (Miller 1980, p. 283). Humphrey made the same trip and the same argument, but with a different leader, when he visited Vietnam four years later. In both cases, the Vice-President went beyond the simple delegate role, pursuing specific administration policies. Unfortunately for most Vice-Presidents, foreign travel usually rests on the delegate function. With State Department officials and White House speechwriters in tow, Johnson and Humphrey were rarely allowed to depart from carefully prepared texts. As one Mondale assistant argued: "We had all seen what Johnson had done with Humphrey, keeping him on a short leash, only letting him out with a muzzle on. We vowed never to do that to ourselves, never to go anywhere without our own national security adviser and our own speechwriters, never to be cloistered like Humphrey."

There are, however, two visible payoffs from the delegate function. First, Vice-Presidents are received with some pomp when they travel abroad. They may be given much greater status in a foreign capital than they can ever gain at home. "The bands will play for you, you get nice food, you sleep in first-class hotels, and meet all the big shots," a Humphrey assistant said. "It's at least something, if you can't get anything back home." When Kennedy sent Johnson to Pakistan and India, he gave him a dramatic send-off. According to Robert Komer, a member of the NSC staff assigned to accompany Johnson: "Of course, when a president sends a vice president on a trip that the vice president doesn't want to go on, he does it with style. At least Kennedy did it with style. There we were at the helicopter on the White House grounds . . . the departure ceremony from the Rose Garden. . . . And we flew in Air Force One. Not Air Force Two or Three but Air Force One. When you're sending the vice president of the United States off on a fool's errand, you send him on Air Force One" (Miller 1980, p. 292). A Johnson aide agreed: "The trips were good for Johnson's morale. Warm receptions abroad played well in the U.S. Made him look awfully big, as if he were a mover and a shaker. I still remember the headlines after the Southeast Asia trip in the New York *Daily News:* VEEP WOWS THEM IN VIETNAM."

The second payoff from the delegate role rests on White House support. As one Carter aide argued: "Mondale's behavior in Yugoslavia had to help on the inside. We all saw how he performed. He was a strong representative for Carter and that raised his stock among some of the foreign policy people." Yet, if delegate activity can help the Vice-President, it can also hurt. Agnew's early trips abroad convinced the Nixon people not to let him travel again. Johnson's first trips to Europe led the State Department to advise against any further trips to "civilized" nations. Moreover, too much delegate activity may actually undermine a policy role, physically keeping the Vice-President away from the White House. And too little activity may be a signal of internal dissatisfaction. As one Mondale aide concluded: "The Vice-President should stay away from any invitations to funerals. Just tell the President they depress him."

Commissioner

The second component of the ceremonial Vice-Presidency is the commissioner duty, and involves the Vice-President's symbolic participation in a variety of task forces, councils, and forums. Though commissions often have impressive titles, they rarely have substantive impact. Humphrey, for instance, was chairman of the President's councils on Equal Opportunity, Youth Opportunity, Indian Opportunity, Marine Sciences, and Recreation and Natural Beauty. He was also chairman of the Aeronautics and Space Council and the Council on Economic Opportunity, while serving on the Smithsonian Board of Regents. According to a Humphrey aide, "the councils all looked good on paper and sounded important, but they really didn't have much to do. Johnson used them to show people he was interested in their problems, but left the policy development to Califano and the departments." A second Humphrey aide agreed, with one qualification: "Humphrey was able to turn some of the commissions into more than just symbols. He used Youth Opportunity to develop some ideas on youth unemployment and worked with the Council on Economic Opportunity on the poverty program. But that was all Humphrey's doing. Nothing in the councils gave him much to do beyond make studies of one problem or another." As such, the commissioner duty rarely involves any formal responsibility. There are few clear policy demands and no line authority. Humphrey's chairmanship on the Council on Indian Opportunity, for instance, did not give him any mandate to generate policy, nor did it give him a chance to administer programs or supervise line staffs. At best, the Indian council was used to express symbolic concerns about Indian problems. Whatever Humphrey's legitimate interests in Indian problems, the council did not provide any substantive opportunities to affect policy. Formal authority remained with the Bureau of Indian Affairs and the Interior Department.

The commissioner function was very much a product of the 1960s. Faced with activist Vice-Presidents, Kennedy and Johnson sought to harness their seconds in relatively harmless assignments. Though Nixon had been chairman of several councils 'under Eisenhower, Kennedy expanded the practice when he moved his Vice-President from Capitol Hill to the Old Executive Office Building. Faced with the prospect of a former majority leader roaming the halls of Congress unchecked, Kennedy moved Johnson to the EOB and gave him several commissioner duties. Initially, Johnson was active on the Space Council, the Peace Corps National Advisory Council, and the Committee on Equal Employment. However, as the term progressed, Johnson became increasingly frustrated in handling the symbolic duties of a commissioner. As one Johnson aide noted: "He had explained his acceptance of the nomination by saying 'Power is where power goes.' It wasn't too long, however, before he realized that he was a long distance from where power goes. The commissions were a slap in the face to someone who had been majority leader. He couldn't pretend that the councils were important." That sense of powerlessness was not lost on others. As Harry McPherson, one of Johnson's aides, said of the Vice-President: "I remember one day I was coming off the Senate floor, and I passed him coming out of an elevator wearing a hat. That was a very unusual thing. He looked distinguished in a hat, should have worn one more frequently. He had a briefcase and looked very businesslike. And I asked him where he had been. He said he had been in a meeting of the Smithsonian Board of Regents talking about the zoo. I thought, 'My God, I don't believe it. Lyndon Johnson and the zoo'" (Miller 1980, p. 305).

Yet, for all his frustration, Johnson showed little interest in his own Vice-President. Humphrey had no shortage of time and energy. He was the caricature of the activist Vice-President. With no substantive outlet for his energy, however, Humphrey accepted a remarkable number of commissions and task forces. No American Vice-President has had more commissioner assignments than Humphrey. Moreover, Humphrey actively sought more assignments over the term. One reason was Humphrey's increasing isolation from policy. As the freeze went deeper, Humphrey moved toward more commissioner duties. "He wasn't exactly the kind of person who could slow down of his own free will," a Humphrey aide suggested. "The colder it got inside the White House, the more he expanded his other activities. He wasn't willing to sit back and get fat like Johnson had done. He wanted to be doing something, even if it wasn't important." A second reason rests on staffing problems in the Vice-President's office before it gained its own line in the executive budget. Commissions were one method for hiring personal staff. Even though these staff members were formally on detail from other departments, they were still loyal to the Vice-President. As one aide remembered: "We used those commissions as a hiding place for Humphrey's staff. I'm not sure Johnson would have been so willing to have Humphrey on all those councils if he'd known what Humphrey was doing. We managed to collect a fairly large staff through the device."

Occupied with the commissions, Humphrey was effectively frozen out of the policy process. By the end of the administration, Humphrey had concluded that no amount of commissioner activity could substitute for the absence of an advisory role. Thus, when Humphrey advised Mondale to accept the vice-presidential nomination in 1976, he warned Mondale to stay away from any commission assignments. However, the end of the commissioner function was already well under way by then. Nixon had entered the Presidency naturally hostile to many of Humphrey's commissions and quickly disbanded most of them. Nor did Nixon perceive much need for controlling Agnew's energy. Agnew was not an activist Vice-President and did not want many assignments, taking the Aeronautics and Space Council and the Intergovernmental Affairs Council as his two commissioner duties. Agnew had trouble with both, recommending a manned space mission to Mars that had to be derailed by the White House. According to John Ehrlichman, Nixon's domestic policy adviser, the White House had been courted by NASA for the mission, "but not to the degree to which they had made love to Agnew":

> He had been their guest of honor at space launchings, tours and dinners, and it seemed to me they had done a superb job of recruiting him to lead this fight to vastly expand their space empire and budget.
>
> I finally took off the kid gloves: "Look, Mr. Vice President, we have to be practical. There is to be no money for a Mars trip. The President has already decided that. So the President does not want such a trip in the Space Advisory Committee's recommendations. It is your job . . . to make absolutely certain that the Mars trip is not in there" (1982, p. 145).

Nixon eventually removed Agnew from intergovernmental affairs following the 1972 elections. When Ehrlichman asked Nixon if Agnew should continue to handle the area, Nixon replied: "He shouldn't have it. He'll just take the gravy and leave the President all the negatives and the problems. He has such a poor staff, too. Give Agnew the bicentennial to look after" (Ehrlichman 1982, p. 142). As Vice-President, Ford continued to shed the commissioner function, dropping the traditional assignment in Indian affairs. As one aide noted at the time, Ford backed away because "he's already stretched too thin. The thing is he has no real authority in those areas; it's mostly just a matter of listening to their troubles, which takes a lot of time without settling much of anything" (*National Journal*, 10 Aug. 1974).

What Nixon and Ford started, Mondale finished. "We did everything we could to kill formal commitments," one Mondale aide said. "They were a waste of time, with absolutely no value in making decisions or affecting policy. We were able to get out of the Domestic Council when Carter changed it to the Domestic Policy Staff, but could never get out of the Smithsonian. That's a dinosaur that'll be with the Vice-Presidency forever." Though Bush accepted two new assignments at the start of the Reagan term—the Task Force on Regulatory Relief and titular control of White House crisis management—both commitments were downplayed within the Vice-President's office. Bush gave most of the responsibility for regulatory relief to his chief counsel, while avoiding public discussion of his crisis-management assignment.

THE POLITICAL VICE-PRESIDENCY

The vice-presidential job description has always included some political responsibilities. As the President's running mate, the Vice-President has usually participated in the nominating conventions and the general election campaigns. Even during the "dark ages" between John Adams and Franklin D. Roosevelt, vice-presidential nominees had some limited political duties. However, it was not until the twentieth century that Vice-Presidents were given political chores *once in office.* At least four separate duties fall into the political arena: the Vice-President as a public liaison officer, a spokesman for administration policies, a campaigner, and a congressional lobbyist.

Public Liaison

Depending on their background and political connections, Vice-Presidents are often asked to act as public liaison officers for the White House. The duty of a public liaison officer is to listen to complaints, encourage support, and massage egos. As former governors, both Agnew and Rockefeller became contacts for the nation's governors and mayors. "Every time a governor would come to town," one Agnew aide said, "we would have to schedule a meeting, show him around the grounds, listen for an hour to all the problems of his state, and give him a vice-presidential pen." As one Nixon aide wrote, Agnew met with mixed success:

> Spiro Agnew had been the Governor of Maryland; we thought it natural that he would take responsibility for our relations with governors, mayors and county officials. But it turned out that he was only an excellent conduit for their complaints—especially the gripes of Ronald Reagan, John Bell Williams and a few other conservatives. Notwithstanding Agnew's 1968 love affair with the Presidential candidacy of Nelson Rockefeller, Rocky soon gave up on Agnew's liaison and began calling me directly. I tried to wean Rockefeller back to Agnew until the Governor went to the President and insisted that I be his avenue to the President instead of Agnew.
>
> "Agnew doesn't play them well," Nixon complained to me (Ehrlichman 1982, p. 146).

As a former mayor of Minneapolis, Humphrey was given liaison with local officials. According to a Humphrey assistant: "At least Agnew met with governors. We had to set aside time for the mayors of little towns all across the country. They were all pretty nice people, but God, what a waste of time. What could Humphrey tell them anyway? That he'd make sure they got the money? He didn't have the authority to make bargains."

Though the public liaison role often involves considerable time, there are some opportunities for influence. Vice-Presidents can use their connections to outside groups to lobby the President on specific issues. If the groups are important to legislative or electoral success, the President may be more willing to listen to the Vice-President's advice. In 1978, for instance, Mondale used his connections to the Jewish lobby to persuade Carter to tone down a speech that the secretary of state, Cyrus Vance, was to deliver to the United Nations. In 1970, Agnew used his connections to the National Governors' Conference to interest Nixon in expanding the budget for revenue-sharing legislation. In both cases, the Vice-President's links to constituency groups led to increased influence. The critical factor, of course, was that neither Carter nor Nixon had his own connections to those groups. Mondale and Agnew were able to supply connections that were important to the President.

Spokesman

Because of their visibility as national figures, Vice-Presidents are often asked to act as spokesmen, defenders, hitmen, and advertisers for administration policies. Depending on the popularity of the given policy, the chore can be a pleasant or onerous task. Humphrey, for instance, found himself to be the major defender of the Vietnam war, an image that haunted him throughout the 1968 campaign for President. As Humphrey wrote in his autobiography,

> Except for the President, I had been the Administration's primary defender of
> the increasingly ugly and unpopular war. I may have been wrong, but I acted
> out of conviction and upon the information made available to me. I was under
> the impression for a long while that what I was reading of intelligence reports
> was precisely what the President was getting. I was told that would be the case.
> As it turned out, it was not so.
>
> I was picketed at almost every meeting. Generally, there were protesters out-
> side the hall, but frequently, too, there would be some within the hall, heckling
> or walking out. In percentage terms, they were few, and the larger audience
> in the auditorium was generally at least polite and often enthusiastic. But every
> speech, every visit became emotionally draining. The harassment, the shouting,
> the interruptions became a little tough to take over a long period of time. By
> mid-term, I had an almost Pavlovian reaction every time students approached, a
> tightening up physically and psychologically. Hammered daily, it was easy to
> become defensive, aggressive, and strident (1976, p. 429).

Yet, Humphrey also argued that the hitman function was part of the Vice-President's responsibility. According to Humphrey: "Henry Wallace was at times Roosevelt's Roosevelt. Lyndon Johnson was at times Kennedy's Kennedy. And I am proud to say that I was a good deal of the time Johnson's Johnson. . . . The fact that a Vice President may take over some of the responsibilities of the President in the political field is not to condemn him but rather to recommend him" (1974, p. 66). Mondale echoed the argument upon leaving the Vice-Presidency: "A President's public education responsibility may be the most important responsibility he has and, when properly conducted, the most significant power a President possesses. Teddy Roosevelt called it occupying the 'bully pulpit.' The public education role goes to the very heart of a President's capacity to lead and to gain the trust and support that he must have. And any President needs all the help he can get" (remarks, 18 Feb. 1981, p. 4). In support of that role, Mondale traveled almost six hundred thousand miles during his four-year term. Mondale addressed the United Nations on the Indochinese refugees, the U.S. Olympic Committee on the 1980 boycott, the Israeli Knesset on a framework for Middle East peace, and eventually gave the energy speech Carter had canceled during the 1979 midsummer crisis. However, like Humphrey before him, Mondale was sometimes forced to defend unpopular policies. At the 1978 midterm Democratic convention in Memphis, Mondale was in the awkward position of defending Carter's tight fiscal policy before an audience already ignited by Ted Kennedy's passionate call for expanded social programs. According to a Mondale aide: "That was one of the most difficult speeches for Mondale. He had to put some kind of gloss on the President's growing conservatism. Those were his people in Memphis, liberal Democrats from wayt back. All he could do was make the speech and hope for applause."

The dangers of the spokesman's role rest on becoming too closely identified with administration policy. As noted above, Humphrey's defense of the Vietnam war affected his run for the Democratic nomination in 1968. Past tapes of Humphrey's speeches were retrieved from news vaults and replayed for the electorate. Though Humphrey worked to shake the hawk label, his energetic support of the war in 1966 and 1967 remained a source of division within the Democratic party. Humphrey's speeches served as evidence to the liberals of his true sentiments. Ford faced a similar problem after the Nixon resignation. Ford had been a vigorous defender of the Nixon White House during the first months of his brief Vice-Presidency. Reading speeches prepared by Nixon writers, Ford had started his term with ample praise for Nixon. Placing the blame on Congress and a band of misguided liberals, Ford quickly established himself as a prime defender of Watergate. According to Ford aides, Ford had been misled by Nixon. Whatever the reason, the early speeches were recalled after Ford's September 1974 pardon of Nixon, as the media searched for any evidence of a deal. As one Ford vice-presidential assistant noted: "The best thing we ever did was hire our own writers. That only happened after we made those first campaigns to clear Nixon, though. If we had had our own speechwriters from the start, none of Ford's speeches would have been so hot. He just got wrapped up in the rhetoric and, at the start, it still looked like Nixon might not go down." Ford eventually made a break with Nixon, accusing the Committee to Re-elect the President (CREEP), Nixon's 1972 campaign organization, of being manipulated by "an arrogant, elite guard of political adolescents." But, like Humphrey's speeches, Ford's remarks had a way of working back into nightly newscasts and retrospectives in the final days of the Nixon Presidency. Nor was Mondale immune from his ties to the Carter administration when he became a presidential candidate on his own in 1983. According to his campaign director, James Johnson, "In the first half of '81, there was no piece of advice more given to us than: Find a way to separate yourself from Carter fast" (*Boston Globe*, 25 Feb. 1983). Even though Mondale opposed the Soviet grain embargo in private he lived to regret his public support when he returned to Iowa to campaign for his own nomination three years later.

Campaigner

The campaigner function has become central in the contemporary Vice-Presidency. According to one report, Mondale gave over one hundred speeches in the 1978 midterm campaign, traveling to twenty states. Agnew also worked the midterm circuit, establishing himself as a vicious campaigner. Agnew's speeches on the 1970 campaign trail became models of attack. Agnew had already made his mark as a political hitman in his October 1969 attack on "an effete corps of impudent snobs who characterize themselves as intellectuals." In a speech carried live by all three networks, Agnew accused a small band of New York and Washington executives of shaping the news against the "silent majority." Agnew continued his assaults into 1970, becoming the most popular campaigner within the Republican party. By the time he was selected to lead the 1970 campaign, Agnew had become the third most popular figure in the nation as measured by the Gallup poll, only trailing Richard Nixon and Billy Graham. No Vice-President had ever placed so highly in a Gallup poll. Agnew continued his hard-hitting campaign into the fall, raising $3.5 million in the process (a large sum in 1972), but was rebuffed when the Republican party lost nine seats in the House while gaining two in the Senate. Given the heavy investment of White House energy and the level of drama, the results were widely viewed as a defeat for Agnew and Nixon.

Agnew's heated campaign style was merely a reflection of Nixon's own vice-presidential style in the 1950s. Though Eisenhower had asked his Vice-President to participate in the 1954 midterm elections, Nixon expanded his mandate into the first major midterm campaign. Henry Wallace had campaigned in midterm elections, too, but spent most of his time on more general defense of administration policy. According to Donald Young, Nixon traveled over 26,000 miles, visited 95 cities in 31 states, delivered 204 speeches, and met the press over 100 times (1972, p. 262), setting records for midterm campaign activity that only Agnew would surpass. Nixon's campaign rhetoric was as hot as Agnew's twenty years later. Nixon accused the Democratic party of being soft on communism, soft on treason, soft on Korea, and soft on China. In a subtle endorsement of McCarthyism, Nixon also praised the Republican effort to root out communists and fellow travelers in government. And, in a harbinger of the 1970 campaign, Nixon's efforts were tied to the loss of the nineteen seats in the House and two in the Senate, ending Republican majorities in both chambers.

Whatever their campaign styles, Nixon and Agnew recognized the value of the campaigner role. First, both saw the midterm elections as a path for their own national visibility. According to an Agnew assistant: "Agnew knew what he was doing in 1970. He was buying some insurance for 1972 and 1976. By all the speaking, he established himself as a legitimate force within the party. No one cared much about his record once he showed he was a flashy speaker." Though Nixon and Agnew had held elective office before the Vice-Presidency, neither gained national prominence until the midterm campaigns. Because of their slashing styles, both were able to gain recognition, even if it was often negative. However, as another Agnew aide argued: "The public probably didn't notice so much what Agnew was saying as how he was saying it. His rise in the polls was the direct result of the campaign. If he had been dry and boring, no one would have noticed him. I admit the attacks were probably wrong, but it did have some impact on Agnew's career." This kind of roadwork is valuable no matter what the style. Mondale and Ford were able to gather support for their own campaigns by stumping for midterm candidates. At least for Democrats, recent changes reserving seats at the nominating convention for uncommitted party officials raise the value of favors earned in the midterm campaigns.

Second, whatever the future political gains, both Nixon and Agnew saw some short-term need to build party support in Congress. Since Vice-Presidents have some stake in their administration's legislative success, there is some pressure to minimize midterm losses. As Ford argued, his frequent absences from Washington in 1974 were required. "Because of Watergate and the Vietnam War, Republicans were in trouble. Virtually no one was speaking up for the GOP. To stave off crushing defeat at the polls that fall, somebody who knew the party's accomplishments and goals had to be willing and available to explain and answer questions about them" (1979, p. 14). Since Vice-Presidents are highly visible figures, their campaign activities have some impact on outcomes. Though political scientists have not measured the value of vice-presidential visits on congressional campaigns, one Mondale aide offered the following assessment: "Mondale was never asked not to come into a state. He was welcomed by all candidates and never stood alone on a podium. He didn't campaign for some of the heavies, but was never told to stay home. I'd guess that he saved four or five close elections in 1978."

Vice-Presidents also campaign for their own renomination. Only then can they campaign for the reelection of the President. One way to gain renomination is to actively participate in the midterm campaigns. If Vice-Presidents are able to establish their value as campaigners, Presidents may look on them as indispensable resources. Moreover, if Vice-Presidents are able to build external followings, Presidents may be unable to drop them even if they try. That was the case with Nixon and Agnew in 1971. Nixon briefly flirted with John Connally as a running mate, but faced still resistance from Agnew's newly found friends within the conservative wing of the Republican party. A second route to renomination is to gether internal capital. By convincing the President of his internal value and expertise, a Vice-President can eliminate most speculation about rival candidates. Since no Vice-President is immune from rumors, they must give some thought to their own campaigns reasonably early in the term. Ultimately, the midterm elections serve as the key for demonstrating ability and effectiveness. The Vice-President's willingness to spend endless nights away from home can serve as the best strategy in renomination.

There is a final role for the Vice-President as a surrogate for the President in the reelection campaign. When Carter adopted his rose garden strategy in 1980, Mondale was forced to carry the load in the initial primary contests. Part of the strategy rested on the Iranian crisis. Carter was deeply immersed in the effort to free the hostages and believed he had to stay near the White House. Part of the strategy rested on Ted Kennedy. By remaining in the rose garden, Carter avoided any direct confrontation with Kennedy, including debates. Carter's plan was to retain his presidential image by not dirtying himself in the primaries. That left most of the campaign duties to Mondale. According to one Mondale campaign adviser: "I can't recall a single early primary that we didn't get involved in. We were on the road almost nonstop from January to May. The whole strategy worked pretty well at the start, but Mondale couldn't carry it all. People started to demand that Carter come out. And the rose garden strategy eventually fell through." In the end, Carter left the rose garden for the last primaries. By that point, however, Carter had won enough delegates to ensure renomination. Mondale's role in the strategy was to play Carter's Carter, taking on Kennedy without losing the early lift in support from the Iranian crisis.

Lobbyist

Of all the political duties, the lobbyist role appears to offer the greatest advantage for the Vice-President. With a Capitol Hill office only a short distance from the Senate floor, the Vice-President has considerable opportunity to affect the course of presidential legislation. With the authority to recognize senators on the floor and break tie votes, the Vice-President has additional power to direct the flow of policy. In reality, however, Vice-Presidents rarely use the Senate office to influence senators, rarely use the presiding gavel to change the outcome of debate, and rarely break tie votes. According to a Johnson vice-presidential aide: "I once did a count of tie breakers. On the average, the Vice-President gets about ten ties a term. Of those ten, only two or three are really very important. Most ties help the President. Even when a tie is important, the Vice-President can't exercise any independence. He'll vote the way the President wants or never be seen again." Vice-Presidents are almost never lobbyists, being forced to remain aloof from the bargaining process. Their main function on Capitol Hill is to act as conduits to and from the administration, relaying information on head counts to the White House and taking reassurances back. As Mondale argued: "Because of the peculiar relationship that a Vice-President has between the executive and legislative branches, while I do discuss issues with senators, I try to avoid any role that would create doubts as to my impartiality as presiding officer and that would appear to be inappropriate for my office" (*National Journal*, 11 Mar. 1979). Moreover, the norms and folkways of the Senate demand fairness. As Humphrey remembered:

> You recognize the majority leader whenever he seeks recognition. You recognize the minority leader following the majority leader. You try to recognize a Democrat and then a Republican, that is on ordinary matters. When you get into a hot debate, when the issues are difficult, you recognize on the basis of who is up first — whether the Vice President's eye catches a particular person. Now, of course, you can occasionally blink. But I think that most Vice Presidents try to play it fair, and, as we say, on the level (remarks, April 1965).

Though Vice-Presidents and their staffs are not involved in lobbying on a day-to-day basis, there are occasional opportunities for impact. Ford was used on the defense budget, but refused to lobby for Nixon as the Watergate crisis deepened. Rockefeller was used on aid to Turkey, but, according to one aide: "You only use someone like Nelson Rockefeller sparingly. Sometimes we used him on a veto. Had him call so-and-so. You couldn't meet with Rockefeller face-to-face and not be persuaded. But it was like handling nitroglycerin. Could be damn powerful, but could also blow your hands off." Mondale was also held in reserve. As a Carter liaison officer noted: "Mondale did a lot of work on the big-ticket items. He was certainly worth a few swing votes on some of the more difficult bills. Panama Canal. Economic stimulus. He was able to fill in where Carter couldn't. He became the lightning rod for complaints about Carter's style, but he wasn't able to change Carter's mind-set about Congress." A Mondale aide offered a slightly different impression. "Yes, Mondale was active on Panama Canal. He camped up on the Hill for two weeks before the showdown votes. He was also the one who broke the natural gas pricing filibuster in 1978, which cost him a lot of liberal friends. Other than that, Mondale didn't particularly like the lobbying role. He didn't like going to old friends as a salesman. I think he felt it was demeaning to send a Vice-President begging for favors."

Vice-Presidents spend very little time presiding over the Senate: of the 178 days that the Senate met in 1977, Mondale spent 19 days presiding for a total of 18 hours. Bush kept a similar pace in his first two years. Yet, despite the underuse, the congressional role can involve some impact, particularly if the Vice-President can become an informant or strategist. As *informants,* Vice-Presidents can act as conduits for head counts and complaints. "I'd say that was our primary function," a Mondale aide said. "We were there to send down any signals of trouble from Congress. Whether the Carter people got them or not, we kept an eye out on potential trouble. Mondale would come up and just sit and listen to these guys cut into Carter." Mondale would then take the complaints back to Carter and his staff. However, as one aide argued: "No one ever listened to what Mondale was saying and, to be honest, Mondale didn't push too hard. Here were all these congressmen and senators ready to mutiny and all we could do was ring up the White House and give the warning. I'm sure Mondale told Carter what was going on, but Carter just wouldn't change." According to a second Mondale assistant: "That was our major area of expertise—dealing with Congress and legislation—and was also our worst mistake, not taking charge of the legislative operation. Mondale just didn't want to get involved in a fight with Frank Moore, Carter's director of congressional relations. That was part of Mondale's effort not to get caught between other players, but it really hurt us on the Hill." Whether or not Mondale should have become more involved in direct lobbying, he did remain a conduit for information. Bush continued the role, attending the weekly meetings of Republican committee chairmen as a representative of the President. As Bush noted, "It's useful, because people can come up to me and say, 'Tell the president you can't do this, or you ought to do that.' They let off steam on personal problems and I get a pretty good sense of the mood that I can share with [the President]" (*Washington Post,* 30 Mar. 1981).

Depending on their experience in Congress, Vice-Presidents also can act as *strategists,* giving advice on legislative tactics. Johnson, Humphrey, Ford, Mondale and Bush all had Capitol Hill experience before entering the

Vice-Presidency. All combined, the five had over sixty years of legislative service. Thus, when Johnson was asked for advice on passing the civil rights bill, the Vice-President had plenty to offer:

> I wouldn't have [Kennedy] go down there and meet Wallace and get in a tussle with him. I'd pick my own time and my own place. The hell with confronting those people. But I think he ought to talk frankly and freely, rather understandingly and maybe fatherly. He should stick to the moral issue and he should do it without equivocation. . . . I know these risks are great and it might cost us the South, but those sorts of states may be lost anyway. The difference is: if your president just enforces court decrees, the South will feel it's yielded to force. But if he goes down there and looks them in the eyes and states the moral issue and the Christian issue, and he does it face to face, the southerners at least respect his courage. They feel that they're on the losing side of an issue of conscience (Miller 1980, p. 306).

Kennedy did not accept Johnson's advice and the civil rights bill remained stalled in committee. Nonetheless, Johnson had briefly acted as a legislative strategist. Mondale also acted as a strategist in urging Carter to veto a $37 billion weapons bill in 1978. Mondale felt that the $2 billion authorization for a new nuclear carrier was a good target for a veto. According to Finlay Lewis:

> When Mondale took it up with Carter, he was badly outnumbered. Defense-authorization bills were traditionally considered veto-proof. Almost all of Carter's major advisers—Jordan, Jody Powell, Eizenstat, Frank Moore—were opposed to a veto. An outraged Congress, they argued, would surely override the president, making him look more foolish than ever.
>
> But Congress was Mondale's special area of expertise. He also had learned to be more direct.
>
> "Mr. President, you've got to veto something," Mondale said, "Here's one where you've got a good case. You said you're for a strong defense but would not take a carrier.
>
> "If you don't do it now, you'll never get control" (1980, p. 248).

In this case, the President accepted the Vice-President's advice—an example of influence—and vetoed the bill. The veto was sustained with relative ease.

Vice-Presidents have varied to the degree that they were interested in the congressional role. Those with legislative experience—Barkley, Nixon, Johnson, Humphrey, Ford, and Mondale—were generally attracted to the Congress. The two without legislative backgrounds—Agnew and Rockefeller—had more trouble. However, though Agnew did not like the Senate and felt out of place, Rockefeller was one of the most active lobbyists among recent Vice-Presidents. As one Rockefeller aide argued: "Nelson loved the Senate. Got very excited about the traditions of the body. His uncle, Nelson Aldrich, was once the majority leader in the Senate. Rockefeller was very interested in the tradition and history of the Senate and worked very hard to learn the rules and customs." Spofford Canfield, a vice-presidential liaison aide under Agnew, Ford, and Rockefeller, offered the following comparison of the three Vice-Presidents:

The biggest difference was in their background. . . . Agnew had only limited experience in Annapolis as Governor (1967-69) and no background in legislative affairs. He seemed to lose interest and did not spend much time in the Senate.

Ford was a creature of Congress but really of the House. He served in a hectic period during Watergate and impeachment and did not have the opportunity to become involved in substantive issues. But he was very popular up here.

The current Vice President [Rockefeller] is unique; he is very interested in the legislative process and enjoys the ceremonial aspects of the job. It is safe to say that he spends more time up here than any other Vice President in the last 20 years (*National Journal*, 23 Aug. 1975).

A second aide noted that "we only had Agnew on the floor or in the cloakroom two or three times during his five years. Ford liked to wander into the cloakrooms all the time; we used to lose him over in the House. Rockefeller was very adept at dealing with members and genuinely liked wheeling and dealing." Agnew had started his term with a major blunder in the Senate. During debate over the tax surcharge extension in 1969, he asked Senator Len Jordan of Idaho whether the administration had his vote. As one aide remembered: "Jordan probably didn't understand the question anyway. He was pretty damn old. But he thought Agnew was putting the squeeze on him for the vote and snapped back 'You had my vote until now.' Agnew was just livid when he came off the floor. He thought he was being friendly. He was already pretty shaky because he had such a lousy reputation. I can count on one hand the number of times he went back up after that." A Ford presidential aide summarized the problems of Agnew and Rockefeller as follows: "It's interesting that the two people who had the most controversy in handling the Senate were governors, Rockefeller and Agnew. They weren't in the same league, though. Rockefeller was more persuasive and genteel. But they both came in and immediately violated Senate norms—Agnew by pressuring a Senator for a vote and Rockefeller by using his gavel to stop a debate on Rule 22."

Rockefeller's chief trouble stemmed from the Vice-President's constitutional authority to give opinions on procedure from the Senate chair. The bulk of past vice-presidential opinions have dealt with cloture, the method used for ending Senate filibusters. Until 1917, the Senate had no rules for ending filibusters. As long as a member or group of members could hold the floor, they could continue talking. With the adoption of Senate Rule 22, two-thirds of the senators present and voting could end debate. Cloture became more difficult in 1949 when Rule 22 was changed to two-thirds of all senators, not just those present and voting. Attempts were made every two

years after, except 1965 and 1973, to reduce that number of votes from 66 to
60. In doing so, the Senate first had to decide how many votes were necessary
to end filibusters over the cloture rule itself. Could a simple majority stop
debate on Rule 22 or was the two-thirds rule still in effect? Five Vice-
Presidents—Nixon, Johnson, Humphrey, Agnew, and Rockefeller—were
asked for their opinions on the question. Once given, the Vice-President's
opinion could be put to a majority vote. In 1957, Nixon advised the Senate
that a majority was enough to end a filibuster over Rule 22, but his opinion
was never put to a vote. In 1963, Johnson was asked the same question, and
ruled that the two-thirds rule carried over from one session to the next and
thereby affected all filibusters on all issues. In 1967 and 1969, Humphrey
took the majority route, but his opinions were rejected in floor votes. In
1971, Agnew returned to the two-thirds position.

Thus, when Rockefeller was asked for his opinion in 1975, he could not
look back to any consistency from his predecessors. Rockefeller ruled that a
majority could decide its rules and was sustained by a vote of 51 to 42. In the
key debates that followed, Rockefeller repeatedly used his power to "gavel
through" the opposition. In one critical series of arguments, he refused to
recognize James Allen, a Democratic senator from Alabama. As one aide
recalled: "Rockefeller eventually became friends with Allen, but he had
that one day when he gaveled down Allen. He hadn't violated any rules, but
had violated a norm. It was inadvertent, but caused quite a stir among
conservatives who were opposed to any changes in Rule 22." Rockefeller's
maneuvers were widely interpreted among conservatives as telling evidence
of the Vice-President's liberalism. Rockefeller's seeming preference for
liberals during the floor debate became the tip of the wedge that ultimately
drove him off the presidential ticket. "And all because of what?" an aide
questioned. "Because he was asked to give an opinion on Rule 22. Hell, the
Senate didn't even stick with it. They compromised with the conservatives
and hammered out a temporary deal. Rockefeller should have kept his
head down, but he wanted to be like his uncle."

THE POLICY VICE-PRESIDENCY

The policy functions of the Vice-Presidency are relatively recent additions
to the office. Though Wallace had temporary control of the Board of Economic Warfare in World War II, his line assignment lasted only eighteen
months and ended with the disbanding of the board. Subsequent Vice-
Presidents received occasional policy assignments in minor areas, but it was
not until Rockefeller occupied the Domestic Council that the policy Vice-
Presidency reemerged. Rockefeller was also able to expand the policy function to include advocacy. In his administrative position on the Domestic
Council, Rockefeller tried to shape the President's domestic agenda. In his

weekly one-on-one meetings with Ford, he used his considerable persuasive talents to push for pet projects, particularly the Energy Independence Authority, a $100 billion research and development program. However, in his activity as both a line assistant and senior adviser, Rockefeller took a position as a policy advocate, adopting highly visible stands on controversial issues. Rockefeller's advisory style created considerable tension in an already divided White House, leading to his isolation from the policy process. By the end of 1975, Rockefeller had been forced off the presidential ticket and had resigned from the Domestic Council. Though he continued his private conferences with Ford, he was effectively isolated from the rest of the White House staff. Before his defeat, however, Rockefeller had occupied both components of the policy Vice-Presidency: line assistant and senior adviser.

Line Assistant

Line assignments give the Vice-President administrative duties, with the delegation of authority from the President. Unlike the senior adviser role, line assignments demand a long-term commitment of vice-presidential time and energy. In the past, vice-presidential line assignments have fallen into three categories. First, Vice-Presidents have been given the responsibility for policy *issues.* Rockefeller was given control of domestic policy, while Ford was given responsibility for privacy issues. Second, Vice-Presidents have been given control of policy *processes.* Mondale was in charge of the White House agenda-setting process, while Bush was responsible for crisis management in the White House Situation Room. Third, Vice-Presidents have been given operating authority for specific policy *agencies.* Rockefeller was the vice-chairman of the Domestic Council, while Wallace was the chairman of the BEW. Whatever the specific category of assignment, the line assistant role involves a presidential mandate for action. The President may ask for a specific product, request a periodic report, or demand a final document. But, regardless of the administrative end, the most important characteristic of a line assignment is that the President actually expects some result.

If the commissioner function was a product of the 1960s, the line assistant role was a product of the 1970s and one Vice-President: Rockefeller. Because of the unusual pressures of Ford's post-Watergate Presidency, Rockefeller was able to bargain for a grant of authority in domestic policy. As one Ford aide noted: "I think the President was willing to yield some ground to Rockefeller because he wanted him on board. I also think Rockefeller wanted the Domestic Council because he wanted a formal guarantee he wouldn't be wasting his time. It was a trade-off: Ford gave the domestic field to Rockefeller, while Rockefeller gave his credibility to Ford." A Rockefeller assistant agreed. "You can't attract a Rockefeller to the Vice-Presidency unless you give up some territory. Rockefeller wasn't about to accept the Vice-

sistant agreed. "You can't attract a Rockefeller to the Vice-Presidency unless you give up some territory. Rockefeller wasn't about to accept the Vice-Presidency without some clear responsibilities."

This is not to suggest that previous Vice-Presidents had never been given line assignments. Technically, Henry Wallace was the first modern Vice-President to act as a line assistant. He was given formal duties, controlled a sizable administrative agency, and had specific targets to meet. However, between Wallace and Rockefeller, line assignments were few. Agnew, for instance, was given responsibility for health policy in 1970. According to Ehrlichman,

> Health experts were to be added to the Vice President's staff, along with a speechwriter and TV specialists. Agnew then chaired a series of interdepartmental meetings on health issues, but he seemed incapable of organizing the work and guiding the staff to a result. I watched the Vice President closely during this health project, trying to discover the cause of his mental constipation.
>
> I concluded that the man was exceedingly narrow; new thoughts were unwelcome to him. As a result, his health project did not gather for the President all the practical alternatives for a final choice. Instead it became a narrow reflection of Spiro Agnew's preferences. One by one the resource people dropped away from the effort (as did I), and it languished. Eventually the quest for a health program was reassigned to Ken Cole, Jim Cavanaugh and a new working group, and some excellent options were forwarded to the President. Spiro Agnew had struck out on health (1982, p. 147).

Thus, when Ford gave Rockefeller control of the Domestic Council on 13 February 1975, Rockefeller became only the second Vice-President in history with a major line assignment. Ford's decision moved Rockefeller to the vice-chairmanship of the council and included the following responsibilities: assessing national needs and identifying alternative ways of meeting them; providing rapid response to Presidential needs for policy advice; coordinating the establishment of national priorities for the allocation of available resources; maintaining a continuous policy review of on-going programs; proposing reforms as needed. As Ford remembers, the decision to cede the Domestic Council involved his promise to the Vice-President:

> When I asked Nelson Rockefeller to be Vice President, I told him that he would be given major responsibility for the formulation of domestic policy, and I intended to keep that promise. Understandably, Nelson wanted James M. Cannon III, a long-time aide, to be executive director of the Domestic Council. He also wanted to reorganize the council as an autonomous unit that reported directly to him. Rumsfeld opposed that. He didn't feel that there was enough time in the day for Rockefeller to do all the things he had signed on to do. The Vice President, Don pointed out, had to preside over the Senate. He had the CIA investigation to worry about, meetings of the Cabinet and the NSC to at-

tend, the trips abroad as my personal representative. He wouldn't have time to come to the morning staff meetings where the day-to-day decisions on domestic policy were made. Similarly, Rumsfeld argued that it would be a serious mistake to allow the council to operate as an autonomous unit outside the organization that he had set up and that he controlled. Rumsfeld bore no animosity toward Rockefeller or Cannon personally. He simply opposed what they wanted to do organizationally. Unfortunately, the end result was that tension developed between Nelson and Don (1979, p. 228).

After winning the line assignment, Rockefeller was able to launch a series of domestic policy initiatives, including an inventory of past Domestic Council activities, a canvass of the departments and agencies for new ideas, and a division of the organizational structure into two parts, one focusing on day-to-day needs and the other working on long-range planning.

Despite the initial victories, the line assignment became a failure. Rockefeller dropped off the council in late 1975, spending most of his time on a series of policy forums in various parts of the country. "Rockefeller thought the Domestic Council would be policy *formulating,* but it was more policy *coordinating,*" a council assistant explained. "OMB had the leverage over policy during the Ford administration. The Domestic Council assignment actually limited Rockefeller's impact by holding him down." A second council aide agreed: "The Domestic Council didn't do for the Vice-President what Rockefeller thought it would do. Rocky thought the domestic adviser would be the counterpart to Kissinger at NSC. Thought there would be long-term policy. It wasn't true. More than 80 percent of our time was invested in immediate problems. Little opportunity for long-range planning. Rocky expected us to be laying out broad policy, but we barely had the time to put out the fires."

Although line assignments carry opportunities for advice and influence, they involve high costs. Rockefeller's Domestic Council assignment exposed him to considerable staff infighting, allowed the media to measure his success and failure, and absorbed great amounts of time and energy. Thus, when Mondale drafted a set of recommendations for his Vice-Presidency, he asked Carter to spare him the line assignments. As Mondale noted,

I decided to recommend to the President that I not be assigned any line functions as such, for several reasons. First, most of the functions would, if they are significant, be already assigned to some Cabinet or key executive officer and why should I handle them? Or, if they weren't significant, they would trivialize the Vice Presidency. I think, in the past, Vice Presidents have often taken on minor functions in order to make it appear that their role was significant when, if they were President, they wouldn't touch them at all. I decided to stay away from that. Also, by staying away from direct line functions, I think you avoid the jealousies and competition that might otherwise develop and affect your role as adviser.

Secondly, I don't have the staff to run a major line function. Nor should I. It takes a lot of time away from your advisory role. The way it is now, I don't have to defend a bureaucratic office. And that's good. I can spend my time else-where. . . . I can, more or less, be where the President needs me most, with not having the continuing responsibility of a staff nature, which is really a misuse of my time (*National Journal*, 11 Mar. 1978).

Yet, even with Mondale's reluctance, he was willing to take limited assignments in a troubleshooting role. Unlike Rockefeller's Domestic Council duties, however, Mondale's troubleshooting function was limited to very specific policy areas and/or very limited periods. Mondale did accept the chairmanship of the White House Executive Management Committee, established in July 1977 under Carter's reorganization of the executive office. Mondale used this assignment to continue his agenda-setting process for the legislative program. As Gail Harrison, Mondale's domestic issues director, argued in 1978, "We take a look across the board as to what we're prepared to do in foreign and domestic areas, whether it is consistent with policy, whether the timing is right and whether it is a high priority goal" (*National Journal*, 11 Mar. 1978). The agenda-setting process generally lasted less than three months, always at the end of the year, and did not absorb much of Mondale's personal time. However, the agenda process did become a tool for securing information and expanding the Vice-President's institutional base. Yet, the line assignment remained a very temporary, troubleshooting responsibility. As a second aide argued: "Mondale was willing to take the agenda thing because he felt that it was essential that somebody do it. He didn't see any potential trouble because it really didn't fit between any departments or players. He clearly felt it was a problem area that needed someone's attention. Nobody in the administration seemed to see the problem of sending up so much legislation without any idea of priorities. Mondale felt it was a vacuum and needed to be done by somebody."

Senior Adviser

At least since Henry Wallace, all Vice-Presidents have had occasional opportunities to act as senior advisers, offering opinions on what should or should not be done on questions of policy. For some Vice-Presidents, these opportunities have been quite rare—a courtesy call from Ted Sorensen to Lyndon Johnson on civil rights strategy, a request from Johnson to Hubert Humphrey on youth employment, an assignment from Nixon to Spiro Agnew on health. Most of the opportunities for advice have been rare, and some have carried high risks. Humphrey's arguments against the bombing of North Vietnam, for example, only succeeded in angering Johnson. Johnson refused to call National Security Council meetings for a time just to isolate Humphrey from his one formal advisory role. For Rockefeller and Mondale, however, advisory opportunities were frequent, coming at least once a week in private meetings. During the weeks of 4 April and 11 April, 1977, for instance, Mondale spent at least eleven hours in conference with Carter, including three private lunches. According to a Mondale aide who kept records of the Vice-President's time: "Mondale spent 25 percent of his White House time with the President and another 10 percent with the senior staff, the NSC, or receiving the President's Daily Briefing. We always received the President's weekly schedule and picked out the meetings that Mondale might have been interested in attending." Though Rockefeller had frequent access to Ford, Mondale outdistanced his predecessor in the sheer amount of time spent in the advisory role. And, though both Vice-Presidents shared in the development of the advisory function, each had a different approach to the role. Rockefeller is a prime example of the *advocate,* while Mondale is an example of the *hidden-hand* adviser.

In his role as an adviser, Rockefeller was the consummate advocate. According to a Ford assistant: "That man always had some idea that he wanted to see Ford about. I don't think he ever went in to Ford unarmed. He'd take in charts and draft legislation and even speeches. For Rockefeller, it was always sell. He just didn't see himself as sitting back and having Ford ask the questions. He was always on the offensive." A second Ford aide echoed the argument. "The problem with Rockefeller was that nobody could say no. He was constantly pressuring for some idea, always an advocate. Great if you're a governor with some money to throw around; not so hot if you're a Vice-President in an administration committed to a tight budget." Rockefeller's major sales effort came with the Energy Independence Authority. Rockefeller worked the inside circuit for months in support of the research and development idea, an approach he had used as governor in urban redevelopment. When Rockefeller failed to win inside support, he used his access to Ford for an end run, working to persuade Ford regardless of administration sentiment. It is still a matter of dispute whether Ford actually signed off on the Rockefeller proposal. However, Rockefeller was able to persuade the President to include the idea in the 1976 State of the Union message. Given the odds against original approval, Rockefeller was able to win a significant moral, if not legislative, victory.

The problem with the advocate's position is that the Vice-President is exposed to counterargument and counterattack. One Ford OMB officer noted,

There is something inherently difficult about the Vice-President wanting to be an advocate. Unless his views and programs are amazingly coincident with the President's, he will be cut down. The President can't submerge his ideas to accommodate the Vice-President. What Nelson had in mind was to control domestic policy, as if he was saying "I know everything there is to know about domestic policy and Ford will have to listen." What Ford was thinking was "I'll listen to Rocky's ideas and make my decisions on the basis of what I think is important."

Unlike department secretaries or OMB directors, Vice-Presidents do not have the troops to sustain an active advocate's role. Rockefeller not only had to win the President's approval, but he had to secure a budget, legislative passage, and implementation. When legislative liaison refused to lobby for his energy bill, when OMB refused to budget the program, and when the Federal Energy Agency refused to staff the hearings, Rockefeller had to fight his battles alone. According to a Domestic Council aide: "Nelson would have been far more successful had he pursued the energy idea through either the Domestic Council or through the energy agency. Instead, he took it on as *his* program. It had to be Rockefeller's success or failure." When Rockefeller worked through the Domestic Council as a hidden advocate, he was more successful. Regulatory reform and drug control were two programs that Rockefeller supported, but that came from the Domestic Council. Rockefeller's problem was not that he supported certain ideas, but that he often became the lead actor within the policy process.

Mondale preferred the *hidden-hand* approach, reserving his arguments for the covert stages of a debate. Though Mondale used his staff as lead actors on several policies—electoral reform, the carrier veto, the hospital cost containment task force—Mondale was rarely the primary advocate for a specific program; thus of all the programs that the Carter administration produced, only the Vietnamese boat people rescue can be identified as a pure Mondale idea. That is not to say that Mondale did not weigh in on policy debates. However, Mondale carefully avoided the high visibility of the advocate's position. As one aide argued: "I can't recall too many times that Mondale got visibly angry about any policy in public. In fact, I can't recall too many times that he was openly involved in any debate. He would sit there and listen, waiting until he got Carter alone." Mondale simply could not maintain the advocate's position and actually viewed Rockefeller's failure as an important lesson on strategy. Using a more subdued, generalist approach, Mondale was deeply involved in administration policy. He was involved in the selection of several cabinet members, reorganization of the intelligence agencies, the search for a new Federal Reserve Board chairman, the establishment of the Department of Education, expansion of child welfare programs, electoral reform, and budget policy.

Which is the best approach philosophically? Should the Vice-President remain silent even when he disagrees? Should the Vice-President argue for ideas which may cost him access in the future? Should Humphrey have stayed quiet on the bombing of North Vietnam? These questions are just as easily paired with a second set. Should the Vice-President hold off on some issues to retain influence on others? Should Rockefeller have stayed quiet on energy to preserve at least some influence for later? Is some influence on some issues more valuable than principled resistance with no influence? A Humphrey aide offered a preliminary answer:

> In politics, you have to be willing to compromise. There's no such thing as a pure right and wrong. I personally believe that Humphrey should have tried a different approach with the bombing. Had Humphrey worked a little different track, he might have been able to have some impact. Maybe he would have been able to slow down the bombing or speed up the peace initiative. Maybe he would have been able to alert Johnson in a different way as to what was going on. Maybe he would have been able to end the war by a couple of days. Who knows? But as it was, he had no impact on the war. He stood up at that first meeting and was closed out from then on. He spoke his convictions, but wasn't ever allowed to speak again. I'd guess I'm a believer in working for whatever you can get whenever you can get it. Humphrey was probably right on the issue, but had no impact.

THE TRAINING FUNCTION

One final function remains in the vice-presidential job description: the training function. Since the Vice-President's major constitutional duty is to remain in waiting for a presidential resignation or mishap, the training function is an important component of the job. Unfortunately, as Schlesinger argues:

> Presidents not only do not choose Vice Presidents to become successors, but, after they make the White House themselves, they do as little as possible to prepare them to be successors. A Vice President can learn only as much as a President is willing to have him learn—which given presidential resentment of vice presidential existence, is not ordinarily very much. . . .
>
> Moreover, seeing things as an ill-informed, impotent, and often sullen outsider, the Vice President will very likely "learn" the wrong things. Lyndon Johnson thought Kennedy too cautious at the time of the Cuban missile crisis and in Vietnam. . . .
>
> A learning office? With Presidents less generous than Truman—and that in this context is most Presidents, however generous they may be in other relationships—the Vice Presidency is much less a making than a maiming experience (1974, p. 485).

A Rockefeller aide seconded the opinion. "The Vice-Presidency isn't much good for training. Here's a guy who happens to be Vice-President because he's the second-best politician in the party. There is no power to decide anything, to vote on anything, to administer anything. The Vice-President is the most senior counselor the President has, but must beg to get even a morsel of power. Unless the President wants the Vice-President to learn, he'll spend his time doing nothing."

Yet, assuming we will continue to have Vice-Presidents and we will also continue to have presidential emergencies, the training function will remain. It may be inadequate, as Schlesinger suggests, but it is training nonetheless. As one Humphrey assistant notes: "Judge the Vice-President on no other measure than his preparation for succession. He is a reservoir for the future rather than a resource for the present." A Carter aide made a similar argument:

> Advocacy is not what the Vice-Presidency is for. Presidents don't need more voices—there are plenty of advocates. Vice-Presidents don't have the staff for advocacy anyway. The best the Vice-President can do is observe and help make an occasional decision. Mondale was prepared to step in. That's it. Mondale received great on-the-job training, but he can't be blamed for any of the Carter mistakes. He doesn't have to defend the Carter administration. He can tell everyone he knows how to do the job, but no one can say "Fritz Mondale was the one who got us into Iran."

As the vice-presidential job description has deepened, the Vice-President's training has improved. As Vice-Presidents have moved from ceremonial duties to policy responsibilities, they have become better prepared for succession. As Mondale noted,

> I think it may be the best training of all. I don't know of any other office, outside of the presidency, that informs an officer more fully about the realities of presidential government, about the realities of federal government and the duties of the presidency that remotely compares to that of the Vice President *as it is now being used.*
>
> I'm privy to all the same secret information as the President. I have unlimited access to the President. I'm usually with him when all the central decisions are being made. I've been through several of these crises now that a President inevitably confronts, and I see how they work. I've been through the budget process. I've been through diplomatic ventures. I've been through a host of congressional fights as seen from the presidential perspective.
>
> I spent 12 years in the Senate. I learned a lot there, but I learned more here about the realities of presidential responsibilities. I learned more about our country and the world in the last three years than I could any other way (*National Journal,* 1 Dec. 1979).

The key phrase, of course, is "as it is now being used." The change in the Vice-Presidency over the past two decades has made the training function more viable. Further, the training has also improved for the Vice-President's staff. As the staff has grown, Vice-Presidents have been able to build experience for emergency transitions. Unlike Johnson in 1963, Mondale would not have been forced to rely on his predecessor's staff during the first crucial months.

TEN VICE-PRESIDENTS

By now, it should be clear that the vice-presidential job description has changed over the past decades. Vice-Presidents now have some hope of taking on substantive policy responsibilities, while shedding their ceremonial mantles. One way to appreciate the change is to look back at the past ten Vice-Presidents: Wallace, Truman, Barkley, Nixon, Johnson, Humphrey, Agnew, Ford, Rockefeller, and Mondale. These ten contemporary Vice-Presidents should illustrate the evolution of the job description.

The Ceremonial Vice-Presidents

Truman, Barkley, Johnson, Humphrey. These four Vice-Presidents spent the bulk of their time performing ceremonial duties, whether as delegates or commissioners. All four had opportunities to give advice, but none was able to formalize that role. Though Humphrey came closest to substantive policy duties in his extensive and exhaustive commissioner activity, his role was generally restricted. Because of his abbreviated term, of course, Truman had few chances for developing an advisory role in the mold of his predecessor, Henry Wallace. Truman had been Vice-President less than three months before Roosevelt's death. In that brief time, however, he was generally ignored within the White House and was not well prepared for the emergency succession. Truman was not told about the Manhattan Project, which produced the atomic bomb that Truman would order dropped on Hiroshima and Nagasaki, nor was he given a full briefing on the Yalta meetings, which set the stage for the cold war.

Upon election to the Presidency in his own right, Truman made several changes in the treatment of his Vice-President, Alben Barkley. Truman actively sought Barkley's participation at cabinet meetings and included the Vice-President in the Korean decision. In 1949, Congress passed legislation at Truman's request to make the Vice-President a formal member of the National Security Council, an assignment that remains a statutory function today. Though Barkley was active in the 1948 campaign, traveling extensively in support of the ticket, his age limited his activity once in office. Barkley was seventy-one when he was inaugurated and preferred the ceremonial Vice-Presidency to an advisory role. A few brief quotations from Barkley's autobiography should demonstrate the point.

> I suppose I traveled, mostly by air, more than any Vice President had up to that time, making speeches in all parts of the country. Many of these speeches were of semi-official nature, for I often represented the President, who, naturally, was limited in his ability to accept engagements. . . .
>
> Of course, for a certain period, I seemed to be much in demand as a crowner of "queens" at various celebrations—Apple Blossom festivals, Cherry Blossom

festivals, and just about every sort of festival that one can think of. It seemed an inevitable—and not entirely unwelcome—part of the ritual that the visiting Vice President should kiss the queen, after crowning her. . . .

The Vice President's principal duty is to preside over the Senate. I enjoyed this, though I came to sympathize with Vice President Dawes' feeling of frustration, as I often itched to get back into the fray of debate. . . .

I was proud to occupy the historical room in the Capitol assigned to the Vice President. I liked to keep a wood fire burning in the fireplace and to smell the good smell of wood smoke which reminded me of the innumerable open hearths at which I had warmed myself in my youth. I enjoyed being surrounded by the priceless relics which enhanced the office. . . (1954, pp. 207-10).

Although Barkley was invited to all Cabinet meetings and attended most of the meetings of the National Security Council, his autobiography does not mention any policy involvement in the Truman administration. And, though Barkley enjoyed presiding over the Senate, he was not a lobbyist for Truman's programs.

As noted earlier, the commissioner function was a product of the Kennedy and Johnson years. However, between the two Vice-Presidents of the period, only Humphrey took the duty seriously. As Johnson's term as Vice-President progressed, he became less and less interested in any activities, regardless of their symbolic value. At the start of the term, Johnson had been reasonably hopeful about a substantive role. Under his direction, the National Aeronautics and Space Council recommended the lunar project. He joined astronaut John Glenn on his triumphant ticker-tape parade in New York. However, in an administration that moved in ad hoc committees and a crisis atmosphere, Johnson could not keep up. As one Kennedy aide remembered:

The president brought me into his office and said, "I want you to take care of the vice-president and Mrs. Johnson. I want you to watch over them and see that they're not ignored, not only when you see them but at all other occasions." I said, "What do you mean?" He said, "Because I'm going to forget. My staff is going to forget. We're all going to forget. We've got too much to do around here. We move so fast from one thing to another that I'm going to forget, and I want you to remember" (Miller 1980, p. 278).

The lack of a substantive role may have hurt most in foreign policy. As this Kennedy aide continued:

He wanted to play on the president's team. He wanted to be a help to him. He said, "I don't want to have any blurring of the image of the United States in foreign policy." He thought I was very close to the president, and he said, "I want you to get that point over to him that I'm not playing any games here. I'm sincere. I would like to be part of his team and to play on the team. If he thinks I'm out playing for myself, carving out areas of foreign policy, it's not so. How can I get that through to him?

"After all, I'm sent out to speak all over the country, and then when I do, I get myself knocked on the head . . . and it's just not fair."
He was like a dog worrying at a bone (Miller 1980, p. 307).

Nor did Johnson participate in the 1962 congressional campaign. The Cuban missile crisis in October eclipsed any major campaigning, but Johnson had few plans anyway. He was already pulling back from any active role long before November 1962. Nor was Johnson involved in the Kennedy legislative program. Part of the problem was Bobby Kennedy, but part reflected Johnson's bitterness following his "defeat" in the Democratic caucus at the start of the administration. Johnson had asked to be chairman of the caucus, an unprecedented role for a Vice-President, even if he happened to be the former Senate majority leader. The issue was brought to a vote in the caucus and Johnson was elected. However, there were enough dissenting votes to challenge Johnson's authority, and the Vice-President reluctantly withdrew. According to one set of observers: "Johnson was so hurt and angry at the large number of votes against him on the Mansfield motion on January 3 that his usefulness as a legislative helper to Kennedy turned out to be minimal. . . . With a few exceptions, Johnson did absolutely nothing to advance the Kennedy legislative program. He did not try to exert his influence on his old friends in the Senate, seldom if ever employing the Johnson Treatment as of old on Richard Rusell or members of the vestigial Johnson network. He did not wheel and deal" (Evans and Novak 1966, p. 311).

The common denominator among these four ceremonial Vice-Presidents is that they all served under activist Democrats. Before concluding that there is a party trend in the use and misuse of Vice-Presidents, note that two of three policy Vice-Presidents also came under Democrats. Perceptions vary on the explanations for the Democratic pattern. As one observer argued: "The strange thing about Kennedy and Johnson was they chose not to use their Vice-Presidents. You'd think they would have wanted all the help they could get to keep the ball rolling. I suppose that both felt threatened or didn't think their Vice-Presidents could keep up." A Humphrey assistant agreed in part: "I'd say Lyndon just didn't think it was worth the trouble. If he was in a meeting about the war or the poverty program or whatever and wanted Humphrey in on it, he'd have to pick up the phone and call him over. The EOB isn't very far away from the White House, but it's still about a fifteen-minute proposition. Why bother to wait? It was more convenient not to use him." In the onward rush of an activist administration, the Vice-President can be a time-consuming commodity. Recall that Mondale saw the EOB as like "being in Baltimore." The lack of proximity to the Oval Office was at least a contributing factor in the four ceremonial Vice-Presidencies. Moreover, as I suggest in Chapter 4, there were few incentives for using the Vice-Presidents in these four White Houses. All four Presidents were insiders, with considerable Washington experience. Regardless of the qualities of their Vice-Presidents, these Presidents had plenty of advice from their own people. Why would Johnson call on Humphrey for legislative strategy? Why would Roosevelt call on Truman for help on the war?

The Political Vice-Presidents

Nixon, Agnew, and Ford. Though these three Vice-Presidents also spent considerable time in the ceremonial arena, they added political duties to their job descriptions. Under Eisenhower, Vice-President Nixon spent every other year on the campaign trail, building a base for his own presidential candidacy in 1960. Under President Nixon, both Agnew and Ford logged several hundred thousand miles on the campaign trail, making hundreds of speeches in search of elusive Republican votes. Though the four ceremonial Vice-Presidents also campaigned, it remained for Nixon, Agnew, and Ford to inaugurate a new level in political activity.

The obvious common element among the three political Vice-Presidents is that they all served in Republican administrations. Once again, there seems to be a party pattern. Several explanations arise. First, Eisenhower was a passive campaigner (though not a passive President according to Greenstein 1979), leaving a large vacuum for his ambitious Vice-President. Eisenhower was generally impressed with Nixon's campaign and speaking abilities, but did not originally conceive of the active political role. Nixon persuaded Eisenhower of the need for a campaign presence. Thus, it was Nixon, not Eisenhower, who saw the potentials of the political Vice-Presidency. Had Eisenhower been an activist President, Nixon might not have been able to shape the new role. Second, once Nixon was elected President in 1968, he had already been exposed to the political Vice-Presidency. As one Agnew aide noted: "I don't think there was much question that Nixon would allow Agnew some running room as a hitman. Nixon had done it himself in the 1950s and it was generally agreed that Agnew could do it in the 1970s. The critical thing was that Agnew had to prove he was at least as vicious as Nixon had been. That was a hard task, but Agnew somehow found it in himself to out-Nixon Nixon." A second Agnew aide concurred. "Nixon had a reputation as being one tough son of a bitch under Ike and I'm sure Agnew realized that it was the way to score points. Nixon never said a thing about not going out to campaign. It was almost an automatic. We were given the speechwriters and let loose."

Once Agnew resigned and the Watergate crisis deepened, Nixon desperately needed a political Vice-President, one who could both defend the administration on the road and build bridges on Capitol Hill. Ford was the logical choice, even agreeing not to run for President in 1976 as part of his nomination to the Vice-Presidency (see Ford 1979). Yet, though Nixon recognized the value of the political assignments, he refused to give Ford any policy responsibilities beyond the Privacy Commission. Nor did he particularly want policy advice from Agnew or Ford, holding both in some disdain, once talking of Agnew as his "insurance" against impeachment. Nixon could see the merits of political Vice-Presidents, particularly as Watergate expanded, but he did not see the value of their policy advice. Such was the evolution of the political role. A passive Republican President gave his Vice-President a campaign role. That Vice-President eventually became an activist President in his own right, but still recognized the value of the political role.

A final explanation for the political Vice-Presidents is that the three Republican Presidents had very slim margins in Congress. Unlike their Democratic colleagues, Eisenhower and Nixon faced the problems of minority support on Capitol Hill. Though the Democrats wanted majorities, just like the Republicans, Eisenhower and Nixon felt the absence of support more sharply. Nixon recognized the problem in 1969 as his domestic agenda stalled in Congress. According to an Agnew liaison aide: "Nixon was madder than hell that his efforts to compromise with the Democrats had failed. He wanted to see if he could clean them out in 1970 and was willing to use any means available. Nixon had concluded by autumn 1969 that he wasn't going to win much in a Democratic Congress and started dreaming about a Republican majority." Moreover, because of the Republican minority in Congress, Nixon had fewer people to draw on for the campaigner role. Once Agnew had demonstrated his abilities in the attacks on liberals, intellectuals, and the media, he was given the lead in the 1970 congressional campaigns. Ford was given the same assignment in 1974.

The Policy Vice-Presidents

Wallace, Rockefeller, and Mondale. The first two policy Vice-Presidents, Wallace and Rockefeller, were the product of unusual circumstances. Wallace's assignment to the BEW came only moments before World War II, with Roosevelt facing a broad range of political and strategic demands. Though Wallace had not been nominated for the Vice-Presidency because of his administrative abilities, there were several incentives for using him in the war effort. First, as the only other nationally elected official, Wallace brought legitimacy to the BEW. Since the BEW was charged with the acquisition of strategic materials—materials that would soon be scarce in the private sector—it may have helped to have the Vice-President at the top. Second, Roosevelt had far more than he could do in handling the war machinery. Wallace had been secretary of agriculture before accepting the Vice-Presidency and had impressed Roosevelt as being an effective administrator. Like many other Roosevelt aides, Wallace possessed certain strengths that made him a logical candidate for an administrative assignment. Despite the line duty, however, Wallace did not become an adviser. Upon losing the BEW, Wallace returned to the relative obscurity of the ceremonial Vice-Presidency, punished for both his support of a U.S.-Soviet alliance and his attacks on Jesse Jones. Though Wallace was the first policy Vice-President, he was not a senior adviser.

Rockefeller's policy Vice-Presidency was also the product of peculiar circumstances. Rockefeller was the second appointed Vice-President in less than a year and the first to be nominated by an appointed President. Rockefeller's policy role emerged from two features in the situation. First, in selecting Rockefeller, President Ford was searching for a national figure, not just a ceremonial Vice-President. In presenting a list of names for Ford's decision—a list which included George Bush, Rogers Morton, Republican Minority Leader John Rhodes, Tennessee senator William Brock, and Nelson Rockefeller—Bryce Harlow suggested that Rockefeller was "professionally the best qualified by far with the added strengths of (a) proving the President's self-confidence by bringing in a towering number two, (b) making available superb manpower resources to staff the administration, and (c) broadening the Ford political base." Harlow concluded that the "choice narrows to Bush and Rockefeller. For party harmony, plainly it should be Bush. But this would be construed primarily as a partisan act, foretelling a presidential hesitancy to move boldly in the face of known controversy. The Rockefeller choice would be hailed by the media normally most hostile to Republicans. It would encourage estranged groups to return to the party and would signal that the new President will not be the captive of any political faction" (Ford 1979, p. 140). As Ford describes his decision:

> Some of my staff felt that Rockefeller was too strong, that he'd try to dominate the administration. That didn't worry me because I was determined to heed the advice Laird had given me shortly after I'd assumed the Presidency. "I have an idea that Nixon picked Agnew because he was insecure and didn't want anyone who would overshadow him," Mel said. "Don't you do anything like that. When you're President, you don't have to worry about being overshadowed by anyone." If Rockefeller was strong, that was all to the good. What the country needed was not just the image but the substance of strength, and Rockefeller could contribute more to that strength than anyone else. Adding up the pros and cons, I concluded that he would be a fine partner (1979, p. 140).

Once Ford selected Rockefeller, he turned to a second problem: how to attract a person who had twice rejected the vice-presidential nomination before. In the negotiations that followed the initial choice, Rockefeller was able to work for a substantive policy role. As Ford remembers:

> I said I wasn't going to ask him merely to carry out the routine functions of his office, which involve presiding over the Senate and travelling all over the world. I wanted him to participate in all meetings of the Cabinet and National Security Council. Additionally, I wanted him to head the Domestic Council and help put together my domestic legislative package. "You've been studying these

issues," I said. "You've had a lot of experience with them, and I think that is one area where you can be very helpful to me" (1979, p. 141).

Moreover, like Wallace, Rockefeller had some skills that were in short supply in the White House. Although Ford had been Vice-President for nine months, his staff was still quite thin in the autumn of 1974. His staff had been weakened by a turf battle between the congressional group (led by Robert Hartmann) and the new vice-presidential team (led by Philip Buchen and William Seidman). That staff fight was heightened by the presence of a large number of Nixon holdovers following the resignation. Further, though Ford certainly grew into the job, he was quite concerned about his own qualifications for the Presidency. As one aide noted: "It would be fair to characterize Ford as insecure at the start. He had never really wanted to be President and was only there because of a fluke of history. He was scared at the start and reached out for help. Rockefeller probably sensed that and pressed for all the territory he could get." Though Ford had considerable Washington experience before the Presidency, he was still unprepared for office, still facing an uphill battle for his own renomination. "Rockefeller had Ford pretty much where he wanted him," a Ford assistant said. "Ford was desperate for some symbol to calm everybody down, including himself. Rockefeller had a patriotic streak and accepted the job for a variety of reasons, but he did some hard bargaining for a major assignment."

Compared to Ford, however, Carter was the extreme in lack of presidential training. He had only limited contact with the federal govenment, serving one term as governor of Georgia before embarking on his campaign for the Presidency. His staff did little to answer the shortage of political skills. Most of Carter's top staff was drawn from Georgia—Hamilton Jordan, Jody Powell, Frank Moore, and Bert Lance. Mondale was the opposite. Mondale had served in the Senate for a decade before reaching the Vice-Presidency. Richard Moe, Michael Berman, Gail Harrison, Bertram Carp, and David Aaron all had similar backgrounds. Mondale entered office surrounded by a well-seasoned staff. Moreover, Carter was willing to have a policy Vice-President.

Once in office, Carter recognized the potential value in Mondale's participation. One payoff was the expertise of the Mondale staff. Several Mondale staff aides were moved into other White House offices, Carp to domestic policy and Aaron to NSC. Other Mondale aides were integrated with the Carter team. Berman, for instance, filled in on legal matters before Lloyd Cutler was hired for the White House counselor's post. A second payoff was Mondale's connection to mainstream Democrats. Until Anne Wexler joined the White House staff as director of public liaison in mid-1978, Carter had few aides who could offer sound political advice and connections with interest groups. A third arose when Bert Lance resigned in 1977. As OMB Director, Lance had access to a considerable store of information. Lance was also Carter's close personal friend, one of the few aides in the President's age range. Once Lance resigned, Mondale helped fill at least part of the void. With Carter's close friend gone, Mondale became more active as a senior adviser. Thus, Mondale's policy role stemmed from his personal and staff resources, as well as from Carter's willingness to listen. According to Mondale and Carter aides, the President simply thought it natural to use the Vice-President. "Like any other officer," a Carter aide argued, "Mondale was there to be used. It made no sense to the President to just let an officer do nothing. It didn't fit with the President's view of an orderly ship."

CONCLUSION

Before turning to changes in the Vice-President's institutional support, it is important to look at three patterns that emerge from this brief history.

First, the political Vice-Presidency arrived *before* the policy Vice-Presidency. It was the political Vice-Presidency that supplied much of the staff and advisory resources necessary for the policy role. It was the political role that allowed Vice-Presidents to demonstrate their value as advisers. The political Vice-Presidency provided the building blocks for the policy function. As a Carter aide suggested: "Whatever Agnew's worth to Nixon or the country, he did show that a Vice-President could do something more besides sit on his ass. He was a bastard of the first degree, but he did prove to be of some political value. Same goes for Ford. Vice-Presidents had to show that they were good politicians before they could be accepted as advisers." Chronologically, the ceremonial Vice-Presidency was present long before either the political or policy role. However, the ceremonial function could do little to enhance the Vice-President's stature inside or outside of the White House. As Vice-Presidents discovered the rewards of campaigning and speaking—primarily nomination to the Presidency at the end of four or eight years—they also demonstrated their value to the White House. The political duty thereby became the driving force toward greater staff support (more speechwriters and advance people), more perquisites (better airplanes and offices), and more responsible assignments (fewer funerals and ribbon cuttings, more advising). Presidents began to recognize the potential value of activist Vice-Presidents in maintaining an ongoing political campaign. No longer would Presidents have to wait to campaign until just the fourth year. Nor could Vice-Presidents be relegated to meaningless White House chores during breaks from the road.

Second, Watergate was a prime catalyst in the growth of the policy Vice-Presidency. The single largest increase in the Vice-President's staff budget, for example, followed Ford's appointment to the office in 1973. Agnew's resignation on the eve of the Watergate crisis created a bargaining opportunity for a new Vice-President. "Nixon had no choice on Ford's staff," an aide remarked. "He was in deep trouble and had to give Ford more freedom to keep him interested in helping the administration. Ford always held that one trump card. By keeping quiet about Nixon's innocence, he could show Nixon's guilt." Following Nixon's resignation, Watergate continued to exert pressure for an expanded Vice-Presidency. In the search for his own Vice-President, Ford had to attract a national figure to shore up his weakened administration. Among the Republicans mentioned as potential replacements, only Rockefeller had not been tainted by past association with Nixon. Finally, it was Watergate that led Rockefeller to accept the position he had rejected twice before, once with Nixon (1960) and once with Humphrey (1968). As Rockefeller told Hartmann after leaving office:

It was entirely a question of there being a Constitutional crisis and a crisis of confidence on the part of the American people. . . . I felt there was a duty incumbent on any American who could do anything that would help contribute to a restoration of confidence in the democratic process and in the integrity of government. I felt President Ford was taking over the job on that basis. He understood the Congressional-legislative side of the issues and I understood the Executive-administrative side. And, therefore, I might be able to contribute something.

He wanted me to give him support in the domestic field and wanted me to head it up as Henry [Kissinger] would in the foreign field. And he wanted me to help him on recruitment, which he said could be very helpful, as I was known for having attracted good people. . . (1980, pp. 230-31).

Without the unique mixture of events following the 1972 break-in, the Vice-President might still be languishing in isolation. The rise of an independent vice-presidential staff, the freedom to organize and reorganize the office, the arrival of greater administrative and political support, even the growth of an institutional identity, all coincided with Watergate. It was an event which created distinct opportunities for vice-presidential bargaining. Though all the trends were moving toward a greater vice-presidential policy role, the impact of this one event cannot be underestimated. Watergate was a turning point in the institutionalization of the office, as much so as the appointment of Rockefeller and the election of Mondale. It involved a step-jump in the vice-presidential job description. And while many contemporary observers look to Watergate as one source of our current political disarray, Vice-Presidents cannot be faulted if they look back to that event as the start of a renaissance in their institution.

Third, whatever Henry Wallace's contributions, the policy Vice-Presidency was the result of the Rockefeller and Mondale experiences. Despite the unusual circumstances surrounding Rockefeller's appointment, he was able to set the precedent for an active advisory role. His weekly meetings with Ford may have been the most important single event in the evolution of the policy function. It remained for Mondale to supply the discipline and the strategies to make the role successful. In Chapter 6, I look at both Vice-Presidencies in detail. For now, it is important to note the impact of Mondale in shaping his own influence. Though institutional support had increased by 1977, Mondale used that support to increase his advisory capacity. He did not use it for better travel plans or patronage. He hired staff members that compensated for Carter's weaknesses. When the option arose to place several staff members in positions inside the White House, Mondale decided to use them to build influence networks. Though the political Vice-Presidency had paved the way for the advisory role, Mondale did not use his campaigning in a threatening manner. In the heavy campaigning of 1978 and 1980, he worked as a team player, never separating himself from the Carter administration. Mondale often refused to advertise programs that he opposed, but he did not "go public" with his dissents. Though Carter was an outsider and needed considerable help, Mondale did not press his advantage. At the start of the administration, Mondale rarely volunteered advice, reserving his opinions for Carter's questions. That simple stylistic difference allowed Mondale to build his internal capital, while cementing coalitions within the White House. Unlike Rockefeller, who sought immediate victories over both policy and process, Mondale started with a low profile and worked toward a more aggressive stance. By the end of the term, Mondale was as active as any of the top four or five Carter aides.

Thus, when Mondale was elected, the Vice-Presidency was already at a threshold. It had the institutional support for an ongoing advisory role. However, the evolution of the office clearly reflected Mondale's personal style and ability. It was Mondale who lobbied for the West Wing office. It was Mondale who refused the long-term line assignments. And it was Mondale who developed new strategies for vice-presidential advice and influence. Like the rise of other White House agencies under staff entrepreneurs—the National Security Council under Kissinger, the Domestic Council under Ehrlichman, the Office of Congressional Relations under Harlow and O'Brien—the Vice-Presidency gained much of its new role under one player: Mondale. Like these other agencies, the Vice-Presidency retained some of the power after Mondale left. Bush kept the West Wing office and adopted many of Mondale's strategies. Yet, the Vice-President's ability to give advice must be distinguished from actual *influence*. The Vice-Presidency has finally achieved an advisory role, but nothing guarantees impact.

3.

The Institutional Vice-Presidency

The Vice-President's policy role starts with the institutional support needed to give advice. That support grew with remarkable speed in the 1970s. From an office with too many payrolls, too many locations, and not enough staff, the Office of the Vice-President of the United States now has a distinct institutional identity. It is now very much a part of the Executive Office of the President (EOP). From an office with fewer than twenty staff members in 1960, the Vice-President's office now has seventy permanent positions. From an office with no executive budget, the Vice-President's office now has its own line with an annual budget of two million. From an office with five or six different locations, the Vice-President's staff is now consolidated on the second floor of the Old Executive Office Building, with outposts on Capitol Hill and in the West Wing.

The Vice-President's office is now a replica of the President's office, with a national security adviser, press secretary, domestic issues staff, scheduling team, advance, appointments, administration, chief of staff, and counsel's office. And, in 1972, the Vice-President's office finally was listed as a distinct unit in the *United States Government Organization Manual*, a major sign of institutional identity. The manual had no trouble placing this "hybrid" office in the Executive Office of the President, acknowledging its status as part of the White House, not Congress. A Humphrey aide perceived these changes in a very simple light. "When I went over to visit some of the Mondale people after their first year, I saw something completely different.

The Vice-President's staff had come out of the closet. They weren't worried about letting the rest of the White House know who they were. They ate in the mess and were proud to work for the Vice-President."

THE INSTITUTIONAL ADVANTAGE

Apart from the aesthetic values of the new-found identity, the institution-alization of the Vice-President's office has at least four advantages.

First, the separate budget makes it easier for Vice-Presidents *to attract staff talent.* In 1960, Lyndon Johnson was unsuccessful in persuading many of his Senate staffers to join him in the Vice-Presidency. Part of the problem was the absence of high-paying positions to compete with the Senate—some aides were unable or unwilling to take the cuts in salary. Part of the problem was the absence of specific positions. The best Johnson could do was offer some the chance to work for him on loan from departments or commissions. For those who had tasted the power of the majority leader's office, Johnson could not match the money, prestige, or potential influence to lure them to the Vice-Presidency. As one Johnson Senate aide remarked: "What was I going to do in the Vice-Presidency? Johnson decided to take his schedulers and some letter writers and one or two policy people—George Reddy and Walter Jenkins. There wasn't any room for the rest of us and none of us really wanted to go anyway. The money was poor and the office wasn't organized to use us." As a result, Johnson left most of his Senate Staff behind, including Bobby Baker.

By 1977, institutional changes allowed Mondale to bring virtually all of his Senate staff to the Vice-President's office. Mondale could offer specific positions to most of his Senate staff and did not have to work out loans with departments. As one observer argued: "As the Vice-Presidency gains strength, it should be easier to get good people on board. No one wants to work for a loser or spend four years doing nothing. Washington staffers look for certain signs of prestige: good pay, nice offices, mess privileges, good travel support, decent assignments. If the Vice-President has those kinds of perks, he'll be able to get better people and keep them longer." A Mondale assistant agreed. "I never once felt that I was wasting my life working in the Vice-President's office. It was reasonably enjoyable, a lot of hard work, fairly good pay. I never felt as if I was less of a person because I was connected to the Vice-President. I never had to beg for anything. I lost some arguments over policy, but I never had to fight for the basic support and dignity that a White House aide should have."

Second, the institutional identity provides *both protection and a vantage point in the White House policy process.* Vice-Presidents are now less vul-nerable to changes in presidential moods. Because the Vice-President's office now has its own line in the executive budget, Vice-Presidents have the ability to protect their staffs against arbitrary presidential cuts. If push comes to shove, the President will always win. However, short of open warfare, the growing institutional strength of the Vice-President's office provides some protection against presidential whims and freeze-outs. If the President cuts the Vice-President off from information and expertise, the Vice-President has at least some alternative sources within his own staff. Nor do Vice-Presidents now have to rely solely on presidential advance teams or speechwriters for travel support. Unlike Agnew, who took most of his texts from the White House writing corps, Mondale had his own team of speechwriters. "We were never in the position of having ten minutes to rewrite a speech that some typewriter jockey had screwed up in the White House," an aide remembered. "We did all our own material. We did our propaganda and our scheduling. We always worked for the Vice-President's interests, but still represented the President on most of the trips." Unlike Johnson, who relied on State Department or NSC experts, Mondale had his own team of foreign advisers. Mondale was never forced to depend on Carter's staff for basic political support. That provided a level of independence not previously found in the Vice-Presidency. According to an assistant: "Mondale wanted an independent staff. He always had access to the White House staff, but wanted a separate staff of his own. Carter had suggested that the Vice-President share the White House staff, but Mondale refused. Mondale wanted an independent source of advice, his own speechwriters, press people, etc. The staffs were integrated function by function, but they were independent."

Though the institutional independence offers some protection against internal isolation, it also provides a vantage point within the policy process. Any adviser who controls seventy staff positions has some weight in the White House. If Vice-Presidents can hire qualified staff members and generate independent advice, they can compete within the White House. They may not win every argument, but the institutional base offers some leverage. Thus, Rockefeller's frustration in the Ford White House was less a problem of institutional support and more a problem of heavy White House opposition. According to a Rockefeller aide: "The very fact that we were being attacked like that was one sign of just how strong we were. We became a very real threat inside the White House. We had good people and plenty of things to say." An observer offered a sports analogy to explain the change from 1960:

> The Vice-Presidency has come a long way since Johnson. It is still not as strong as NSC or DPS or the departments, and I doubt it will ever get to that level. It is, however, much stronger; strong enough to have some level of influence. It's kind of like an expansion baseball club. When it started out, it was pretty

damn bad, using second-rate players and old pitchers. Now, twenty years later, the team has gotten a lot better; younger players, better arms, better coaching, a good farm system. Maybe it won't win a pennant, but it'll still do better than .500. And the other teams will have to play better to win.

This leverage increases as the Vice-President's staff is functionally integrated with the President's staff. Avoiding needless duplication of effort, the Vice-President's office, while still retaining its independent status, can build networks of advice and influence. Mike Berman, Mondale's counsel, worked closely with Lloyd Cutler, Carter's counsel; Gail Harrison, Mondale's domestic policy adviser, worked closely with Stuart Eizenstat, Carter's domestic policy adviser; Richard Moe, Mondale's chief of staff, worked closely with Hamilton Jordan, Carter's chief of staff. Because the Vice-President's office now has enough positions to cover the political function, the policy staff can spend the bulk of its time on the advisory role. And, when the Vice-President travels on some foreign or domestic chore, the Vice-President's staff can continue its effort to advise and influence. Depending again on the President's willingness to listen, the Vice-President's office can act as a powerful source of advice.

A third advantage of the institutionalization of the Vice-President's office centers on *the resources needed for an advisory role.* The Vice-President's office now provides a stable, reliable source of both information and expertise. With the addition of a national security adviser and domestic issues staff, the Vice-President's office is equipped to supplement White House information. The Vice-President's office still needs access to presidential paper, but now has the capacity to analyze and interpret that information with a separate staff. As a Mondale domestic policy aide argued: "Our job was to take a hard look at the issues that were circulating throughout the White House. Our main interest was in giving the Vice-President a set of options and adding to the arguments he supported. We weren't just a conduit for a stack of paper. We added our own analysis to the material we received and cooked up a number of our own initiatives." Part of the institutionalization of the Vice-President's office involved regular access to presidential information—gaining a position in the White House paper loop. Vice-Presidents now receive most of the paper that Presidents receive. But paper alone does not always equal information. The Vice-President's office acts as a second source of information and serves as both a backup and a screen for presidential paper. The office also acts as a reservoir of expertise for the Vice-President. In Mondale's case, for instance, the staff had considerable Washington experience to add to the Vice-President's own abilities. Yet, according to a Mondale assistant: "The most valuable part of the office is the administrative staff, the people who handle the paper. Most of those people stay on from one Vice-President to the next and retain a good deal of ability. They allowed us to concentrate on the more important issues, and took care of the paper flow and the clerical problems. It was really the only source of institutional memory beyond the military aides."

As the Vice-President's office expanded, the greatest growth occurred at the lower levels, particularly in the political and administrative sections. The number of top aides has remained reasonably stable since Humphrey, averaging around twenty staff members. As the number of support troops increased, the top aides were released to work on the substantive issues. And, as a Rockefeller aide noted: "It's not enough to ask only where the Vice-President is. He may be in the middle of China, but if his staff is still hard at work in Washington, he'll be represented. One of the biggest mistakes a Vice-President can make is to haul his top people with him on the minor trips. Leave them at home to keep the work going." The growth in the political and administrative staffs allows Vice-Presidents to take more trips without risking a great loss in potential influence. Thus, even though Mondale was out of town during the cabinet firings in the summer of 1979, his senior staff remained in Washington and lobbied on his behalf. Certainly, their voices were not as strong with Mondale gone, but they did continue the advisory role. At the very least, the institutionalization of the office has reduced the amount of time and energy Vice-Presidents must spend on routine matters, thereby increasing the amount available for advice and influence.

A fourth advantage of institutional strength rests on *preparation for emergency transitions.* By giving the Vice-President's staff an opportunity to work together and develop White House networks, institutionalization adds to the training function. Had Mondale been forced to take over the Presidency, he would have been ready to plug his own staff into key positions. Moreover, because Mondale's staff had been integrated into the White House, they were better prepared to take over. As one staffer noted: "There would have been no surprises. And I don't just mean national security. We knew how things got done, how the Presidency worked. Mondale would have been given a number of choices. He wouldn't have had to take Carter's people, but would have known how they all worked and who he would want to keep." Though institutionalization offers the Vice-President better information and expertise in the short run, it also offers greater preparation for emergency succession. Because the Vice-President's office is a replica of the President's office, institutionalization offers the staff an opportunity to train for the future.

AN INSTITUTIONAL HISTORY

Institutionalization is a process of increasing size, specialization, and organizational structure. It is a process that creates a distinct institutional unit, along with a set of characteristics that show an organization to be established and surviving in its own right. It is also a process of aging, with the organization adapting to changes in its external surroundings. Whether institutionalization is marked by increased budgets, hierarchy, or a changing mandate, it is a process that produces a separate White House entity.

The institutionalization of the Vice-Presidency occurred in a number of steps during the 1960s and 1970s. It was the result of more money, more staff, an esprit de corps, and an administrative unit. Some of the steps were accidental, some were presidential initiatives, but most came from the efforts of Ford, Rockefeller, and Mondale.

1961. The first step toward an institutional identity came when Kennedy moved Vice-President Johnson from Capitol Hill to the executive compound. The Vice-President's office became more a part of the Executive Office of the President (EOP) because it was housed with the rest of the President's entourage in the Executive Office Building (EOB). Though Kennedy was said to have moved Johnson closer to keep him under tighter watch, the consolidation of the Vice-President's office on the second floor of the EOB helped give it an institutional identity, with physical boundaries and presidential reference points. No longer would the Vice-President belong to Capitol Hill. The office staff is now located less than one hundred yards from the Oval Office. Though Vice-Presidents continue to occupy quarters in the Dirksen Senate Office Building and an office directly off the Senate floor (Ford also kept a small office in the minority leader's suite, while Johnson kept his majority leader's office, then known as the "Taj Mahal"), the Vice-President's main office staff is now located in the presidential compound.

The move to the EOB had several effects. It certainly increased the Vice-President's proximity and visibility within the White House, though Vice-Presidents still remained outside of the West Wing untill 1977. Unfortunately, as a Humphrey aide noted: "We were close, but not close enough. We could see what was going on, and I suppose that was an improvement from being in Congress, but we couldn't get into the White House without clearance. We were still about fifteen minutes away from the action." The EOB office was, however, much more elegant than the congressional office. As the former office of the secretary of war, the suite has high ceilings and a panoramic view of the White House. With hardwood floors and fireplaces, the Vice-President's office suite offers at least some reward to the second-in-command. Even after Mondale moved over to the West Wing in 1977, he retained the office for ceremonial functions and interviews. "It's a very impressive office," an aide argued; "if you were only interested in pomp, it would be more than enough. I still think it's much nicer than anything over in the White House. But, then again, it's not worth anything if you want any policy impact."

1969. The second step toward institutionalization was the acquisition of a line item in the executive budget. The Vice-President's office became more a part of the EOP because it was funded from the President's budget. Though Vice-Presidents still receive part of their support from the Senate, averaging $350,000 during Mondale's four years, they get the lion's share of their budget from the executive line, averaging over $1 million per year under Mondale. The line-item was not labeled as "The Vice-President's Office," but "Special Assistance to the President," and remains so labeled today. The change in funding came almost by accident in 1969 with the passage of the fiscal year 1970 budget. Agnew was not particularly involved in the decision, giving his legislative liaison team freedom to negotiate the specifics. According to a staff member,

> All we did was go to the chairman of the Appropriations Committee and ask for permission for a line item. The Appropriations Committee didn't usually handle these kinds of legislative changes, but it was willing to sign off in this case. It happened in less than a day and wasn't really that difficult. No one had ever thought to ask for a budget line and Vice-Presidents had been subjected to the President's discretion. We just went in and asked. We checked it out with OMB and the White House, but no one thought much about it at the time.

Whatever Agnew's knowledge of the change, it was a significant grant of institutional independence. Up to 1970, Vice-Presidents had been forced to use their Senate budgets and loans of staff from departments as their prime sources of personnel. In 1961, Johnson had been able to place thirteen full-time assistants on his Senate payroll, and had added another eight to ten on detail from departments and commissions. It was an awkward arrangement that continued under Humphrey. According to a Humphrey aide who had been hired on the Agriculture Department payroll:

> It was harder than hell to get Humphrey's staff on the payroll. We had some money from the Senate, but not enough. Humphrey's press secretary was once paid on the Space Council payroll. We didn't have our own executive money and had to fight with bureau chiefs for money and our own people. Every aide had to come off someone else's payroll. It would never work today. With all of the reductions in staff around the executive branch under Reagan, no agency head would give up a position to help the Vice-President. It barely worked for Humphrey.

A second assistant argued that the hiring system did not hamper Humphrey's preparation, but kept the staff off balance. "I'd guess we had about thirty people working for us by 1968. They did just about everything, though it was much less organized than Mondale's office. The problem was that we just didn't have enough people on administration, but Humphrey was very well backgrounded for his work." Yet, even if Humphrey was well backgrounded, the office structure was weak, forcing needless duplication of effort between the Vice-President's staff and the White House, wasting time and effort that could have been spent on policy.

The executive line allowed the Vice-President's office to expand with the President's staff. From twenty aides in 1960, the Vice-President's office grew to seventy under Rockefeller. It then dropped to sixty under Mondale, as Carter tried to reduce the White House staff, but rose again in the first months under Bush to seventy. Of the sixty to seventy staff members, approximately two-thirds are hired with presidential funds. Asked if the line budget made any difference, a Mondale aide replied: "It would only have made a difference if we had lost it. We'd have lost a number of people and it would have vastly complicated our work. It obviously made for easy administration and helped us with our planning. Knowing the people were included in the budget gave us more of a guarantee than relying on Carter's grace." From the perspective of a long-term vice-presidential servant, the line was critical:

> I watched Agnew, Ford, Rockefeller, and Mondale all prosper with that line. It was no small accomplishment, but Agnew wasn't bright enough to notice. The line was such a signal inside the White House. Here was the absolute perquisite. The Vice-President would have his own money and, henceforth, his own staff. It gave the Vice-President what he had never had: the power to hire and fire and spend. It seems like such a small thing to Vice-Presidents now and it was so simple. But it makes a difference as one of those many signals that insiders watch. If the Vice-President has to go begging for people, why listen to him on anything else?

1972. The third step toward an institutional identity was also simple: a listing in the *United States Government Organization Manual.* The Vice-President's office became more a part of the EOP because the General Services Administration, publisher of the manual, finally said it was part of the EOP. The one-page description of the 1972 Office of the Vice President included an address (Executive Office Building, Washington, D.C. 20501), a phone number (202-456-2143), a list of Agnew's top aides (Victor Gold, Press Secretary; Arthur Sohmer, Administrative Assistant; C. D. Ward, Intergovernmental Affairs; Brig. Gen. J. M. Dunn, International Affairs), and a brief description of duties:

> Article II, section I, of the Constitution provides that the President "shall hold his Office during the Term of four Years * * * together with the Vice President. . . ." In addition to his role as President of the Senate, the Vice President is empowered to succeed to the Presidency, pursuant to Article II and the 20th and 25th Amendments to the Constitution.
>
> The executive functions of the Vice President include participation in all Cabinet meetings, and, by statute, membership in the National Security Council and the Board of Regents of the Smithsonian Institution, and chairmanship of

the National Aeronautics and Space Council and the National Council on Indian Opportunity. By Executive Order 11541 of July 1, 1970, the Vice President is a member of the Domestic Council.

In addition, the President has assigned the Vice President primary responsibility for liaison with State and local officials and has given him supervisory responsibility for the Office of Intergovernmental Relations (*United States Government Organization Manual*, 1972/73, p. 89).

The listing was little more than a symbolic step toward institutionalization of the office. Just like signs on the doors saying "Vice President's Office," the listing helped define the boundaries of an executive agency. And, as one vice-presidential aide said, "It was a nice gesture. We weren't exactly overwhelmed with questions and interest from the Nixon staff. It was nice to see that at least somebody took us seriously."

1974. The fourth step involved the arrival of a vice-presidential support staff. Until Ford became Vice-President, occupants had been forced to rely on White House administrative support, while using their own policy aides for routine speechwriting and advance chores. According to an Agnew aide, for instance: "Nixon told the Vice-President that the White House staff would serve at his disposal. You bet. Agnew was given some money for a couple of personal aides—press, congressional relations, intergovernmental relations—but speechwriting, scheduling, administration, as well as policy came through the White House. In fact, even our congressional relations people were working for Max Friedersdorf, Nixon's liaison director. That was their first loyalty. Not Agnew." A Nixon presidential aide confirmed the pattern. "We were generally responsible for outfitting the Vice-President with some basic services. But on a list of one to ten, Agnew was at the bottom in priority. If he wanted something printed, he had to wait. If he needed office supplies, he had to use his own funds. We were working for the President first."

According to Robert Hartmann, Ford's chief of staff in 1973-1974, Nixon offered the same arrangement to the new Vice-President. Hartmann reports that "two things were quickly obvious to me, but I bit my tongue. . . . These guys figured the Vice President for an empty headed neophyte who knew little or nothing about what was going on. They also intended to integrate his supporting staff so completely with the White House that it would be impossible for him to assert even the little independence Agnew had managed for five years" (1980, p. 82). A second Ford assistant confirmed Hartmann's impressions. "The Nixon people wanted to loan most of the staff to Ford, give him one of their speechwriters, one of their legal guys. Ford refused. He wanted to bring in his own people. We built the staff from seventeen at the start to seventy by August 1974. Tried to build a smooth staff system for the transition. We kept hoping that the resignation or impeachment wouldn't come until later, until we had time to build up the staff." Thus, as a third aide concluded:

One of the first things we did was refuse Nixon's generous offer of staff. We knew that we had to have our own people. That set a certain precedent which Rockefeller and Mondale both followed. You really must have your own support group. It frees you up from being dependent on the President. You don't have to waste any of your political capital fighting for a speechwriter or some policy people. You already have them with you so at least if you are cut off, you'll have some people to backstop you for the rest of the term.

In a series of early maneuvers at OMB and on Capitol Hill, Ford was able to boost the appropriation for the Vice-President's office to $920,000, an increase of $228,000 or 33 percent over the previous year. When coupled with a $40,000 increase in the Senate budget to $475,000, Ford was able to find the money for approximately ten new full-time assistants. Moreover, Ford was also able to place Philip Buchen as the staff director of the Privacy Commission, adding still more staff at the Vice-President's disposal. Roughly half of the new aides were added at the senior level. Ford was the first Vice-President with a counsel's office and a national security adviser. The counsel's office was particularly important given the unusual nature of Ford's term. "We needed the best advice we could get on legal matters pertaining to both Ford's appointment and Nixon's resignation," a Ford aide remembered. "It was all new territory under the Twenty-fifth Amendment. We wanted to make sure we were clean on everything." The other half were added in administration and political support. Ford hired his own speechwriters, and built his own scheduling, advance, and administration teams. Unlike Agnew, who was forced to turn repeatedly to the White House for support, Ford built the first self-contained Vice-President's office. A media observer offered one interpretation:

> The office itself had grown somewhat over the previous three Vice-Presidents, just barely keeping up with the expansion of the EOP. Johnson and Humphrey both had staffs anywhere from twenty to forty people, though most of their people were working on too many minor things. Agnew was able to expand somewhat, but still didn't have his own issues staff beyond the intergovernmental affairs group. Ford was the first Vice-President who really used the office as a power base. He added a whole new layer of staff on substantive issues — legal, domestic, foreign, even economic. He added a much deeper political side, bringing on the first speechwriters whose only jobs were speechwriting. When you look at the organization of the Ford Vice-Presidency, you'll see that it was a mirror of the President's office. It was build to provide everything Ford needed.

With the line budget, the Vice-President's office became an *independent* source of information and expertise. With the addition of a political and administrative support team, the Vice-President could begin converting his newly available resources into an advisory role.

1974. A fifth and highly related step toward institutionalization involved

the Vice-President's freedom to hire and fire the staffs of his choice. It was not enough merely to add substantive and support staff. Vice-Presidents had to have the authority to bring their own people into office. Agnew, for instance, allowed the Nixon White House to appoint his legislative liaison staff. Though Agnew's liaison team was strong, it was more an arm of the White House than of the Vice-President. Its first loyalty belonged to Nixon and Max Friedersdorf. According to an Agnew aide: "We never really trusted the Capitol Hill staff. They weren't our appointees and were mainly working for Nixon. I don't think we talked more than two or three times over the entire five years. They weren't comfortable coming down to the EOB because they weren't Agnew's choices." One of the liaison aides agreed. "I didn't consider myself an 'Agnew person.' I worked for the President and that's how it should've been. Max Friedersdorf believed that the Vice-President's legislative office should be staffed by pros and should be used by the President." Ford was much less willing to appoint Nixon people to vice-presidential posts, reserving the key slots for Ford loyalists.

1974-77. The sixth step centered on the formal organization of the Vice-President's office. Starting with Ford and continuing with Rockefeller and Mondale, the office began to look more like other White House agencies. Instead of the loose collections of individuals under Humphrey, the Ford and Mondale offices became quite hierarchical, involving specific chains of command and functions. As the staff increased and assignments expanded, the Vice-President's office needed tighter organization to operate. Under Humphrey, the office had not needed stronger organization, running on an ad hoc basis. Because aides often performed a variety of political and administrative duties, Humphrey could not afford a specific line and staff arrangement. Ford and Mondale, however, decided that they needed a clear organizational chart, with, as one aide noted, "a place for everybody, and everybody in their place." The preoccupation with organization reflected each Vice-President's style, but was also a product of size. Within the White House, this tighter organization allowed for better communication between the Vice-President's office and the rest of the EOP. The President's scheduling office knew whom to call about the Vice-President's schedule; the President's domestic policy staff knew whom to contact about the Vice-President's domestic policy position. More importantly, the tighter organization focused more vice-presidential energy on the advisory role. Political and administrative subsections were given increasing responsibility for routine decisions, leaving more time for policy specialists to ply their trades. Whether the organization created better efficiency or better advice is arguable, but it did raise the institutional identity of the Vice-President's office. It gained its own organizational chart to go with the charts from OMB, NSC, DPS, CEA, legislative liaison, and so forth.

1977. A seventh step involved the perquisites to reward the institution.

White House mess privileges, better aircraft, better offices, fast printing support, and limousines are all signals of institutional prestige. Airplanes are just one example of how the Vice-President's position changed inside the EOP during the 1970s. According to a Humphrey aide: "Mondale was treated 1,000 percent better than Humphrey. By the time Mondale got there, he had a separate appropriation for the Vice-President's office. He didn't have to go begging to Marvin Watson (Johnson's chief of staff) for money. There are several airplanes now. Every time we needed an airplane, we had to kiss ass. We were usually given a small jet with room for ten or twelve people, never room for the media." Agnew moved up a step to a windowless Air Force transport, often called Air Force Thirteen by the staff. "The damn thing didn't even have windows," an Agnew travel assistant joked. "Ever fly to Europe in a plane without windows? Talk about a flying coffin. When we'd get near our destination, a green light would flash and some second lieutenant would throw open a door and push Agnew out." Ford's comfort did not improve much. As Ford remembers: "The aircraft provided for the Vice President's use that summer of 1974 was called Air Force Two, but it was hardly luxurious. It was a squat and aging Convair, a turboprop that creaked and groaned its way through the skies" (1979, p. 13). By the time Mondale arrived, the situation had improved dramatically. Mondale had one plane always on standby, plus access to other aircraft. When he traveled in the campaign, he was equipped to carry the press. As one aide noted: "We had two or three planes that could not be moved without our permission. And they were decent airplanes. Windows, engines, wheels, the whole package. We didn't have to leave in the middle of the night either, like Humphrey."

The growth in vice-presidential "perks" was seen by many staffers as an important symbolic change. Though perks cannot be easily converted into influence, they do act as a signal to other staff members in the White House. If the Vice-President's staff is allowed to eat in the mess side-by-side with the President's staff, it is a signal of increased institutional strength. "This is a city of symbols," a Mondale aide argued. "Little things can make a great deal of difference to the staff. If you've got good perks, it's a symbol of where you stand in the White House. If your office is in the basement of the West Wing, you're not taken as seriously as someone with an office next to the President." A second Mondale aide agreed. "All the little changes in perks can't be as important as Mondale's relationship with Carter. But they brought us to a higher level in the White House. When you can sit down and have lunch with people who are making decisions, it's got to have some impact." One Humphrey assistant offered the following analysis of perks:

> It used to take an act of Congress to get us into the White House. We had to get cleared in by somebody because we didn't have White House passes. Half the

business in Washington is conducted over lunch and we couldn't get into the mess. We were treated like little children, allowed to look but not touch. We had none of the keys to unlock the White House gates and never got to know any of the Johnson people—except to dislike them. We never sat down for a drink or threw the bull around. We didn't have any symbols of power and that was the currency in the White House.

1977. The eighth step toward an institutional presence involved the integration of the Vice-President's staff into the White House policy process. Once the Vice-President's office became self-reliant for political and administrative support, it needed networks into the President's office for any policy impact. As a Mondale aide suggested:

The number of staffers doesn't make as much difference as who they know and how much access they have into the White House. We had between fifty-five and sixty-five people, but not much more than Rockefeller and a little less than Bush, but those people were tied into the Carter staff, freeing them up to do different things. There was very little duplication of effort in the Mondale office. We had access to the senior staff meetings, the deputies' meetings, everything. We didn't have to use our domestic or foreign policy staff repeating the analyses of the Carter staff.

Instead of depending on the White House for basic support, the Vice-President's office could turn to the problem of building influence. "Instead of talking to some midlevel assistant about paper clips or typing ribbons," an assistant noted, "I talked to upper-level aides about education or health or energy policy. I had no problems getting administrative services from our own staffs and could spend my time arguing for more important issues. I wasn't asking for help getting a better airplane. I was using my meetings to suggest different alternatives." Unlike Humphrey's staff, which generally contacted Johnson aides only when looking for support, Mondale's staff could participate in substantive policy debates. Richard Moe, for instance, was chairman of the hospital cost control task force in 1979, chairman of the task force on electoral reform in 1978, chairman of the defense appropriations bill veto task force in 1979, chairman of the task force opposing a constitutional amendment on a balanced federal budget, and a member of the Strategic Arms Limitation Treaty (SALT II) task force. Moe viewed his role as a "kind of rower around the White House. I make myself available to Hamilton Jordan and take on whatever chores he has in mind. It is usually something different every day" (*National Journal,* 3 Feb. 1979). Moe did not have to commit his time and energy to finding a xerox machine or placing a staffer on a commission. And, because the Mondale staff had ties into the Carter staff, the Vice-President's office had an outlet for advice.

The integration of Mondale's staff occurred on four different levels. First, Mondale always received the President's schedule and had an open invitation to attend any meetings of interest. Though Mondale generally did not attend any meetings without specific invitations, the schedule provided an opportunity to track upcoming decisions. "The Vice-President received the schedule with plenty of time to prepare for important discussions," an aide said. "It gave him the lead time to work up his ideas and direct his staff." Mondale also met regularly with Carter, averaging three to six hours a day in both public and private forums in 1977. The schedule and meetings provided ample opportunities for the coordination of vice-presidential advice. Second, Mondale's top aides attended the senior staff meetings each day. These meetings focused on the President's agenda and calendar, generally running from 9:00 to 10:00 each morning. According to a Carter aide: "The Mondale staff presence at those meetings allowed them to keep up with what was going on. It was an important step toward ensuring Mondale's active participation. They never missed any meetings that I can remember." (Ford and Rockefeller aides had also attended senior staff meetings, but were eventually discouraged from coming.) If these meetings allowed Mondale's staff to keep up, they also offered an opportunity to present advice.

Third, Mondale's midlevel aides attended the deputies meeting each day. These meetings focused more on what each agency or unit in the White House was doing and less on the President's agenda, generally running from 8:30 to 9:00 each morning. The meetings allowed midlevel deputies to exchange information on current problems and represented an intelligence-gathering activity for most offices. As an aide remarked: "We didn't spend that much time scoping out the coming day for the President. It was more asking what everyone was doing this week, trying to see what everybody was up to." The regular deputies meetings were new to the Presidency, coming during Carter's first year as a way to keep up with the numerous issues on the agenda and the lack of an acting chief of staff. Fourth, with the appointment of Carp to the Domestic Policy Staff and Aaron to the NSC, Mondale's office was tied into the White House on an informal basis. Carp and Aaron kept their former Senate colleagues posted on any issues that were being hidden from the Vice-President, preventing any end runs around the Mondale staff. As we will see later, Carp and Aaron ensured that Mondale would be included on substantive policy issues. That institutional advantage continued under Bush with the appointment of James Baker III as Reagan's chief of staff.

1977. The ninth step toward an institutional identity came when the Vice-President moved from the EOB into the West Wing. Mondale was not, however, the first Vice-President with West Wing quarters. In the first months of the Nixon administration, Agnew occupied the relatively prestigious corner office that eventually belonged to a string of chiefs of staff (Haldeman, Rumsfeld, Cheney, Jordan, and Baker). Agnew did not stay long, in part because Haldeman wanted him out, in part because of his isolation from his own staff. This ironic situation came from the lack of integration between the Agnew and Nixon staffs. Though Agnew was only yards from the President, he was inaccessible to his own staff. As one aide remembered: "Agnew had the West Wing office, but wasn't doing anything over there. Sat just reading magazines. If he wanted to see his staff, he had to clear us in. We did not have White House passes." A second agreed: "It was a miracle to see Agnew in the West Wing. Security was tight and the clearance process was slow. Agnew didn't like the clutter, either. He preferred the expanse of the EOB office. Had it carpeted in royal blue." Without White House passes for his staff, Agnew was stripped of contact with his own sources of information. Agnew found himself lonely in the West Wing, with no friends on the White House staff. "He wasn't well liked anyway," an assistant remarked. "No one over there thought he had a brain in his head. He couldn't skip between offices and decided, with Haldeman's support of course, to move back to the EOB." Mondale's move was quite different. Aaron was right down the hall, with Carp upstairs. Mondale's staff had White House passes and moved freely between the EOB and the Vice-President's office. In Chapter 5, I return to the importance of the West Wing office for advice and influence. Here, it is important to note that the office increased Mondale's proximity and inside prestige, moving the Vice-President to the physical level of other senior advisers and setting a precedent that Bush followed. Unlike Agnew, however, both Mondale and Bush took offices in between the two valued corner offices, avoiding any conflicts with chiefs of staff (south side) or policy directors (north side).

1977. The most recent step toward institutionalization was the rise of an esprit de corps among the Vice-President's staff. No longer was it the worst moment of a career to work for the Vice-President. Mondale's staff was committed to the office and expressed a desire to work with the Carter team. One Mondale aide noted that "it was a very difficult and tiring experience. We worked hard and were hot-wired for four straight years. Yet, that's one sign of our involvement. We were proud to work for Carter and Mondale. Speaking for myself, it was a very good time."

Esprit de corps is not the most important factor in the institutionalization of the Vice-Presidency and may even be a product of the evolutionary process, but it is a signal of change. As the Vice-President's office grew and prospered, staff members began to think of themselves as more valuable members of the presidential establishment. "At the start of the term," a Mondale assistant remembered, "we held back at meetings and didn't talk much. By the second year, we were talking more and fighting more. We started to act like full-fledged members of the administration." That esprit led to greater solidarity during periods of internal crisis—for instance, during the midsummer crisis in 1979—while adding to job satisfaction. There was less turnover in key staff positions and more willingness to work with the President's staff. Working for the Vice-President was no longer unbearable.*

All of these institutional changes—the move downtown, the executive budget, the support staff, the West Wing office, the organizational charts —contributed to a greater vice-presidential status within the EOP. But none of the changes guarantees the Vice-President an active advisory role. The institutional Vice-Presidency does provide resources for a policy role, increasing the Vice-President's information and expertise, releasing more staff time and energy for substantive issues. If future Vice-Presidents can retain the West Wing office, they will retain their proximity. However, nothing in the institutional framework ensures presidential willingness to listen. The Vice-President's office is now certainly better prepared to provide advice when the President asks. It is not designed to force the President to listen. Just like other advisers, the Vice-President must have the President's participation to complete the advisory connection. Yet, even though the institutional apparatus cannot coerce presidential interest, it can make the Vice-President's participation more inviting. If the Vice-President has independent sources of information and expertise and is prepared to give advice when called, the President may learn to ask more frequently. As a Carter aide noted: "After a while, it was almost automatic for Carter to ask 'What does Fritz Mondale think about this?' It doesn't take too many questions like that before the staff goes to Fritz before the President asks."

*Two other minor events deserve mention before looking at the organizational chart. The first was the vice-presidential mansion, purchased in the early 1970s. Instead of staying in their own homes, Vice-Presidents now live in the refinished Naval Observatory on Embassy Row. The mansion provides the first official Vice-President's residence. Whereas Agnew and his wife lived in a hotel during their five years in Washington, Vice-Presidents now have the luxury of the Naval Observatory. As a Mondale aide argued, "It was a very lovely home and a fine place to entertain. It was fully refurbished and had a complete staff at the Vice-President's disposal. It was a very nice step for the Vice-Presidency." Like the growth in other vice-presidential perquisites, the mansion was a symbolic gesture, giving the occupant additional stature in the Washington community. The second, and again symbolic event, was the redesign of the vice-presidential seal under Nelson Rockefeller. Rockefeller was distressed at the original seal, first adopted in 1948 under Alben Barkley. Rockefeller thought the eagle was sickly, perched at half rest with only one arrow and one olive branch. At his own expense, Rockefeller had the seal redrawn, with the eagle at full wingspread, a claw-full of arrows and a series of bursting stars at its head. As one Rockefeller aide remembered the change, "One day after a particularly long series of defeats, I walked into the Governor's office with yet another piece of bad news. The Governor turned to me and pointed at the new seal and flag, sighing, 'See that goddamn seal? That's the most important thing I've done all year.' And I thought, Jesus, he's probably right." It is doubtful that either the mansion or the new seal made much difference in Mondale's advisory role. They were incidentals in the evolution of the institutional presence. Yet, as one aide remarked, "Everything helps in an office like the Vice-Presidency. You can't have too many perks. You didn't see Mondale moving out of the observatory."

THE VICE-PRESIDENT'S OFFICE

One way to understand the importance of the institutional Vice-Presidency is to look at what the office does and does not do. As noted earlier, the Vice-President's office has evolved from a rather loose collection of individuals to a reasonably organized structure. The office now has clear channels for information and specific chains of command. Though future Vice-Presidents may change the structure at the top—Mondale, for instance, had a triumvirate at the top of the office, while Rockefeller relied on a single chief of staff—the basic hierarchy has remained constant from Ford to Bush. The organizational structure for the Ford Vice-Presidency is summarized in the Appendix. Altogether, there are twelve units that have become more or less permanent fixtures in the Vice-President's office. Generally, these units support one or more of three main functions: (1) administrative, (2) political, and (3) advisory. Using interviews with staff members from all twelve units in the Mondale office, each function will be examined separately. However, though each office is distinct, the Vice-President's staff interact frequently. The issues staff talks with the counsel's office; the national security adviser works with the chief of staff; the scheduling operation coordinates the Vice-President's calendar with appointments, speechwriting, and advance; press seems to talk to everyone. The two offices that exist in relative isolation are constituent relations and congressional relations.

Administrative Support

Administrative support comes from three offices: appointments, scheduling, and, not surprisingly, administration. Approximately 25 percent of the Mondale staff worked in the administrative area. Because these offices *organized or scheduled* vice-presidential activity, they are seen as administrative, not political or advisory.

Appointments. The appointments office handled most of Mondale's time in Washington. The Vice-President's calendar was built around the President's schedule. Mondale's appointments office received Carter's weekly calendar and budgeted the Vice-President's time around important meetings and events. As noted earlier, Mondale had an open invitation to attend any meetings with the President. Mondale's appointments office was one of several offices responsible for picking the more interesting or important meetings. According to one aide: "We selected meetings on the basis of the subject matter, whether the Vice-President was interested in the specific policy or topic, and on the basis of who was going to be in attendance. The Vice-President was not very interested in attending large meetings with Carter's deputies. We looked for meetings that would give the Vice-President a chance to participate." A second aide confirmed the pattern. "Mondale felt he would inhibit most discussions among the Carter people, he felt he carried too much weight. He also wanted to avoid any meetings where his opinions might be leaked. He knew that the press would always be looking for signs of disfavor and didn't want to be involved in huge meetings where he might be put on the spot." When Mondale was in Washington, certain meetings were automatically scheduled: the Monday lunch with Carter, NSC meetings, the Tuesday congressional leadership breakfast, and the Friday morning foreign policy breakfasts.

The appointments office was also responsible for tracking Mondale's time, splitting each hour into six-minute segments for computer analysis. Each segment was broken into one of three categories: (1) time spent with the President, with ten levels; (2) time spent on foreign policy, with six levels; and (3) time spent on domestic policy, with five levels. The levels in each category referred to the quality of the time spent, ranging from private meetings with the President to briefings from cabinet officers to bill signings, and so forth. As one aide remarked: "We did that mostly out of curiosity, to reflect on it and make some judgments. We would periodically take the printouts and see what Mondale was doing. Too much time up at the Hill, too much in meetings with constituents, that kind of thing. We had the computer there in the White House and thought why not do it." According to another assistant: "We used it more at the start of the term to try and figure out what Mondale should be doing. How much time was he on the road? How much on the Hill? How much on foreign issues? How much in meetings? We'd look at the administration's priorities and see if Mondale ought to be doing something different. It was never that formal; we never set guidelines for X percentage in meetings with the President, X for Congress." The computer tracking allowed one assistant to give a very confident description of Mondale's time at the end of the term:

> Substantively, the Vice-President spent about a quarter of his working time on matters relating to foreign policy, defense, and intelligence. Another quarter of his time was spent on domestic policy matters. About 15 percent was spent on congressional matters, including time spent in presiding in the Senate (very little), and working with members of Congress on behalf of administration initiatives. Just under a quarter of his time was devoted to private work and study time and meetings with his staff. The balance of his time in miscellaneous meetings, dealing with the news media and political party matters (remarks, 21 Feb. 1981).

The computer analysis also became one of several tools for drafting strategies for advice and influence. The arrival of the computer age in the Vice-President's office gave Mondale's staff the chance to step back from the day-to-day problems and look at broader priorities. It was one more source of information and expertise in the institutional Vice-Presidency.

Scheduling. The scheduling office handled most of Mondale's time once he left the White House compound, whether on foreign or domestic travel. In the words of one aide, "Our job was to put him in the best position to sell administration goals. After he decided *what* he wanted to do, we decided *when, where,* and *how.* We had to clear his calendar, notify the various staffs, schedule the travel, and work out some of the details." Though scheduling did have some political duties, most of its time was spent on the mechanics of getting Mondale to and from his destination. Scheduling generally operated as a "desking" office, arranging for the logistics of the Vice-President's travel, but usually staying home. According to an aide: "When Mondale would say 'I want to go to Minnesota this week,' we would start blocking the time and cueing the necessary people. The travel logistics were our responsibility, but we didn't work on the advance and didn't deal that much with the substance of the travel. We had to get Mondale there and back. What happened once he touched down was left to advance and the political shops."

The scheduling of any trip would start with calls to the Carter staff alerting them to the Vice-President's plans. However, that did not mean the Carter White House had a veto over Mondale's trips. "We never went begging to the Carter people," an aide remarked, echoing several other interviews. "We were autonomous. If Mondale wanted to take a trip, it was his decision. We did consult with the Carter staff on most trips. Did they want us to meet with anyone special? Should we watch out for anything down South? But that's different from a veto." Moreover, because the Vice-President's office now had access to aircraft and support staff, scheduling did not have to ask for help in setting up the trips. Unlike Humphrey, who had to submit travel manifests to Johnson's chief of staff for permission, Mondale was free to travel when he wanted and with the press. That freedom, of course, was based on Mondale's relationship with Carter and the White House staff.

Administration. In absolute terms, the administration office had the largest number of aides directly involved in the day-to-day operation of the Vice-President's office. Administration was responsible for accounting, purchasing, leasing of equipment, and the paper flow. On the average, the office handled seven hundred letters and documents a day. According to an administration aide: "Mondale had ten people working in the office. We monitored travel funds, handled the central files, took care of any mass mailings, pulled together documents, xeroxed materials, and drove the cars." Traditionally, Vice-Presidents have had second priority in the White House administrative queue. If the Vice-President wanted xeroxing or printing, he had to wait behind the President and the rest of the EOP. The administration office became a key to speeding up White House service. As the office expanded under Ford, Rockefeller, and Mondale, the technical problems became less and less burdensome.

With a separate administrative core, the Vice-President's office had the freedom to purchase its own supplies and hire its own specialists. As a Mondale aide noted: "We decided not to tamper with the administration office once we came in. We thought it best to keep the old office going for purchasing and accounting, rather than turning it back over to the White House. That meant when something went wrong, we could jump all over our *own* people. We didn't have to apologize to the President's administrators." The Vice-President's priority remains number two behind the President and ahead of the White House staff, but at least now the Vice-President has several alternative sources of services. For someone like Rockefeller, of course, the problems were minor. "If Rockefeller didn't like the service," an aide noted, "he'd go outside and pay for it out of his own pocket. I remember coming in one day and finding that the White House had taken away my parking space. Rockefeller gave me $100 and told me to go down the street and buy the best damn parking space that I could find."

The addition of an administrative core was a major step in the institutionalization of the Vice-Presidency. Mondale's top staff did not have to waste their energy tracking down a spare typewriter or finding a new limousine. As one assistant argued: "It was just taken for granted that we would be able to spend our time working on policy or politics. No one ever thought much about what it would have been like without the administrative people. They were invaluable, not so much for what they did for Mondale, but for what they allowed *us* to do for Mondale. They gave us our freedom."

Political Support

Political support comes from all of the Vice-President's top staff, but is concentrated in five offices: constituent relations, advance, speechwriting, congressional liaison, and press. Together, roughly 30 percent of the Mondale staff worked in the political area. Because these offices *marketed* presidential or vice-presidential policies, they are seen as political, not advisory.

Constituent Relations. Constituent relations was the smallest office in the Mondale Vice-Presidency, consisting of three people and a word processor. The office was responsible for handling casework for the state of Minnesota —Mondale's old constituency—as well as any other nonmilitary problems that came to the Vice-Presidency. Located in the Dirksen Senate Office Building, the constituent relations staff had very little contact with either the Mondale or Carter staff. They received their work directly from administration and answered most letters without the Vice-President's direct involvement. As one aide argued: "We would give the constituent staff any letters needing casework and they'd take it from there. Anne Wright, the director, had been with Mondale for sixteen years and knew her way around the city. The only time she would come downtown to the EOB was when she had a very difficult case that needed Mondale's personal pressure." Child stealing, social security shortfalls, lost welfare checks, passports, immigration, pensions, education loans, and Medicare errors were among the thousands of cases that would pass through the office each year, with final answers for 75 percent, according to a Mondale assistant. However, constituent relations did not operate on a policy level and did not add information or expertise for the advisory role. It was a purely political operation that has remained in the Bush office.

Advance. Compared to constituent relations, the advance office had much more contact with Mondale. Advance was generally responsible for the details of the Vice-President's travel once the airplane landed. Whereas scheduling handled the overall routes, advance teams actually went over every mile to and from the destination. Whereas scheduling booked the hotels, advance actually checked them out, sleeping in the beds and eating the food. As one advance aide argued: "Scheduling always stayed home in Washington. Advance was always out in front of the Vice-President. Before Mondale would arrive in a city, every footstep had been walked. The secret service would protect the Vice-President, scheduling would block out his time, military affairs would handle the protocol, but we were the ones who set up the podiums, booked the auditoriums, checked the lighting, and found the closest bathrooms." Thus, appointments was generally responsible for Mondale's White House time, scheduling was responsible for travel time, but advance was involved in watching the minute-to-minute activities for both. As Hartmann described Ford's advance staff:

> They fend off publicity hounds, eccentrics, minor celebrities and—not always with the same degree of success—the throngs of pretty girls who throw themselves into political campaigns. After all, they have dutifully sewed up a luxurious Presidential suite days in advance and stocked it with all manner of booze and viands.
> They hire fleets of cars and carefully go over every mile of the arrival and departure route, timing it with stop watches down to a split-second schedule. When the great man arrives, they hover at his elbow, telling him just where the microphones have been set up and where the most boisterous crowds—and the most television cameras—can be expected. They pack the meeting hall and connive with the cops to blockade protesters and get their friends in for a handshake with the hero.
> Advance men even tend to look alike. They wear natty junior-chamber-of-commerce fashions for the young executive; they speak a special walkie-talkie lingo even when relaxing in the bar; and it is perfectly natural that they come to

regard themselves even more highly than most bright, aggressive, energetic, resourceful, rootless, and ruthless young achievers (1980, pp. 86-87).

Yet, whatever Hartmann's opinion of Ford's slick advance team, they were a critical component of the political operation. Vice-Presidents cannot travel without advance.

In contrast to scheduling, the advance office under Mondale did not distinguish among White House, domestic, and foreign time. Instead, the office viewed travel as either "inside-compound" or "outside-compound." Inside-compound advance merely involved making sure that appointments were set up on time and the press was notified. Outside-compound was much more complex, involving questions of who went with Mondale in the motorcade, who appeared with Mondale on the podium, who ate with Mondale at the dinner, who briefed the press, and who handled the suitcases. Generally, the Mondale advance office sent three people to each stop. They would coordinate all of the details and meet the Vice-President's plane. The minute the Vice-President stepped off the plane, however, the advance team was finished. They would give the trip coordinator—sometimes Mondale's personal aide, James Johnson, sometimes another advance assistant—a list of plans and leave for the next destination. Their job was to set the stage for the Vice-President, arriving several days ahead. Hence, the term *advance*. Though advance was certainly important in off years, it became especially important during the Mondale campaigns. According to an advance staffer: "We had over three hundred people working on a volunteer basis in the 1980 campaign. We had to get them to the destination four or five days before Mondale. One handled the press, one handled the hotels, the third set up a coordinating council for the trip. The most important job was to look at the sites. A million things can go wrong and advance gets the blame for all of them."

Though advance provided administrative support for travel, some of the work involved political negotiation. As one advance assistant remembered: "Mondale had one rule for his advance people: never leave any enemies. When you've got a hundred politicians asking to stand with the Vice-President and you've only got room for ten, you've got to make some very gentle choices. Mondale preferred to make his own enemies and didn't want advance to screw up." The broad contours of a vice-presidential trip could be mapped in Washington, but the details often had to be handled at the last minute. When asked about the administrative aspects of the job, a Mondale advance officer offered the following view:

> We did work pretty close with scheduling and appointments, but we were involved in outreach. It was our job to fill the auditoriums and to get the local press involved. It was our job to find the TV stations and get the lighting set up. It was our job to make sure the halls were full of enthusiastic supporters. We had to stroke the locals and get them interested. We had to handle the blacks

who wanted to protest the Carter economic program. We had to handle the
Jewish community and labor. Our job was more negotiation than planning. We
had to prepare for a successful visit, not a catastrophe. If that wasn't an administrative function, it's news to me. Maybe political administration would be
a better term.

Under Mondale, the office eventually included five full-time aides and was
continued in the Bush Vice-Presidency.

Speechwriting. Though the speechwriting office was technically part of
Mondale's domestic issues staff, it operated as a distinct unit. Unlike Agnew,
Mondale was not willing to take his speeches from the President's writers.
He wanted his own people working on drafts and had three speechwriters
by 1980. The office was responsible for every remark during the term,
ranging from toasts on NATO trips to brief speeches before constituents to
major addresses on administration policy. Even when Mondale was asked
to deliver a speech in Carter's absence, the Vice-President's writing team
was used. "Mondale considered that one of the parts of his independence,"
an aide noted. "He didn't want the Carter people writing his speeches. He
wanted people who knew him and knew his style to put the words together.
The Carter staff never complained, either. Mondale gave some awfully
damn good speeches." However, on major foreign and domestic addresses,
Mondale's staff circulated drafts to key Carter aides. Mondale's speech to
the Israeli Knesset, for instance, was read and critiqued by several White
House offices, including NSC and the press secretary. That was a standard
approach for all major speeches, including those of Carter and members
of his cabinet. Like those of other spokesmen, Mondale's speeches were
sometimes rewritten to meet potential criticism. Like the others, Mondale's
speeches had to clear a number of hurdles before the final draft. Yet, the
clearance process was not designed to control or inhibit Mondale. It was a
standard operating procedure for all staff members.

According to the speechwriting staff, Mondale gave over a thousand
speeches during the term. Most were delivered in 1978 and 1980, during the
election campaigns. That is not to argue that Mondale did not give any
substantive addresses. One aide listed Mondale's best speeches as follows:

1. The United Nations Conference on Indochinese Refugees: "A tremendous speech, well-written, powerful. Set Mondale apart as a very compassionate leader, raised his stock in the administration. Effective
   address for mobilizing world opinion. Produced results in Washington,
   too."
2. The Israeli Knesset: "Top effort of the term. Good writing. Got through
   to Israelis and Begin. Got ball moving again. Good substance, but
   better passion. Made sense and made important contribution. Established Mondale as the administration person who could communicate
   with Begin."

3. 1980 Democratic Convention: "More time spent on this one than any other. Tough speech. Carter was not going to look good following Kennedy. Mondale only powerful speaker in the administration. Good orator. Needed strong material defending administration. Excellent delivery. Mondale is still one of the best speakers in the country."

4. China Address: "Televised live to one billion people. Major policy statement on China relations. Had to make it personal for TV. Not too hot for Chinese. What an audience, what an opportunity to make the words work."

5. Colorado Springs U.S. Olympic Boycott: "Toughest speech of the term. It was the most difficult idea to sell. Hostile audience, disappointed by decision. Mondale had to be compassionate, but hard on Soviets. Try to convince American public that it was the right thing to do."

6. Lagos, Nigeria, on Africa Policy: "Another good effort. Well-written. Good forensic effort."

7. Oslo, Norway, on NATO: "Also good effort. Good sell on tough issues. Hard to communicate in so many languages. Try to keep the speech simple and direct, but not too hot. Try to bring NATO along faster with their own money and troops."

Though Mondale had his share of major speeches, he made few first announcements of new programs. According to one speechwriter, "Mondale was always eager to make news, just like any politician. But the President had every right to reserve the goodies for himself. Mondale did announce the electoral reform and started the refugee program. Most of his time was spent on raw politics, though." Because of his speaking skills, Mondale was used more and more as the key defender of the Carter program. Once Carter adopted the rose garden strategy in early 1980, Mondale's speechwriting staff was working full time on campaign speeches. Mondale's activity, of course, reflected Carter's inactivity.

Congressional Relations. The congressional relations office has a mixed history in the Vice-Presidency. Like constituent relations, congressional liaison is located some distance from the main EOB headquarters. "I don't remember too much contact with the Vice-President's staff," one Agnew aide said. "Most of my work was with the President's people, not the Vice-President's staff. I saw him every so often when he'd come up to the Hill, but didn't spend too much time with him." Because the congressional relations staff rarely comes to the EOB, they sometimes see themselves as cut off from the Vice-President. Moreover, because of the relationship with the presidential liaison staff, the congressional relations staff sometimes loses the trust of the Vice-President's EOB staff. As a Rockefeller vice-presidential aide noted: "it was natural for us to drift apart. The congressional people had worked for Agnew and Ford and were originally hired by Nixon. They weren't our people and weren't working for us. They were decent staffers, I suppose, but they didn't represent Rockefeller." The Vice-President's Senate floor office usually serves as the headquarters for the White House liaison operation, reducing travel to and from the White House, while facilitating the lobbying effort. As a quid pro quo for using the office and out of simple courtesy, the President's liaison staff includes the Vice-President's liaison staff in most discussion and strategy sessions. That is an advantage for the Vice-President. However, during the Agnew, Ford, and Rockefeller terms, the congressional relations office was more an arm of the White House than of the Vice-Presidency. That created a climate of hostility between the Vice-President's Hill staff and the EOB staff.

The relationship between the two units improved under Mondale. The congressional relations office was rarely put in the awkward position of choosing between the Vice-President and the President. According to a Carter liaison aide: "The Vice-President's liaison person has to decide who he's going to work for. If the Vice-President never comes up to Capitol Hill, he's got to fend for himself and make some friends with the President's staff." Mondale did spend considerable time lobbying for several administration priorities—including the Panama Canal treaties and the Department of Education—but did not enjoy the presiding function. After breaking a natural gas pricing filibuster, Mondale spent less and less time in Congress, leaving his congressional relations office to negotiate a role with the Carter staff, a role which involved head counts and occasional lobbying. Like previous liaison staffs, Mondale's congressional relations office sometimes walked a tightrope between the Presidency and Congress. As one past aide argued: "Congress never really trusted us. They readily accepted the President's lobbyists, but didn't know what to do with us. We were paid by the Senate. Did that make us one of them? We were never sure ourselves. We just didn't quite fit."

Mondale's congressional relations office eventually performed three functions. First, the staff handled appointments for Mondale when he journeyed up Pennsylvania Avenue. Second, the staff prepared head counts on key votes. Because the Carter staff had limited experience at the start of the term, the Mondale congressional relations office became an important source of legislative information. As one Carter aide remarked, "There's no question that they served us well on intelligence. We needed their background early on. They supplied very good information on the economic stimulus package in 1977 and were equally valuable on Panama Canal and civil service." Third, the staff kept Mondale posted on legislative problems. Though Mondale was well aware of administration failings in Congress, the congressional relations office acted as one more conduit for complaints. On some issues, the staff was able to highlight major errors—e.g., Carter's water projects veto at the start of the term—and handle liaison with congressional liberals. These functions were all continued in a slightly larger congressional office under Bush.

Press. Unlike congressional relations, Mondale's press office had a very clear mandate: maximum exposure for the Vice-President, with minimum threat to the President. In doing so, the press office was responsible for arranging interviews, distributing handouts, publicizing trips, supervising press conferences, and protecting the Vice-President. According to one Mondale aide, "Our time was divided between working on internal problems—what was going to be said, how the Vice-President would handle a problem, how much coverage would we get, etc.—and external problems—actually getting the press in to see the Vice-President, typing up releases, answering questions, etc. Our time was split just about equally between both." There was considerable contact with Jody Powell, Carter's press secretary, on major news. Unlike Agnew, however, Mondale rarely had major problems with the press. The press office scheduled most requests for interviews and saw little need to protect Mondale from hostile reporting. The only problem during the term was the inevitable question of Mondale's involvement in administration policy. During the midsummer crisis in 1979, reporters picked up on a "dump Mondale" rumor and pressed for information. Because Mondale had left Washington during the cabinet shakeup, the media assumed he was on the way out. "Our problem was to stop those rumors," an assistant argued. "If they go on too long, they become self-fulfilling. There was no evidence of any dump Mondale sentiment in the staff, but there was enough circumstantial material to lead to the rumor. We had to bring the press in and give them the standard routine on Mondale's importance. We also had to get Jody to cooperate with his own briefing."

Though the press office hoped for maximum coverage, there were several caveats. First, Mondale did not want to claim credit for any administration policies. He did not want to be seen as searching for publicity for himself. According to an assistant: "We did not come out with a monthly list of Mondale's achievements. That would have been seen as grandstanding and would have hurt Mondale inside the White House. When a reporter would ask if Mondale had been responsible for such and such, the standard response was that he was a team player and the policy was a Carter idea." That strategy protected Mondale from charges of disloyalty, but also kept his name away from unpopular decisions. Second, Mondale did not want to upstage the President. News conferences, interviews, press releases, and public appearances were scheduled around the President's activities. Mondale's press office worked closely with Powell to avoid any overlap of coverage. Third, Mondale did not want the press to know what he was saying on the inside. He did not want any leaks about his positions. "The press is always looking for measuring sticks," an aide noted. "Anytime the Vice-President would say 'I am in favor of this,' the press could eventually find out if he won. If he won, the press would say he was controlling the

President. If he lost, the press would say he was on the way out. It was essential that Mondale's activities be kept quiet."

Regardless of the strategy, the press office remains the Vice-President's major link to the public. One press aide usually travels with the Vice-President, another is the official photographer. Though the press office must be careful not to overshadow the President, the staff is responsible for keeping the Vice-President visible. Thus, when Bush received a letter from a grade-schooler in 1981 asking if he was still alive, the press office turned it into publicity. As one past aide said: "There's not too much to advertise in the Vice-Presidency, not much breaking news. The job becomes a challenge when you're trying to get the Vice-President at least some notice. Sometimes, you're between a rock and a hard place. You want to keep the Vice-President alive and visible, but you don't want to threaten the President. The best stories become the 'team player at work' kind."

Vice-Presidents have had a political core in their staffs at least since Humphrey. However, the past ten years have witnessed a considerable increase in the number of aides providing political support. As with administrative support, the political core frees top aides for advisory activities. Under Humphrey, the political staff was also the advisory staff. When it came to a choice of staying in Washington to work on policy or flying with Humphrey to write a speech, the staff had to provide the political services first. The growth in the political core has meant greater time, energy, information, and expertise for the advisory role. Mondale's top aides still worked on politics, providing advice on trips and campaigns, but they did not have to leave their policy jobs whenever Mondale left Washington or received a letter.

Advisory Support

Advisory support comes from four units in the Vice-President's office: national security, domestic policy, the counsel's office, and the chief of staff. In all, over 40 percent of the Mondale staff worked in the advisory area. Because these offices provided support for a vice-presidential *policy role,* they are seen as advisory. The offices often provided support for Mondale's direct participation in policy making, but also maintained separate lines into the White House for hidden-hand input.

National Security. Mondale's national security office was split into two sections: the national security adviser and the military affairs group. Mondale's national security adviser, A. Denis Clift, was responsible for liaison with the NSC, the CIA, and the departments of State and Defense. Clift was also responsible for preparing background briefings and issue papers, and gave Mondale his daily briefing on national security, updating the materials at midday and in the evening. However, because Clift was located in the EOB and not the West Wing, Mondale often turned to David Aaron, his former Senate assistant at NSC, for his foreign policy advice. "Aaron was just down the hall," a Mondale aide said. "It was just much easier to go to Aaron with questions. It wasn't that Clift was unqualified—actually, he was very good. It was a question of Mondale's familiarity with Aaron and the proximity." Beyond the briefings, Clift also handled some speechwriting and worked on foreign trips. In concert with scheduling and advance, Clift helped set up several of Mondale's most visible trips: China, Geneva, the Middle East, and Oslo. Moreover, at the beginning of the administration, Mondale had attended meetings of the NSC Policy Review Committee (PRC) and Special Coordinating Committee (SCC) as a learning device. As the term progressed, those responsibilities fell to Clift.

Mondale's national security adviser also supervised the military affairs staff. That office was responsible for maintaining communication between Mondale and the intelligence community. According to one aide: "We would begin each morning with a briefing, answer the Vice-President's questions, obtain any information that he wanted, and present position papers for upcoming events. My job was as a reporter, not an adviser. It was a current events job, with the material coming from the last twenty-four hours exclusively." Military affairs was also responsible for what some staffers called the "football," the briefcase containing the codes the Vice-President would use to initiate a United States nuclear response in the event of the President's inability. Military affairs carried the football whenever the Vice-President left Washington. Both of these functions were nonpartisan. As one officer noted: "I viewed myself as a neutral participant, much like a foreign service officer in the State Department. It was not my job to offer advice, only information. I was to be present whenever the Vice-President left Washington proper and to keep him informed on anything that was happening from a crisis standpoint." As a Mondale aide noted: "These guys took their jobs very seriously. It was always a little unnerving when one of them would show up on the plane with that little black briefcase. I always wanted to look inside, but I also wanted to live past forty."

Military affairs also handled the protocol and some planning for the Vice-President's foreign trips. Though Mondale often traveled with NSC or State Department support, military affairs took care of most of the logistics. According to one officer, "Our office set up the ceremonies at the bases, transportation to the Vice-President's quarters, protection of the aircraft, establishment of secure communications, protocol, refueling, security, and just about every aspect of the visit." Beyond the travel duties, military affairs also handled a number of lesser chores. Because Vice-Presidents often keep their old constituents even after election, military affairs is one focal point for casework involving the Department of Defense and the

Veteran's Administration. Staff members may be asked to solve a passport problem or to speed the transfer of a soldier back home. "We got to know the people of Minnesota very well," an aide said. "We were responsible for most of the problems that came to Mondale on military issues. Suppose some kid had to get a leave to come home for a parent's funeral. That might come our way. Suppose some other kid needed a break on an assignment or discharge. That was our job, too." Finally, military affairs was responsible for helping the Vice-President choose appointees to the service academies. Like members of Congress, Vice-Presidents are allowed to select nominees for West Point, Annapolis, the Air Force Academy, and the Coast Guard Academy. Mondale generally left the appointment process to military affairs, screening applicants through a competition.

Unlike the rest of the Vice-President's office, military affairs was staffed almost entirely by career officers from the Department of Defense. These officers generally stay from one administration to the next, constituting a pool of expertise for the incoming occupant. Within the Vice-President's office, military affairs is a major source of institutional memory. However, because the military staffers see themselves as nonpartisan, they rarely offer advice on vice-presidential policy. "It was not my job to instruct Mondale on how to be a better Vice-President," one aide argued. "I was to provide information and protect him abroad." Military affairs remains more important as a conduit for information than as a source for advice.

Domestic Issues. All recent Vice-Presidents have had access to national security advice, and military affairs remains the oldest office at the Vice-President's disposal. But Mondale was the first Vice-President to build a domestic policy staff. The Mondale issues office acted as a smaller version of Carter's Domestic Policy Staff (DPS), originally the Domestic Council under Nixon and Ford, known as the Office of Policy Development under Reagan. Though Mondale needed domestic policy information, he also recognized Rockefeller's mistake in trying to control the Domestic Council. According to one Mondale aide: "We had no intention of having a domestic staff as large as DPS or coopting the domestic operation. What we wanted was a staff for interpreting DPS issue papers and supplementing Mondale's information. There was no need to compete with DPS." It was much better to work closely with Stuart Eizenstat, Carter's domestic policy adviser. To do so, however, Mondale decided to construct his own domestic staff, giving him alternative sources of information and conduits for absorbing DPS analysis. Since domestic policy is generally the area where Vice-Presidents have their greatest impact, the institutionalization of a domestic issues staff was an important step toward an advisory role.

Mondale's issues staff was built around a director and three policy specialists. One specialist handled human services, including minority policy, urban affairs, justice, and health. A second specialist was responsible for economic policy and was Mondale's representative to the Carter Economic Policy Group. The third aide covered energy, agriculture, commerce, and the environment. As one domestic aide argued, "Obviously, we couldn't cover every issue with four people. We looked for areas where the Carter staff was weak or where Mondale was especially interested. We also had to cover areas where the administration was heavily invested, like energy and health." A second aide agreed, noting that "we tried to avoid duplication of effort. Since we had good relations with DPS, there was no need to redo their work. We would supplement it and sometimes reinterpret the conclusions, but we usually agreed with their findings anyway." Recall that Bert Carp, Mondale's long-time Senate aide, had been appointed as one of Eizenstat's deputies, again providing a link to the Carter White House. Moreover, Mondale and Eizenstat usually ended up on the same side of arguments, forming a coalition in support of liberal policy.

Mondale's issues staff was primarily responsible for briefing the Vice-President on domestic policy. Sometimes the briefings preceded a campaign swing; other times they preceded the Monday lunch with Carter. Like the national security office, the issues unit was charged with providing information on current issues. As Gail Harrison, the director, noted: "Our role was one of providing advice and staff assistance to the Vice-President on domestic issues and coordinating with the President's policy staff, OMB, and the Cabinet departments. We prepared domestic issue briefings for the Vice-President in connection with his official travel. We also met with members of Congress, Congressional staff, state and local government leaders, constituent groups and citizens on domestic issues" (personal communication, 18 Mar. 1981). The effectiveness of the issues staff rested on the relationship with DPS. Though the issues office was equipped to produce independent analysis, there was a conscious effort to avoid needless repetition. Had Mondale been frozen out of the White House, the issues staff would have acted as a separate vice-presidential Domestic Policy Staff. However, because Mondale remained firmly positioned in the policy loop, the issues office often became an extension of the Carter DPS. That integration had its advantages. Mondale's staff could spend more time working on new alternatives and less just keeping up with current issues. Mondale's staff could also spend more time working deeper into the policy process, blurring the distinction between the Vice-President's staff and the President's. That allowed for greater hidden-hand influence. As one aide argued: "We became such frequent participants in the domestic process that we were no longer seen as Mondale's people. We were all from the White House and all represented the President. We still worked for Mondale and still represented his views, but we were never excluded because our employer was the Vice-President."

That integration was the product of several factors. First, the Mondale staff spent a great deal of time in direct contact with the Carter DPS. The staffs were both located on the second floor in the EOB and, according to one aide, "ate lunch together, argued about policy together, saw each other in the john, and looked at the world in similar terms." According to Gail Harrison: "I spent a great deal of my time coordinating with Presidential policy, Congressional liaison, intergovernmental relations, and budget staff. This included regular meetings on the Presidential agenda, coordination of major legislative priorities, participation in the preparation of new policy initiatives, and the budget review process. Out of each day, roughly 20% of my time was devoted to meetings and exchange of information with Carter aides" (personal communication, 18 Mar. 1981). Second, as noted earlier, Mondale and Eizenstat shared many of the same positions on domestic policy. As the Carter administration aged and the budget tightened, Mondale and Eizenstat increasingly found themselves partners in the policy process. Though other Mondale aides were tied into the White House, the issues staff had the closest contact with the Carter policy operation. As a Carter assistant said: "No small part of that was ideological. If Jim McIntyre, OMB director, had been in charge of domestic policy, there wouldn't have been any basis for agreement. Mondale and Eizenstat were the strongest liberals in the White House and naturally teamed up when possible. They fought against the budget cuts and usually argued for the liberal cause." Third, Mondale's main strength coming into the Carter administration was domestic policy. Though Mondale was certainly interested in foreign and economic affairs, he had spent much of his Senate career working on domestic issues. Eizenstat was regarded as a persuasive adviser, well prepared and thoroughly briefed, with a strong staff. However, Mondale's staff also brought considerable expertise into the White House. There were advantages to be gained by both sides in the integration of Mondale's domestic issues staff.

That integration, however, was given its greatest boost when Mondale's staff assumed responsibility for the executive agenda process. The agenda operation received the go-ahead during the transition. Meeting with the cabinet on Saint Simons Island, Georgia, Carter encouraged Mondale to organize a periodic review of priorities and timing. During the first six months, however, the agenda process was not taken seriously. As the administration moved ahead with a broad legislative program, few aides saw the need for priority setting.

Though the Mondale staff had prepared a detailed timetable for the first six months (see Light 1982b, p. 191), it was ignored. As congressional complaints about overloading mounted and the defeats multiplied, the agenda process gained more strength. By the end of the first year, it had been accepted as a necessary part of the policy process. As one Mondale aide argued: "Mondale saw a major gap in the administration's operation and wanted to take advantage of the opportunity. He knew that the agenda was one source of influence inside the White House and filled the vacuum with the issues staff. By the end of 1977, the rest of the administration had no choice but to go through the agenda process. The damage from the first six months had been so deep that Carter had given primary control of the priority-setting operation to Mondale." Though Mondale did not exercise that power frequently, the mechanism was an important source of bargaining leverage in the administration. By determining the order of issues presented to both Carter and Congress, Mondale had a potent source of rewards and sanctions.

The agenda process itself was simple. The mechanism produced a yearly document listing administration priorities. According to a Carter aide:

> We started the canvass for proposals in the fall, around September or October. We organized papers in November and asked for comments from the cabinet and leaders in Congress by Thanksgiving. We offered appeals and finalized the document in December. The document was then sent in to Carter for his signing. It was a very intense process in 1978 and 1979, with a lot of people willing to spill some blood for position. Most of the analysis was done in the agencies and we spent only three or four months on the agenda each year. The President usually gave the players a chance to lobby and then put the priorities into the State of the Union address. I'd say it was a very potent source of influence for Mondale. He controlled the agenda-setting process. And, in the White House, the one who controls that machinery has a lot of clout.

The document resulted in three levels of priorities for programs: (1) Presidential Lead, (2) Cabinet Secretary or White House Staff Lead, (3) Department or Agency Lead. The top priorities were to be handled by Carter himself, while the rest of the program would fall either to the staff or the departments. According to most staff members, the battle between levels one and two was often the hardest fought. As the referee and arbiter, Mondale gained some advantage by deciding who would speak, how issues were to be phrased, and which topics were to be debated first. As one assistant noted: "The first item adopted has a bearing on everything else. If you take welfare reform first, then national health insurance might have to wait. The order of presentation is an important factor in determining the priorities. By setting up a 'go or no-go' decision on welfare reform first, you could affect the rest of the process." In theory, the agenda process was designed to consider all issues simultaneously. In practice, it was never so strict.

As a line assignment with recurring responsibilities, the agenda process did expose Mondale to increased conflict. The process was not new to the Presidency—Califano was in charge of the domestic agenda process under Johnson, and Ehrlichman ran a similar process under Nixon—but it was new to the Vice-Presidency. In previous administrations, the President's top staff had handled agenda setting, not the Vice-President. Mondale's control of the process was a sign of his expertise in bureaucratic politics, as well as an indication of the relative inexperience of the Carter staff. According to an observer: "Mondale did not fight for the agenda job. It was just there to be filled. No one else inside the administration thought it was important or needed to be done." Though Mondale was elevated into a position of higher visibility, an assistant suggested that "it was not a line assignment in the sense that the Domestic Council was for Rockefeller. It allowed Mondale to manage conflict to a certain extent. It also allowed him to get to know both the cabinet and the programs. He was a professional politician and used the agenda to push the programs he advocated, but not in the visible, open sense of Rockefeller." And, though the process was active in 1978 and 1979, it lost momentum in 1980. Once the agenda was set and presented to Congress, attention shifted to the lobbying process. By 1980, Mondale had also turned to the problems of reelection and spent the first six months campaigning. As the administration went through the natural aging cycle, the agenda process withered. Assuming that Carter and Mondale had been reelected, the agenda process would have returned in the second term.

Counsel. If the issues staff was a product of Mondale's term, the counsel's office was a product of Ford's Vice-Presidency. Ford wanted a strong legal staff both because of his unusual status as the first appointive Vice-President and because of Watergate. "Everybody had a lawyer in 1974," an aide remarked. "It was a great year for the legal profession. Why should Ford be different?" As the heir apparent to Richard Nixon, Ford also wanted to avoid any hint of scandal. The Agnew and Nixon problems had sensitized all of Washington to the advantages of sound legal counsel. Thus, in hiring William E. Casselman II as vice-presidential attorney, Ford's chief of staff ordered him to draw up a code of standards for the staff. "I want it to be the strictest in town," Hartmann reportedly said. "You can draw on White House and Civil Service codes and House and Senate rules, but in no case should our standards be less than the most rigid that now exist" (Hartmann 1980, p. 89). Ford also hired Philip Buchen as staff director for the Privacy Commission. As Ford's former law partner, Buchen became the first source of legal advice in the brief term. As Buchen prepared for the legal problem of the transition to the Presidency, Casselman was stranded with few duties. The Vice-President had few legal issues to review, and the counsel's office was not even remotely integrated with the White House.

The counsel's operation continued in the Rockefeller and Mondale Vice-Presidencies. As an outside observer suggested: "No one can be without legal support in this town anymore. That is one of your most important appointments. You've got to find someone who will protect you and keep you. Things that used to be simple, like a brother who worked for the

Libyans, now create great interest." But whereas both Ford and Rockefeller needed legal help to navigate the waters of the Twenty-fifth Amendment, Mondale's office had a different set of responsibilities. First, Mondale's chief counsel, Michael Berman, was the administrative workhorse of the Vice-President's office. Though Mondale had a chief of staff, Berman handled the day-to-day operation of the office. Berman was in charge of hiring and firing, budgeting, supervising the staff, and following through on policy. Most of the staff reported to Berman. Second, during the brief tenure of Robert Lipshutz as Carter's chief counsel at the start of the term, Berman spent considerable time doubling on White House legal problems. According to a Carter aide: "Lipshutz was not always on top of the ball and needed some help. With the Lance resignation in 1977, Lipshutz was over-whelmed and had to call in some support. Berman was a logical choice, especially for questions of campaign finance. There was nobody better in Washington to look at those issues." Once Lloyd Cutler replaced Lipshutz, Berman's White House activities dropped slightly. However, Berman re-mained an active participant in legal issues and was the lead actor in Carter's electoral reform package.

Third, the counsel's office spent some time thinking about emergency succession and the transfer of power. No Vice-President wants the White House or press to know that he is studying the problem, but the questions arise in every term—Eisenhower's heart attacks, Johnson's heart problems, Nixon's phlebitis. When Carter went into the hospital for surgery on his hemorrhoids, Berman had to review the procedures for succession. Carter was obviously unable to discharge his duties while he was anesthetized. In Carter's absence, even for three hours, should Mondale have been in charge? From a political standpoint, the answer was no. It would have been viewed as grandstanding and superfluous. The succession machinery would have hardly started moving before Carter awoke. From a technical standpoint, the answer was yes. The Constitution says nothing about a Hamilton Jordan or an H. R. Haldeman standing in during disability. A similar question arose during Reagan's emergency surgery following the assassination attempt. Again, the problem had to be addressed by the counsel's office. Again, the Vice-President decided not to proceed with the formal process of succession. Yet, unlike Carter's hemorrhoids, it was a case where succession might have been given much greater consideration.

Chief of Staff. The chief of staff in any office operates as an organizational troubleshooter, handling problems as they arise and supervising the staff. Mondale's chief of staff did perform these duties, but also spent time working on the relationship between Mondale and Carter. Mondale's top staff gen-erally worked as a triumvirate: Berman handled day-to-day administration; James Johnson was Mondale's personal assistant and, in the words of one aide, took charge of the "care and feeding of the Vice-President"; Richard Moe was the chief of staff, chairing a number of White House internal task forces and working closely with Hamilton Jordan, Carter's titular chief of staff. All three Mondale aides cleared major decisions and met frequently to discuss Mondale's activities. According to a Mondale assistant: "Richard Moe was Mondale's most active staff member at the upper levels of the White House. He chaired the nuclear carrier veto task force and the hospital cost containment task force. He was as much a member of the Carter senior staff as anybody else. He spent about 90 percent of his time working with the Carter people to make the relationship work. He was still part of the Vice-President's staff, however, and worked as a liaison between the Carter and Mondale people." Moe was the Vice-President's representative at the senior staff meetings, and encouraged greater integration of the two staffs. In other Vice-Presidencies, the chief of staff has had a much stronger role in the operation of the office. However, even in the most structured offices, the chief of staff operates as a floater, drifting from issue to issue as the need changes. Both Moe and Berman had been chiefs of staff in the Mondale Senate office and evolved a working relationship that emphasized their individual strengths. Berman was much stronger on the details of adminis-tration and was generally regarded as the tougher manager. Moe was much stronger on building ties with other political entrepreneurs and was gen-erally viewed as a stronger negotiator. Throughout the administration, Moe saw his job as supporting Mondale's advisory role. Though Moe did circulate among the Vice-President's staff, his main goal was the integration and working relationship between the two offices.

Moe was also responsible for assembling the weekly agenda for Mondale's meeting with Carter. The list of "talking points" for the lunch was a joint project of the four policy offices—issues, national security, counsel, and chief of staff—but was coordinated by Moe and his staff. According to the Mondale staff, nothing was out of bounds for the private meeting with Carter. Any issue was a potential topic and, as one aide noted, "It was generally whatever was hot that week." The talking points—that is, brief capsules of issues for discussion—were assembled into a briefing book that Mondale could study and use in the meetings. Though Mondale avoided certain issues over the term and did not talk to Carter about either Bert Lance or Billy Carter, he felt free to tackle any subject of interest.

The growth in the policy staff has increased the resources for the Vice-President's advisory role. The arrival of a domestic policy staff and the counsel's office in the mid-1970s gave the Vice-President new sources of in-formation and expertise. With the coinciding growth in administrative and political support, the Vice-President's office was finally equipped to sustain an active policy presence in the White House. Even if the Vice-President is frozen out of the policy process, the office is now prepared to keep the occupant informed.

WHITE HOUSE CONTACT

Although the structure of the Vice-President's office has remained reasonably constant since Ford, the amount of contact with the White House has varied greatly. Rockefeller aides report that there was rarely much contact with the Ford presidential staff, while Mondale aides report a much higher level of interaction. Since staff contact is one avenue for advice and influence—particularly when the Vice-President travels 30 percent of the year—it is an important question here. If the staffs never meet or talk, it is far more difficult for the Vice-President to play an advisory role. Even if the Vice-President retains the weekly meeting with the President, there is less opportunity for advice and influence if the staffs remain separate. This is not to suggest that Vice-Presidents ought to merge their staff with the White House. Rather, by encouraging frequent contact between the two staffs, Vice-Presidents can minimize duplication of effort, while generating greater channels to the President. If a Richard Moe or a Gail Harrison can force an issue to the agenda at the staff level, the Vice-President can reserve his internal capital for other issues.

When asked about the frequency of contact at their levels of the Vice-President's office, only 7 percent of the Rockefeller aides reported daily interaction with the White House. Another 14 percent had weekly contact, 45 percent had monthly contact, and 34 percent never had contact. Though Rockefeller had several former aides on the Ford Domestic Council, his vice-presidential staff remained isolated from the White House. As one aide remarked: "We weren't exactly the first people they called with a problem. The White House was already so divided that they didn't need any more conflict." The Mondale staff had much more contact with the White House: 31 percent reported daily interaction, 27 percent had weekly contact, 22 percent had monthly contact, and only 20 percent never had any contact. In all, 58 percent of the Mondale staff had some contact with the Carter White House on a weekly basis, compared with only 21 percent of the Rockefeller staff.

Did the differences in contact affect vice-presidential advice? One way to answer is to look beyond just the quantity of contact to the quality of contact. Of the Mondale aides who had some contact with the White House —whether daily, weekly, or monthly—49 percent worked on policy issues, 35 percent worked on the coordination of travel and statements, and 26 percent worked on administration. Of the aides who had *daily* contact with the Carter staff, however, over 70 percent were involved with policy issues, with

20 percent working on coordination. That amount of policy contact increased Mondale's advisory presence. The level of contact can be used as one indication of the depth of vice-presidential participation in the presidential process. According to a Mondale aide: "Hardly a day went by without some kind of contact. I attended the deputies meetings, Moe attended the senior staff meetings, Harrison attended issue briefings, Berman went to legal meetings, the press people went over to Powell, national security talked to NSC, administration pushed the paper around, scheduling talked to scheduling, etc." A second aide agreed. "We had the most contact with the people who were doing similar things for the President. There was a good level of informal talk, plus a great deal of memo shuffling. At least on the policy level, we were very well connected."

Of the 7 percent of the Rockefeller staff with daily contact with the Ford White House, almost all were involved on coordination or administration. As an aide concluded:

> From the very beginning, we couldn't seem to click with the Ford staff. We couldn't work out any arrangements for information sharing and had to rely on our own staff for most of the backgrounding. We did get some paper and Rockefeller was prepared for anything that might happen to Ford, but we couldn't get lines into the White House. We didn't talk that much and found it very frustrating. By the time Rockefeller was confirmed, the administration was already in place. That first four-month shakedown was critical, and we weren't involved. That was when the relationship evolved and we were on Capitol Hill fighting for confirmation.

Not only did Rockefeller have to duplicate the efforts of the Ford staff, but he lost potential channels for hidden-hand advice and influence.

CONCLUSION

Institutionalization is an ongoing process, with each new Vice-President adding or subtracting something from the office. At the very least, the institutional growth of the Vice-President's office has provided an increase in the basic resources for the advisory role. The office now has specialized subdivisions to supply administrative, political, and policy support. The office now has the budget to hire more top-level staff. The office now has a hierarchical structure and at least some institutional memory at the administrative core. These changes have given Vice-Presidents more access to information and expertise, while freeing more time and energy for the policy role. The initial steps on this road to an institutional identity were almost accidental—Johnson moved downtown, Agnew won the separate budget line. Had Kennedy and Nixon known what was happening with the Vice-Presidency, one wonders whether they would have made the same decisions.

Unlike that of some institutions, the growth of the Vice-President's office was not incremental. It occurred in a very brief period and stabilized quickly. From twenty or so aides in 1961, the office reached a peak of seventy in 1974 and has remained there since. The greatest expansion of the office took place between 1973 and 1977, and was the result of the unusual circumstances surrounding the Ford and Rockefeller appointments. As already noted in Chapter 2, Watergate may have been the turning point in the evolution of the Vice-Presidency from a ceremonial fixture to a political and policy support agency. Though changes in the external environment—weakening parties, complex issues, etc.—and the electoral connection between Presidents and Vice-Presidents had an important impact on institutionalization, Watergate may have been the key catalyst. Nixon was forced to make concessions to his second Vice-President to bring him on board, concessions that he might not have made before the Watergate crisis. Ford was then forced to make similar concessions to his first Vice-President to attract him to the job, concessions that Ford did not make to Dole in the 1976 Republican convention. Among recent Presidents, only Carter deliberately aided the institutionalization of the Vice-Presidency, inviting Mondale to take a West Wing office and encouraging an expanded job description.

The Vice-President's office is now structured to provide a broad range of political, administrative, and policy services. It has a strong administrative core and a deep political section. The office is equipped to travel on short notice, while also supplying long-range planning. The office is better prepared for emergency succession, while supporting an advisory role across the full term. The office is able to staff short-term crises, while providing a steady source of information and expertise on both foreign and domestic affairs. By itself, the office is not enough to ensure an advisory role, but it does provide the minimum support necessary for the Vice-President's policy involvement. Though the office is only as good as its staff—and some recent staffs have been better than others—it is one key to the evolution of the vice-presidential job description. If the Vice-President *wants* an advisory role, the office can provide the initial support.

4.

Presidents, Vice-Presidents, and Staffs

Once the Vice-President has the necessary institutional support to give advice, the policy role rests on goals. Presidents, Vice-Presidents, and the assorted White House staffs often have very different ideas on what the Vice-President should and should not do. Some Vice-Presidents may not want an advisory role, preferring the campaign trail or the ceremonial trappings instead. Some Vice-Presidents may even avoid activity altogether, opting to wait for their own opportunities. Presidential goals also change. Some Presidents may be more interested in isolating their Vice-Presidents than in listening to their advice. Some may be more concerned with what their Vice-Presidents can do for reelection or constituency relations. The degree to which these presidential and vice-presidential goals are compatible has a significant bearing on the advisory role.

GOALS AND THE JOB DESCRIPTION

Goals involve some desired outcome—whether reelection, lower inflation, more party support in Congress, welfare reform, a place in history, or nuclear arms control. If Presidents want to be elected to a second term, they might ask how Vice-Presidents could help. If Vice-Presidents have some policies they support, they might ask how to build advisory roles.

There are at least four sets of goals that affect the vice-presidential advisory role. *Presidents* certainly enter office with a number of goals that affect what they want their Vice-Presidents to do. These goals are the most important, if only because an advisory role is impossible if the President will not grant access. *The President's staff members* also have goals that shape vice-presi-

101

dential duties. These goals often reflect the President's signals, coupled with the staff's anticipated reactions. If the President has goals which support an advisory role, the White House staff may invest the time building relationships with the Vice-President. If the President ridicules and belittles the Vice-President, the White House staff will be happy to join in. *Vice-Presidents* also enter office with goals that affect their interest in an advisory role. Obviously, Vice-Presidents do not have to do anything during the four-year term. They are invited to National Security Council meetings by statute, but do not have to attend. They are invited to preside over the Senate, but do not have to take the gavel. If, however, Vice-Presidents have programs they support, they must often take unpleasant duties along with the advisory role. Finally, the *Vice-President's own staff members* have goals that affect their interest in the advisory role, whether because they want to expand their own territory or protect their boss from political embarrassment.

The President's Goals

The President's goals are the first and foremost ingredient in the vice-presidential advisory role. As Rockefeller noted shortly after being nominated: "The role of the Vice-President totally depends on the President. If he wants to use him, wonderful; if he doesn't want to use him, fine" (*National Journal,* 24 Aug. 1974). In short, Vice-Presidents are whatever Presidents make them. The President's goals become the first hurdle to an advisory role.

In the past, there have been at least four presidential goals that have affected the Vice-President's role: (1) *reelection,* (2) *good policy,* (3) *resource management,* and (4) *isolation of competition.* In the following pages I am most interested in how these four goals shape the Vice-President's role—that is, how the President's drive for reelection might involve vice-presidential political activity, how the President's search for good policy might involve a vice-presidential advisory role.

Reelection. Like congressmen and senators, all first-term Presidents spend considerable time thinking about reelection. Though the Twenty-second Amendment now limits Presidents to two consecutive terms, reelection is a powerful first-term goal. It affects the choice of issues and alternatives for the policy agenda, the President's travel schedule, cabinet appointments, and press conferences. It also shapes the vice-presidential job description. Vice-Presidents can be powerful weapons in a reelection campaign, defending the administration from attack and promoting the President's program. Because most reelection campaigns start the first day of the first term, Vice-Presidents often spend considerable time on the road. The President's drive for reelection is the major force behind the political Vice-Presidency. As one vice-presidential aide noted: "I can't imagine any President not wanting the Vice-President out on the campaign trail. If the President is smart, he'll push the Vice-President hard. If the Vice-President is smart, he'll go along. It's a great opportunity to carry your own flag in the party."

Most Vice-Presidents have the necessary campaign skills to perform the political function, having risen to the office by being at least the second best campaigners in their party. Only one of the modern Vice-Presidents —Henry Wallace—had not held elective office before joining the party ticket. At least five—Johnson, Humphrey, Rockefeller, Mondale, and Bush —had already run for the presidential nomination before entering office. According to a Mondale assistant: "Mondale was a pretty damn strong campaigner. I think he proved that in the debate with Dole [Ford's running mate in 1976]. He was a good speaker, had reasonable interpersonal skills, but had some problems convincing the Carter people he was interested in the whole process." An Agnew aide offered a similar assessment from the Nixon term. "Agnew's first problem was showing the White House he was a good campaigner. That was solved in November 1969 with the media speech. Agnew had been in only one campaign before the Vice-Presidency, for governor of Maryland. He had to show Nixon he could cut it."

In theory, the reelection goal should dissipate in the second term. Once the President is reelected, the campaign fixation should abate. That happened in Eisenhower's second term, as he turned his attention to other goals. However, Vice-President Nixon continued his campaign activities in the 1958 midterm elections. Eisenhower's first-term goal of reelection had provided the precedent for vice-presidential campaigning, while Nixon's own goal of future election provided the stimulus for continued political activity. Once Nixon reached his own second term as President, his campaign machinery also slowed down. However, with the rise of Watergate, Nixon pressed his second Vice-President, Ford, into service as a campaigner and defender. "It was not a case of wanting reelection, obviously," a Ford aide remarked. "It was a case of political survival. Nixon was desperate for someone to rise to his defense, especially when the impeachment proceedings began in 1974." A second aide concurred: "There was tremendous pressure on Ford from the White House to be the leader of Nixon's defense on Capitol Hill. More than that, they wanted Ford to be a high-level negotiator between Congress and the President. That was a major consideration in Nixon's selection of Ford. First, Ford could be confirmed, no small feat in that Congress. Second, having been a member of Congress, Ford had credibility and friends. He was to be a superlobbyist to Capitol Hill and the country."

Thus, if the President wants to be reelected, the stage is set for a strong political role in the vice-presidential job description.

Good Policy. All Presidents enter office with policies they want to see enacted. Part of the search for good policy involves advice from staff members. Some Presidents build advisory systems to produce more options and inputs, others prefer to see only the final ideas. Depending upon how each President structures the search for good policy, the policy process can include a vice-presidential advisory role. In the Carter administration, the policy process was designed to elicit multiple options for most decisions. Carter preferred to be bracketed by advice from both sides of a question, reserving the final decision for an on-paper review of the major positions, thereby giving Mondale and other advisers frequent opportunity for advice giving. In the Nixon administration, the policy process was structured to produce one major option with a "go" or "no-go" decision. Instead of balancing different ideas against each other, Nixon wanted to have one final option presented for his signature. Nixon was generally uncomfortable with the give-and-take of debate and adopted an on-paper decision structure that produced separate choices on each option, leaving little opportunity for advice from Vice-Presidents or other outside advisers.

In the search for good policy, presidential management styles have an important bearing on the vice-presidential advisory role. A *formalistic* or hierarchical style, with tightly structured decision chains, reduces the opportunity for vice-presidential advice. Since a formalistic system relies on a hierarchical chain of command, the Vice-President can be easily excluded. A *competitive* style, with overlapping assignments among different staff members, offers more opportunity for vice-presidential advice, but also raises the potential for conflict. A *collegial*, or "spokes-of-the-wheel," style, with ad hoc meetings among the staff and free-flowing exchange with the President, offers the most opportunity for vice-presidential advice. The Vice-President can move in and out across the issues, avoiding conflict when it arises, but not sacrificing future participation. Though Johnson was unable to penetrate the closed network of Kennedy's collegial system — in large part because of Bobby Kennedy — both Rockefeller and Mondale achieved greater success under that style. The openness of the collegial system gave both Vice-Presidents more opportunity for an advisory role. Unfortunately, Rockefeller may have actually pushed the Ford system into a more competitive style, duplicating assignments from other staff members and fighting for agenda space. Rockefeller's decision to enter the White House as an advocate pressed the already fragile system to its limits, creating opposition within the White House. Initially Rockefeller had favored a hierarchical system for the Ford White House, but only with the Vice-President at the top of domestic policy and Henry Kissinger at the top of national security. Unfortunately, when a modified version of the system was finally adopted to control increasing staff conflict, Donald Rumsfeld emerged at the top, not Rockefeller. Once again, because Vice-Presidents are unlikely to rise to the top of the hierarchy, a more permeable staffing system yields the greatest advisory opportunities.

It is important to recognize that the goal of good policy has a strong ideological flavor. A President and a Vice-President may both want good policy enacted, but they might not agree on just what good policy is. Since presidential nominees often choose Vice-Presidents on the basis of ideological balance, there is considerable potential for policy conflict. A moderate Nixon selected a conservative Agnew, a liberal Kennedy chose a moderate Johnson, a moderate Carter picked a liberal Mondale, and so forth. Thus, in comparing goal compatibility on policy, we must look at both the intensity of the goal and the ideological content of the search for good policy.

Thus, if the President wants good policy and adopts an open system for generating advice, the incentives exist for a stronger policy role in the vice-presidential job description.

Resource Management. All Presidents enter office with resources that ebb and flow over the term. Some resources are internal to the White House —time, information, expertise, and energy—and are expended inside the White House. Other resources are external in nature, what many staff members call "capital"—public approval, party seats, reputation—and are committed in the legislative process. Presidents enter office with different levels of both internal and external resources. Johnson had more capital than Ford, while Kennedy had more expertise than Carter. Yet, regardless of the initial level, these resources have an important impact on presidential policy. Resources shape the number of programs a President will send to Congress, the kinds of alternatives a President can afford, the degree of internal conflict over administration priorities, and the ultimate success in passing the legislation.

Because these resources are generally scarce, Presidents often look for ways of conserving them. Controversial programs may be delayed until later in the term, dissenting advisers may be asked to leave, internal gate-keepers may emerge, multiple advocacy may decline. The Mondale agenda-setting process, for instance, was designed to develop presidential priorities to conserve political capital. Ehrlichman's rise within the Nixon administration reflected a similar pattern. One way to conserve scarce resources is to put the Vice-President in charge of administrative chores. As one Nixon aide argued: "You can save the President a lot of time by delegating the routine matters. A John Ehrlichman can screen the programs, an H. R. Haldeman can screen the people, a Spiro Agnew can handle Indian affairs and the governors. The President should save time for the more important problems."

Assuming that Presidents want to conserve their time and energy for the top issues, Vice-Presidents may be asked to perform administrative errands that might otherwise occupy the President's staff. Johson's Aeronautics and Space Council, Humphrey's Economic Opportunity Council, Agnew's Intergovernmental Affairs Council and Mondale's agenda-setting activity all contributed in some way to the President's store of resources. Johnson's work created greater public interest in a lunar landing, Agnew's work generated greater interest in revenue sharing. Yet, as one observer noted: "On a scale of one to ten, Agnew would be a two for helping Nixon. I'll grant that Agnew did save some time by talking to the governors, but it wasn't that great. Ehrlichman probably spent just as much time watching Agnew as he saved by giving intergovernmental affairs to the Vice-President."

At the ceremonial and political level, Vice-Presidents can add to internal resources by reducing the time needed for the President's speaking, lobbying, and liaison activities. At the policy level, they can add to the President's internal resources through the line assistant role. However, even if Vice-Presidents can add to scarce *presidential* resources by performing routine administrative chores, they must commit considerable *vice-presidential* resources in the effort. The President's goal of resource management often conflicts with the Vice-President's goal of becoming a senior adviser. The very activities that meet the President's goal undermine the Vice-President's advisory role.

Thus, if the President wants to conserve scarce time, energy, and capital, the opportunity arises for a greater administrative role in the vice-presidential job description. The chances also increase for greater vice-presidential role conflict.

Isolation of Competition. Few Presidents enter office with the explicit goal of isolating the Vice-President. Yet all Presidents try to anticipate potential competition. Though most of the political competition comes from outside the White House, Presidents sometimes focus on their own Vice-Presidents as potential enemies. The Ford staff was concerned about the role of Nelson Rockefeller as a spoiler in 1976, while rumors about a possible Mondale candidacy arose during the "dump Carter" movement just before the 1980 Democratic convention. Of recent Vice-Presidents, perhaps Agnew was hurt most by his rise as a potential competitor. As an Agnew aide remarked: "You've got to relax the President that the Vice-President is not a competitor. A successor, perhaps, but not a competitor. Agnew made the mistake of appearing as a competitor. Nixon had the weapons to isolate Agnew. He disliked Agnew that much."

There are ample reasons why Presidents worry about vice-presidential competition. Vice-Presidents have access to party officials through their campaign, liaison, and lobbying activities. Vice-Presidents also gain valuable experience over the term, becoming better politicians, honing their speaking and handshaking abilities. As I argue shortly, Vice-Presidents often enter office with the goal of future election in their own right. Presidents are rightly concerned about just when that future will arrive. The concern is heightened, of course, by the fact that many Vice-Presidents are former political competitors, having accepted the second spot only after trying for the first. Johnson, Humphrey, Rockefeller, and Bush were all former competitors for the presidential nomination, with Bush coming closest to defeating his eventual boss. According to a media observer: "Here's a situation where the President is sitting across the table from someone who probably called him a boob and an idiot, someone who probably called his family stupid and his programs pitiful, someone who made jokes about his clothes and his speech impediment, someone who probably beat him a couple of times in the primaries and gloated about the wins. Would you want that guy sitting across from you every day?"

Presidents may also isolate their Vice-Presidents for other reasons. In 1972 Agnew stood in the way of John Connally, Nixon's chosen successor. According to Ehrlichman, Nixon often considered dropping Agnew from the ticket, one such instance coming in July 1971:

> Nixon asked me my opinion of Agnew, and I told him it was my hope that the Vice President would resign soon. He was obviously not happy in the job, did not get on well with the President or the rest of us and was not suited to what he was expected to do.
>
> "I talked to John Connally for three hours yesterday," Nixon told me. "I offered him the Vice Presidency or, if that's not possible, then Secretary of State. I want to position him as my logical successor. . . ."
>
> "Connally told me," Nixon said, "that he had no complaints about you or Bob (Haldeman). But I want you to meet often with Connally. You woo him. And I want you and Bob to meet with Connally and Bryce Harlow to figure out how the hell we can get Agnew to resign early" (1982, p. 261).

Though Agnew survived the purge, in part because of John Mitchell's support, Nixon's interest in Connally did little to expand Agnew's advisory role. "It's like being saved from drowning," one aide joked, "only to be shot for swimming." Thus, following the 1972 election, Agnew was removed from the intergovernmental affairs position. According to an Agnew assistant, "They thought it was a power base for Agnew and wanted to push Connally ahead. They saw it was important and took it back. Nixon wanted to completely reorganize, wanted to consolidate all the substance into the Super-Cabinet. It was very cold in the EOB that January."

Among recent Presidents, perhaps Johnson was most concerned about limiting his Vice-President's participation. According to a Johnson aide:

> Johnson had become very conscious of his own mortality. Maybe the heart attack did it. He didn't like to see Humphrey walking around, feeling healthy, because Johnson didn't think he would make it past a second term. He didn't like staring at Humphrey knowing that man would be making love to the Presidency after he left. The peculiar thing about it was that Johnson had really liked Humphrey in the Senate. Both had been state NYA [National Youth Administration] administrators under Roosevelt and felt a common bond. LBJ went

out of his way to favor Humphrey in the Senate, not just to build a power base either.

An Agnew aide echoed the argument. "There is a psychological block built in. Presidents don't like meeting with their successors. It's morbid to be training your own heir." A second Agnew aide agreed. "The final obstacle for a strong role for the Vice-President is the President himself, who may want such a role for his Vice-President, but may subconsciously relieve his own anxiety of being replaced by not pushing for it." As Vice-President, Johnson had complained about feeling like a "goddamn raven hovering around the President's neck." It should not have been a surprise that he would see Humphrey in the same light. Johnson may have also suffered from what might be called the "abused child" syndrome. Having been humiliated and isolated by Kennedy, Johnson may have projected his anger onto his own Vice-President. Of the Presidents who inflicted the greatest pain on their Vice-Presidents—Kennedy, Johnson, and Nixon—two had been former Vice-Presidents themselves.

Thus, if the President wants to isolate the Vice-President, the ceremonial role offers little vice-presidential visibility and plenty of trivial work. The political and policy roles are less effective for purposes of isolation, since they invite greater public attention.

The President's Staff

The President's staff is the second major ingredient in the vice-presidential job description, often rivaling the President in importance. The staff often isolates the Vice-President from the policy role and reacts to the slightest presidential signal to do so. As one Rockefeller aide argued, "The President's men are always ready if the President wants to cut the V.P. out, but are deaf if the President wants him involved." If the President wants a vice-presidential policy role, he will often have to force the staff to give ground. A number of White House aides and outside observers agreed on this point:

> White House staffers won't give their territory to anyone without a fight. The President has to step in to let them know that he intends to have the Vice-President included. Without that presidential signal, the White House staff will take the cue from the past and ice the Vice-President out (Humphrey aide).

> The President must make it known to his Cabinet and staff that he emphatically intends to monitor the Vice President's progress and is prepared to change personnel to insure that it works. Nothing but a forceful measure such as this can penetrate the intoxicating atmosphere of power which surrounds the Presidency (C. D. Ward, Agnew intergovernmental affairs aide, *Washington Star*, 12 Dec. 1976).

Ford thought all he had to do was tell the staff once and that would do it. But if the staff doesn't obey, you've got to fire them and Ford wouldn't do that. Sometimes Rockefeller would bitch and complain to Ford about the staff icing him out and Ford would call his top aides in to tell them to stop, but it didn't change (Ford presidential aide).

When I was frozen out, the symptoms were everywhere. The staff took their cues from the boss. It meant sitting outside Joe Califano's office, while he, pretentiously, went about his work inside at his own pace. Or Marvin Watson instructed to cancel the use of a boat on the Potomac just before my guests were to arrive (Humphrey 1976, p. 427).

Individuals join the White House staff for many reasons. Some want higher salaries after low paying campaign jobs (a reason that applied to many of the Carter aides but to few of the Reagan team). Some want better credentials, a reason that becomes evident as staffers leave to form consulting groups and new law firms. Some support certain ideas and want to make them into presidential policy. Though the White House staff is composed of different individuals with different goals—legislative liaison, for instance, does not have the same goals on policy as OMB or NSC—there are at least two major goals that apply to all of the President's White House assistants: (1) *protection of the President* and (2) *protection of staff territory.* Since both goals focus on the isolation of the Vice-President from the advisory process, the staffs can become a critical obstacle to substantive assignments. It is not enough for the Vice-President to have a good relationship with the President.

Protection of the President. Staff members try to protect the President from potential damage, spending considerable time on fire fighting and minor crises. The damage may come from a Cabinet member's end run to Congress, an agency's leak to the press, a staff member's accident at a local bar, a brother's relationship with foreign interests, even a President's mistake at a press conference. The damage can also come from the Vice-President. Agnew was generally viewed as an embarrassment to the White House—too hot on the campaign trail and too cold on policy ideas. Rockefeller was generally perceived as a threat inside the White House, too strong to be satisfied with a subordinate's role. Humphrey was seen as too talkative and cheerful, as if in the words of one aide, "something was wrong with him if he was happy being Vice-President." Johnson was viewed as a nuisance, drinking and complaining too much. According to one Johnson aide: "The relationship with Kennedy was OK. The relationship with the Kennedyites was terrible. The staff regarded him as an oaf, an influence to be avoided, embarrassing when he whooped in the Taj Mahal, a waste of time. Bobby, Arthur Schlesinger, Jr., those types couldn't stand Johnson. They walled him off from the President."

As a Mondale aide argued, such images work to undermine the Vice-President's potential impact. "One of the things that has hurt past Vice-Presidents is the staff insecurity. The staff cut Humphrey off at the knees and wouldn't give him the necessary access. The Vice-President has to come to grips with the natural staff protection of the President. He's got to massage them a little, not come on too strong. And never, ever pull an end run around the President's top aides." In the "us-versus-them" world inside the West Wing (see Rockman 1981), the Vice-President must work to convince the staff that he is one of the team, a part of the solution and not the problem.

At no time was the us-versus-them mentality more damaging than with Rockefeller's rise to the Domestic Council. The problems started long before Rockefeller even arrived in Washington following his confirmation. Rockefeller's image as a dynamic, persuasive, and influential politician was contrasted with Ford's image as an unprepared, unwilling, and unimaginative congressman. As one Rockefeller aide maintained: "The image was just as important as the reality. There were stories of Rockefeller preparing to invade Washington with planeloads of staff, ready to take over the government from Ford. That frightened the Ford people into some pretty serious efforts to keep control." A second aide offered a similar perception: "Rockefeller clearly had a stronger national reputation than Ford. Everybody had heard about Rockefeller, but nobody knew about Ford. There was this fear of a monster machine rolling in from New York. It was a misplaced fear with no basis in fact." These natural fears were heightened by the national press corps. Editorials acclaimed Rockefeller's nomination as the first right thing Ford had done. As a Rockefeller assistant noted, "The press really exaggerated the threats and insecurities in the first months of the Ford Presidency. The press flocked around Rockefeller because he was so damn exciting and charming. The Ford people were naturally outraged at the attention for Rockefeller."

Protection of Staff Territory. Most White House aides want to enhance their personal prestige and influence as far as possible. When White House aides see a threat to their jobs or influence, they have several tools to protect their territory. They can deny access to competitors, undermine the paper flow, distort information to a from the President, release embarrassing items to the press, withhold perquisites, and make a competitor's life generally miserable. According to C. D. Ward, Agnew's intergovernmental affairs adviser: "Many White House staffers are particularly opposed to any activity which they perceive as reducing their own power, now or in the future. They also don't like to be reminded of the possibility of their losing their positions close to the leader. Therefore, they resist dealing with the vice president in a manner that carries with it the possibility of his immediate assumption of power." As Ward continues, the problem also applies to cabinet members: "Cabinet officers and other officials who want to deal with the president on a one-to-one basis—'kings only want to talk with other kings'—are reluctant to afford the vice president the same rapport that they strive to establish with the president, as they fear a situation in which the vice president would be substituted for their contacts with the President" (*Washington Star*, 12 Dec. 1976).

For Humphrey, the problems centered on Joseph Califano, Johnson's domestic policy adviser. As an aide argued: "Califano was the source of most of Humphrey's unhappiness. Califano was a power broker and was trying to build his own fiefdom. Humphrey would go to Johnson and propose a new program or whatever and Johnson would say 'Go see Joe Califano about it.' And Califano would deep six the idea." For Rockefeller, the problems centered on Donald Rumsfeld. "I never had much doubt," a Ford aide noted, "that Rumsfeld had his own ambition for the Vice-Presidency and then the Presidency. He was a very cunning politician—still is—and knew that his main competition for the future would come from Nelson Rockefeller." For Johnson, the problems centered on Bobby Kennedy; for Agnew, the problems centered on Ehrlichman. As gatekeepers to the Oval Office, all of these players came to hold considerable power over the vice-presidential advisory role. Since Presidents cannot see to every detail in the day-to-day operation of the White House, their top aides have great influence over the paper flow, the agenda, and the President's own time and energy. As a Rockefeller aide noted, if the chief of staff does not want the Vice-President to participate in a decision, and if the President does not make his wishes clear, "the Vice-President will end up reading about administration decisions in the *Washington Post*."

Once again, at no time was the President's staff more powerful in isolating the Vice-President than with Rockefeller. The problems started when Rockefeller placed his own appointees on the Domestic Council, forcing Rumsfeld to withdraw his nominees. According to most accounts, Rumsfeld hoped to move Phillip Areeda, one of Philip Buchen's aides, to the Domestic Council, but had to back down after Ford gave control to Rockefeller. According to one Rockefeller aide, that first victory also became Rockefeller's last.

> Rumsfeld was determined to keep Rockefeller out of the inner circle—partly from his own ambition, partly from loyalty to Ford. Rumsfeld worked to see that his turf was not cut out from under him and opposed Rockefeller's takeover of the Domestic Council. Rumsfeld had his own person ready to take control of the council, but lost that skirmish. Rumsfeld was still good at palace politics and eventually took the territory back. He was doing the natural thing, looking out for number one.

Part of the trouble came from the high level of conflict in the Ford White House itself. There were at least four concentric circles of aides fighting for influence: Ford's old congressional staff (headed by Hartmann), Ford's new White House team (headed by Rumsfeld), the Nixon holdovers (headed by Haig), and the new Domestic Council staff (headed by James Cannon). In a united administration, Rockefeller might have been more successful maintaining cordial relationships. "We worked well with the substantive policy staff," a Rockefeller aide suggested, "but not with the political boys. Ford inherited Nixon's holdovers and was in the process of purging them. None were superheavies and there were few around who knew much about substance. They were the Chinese Wall that killed Rockefeller. He could not cut around them." Part of the problem was Rockefeller himself. According to a Rockefeller assistant: "Rockefeller didn't want to fuss around with the White House staff. He'd just pick up the phone and call Ford. He'd been a Rockefeller for sixty-seven years and didn't want to compete with the Ford staff for the President's attention. After all, he was serving the President and not Donald Rumsfeld. But if you are anywhere near the President, you want to protect him and your own access. And here was this New York juggernaut coming in from left field, violating all the organizational rules." As a second Rockefeller aide argued: "You have to understand the paper flow that Rockefeller wanted. An idea had to go up to Rockefeller, back to the Domestic Council, up to Rumsfeld, back to the Domestic Council, and in to Ford. And if Rockefeller lost any of those rounds, he would still take the idea in to Ford through the back door. That's just no way to run an agency." Nor did Rockefeller work to allay the fears of the Ford staff. "He had no strategy for winning them over," an aide said. "He didn't feel obligated to kowtow to the Ford staff. He thought they were neophytes, third- and fourth-rate bureaucrats, and didn't miss a chance to tell them so to their faces. Needless to say, they didn't like it." And, as this aide concluded, fears of a takeover weren't entirely groundless. "Had Rockefeller become chief of staff, driving Rumsfeld out, and controlling domestic affairs, he might have taken over the government. He would have been the one icing out Ford. He thought he knew what needed to be done and would have done whatever was necessary to do it."

Rockefeller's problems serve as a lesson on conflict with the White House staff. Just like Congress, the White House has certain operating norms. Advisers are expected to fall in line behind a decision once the President has signed off. Advisers are expected to maintain silence on highly sensitive decisions, while defending the President against outside criticism. Whereas Rockefeller ignored many of these norms, Mondale scrupulously adhered to the unwritten code of staff conduct. He did not criticize decisions in public; he did not make end runs to Congress or the press; he worked to remain a team player. Moreover, Mondale tried to avoid any extended conflict with other entrepreneurs. Though Mondale fought against budget cuts and cabinet crises, he never became involved in a turf fight with other staff members. As we will see in Chapters 6 and 7, one of Mondale's strategies for advice and influence was discretion. It was a strategy that Bush adopted early in the Reagan administration. As Bush argued in 1981: "If I'm another player in the field, protecting my turf and bragging about how close in I am, that inevitably strains things. That's exactly why I've never wanted to talk to anybody about the way my job is developing" (*Washington Post*, 30 Mar. 1981).

Thus, if the White House staff perceives the Vice-President as either disloyal or a threat to internal territory, retaliation will occur at the staff level. Even if the Vice-President develops a strong personal relationship with the President, the White House staff can still freeze the Vice-President out of the policy process.

The Vice-President's Goals

Vice-Presidents often give different explanations for accepting the nomination to the second spot on the ticket. Gerald Ford remembers the Vice-Presidency as "a splendid cap to my career—not the office I'd sought, but one that would also constitute recognition of my long service in Washington" (1979, p. 101). As Ford told the *National Journal*, the Vice-Presidency was never his life's ambition. His first goal was the speakership of the House. "I got sidetracked in that regard by ending up as Vice President, but it was fortuitous, because I think I was foreclosed from ever being Speaker by the political realities. And I think I needed the change. This was an ideal sort of capping to—of the climax" (10 Aug. 1974). Rockefeller may have accepted for a similar reason, but he also saw the Vice-Presidency as one last opportunity for gaining the ultimate power of the Presidency. According to one Rockefeller aide: "He still hungered for the Presidency. He never did anything disloyal to strip the office away from Ford, but he was definitely willing to be the right man in the right place at the right time. He took the nomination because Ford asked him at the most difficult time in our recent history, but that didn't mean Rockefeller didn't want one last shot at the Presidency."

Among recent Vice-Presidents, perhaps Johnson had the most unusual mix of goals. Johnson actually won two elections in 1960, each reflecting a different set of goals. He was elected to the Vice-Presidency and reelected to the Senate. As a Johnson aide remarked, "The Senate campaign was insurance against Kennedy's defeat." Johnson was sworn in for his third Senate term on 3 January 1961. He served for three minutes and resigned. He was sworn in as Vice-President seventeen days later. He served for three years, but thought of resigning in 1964. For the majority leader who vowed never to trade his Senate vote for a presiding gavel, the 1960 election reflected a mixture of personal and political goals. As majority leader under Eisenhower, Johnson had been the most powerful Democrat in Washington. As

Vice-President under Kennedy, Johnson became one of the least powerful. Yet, Johnson wanted to be President. He was willing to accept a loss of power in the short run if he could step up to the Presidency four or eight years later. Several aides also suggest that Johnson took the Vice-Presidency as a chance to rest. After his heart attack in the mid-1950s, Johnson had gone full speed as majority leader and presidential candidate. As one assistant noted: "Mrs. Johnson insists to this day that LBJ accepted the nomination because he was sick and needed a few years off." Other Vice-Presidents have recited the standard list of reasons for accepting: duty to country, duty to party, duty to constituents, blacks, labor, liberals, conservatives, states, the poor, an opportunity to serve, and, most frequent, "The party asked and I could not refuse."

Whatever the reason given at the time of nomination—usually a response to a question about why anyone would want to be Vice-President—there are at least four goals that affect the Vice-President's view of the job description: (1) *future election*, (2) *good policy*, (3) *isolation from the President*, and (4) *pomp and perquisites*. The degree to which these vice-presidential goals match presidential goals, without unduly threatening the White House staff, has a significant bearing on the job description.

Future Election. All Vice-Presidents want to be Presidents some day. With the political functions of their office, Vice-Presidents can establish themselves as front-runners for the future. Of the political roles in the job description, the campaigning function is the most attractive for future election. Campaigning not only exposes the Vice-President as a national figure, but allows the officeholder to make contacts that can be used in the future. "There's nothing like having people acknowledge your value," one Agnew aide remarked. "If the Vice-President can convince a few congressmen that they owe him something, he can use that to his advantage in the party. Not only that, but campaigning gives the Vice-President practice at the one activity that can really help him win the nomination. Agnew learned a hell of a lot about campaigning during his first couple of years as Vice-President." A Carter aide made a similar observation about Mondale. "Mondale was a fairly good campaigner to start with, very effective in the 1976 campaign. Over the four-year term, he just got much better, honed his speaking style, worked on his public presence. His one biggest problem is projecting political charisma and he definitely improved over the term. He used those hundreds of speeches to become a better politician, to become a better campaigner. It was just good practice." Campaigning helps Vice-Presidents build potential electoral coalitions. Agnew used the 1970 elections to solidify his support among Republican conservatives, while Mondale collected chits from Democratic moderates and liberals. Not only does campaigning help the Vice-President hold on to the second spot in the short term, but it allows the Vice-President to build support and organizational expertise for the long term. According to one observer, "Mondale's staff was already strong from the Senate campaigns, but they developed a good feel for how to run a national operation. Remember that Mondale dropped out of the 1976 campaign pretty early, before his staff really jelled and learned much about that kind of campaign. Mondale was able to put together a skeleton campaign organization that was ready to be used for 1984."

While the spokesman role gives Vice-Presidents the opportunity to pursue public support, it carries great risks. Whereas campaigning generally involves references to broad themes and party duty, the spokesman role includes defense of administration policy. The more the public comes to identify the Vice-President with specific administration policies, the more the Vice-President can be blamed for administration failures. Humphrey, of course, suffered most from this problem. His active defense of the Vietnam war cost him considerable support among party liberals, leading him to briefly consider resigning from the Vice-Presidency in 1968 to demonstrate his disaffection with Johnson's policies. As one aide argued: "Humphrey never held back on anything. When he went out to make a speech on poverty or blacks or the war, he would give it everything he had. He'd talk as if Vietnam was the most noble cause ever, attacking opponents and waving the flag. He didn't hold back, even though he should have toned down his support." In most of Mondale's public appearances, he generally avoided a rousing defense of specific policies, adopting a generalist theme in most of his addresses. According to one observer,

> There is not a single program in the entire Carter term that you could get the public to list as a Mondale failure. He was that clean. He did not get tangled up in the arguments over the economic program or Iran. He stayed in the background, moving in the shadows of the administration. The public never blamed him for anything—not double-digit inflation or high interest rates or Iran or Afghanistan. Nothing. He didn't take anything that would damage his reputation, but he did spend an awful lot of time on the road.

The public liaison function also adds indirect support to the Vice-President's goal of future election. During the 1970s, as the Democratic party moved toward a more open nominating system, public liaison was less important as a tool for future rewards. Frequent contact with governors, mayors, and other party officials was important to the President, but had few direct payoffs for the Vice-President. With the adoption of the Democratic reforms in 1982, public liaison became much more important. The Democratic reform commission, under the leadership of James B. Hunt, governor of North Carolina, recommended a much greater role for party officials and government leaders in the nominating system. Fifteen percent of the seats were reserved at the 1984 Democratic convention for party officials. Moreover, the seats for the party leaders—whether senators, House members, governors, or mayors—were uncommitted. "Now tell me that Mondale was a fool to spend time with these people," one Mondale aide challenged. "He made a lot of friends as Vice-President, many of whom will be in attendance at the 1984 convention. If push comes to shove in 1984, all those hours of listening as Vice-President will pay off." Indeed, whereas only one-quarter of the 1980 Democratic delegates were chosen by caucuses, almost half of the 1984 delegates would emerge from the same route, where organization and old friends make a greater difference than in primaries.

Vice-Presidents can also pursue their election goals by remaining quiet, proving they can be team players in their President's party. Depending upon the Vice-President's background—whether liberal, moderate, or con- servative—it is often necessary to convince party constituencies of loyalty to the President. That was certainly the case with Rockefeller. Widely perceived as a liberal in an increasingly conservative Republican party, Rockefeller needed to demonstrate his support of Ford. Unfortunately, Rockefeller was not willing to wait for four or eight years for yet another bid at the Presi- dency. He wanted to have his success immediately, arguing for liberal programs on the Ford agenda. Republican conservatives mounted a cam- paign to force the apparently disloyal Vice-President off the presidential ticket. Had Rockefeller remained silent over his brief term, cultivating support with the conservatives, avoiding fights with Rumsfeld, he might have survived the purge. That may be the strategy that Bush adopted early in the Reagan administration. As one media observer argued:

> Bush likes to be with his staff and I underline *his.* The Bush staff is not well integrated into the Reagan staff and I think Bush recognizes that. I'm sure Bush doesn't agree with many of the budget cuts, but wants to wait it out. If he can just spend four years as Reagan's Vice-President without pissing off the right wing, he just might be able to persuade them that he isn't all that dangerous when Reagan steps down. He's got Jesse Helms out there challenging him for the top spot after Reagan goes, but he's trying to let the right wing know he's a team player. He's willing to swallow a lot of the Reagan dogma in order to be loyal.

Unlike Rockefeller, Bush was young enough to wait. By remaining quiet, leaving most policy disputes to a hidden-hand effort through his former aide James Baker, Bush could still pursue his own goal of future election. As a former Rockefeller assistant noted of Bush: "He's very conscious of being number two. Outstanding example was the shooting. He refused to land on the south lawn. He landed at the Naval Observatory instead, and motored to the White House. Bush is very conscious of being an outsider and has been working very hard to prove that he is a potential candidate for President in his own right."

Thus, if the Vice-President wants to be President some day, the political role is very attractive. The goal of future election can also be pursued in the advisory role. However, nothing helps a Vice-President look quite as presidential as campaigning, speaking, and public liaison. Since Vice-Presidents cannot make decisions that the public can see, the political role becomes the best vehicle for gaining name recognition and visibility.

Good Policy. Like Presidents, all Vice-Presidents enter office with policies they want to see enacted. The problem is that Vice-Presidents have very few tools in that effort. Unlike senators or representatives, Vice-Presidents cannot introduce legislation; unlike cabinet secretaries, Vice-Presidents cannot shape outcomes through administration.

Once the Vice-President has a program to support, the White House policy process provides only limited opportunities for advice giving. The first stage is agenda setting, which involves the President's decision to adopt and announce a policy. If Vice-Presidents cannot win at the agenda-setting stage, there is very little opportunity for victory later. Vice-Presidents have few opportunities for end runs to Congress and must generally secure the President's interest early in the process. At the agenda stage, the Vice-President's policy goals are enhanced by an advisory role. The Vice-President must have opportunities to present arguments and ideas. Those opportunities might arise in weekly meetings with the President or in line assignments, but must involve access to the presidential policy process. Rockefeller, for instance, tried to secure access by controlling the domestic agenda-setting machinery. By screening ideas coming in from the departments and staffing issues coming out of the Oval Office, Rockefeller hoped to have the final say on the President's agenda. According to one aide: "Rockefeller thought that getting the policy-making machinery meant getting the policy-making responsibility. Ford's people didn't agree and wouldn't lay down. Rockefeller underestimated the toughness of the Ford staff. He thought he was a New York Giant in a high school football camp." Rockefeller's problem was less that he wanted to influence parts of the agenda than that he wanted to control all of the domestic program. Instead of selecting several vacuums and concentrating on developing new programs, instead of choosing two or three major issues and pushing for adoption, he wanted to be the domestic fulcrum. He did succeed in winning Ford's signature on the Energy Independence Authority, but lost the program in Congress.

The second stage of the policy process involves legislative decision making. If the Vice-President wins at the agenda level, the battle turns to the legislative arena. Once Rockefeller persuaded Ford to introduce his massive energy program, he spent considerable time trying to convince Congress to pass the legislation. According to one aide: "Rockefeller single-handedly tried to force Congress along. He was on Capitol Hill every day talking it up, trying to interest sponsors, trying to schedule hearings, doing everything possible to move the program through the Congress. The trouble was that he was completely alone." Though Ford announced the program with suitable fanfare, he did not instruct his liaison staff to push for passage. It was a symbolic victory for Rockefeller, not a presidential priority. Rockefeller had won at the agenda stage, only to find that he had still lost.

The legislative stage can also involve the effort to sabotage presidential proposals on Capitol Hill. If Vice-Presidents lose a battle in agenda setting, failing to halt the progress of other advisers, they can either withhold lobbying support or work to undermine the lobbying effort. Obviously, the easiest strategy is simple inaction. By *not* lobbying, campaigning, or speaking, Vice-Presidents do not contribute to programs they oppose. Both Mondale and Bush engaged in just such a strategy on budget cuts in their respective terms. Deliberate sabotage is much riskier. Vice-Presidents court severe retribution if they openly work against presidential initiatives. According to a Carter aide: "Everything eventually works back to the White House. Even if the Vice-President is talking in private to an old friend somebody is bound to find out and it will come back. If the White House ever finds out, the Vice-President will disappear from the face of the earth for the next four years."

The third step of the presidential policy process involves implementation and offers the least potential for vice-presidential impact. Vice-Presidents have virtually no opportunity to influence implementation. They are not involved in administration or rule making, and have only rare chances to offer advice to cabinet members and agency chiefs. As one Mondale aide remarked: "The last thing a Vice-President would want is to be left working with a cabinet secretary to get some policy adopted. Those people are even more territorial than the White House staff. Even though Mondale knew both Califano [health and human services secretary] and Bergland [agriculture secretary], he never asked for favors. There were times when he made suggestions about some policy or regulation, but he saw the limits of that strategy." If the Vice-President fails at agenda setting or on Capitol Hill, implementation will not offer much help.

There is one final opportunity for vice-presidential advice at the budget stage. As deficits have grown over the past decade, the budget has become a primary vehicle for presidential policy. Ford, Carter, and Reagan transformed the budget into the central expression of the President's agenda. As the budget has increased in importance, the annual fight over funding has offered some opportunity for vice-presidential impact. In the final two years of the Carter administration, for instance, Mondale was deeply involved in the budget process. According to several Carter and Mondale aides, the Vice-President was responsible for the restoration of several billions in social service spending in both 1979 and 1980. As Carter moved to cut domestic funding, Mondale teamed up with Eizenstat and other administration liberals to fight the cuts. In a prime example of defensive influence, Mondale worked to stop cuts in welfare, legal services, health, and education. According to a Carter domestic policy aide: "I'd guess Mondale was worth $3 to $5 billion in domestic spending in 1979. He was quite effective in persuading Carter to restore some of the cuts that McIntyre [OMB Director] had suggested. He saw his role more as preventing cutbacks, not as arguing for more spending. He recognized the changing times and worked to reduce the sting on social programs."

Thus, if the Vice-President has some policies he supports, and if he can enter the process early at the agenda-setting stage, the advisory role offers the greatest attraction.

Isolation from the President. No Vice-President enters office with the intention of hiding from the President. Vice-Presidents generally arrive with some expectations of meaningful work. There are, however, instances where they deliberately avoid contact with the White House. If a Vice-President has been systematically excluded from meaningful employment or humiliated by the President's staff, there is a natural withdrawal. "No one likes to be put down," one Humphrey aide noted. "If you get the shaft enough times, you finally say 'forget it.' There's only so much a person will take; even a politician has limits." The best place to withdraw is the ceremonial Vice-Presidency, with the commissions, occasional funerals, and pomp. Vice-Presidents have considerable opportunities to disappear if they wish. They can hide on Capitol Hill or in the EOB. They can travel to boy scout jamborees or attend museum board meetings. Moreover, if the Vice-President does not want to be involved, the President cannot compel activity.

There are several reasons why a Vice-President would choose isolation. Lyndon Johnson, for instance, saw White House plots against him. As a Johnson vice-presidential assistant suggests: "Johnson was intensely paranoiac. He felt he was always being set up for a crash. He fought the travel assignments all the way. He thought Kennedy was trying to send him to Vietnam so that, when Vietnam fell, Johnson would be the scapegoat. He slowed down over the three years, not because he was tired, but because his trips started going places where he wasn't welcome." A second Johnson aide offered a similar perception:

Johnson always suspected that Bobby Kennedy was working on some plot against him. He thought Bobby was trying to embarrass him, always felt that the Kennedy people hated him, thought he was somehow inferior, never trusted them. The basic problem for Johnson was that he was selected out of the political ranks. Even when he was given power, it was still not his. Kennedy went out of his way to keep Johnson occupied, but LBJ didn't view it that way. For example, Kennedy suggested that Johnson go to Mexico during the transition, a great opportunity for some visibility, a good sign of trust. Johnson wouldn't go, suspected it was a plot, suspected that Bobby wanted him to have the same kinds of problems Richard Nixon had had in Venezuela [when angry crowds attacked the vice-presidential motorcade].

What did Johnson do instead? As this aide concluded: "The Kennedy White House finally reached a point where they didn't quite know what to do with him. Johnson still wanted to be involved, but he was so intimidated that he kept his head down."

Other Vice-Presidents have avoided contact with the White House to protect their options for the future. Vice-Presidents have some discretion to pick the topics in their speeches, separating themselves from potentially damaging policies. As a Carter assistant noted: "Mondale stayed with very general themes in most of his speeches; you know, party and country. He didn't want to be the one to tell the American people they had to suffer." Among recent Vice-Presidents, Ford worked hardest to distance himself from the White House. At the start of his brief term as Nixon's second Vice-President, Ford had actually been quite active as a campaigner and defender. He gave a number of early speeches attacking Nixon's opponents as misguided and bloodthirsty, including the famous Atlantic City address placing the blame for Watergate on his former congressional colleagues. By 30 March 1974, however, Ford had changed the tune, criticizing the Nixon campaign staff for the Watergate excesses. By May 1974, Ford had asked his chief counsel for information on the House impeachment process and had started to think seriously about his own candidacy in 1976. As Hartmann remembers:

> In the short four months since his Atlantic City attack on the impeachment lobby, Jerry Ford had changed his primary purpose. No longer was it to save the President who appointed him but to save the Presidency he might inherit. No longer was it to prevent a Constitutional confrontation (which was already here) but to get the crisis over with as soon as possible.
>
> He never said this to us in so many words. But it became clear in an address he . . . worked on for May 9 at Eastern Illinois University, in which he warned of a "crisis in confidence."
>
> Ford called upon "all public officials" to speak frankly and publicly. He said legal processes already begun would settle the guilt or innocence of those involved. "This cleansing process," he declared, "would bring about needed recognition that the law applies to holders of high office as well as to the citizen who elects the office-holder."
>
> Repeating his belief that "truth is the glue that holds government together," the Vice President conceded that truth can be "brutal" and cited the tape transcripts as a painful example. But he warned: "The time has come for persons in political life to avoid the pragmatic dodge which seeks to obscure the truth" (1980, p. 120).

The next day, Nixon called Ford into the Oval Office and suggested that the Vice-President slow down in the coming months.

Ford's change reflected his desire to protect himself from Watergate. Though Ford now admits he agreed not to be a presidential candidate as part of his vice-presidential appointment in 1973, he had begun to entertain a goal of future election in his own right by 1974. Moreover, as Watergate tightened its grip on the Nixon White House, Ford realized that his own Presidency might come much earlier than 1976. As one Ford vice-presidential aide argued: "Ford knew the resignation or impeachment was coming early in the summer. I remember when Barry Goldwater told him to get off his ass because he was going to be President soon. Ford was as white as a sheet, but knew it was the truth." The realization put Ford in an awkward position. According to a Ford assistant: "Ford was concerned that if he did anything to be prepared substantively, it might be construed as disloyal. So he tried to do nothing. He did get briefings and did meet with Nixon occasionally, but it was a very compressed period. Those nine months went by like nine weeks." A second aide concurred. "He was the only person who could have become President by simply saying 'The President is guilty.' He had to balance getting close enough to Nixon to be prepared for succession while getting enough distance to stay clean. He had to dispel the notion that he was trying to encourage impeachment, but had to avoid being dirtied by the whole Watergate affair. As it was, people thought he had made a deal when he gave Nixon the pardon."

Ford had originally accepted Nixon's explanations of Watergate, only to regret his confidence later. Once Ford found out about the "smoking gun" in the Watergate transcripts, he removed himself from any further activity in support of the Nixon Presidency. As Ford recalls the August 5 confrontation:

"Everyone here recognizes the difficult position I'm in," I said. "No one regrets more than I do this whole tragic episode. I have deep personal sympathy for you, Mr. President, and your fine family. But I wish to emphasize that had I known what has been disclosed in reference to Watergate in the last twenty-four hours, I would not have made a number of statements I made either as Minority Leader or as Vice President. I came to a decision yesterday and you may be aware that I informed the press that because of my commitments to Congress and the public, I'll have no further comment on the issue because I'm a party in interest. I'm sure there will be impeachment in the House. I can't predict the Senate outcome. I will make no comment concerning this" (1979, p. 20).

Even then, Ford would not admit his thoughts about succession. As he told the *National Journal* only days before Nixon's resignation: "If I think about it, I wouldn't admit it, because I think it's wrong to make any public statement to the effect that I am thinking about this or that. But you can't help it once in a while, wake up when you're alone. It's not that you do it deliberately, it's just human nature. But I don't talk about what I think about" (10 Aug. 1974).

Thus, if the Vice-President is concerned about being identified with damaging policies, the result may be an "invisible" Vice-Presidency. At the very least, the Vice-President always retains the power of inaction. The office provides ample hiding space if the Vice-President wants to disappear.

Pomp and Perquisites. All Vice-Presidents want at least some of the trappings of office. Vice-Presidents like to have limousines and red carpets. They like to fly in jet aircraft and stay in first-class hotels. They like to be saluted by the troops and covered by the press. The past twenty years have witnessed a dramatic increase in the Vice-President's perquisites. Vice-Presidents now have automatic access to airplanes and White House mess passes. They have a more prominent seal and their own mansion. Yet, among the duties in the vice-presidential job description, some offer more pomp and perquisites than others. For Vice-Presidents interested in the trappings of office, the ceremonial Vice-Presidency is the most attractive arena. "The West Wing office is actually quite grubby," a Mondale aide remarked. "It is cramped and closed in. There's a lot of traffic and the view isn't so hot out the back window. It's got lots of advantages if you want to be a player, but it isn't that great if you're into offices." A second Mondale aide continued: "That EOB office is nothing less than magnificent. Royal blue carpeting. Two entrances, both protected by huge mahogany doors. Great view of the White House and monuments. Good location. Balcony. High ceilings."

Pomp and perquisites are generally highest when the Vice-President travels abroad. According to a Humphrey aide: "It's very heady to run around with the vice-presidential seal and the secret service. It makes you feel very important. The imperial Vice-Presidency. It's something you can only get when you're on the road. Who's to know what the Vice-President really does when you're at a state dinner in Thailand? It's one of the few things that can be really satisfying." Foreign travel offers a rare vice-presidential opportunity for prestige. According to Doris Kearns, such travel was Johnson's only escape as Vice-President:

> He was once again the spoiled, demanding, and exuberant child. Before each trip he compiled a long list of the things he needed to have with him: an oversized bed to fit his six-foot, four-inch frame, a shower attachment that emitted a hard needlepoint spray, two dozen cases of Cutty Sark, five hundred boxes of ball-point pens, six dozen cases of cigarette lighters. The pens and lighters were brought along by the thousands as gifts. In the poorest slums of India, on the crowded streets of Dakar, in the markets of Thailand, Johnson passed among the people distributing LBJ-inscribed pens, shaking hands, patting heads, inviting a camel driver to America. The Vice President's personal diplomacy and impulsive behavior appalled many officials in the Foreign Service. He provokingly refused to take their rules of etiquette seriously; he was, they believed, confusing diplomacy with campaigning. Yet, with all the confusion of pens and crowds and abrupt changes in plans, Lyndon Johnson was clearly

successful as an ambassador of goodwill, though none of this restored even a measure of authority. His energy and his friendly manner were contagious; but then he came home, ending his brief return to center stage and retiring to his cage once again (1976, pp. 167-68).

Among the ten contemporary Vice-Presidents, Barkley may have been most interested in pomp and perquisites. According to a Johnson vice-presidential aide: "Barkley actually loved the Vice-Presidency. At that stage in his life, that's all he wanted. To run around being called a 'Veep' and being asked to ribbon cuttings. The fires of ambition were out." As the oldest recent Vice-President, Barkley focused his energy on presiding in the Senate, telling jokes, and soaking in the ceremonial Vice-Presidency. Though Barkley did have some formal duties—attendance at National Security Council meetings, etc.—his term was devoted to nonsubstantive assignments. And, according to most observers, that is precisely what Barkley wanted. Other Vice-Presidents have emphasized the pomp and perquisites of the ceremonial office only when other channels have failed. Foreclosed from any policy or political duties, Johnson initially turned to travel as one escape; foreclosed from any input on Vietnam, Humphrey turned to the commissioner function. Today, Vice-Presidents have ample pomp and per-quisites without turning to the ceremonial duties. As part of the institu-tionalization of the office, Vice-Presidents now have access to most of the symbols that past occupants lacked. The mansion, the airplanes, the limos, the White House office, the mess privileges, and the seal are all automatic now. Foreign travel is no longer the only opportunity for vice-presidential pomp, but may still remain the best chance for Vice-Presidents to strut.

Thus, if the Vice-President wants the pomp and perquisites of office, the clear choice is the ceremonial Vice-Presidency. The delegate and commis-sioner roles continue to offer the greatest ceremonial trappings. "Where else but the Smithsonian Board can the Vice-President wear a bowler during the middle of the day?" a Johnson aide asked.

The Vice-President's Staff

Since the early 1970s, Vice-Presidents have been able to take their personal staffs into the executive branch. Mondale moved most of his Senate staff to the Vice-Presidency, while Bush took most of his campaign aides. Because most of these aides have long personal ties to their boss, they often exhibit the same loyalty to the Vice-President as the White House staffs show to the President. The Vice-President's staff can be just as protective as the Presi-dent's staff, just as angry about imaginary insults. The difference, of course, is that the President's staff can retaliate for leaks and embarrassments, while the Vice-President's staff must walk a tightrope between maintaining some level of contact with the White House and protecting the Vice-President.

As one Rockefeller aide argued, "We knew that we had to be civil to the Ford staff if we wanted to keep getting the paper, but we also couldn't help but hear what they were saying about Rockefeller behind his back. It was a tough situation because we didn't want to cut our throats, but we didn't want to keep quiet either." In the end, most vice-presidential aides express allegiance to the President. As Rich Bond, first a Bush aide and next deputy director of the Republican National Committee, argued: "Bush would not tolerate me being on his staff if I weren't prepared to work fully and cooperatively with Reagan and his staff. I'd be gone tomorrow if George thought I was spending one second on anything but making this administration a success. He's made it very clear that if we don't like the arrangement, we should go some place else" (*Washington Post*, 30 Mar. 1981).

The staff is an important link to the policy process during the Vice-President's absence. As noted in Chapter 3, Mondale's staff maintained frequent contact with the Carter staff, while Rockefeller's staff was effectively isolated. Fifty-eight percent of the Mondale staff had at least weekly contact with the Carter White House, while only 21 percent of the Rockefeller staff had the same level with the Ford White House. Thus, when Mondale traveled, his staff was able to continue collecting information and ideas, while Rockefeller remained frozen out. Though Mondale gave up his private meetings whenever he left Washington, his staff was able to generate hidden-hand advice and influence. The strength of the relationship between the Vice-President's staff and the President's staff also had an important impact on the evolution of the Mondale advisory role. Both staffs were able to minimize conflict while building effective policy coalitions inside the White House. This is not to suggest that Mondale's and Carter's staffs agreed on all issues. Mondale's staff took exception to some Carter policies, while supporting others. Usually, Mondale's staff worked closest with Eizenstat's Domestic Policy Staff. There was a common bond ideologically and the two staffs merged well together. The search for good policy was enough to balance the staff divisions.

In the past, most staff conflict has come from the natural protective instinct. Vice-presidential staff members want to keep their jobs and expand their influence. The Vice-President's assistants want White House mess privileges and decent offices. The Vice-President's people want phone calls returned and parking spaces. Beyond the normal desire for the accoutrements of office, the Vice-President's staff has two additional goals that shape the job description: (1) *protection of the Vice-President*, and (2) *expansion of staff territory*. Since both goals involve higher visibility for both the Vice-President and the staff, they often conflict with the President's goals and the protective nature of the White House staff.

Protection of the Vice-President. No vice-presidential staff member likes to see the Vice-President humiliated. It reflects on the staff as well as the

Vice-President. According to a Humphrey assistant: "All of the slights and insults affected the staff, too. It was hard not to be embarrassed by Johnson's jokes about Humphrey. Those jokes were about us, too. It was hard not to be angry when we couldn't get into the White House to talk about programs or when we couldn't get supplies or airplanes or secretaries or printing." Moreover, such embarrassments may undermine the Vice-President's own goal of future election, a goal that is shared by most if not all of the vice-presidential staff. "If the Vice-President has been the butt of all those jokes for all that time," an observer noted, "it can't help in his own nomination campaign. What the Vice-President wants is some kind of job where he can claim special training, not a job where he is ridiculed for being dumb enough to give up real power for nothing."

There are a variety of tools for protecting the Vice-President. The most attractive is to push for substantive assignments. The Vice-President's staff has a vested interest in keeping the Vice-President actively involved in policy issues. "For one thing," a Mondale aide argues, "it is more interesting for the staff. Nobody wants to spend their time doing nothing. We were trained to provide support for a politician and that's what we like to do." Another Mondale assistant agreed:

> Obviously, we wanted to see Mondale succeed. It was in his best interests and ours, too. Most staff members go with a candidate for two or three reasons: (1) they want to get some experience that will help them get jobs outside of government, (2) they want to work on some policy issue that they think is important, and (3) they want to move up the ladder inside government, maybe even run for office in the future. It's important, therefore, to work for people who are involved in daily decisions and have some measure of influence. It's useless to work for a lightweight. People in Washington know who's who and won't be particularly impressed if you've worked for a loser. Ask the Agnew people about the difficulties of that. More than that, it's important to keep your mind active. You don't want to spend four or eight years just sitting around doing nothing. That was why we all wanted Mondale to remain active in the administration. That's probably why most of us worked for him in the first place. We knew that he would be one of the key players wherever he went and he was. We also knew that at least some of the Carter people would be interested in our ideas and they were.

A second tool is the timely leak. If the President has embarrassed the Vice-President, why not embarrass the President? "If the Vice-President is being savaged by someone in the White House, one way to get back is to plant some of your own material," a Rockefeller aide argued. "Have Lyndon Johnson criticize the President's congressional operation in public; have Nelson Rockefeller attack the President's domestic budget in the press. It won't stop the problems, but it will give the staff some satisfaction." If all else fails, the third approach is to withdraw. Instead of openly taking the insults, the Vice-President and his staff can pull back, waiting out the administration. This option is the least attractive for the Vice-President's staff. It is the least exciting alternative, ensuring long periods of inactivity and a loss of perquisites. From the staff perspective, the political and policy Vice-Presidencies offer the greatest rewards. Both offer an opportunity to remain involved in the business of government.

Expansion of Staff Territory. Beyond the protection of the Vice-President's political and policy interests, the vice-presidential staff often seeks to expand its territory. Because so many of the Vice-President's aides work in substantive offices before joining the administration, they try to avoid constituent letter writing as their main duty. Top vice-presidential aides want to be involved in substantive policy. Sometimes, this goal involves *coalition building* with White House staff members. Mondale's staff, for instance, was integrated into the White House on several levels. By forming ties with a variety of policy offices—NSC, domestic policy, press—Mondale's staff was able to subtly expand its territory without threatening the President's staff. As one observer noted: "It was all done by infiltration, not by direct confrontation. Rather than try to take over domestic policy, like Rockefeller, Mondale's people made friends with Eizenstat's people. It was very indirect, but wasn't subterfuge. They managed to become quite involved without ever frightening the Carter people." Sometimes, this goal involves *direct conflict* with the White House staff, putting the Vice-President's aides on a collision course with the territorial imperative. As a Rockefeller aide noted: "Here was a staff that had once run the government of the largest state in the country. It was like asking a thoroughbred to hold back in the middle of a race. Many of the staff believed Rockefeller should have been President, not Ford. They just couldn't adjust to being number two. Coming from New York to the Vice-Presidency was just too hard. They couldn't take the demotion and became very isolated, began to circulate rumors about how naive the Ford staff was. Then they made the grab for the Domestic Council and were shut out."

Of the two strategies—coalition building or direct conflict—the former will usually be more successful. Vice-presidential aides do not have the resources to sustain a prolonged fight within the White House. Even if the Vice-President has a strong relationship one-on-one with the President, the vice-presidential staff cannot win. Coalition building offers more opportunity for long-term success, but has its own price. "Sometimes we just wanted to make a stand," a vice-presidential aide reflected, "but it wouldn't have worked. Sooner or later, you have to ask whether an issue is important enough to fight about, even if you lose and spend the next four years rearranging your office. Most of the time, however, you just try to get along."

Thus, for both protecting the Vice-President and expanding substantive territory, the staff will push for a vice-presidential advisory role. Depending upon just how the push comes, the President's staff may counter with isolation.

GOAL COMPATIBILITY

Goal compatibility among staffs and principals is a key to the advisory role. However, what looks like compatibility from outside the White House may be conflict on the inside. Goal compatibility is best viewed as a continuum. Goals are either more compatible or less compatible. If the President, Vice-President, and the two staffs can agree on the basic goals in the administration—reelection, good policy, resource management—conflict can be minimized. The key word here is conflict. When goal compatibility is high, there are lower levels of conflict; when goal compatibility is low, there are higher levels of infighting. In the past, considerable vice-presidential unhappiness has emerged from mismatching White House goals. Vice-Presidents have often pushed for substantive roles only to encounter stiff resistance from Presidents or their staffs. Thus, if a vice-presidential nominee wants to have an advisory role once in office, the time to start lobbying is before the convention and during the campaign. As one Carter aide noted: "Mondale had some impact on Carter's thinking about the Vice-Presidency. Carter had given some thought to the office before calling Mondale down to Plains [for a preconvention interview], but Mondale was fairly successful in pushing Carter towards an active Vice-Presidency. You might even say Mondale raised Carter's consciousness about the job."

One way to understand the impact of goal compatibility is to look back over the past ten Vice-Presidents, excluding Bush. For the advisory role three sets of goals must match: (1) President/Vice-President, (2) President's staff/Vice-President, and (3) President's staff/Vice-President's staff. Because Presidents have so little contact with the vice-presidential staffs, the goal match is not particularly important in determining the advisory role.

Presidents versus Vice-Presidents

In this first combination, the following goals are generally compatible: reelection for Presidents versus future election for Vice-Presidents, good policy for Presidents versus good policy for Vice-Presidents, and isolation of competition for Presidents versus isolation from the President for Vice-Presidents. Surprisingly, of the ten presidential/vice-presidential goal sets over the past forty years, at least six started moderately compatible. Roosevelt-Wallace, Truman-Barkley, Eisenhower-Nixon, Nixon-Agnew, Ford-Rockefeller, and Carter-Mondale all had some compatibility at the start of their administrations. The problems occurred as each administration aged. Whereas Nixon and Agnew were in some agreement in 1968, the following year Nixon had changed. As Nixon saw Agnew's rise in the Republican party, he began to push for isolation of his competition. When Nixon chose John Connally as his successor, Agnew found his public visibility threatened by increasing isolation.

Thus, it is not enough to ask what the goals are at the start of the term. Since both Presidents and Vice-Presidents change over time, particularly as both move closer to the reelection campaign, we must continually reassess goal compatibility. At the start of an administration, the primary focus will often be good policy. As the President sets the agenda, the search for issues and alternatives may take precedence. It is at the very beginning of the term that the chances are greatest for a vice-presidential advisory role. With the midterm elections approaching, the President's interests may change. It is in this second year that the Vice-President's political duties will grow. By the third and fourth year, the President's goals will lean heavily toward reelection. Depending upon the Vice-President's public standing, the pressure will turn to either increased political duties or isolation. Interspersed in the final three years will be some interest in the Vice-President's contribution to the congressional lobbying effort.

The best example of this goal cycle was Ford-Rockefeller. At the start of the abbreviated term, Ford expressed genuine interest in using Rockefeller as a policy adviser. These first months were also Ford's "liberal" phase. During the first days of his term, Ford actually moved left, pushing for national health insurance, amnesty for draft resisters, and labor law reform. Rockefeller fit quite well into that ideological framework, coming to Washington with the belief that Ford wanted a progressive administration. By January 1974, however, Ford was already moving to the right. The economy had soured, Reagan was gearing up for a lengthy campaign, Republicans had suffered massive losses in the midterm elections, and the stage was set for a conservative Ford administration. As Ford looked toward the 1976 elections, and as Ford's goals shifted more toward reelection, Rockefeller's stock inside the White House fell. Still, throughout the term, Rockefeller maintained a close personal relationship with Ford. The President continued to meet on a weekly basis with his Vice-President, and though Rockefeller was no longer a policy advocate, he remained a senior adviser to the end of the administration. Thus, at least for the goal of good policy, it is not enough to argue that a President and Vice-President both have ideological commitments to programs. We must also look at the content of those programs. Rockefeller's goal of good policy had a distinctly liberal flavor, while Ford's goal of good policy changed from liberal to conservative over time.

Of the three least compatible presidential/vice-presidential combinations —Kennedy-Johnson, Johnson-Humphrey, and Nixon-Ford—at least two involved strong resistance on the Vice-President's part. Both Johnson and Ford pulled back from major political policy responsibilities, one because of a fear about becoming a scapegoat for administration failures, the other because of a natural desire to avoid the damage of Watergate. However, before blaming vice-presidential isolation on the victims, it is important to note that Kennedy never wanted an active Vice-President, while Nixon openly pressed Ford to sacrifice his reputation on Capitol Hill for Watergate. Vice-Presidents cannot be blamed if Presidents ask for too little or too much. Their problems arise when they enter office unwilling to compromise over their goals. As one Ford aide argued: "The Vice-President shouldn't expect the President to do all the compromising. It's a question of give-and-take. If the President wants another adviser, fine, but there are other things to be done. The Vice-President can't just wait for the gravy." Thus, Mondale was willing to spend a considerable amount of time in Holiday Inns—something he vowed he would never do again back in 1974—as part of a broad package of vice-presidential duties. He was willing to use the chits from the travel to create and maintain an advisory role.

Presidential Staffs versus Vice-Presidents

The White House staff's protective instinct is compatible with only one vice-presidential goal: isolation from the President. In short, the President's staff generally works to seal off a strong vice-presidential advisory role. According to most of the vice-presidential staff members interviewed for this book, the President's staff is the main source of problems in gaining substantive responsibilities. When asked what caused the most difficulty during the vice-presidential term, 59 percent of the vice-presidential aides pointed at the President's people as the problem. Not surprisingly, when asked the same question, 70 percent of the President's staff pointed to the Vice-President as the problem. Though both groups were willing to put some of the responsibility on the President—34 percent of the vice-presidential staffs and 21 percent of the presidential staffs pointed to the Oval Office—there was a remarkable degree of mutual hostility.

Among recent presidential staffs, only the Carter staff could be characterized as open to a larger vice-presidential role. Even then, the signals had to flow down from Carter before the staff would fall into line. According to one observer: "Carter had to make it absolutely clear several times that the staff was to treat Mondale with the same respect as the President, that the staff was to give him whatever he wanted. It wasn't enough for Carter just to say it once. The staff will never hear it. It has to be said over and over and over, until it sinks in and until the staff is positive the President means business." A Carter aide agreed. "There's just a built-in thing about the Vice-Presidency. You want to keep the guy happy, but you only have so much time in the day. The President has to make sure everyone knows what he wants. And that's true for the cabinet, too. Unless the President really pounds it in, the staff will take the easiest way out. And there's nothing wrong with that either. It's whatever the President wants, but he has to make it clear." The President's staff remains adept at anticipated reactions, or what one assistant called "reading lips." As this aide argued: "The minute Johnson told us not to tell Humphrey something, we knew that was one call we'd never have to make again. He didn't tell us not to inform Humphrey on everything, but it was clear that he didn't care anymore." Like Presidents, White House staff members have limited resources. When given a choice of including or excluding a Vice-President or cabinet member, the decision will be isolation.

That kind of isolation can be reduced, of course, if the Vice-President can place some of his own people on the White House staff. Mondale's success in moving two former aides, Carp and Aaron, to the Carter staff was an important step toward increasing goal compatibility and reducing conflict between the two offices. Carp and Aaron acted as conduits for information and expertise to Mondale while preventing end runs around the Vice-President. They also acted to bridge the gap between Mondale and the White House, working as socializing agents both ways. "Carp and Aaron explained Mondale to us," a Carter aide remarked, "and we explained Carter to them." Carp and Aaron were also able to retain their friendships on the Mondale staff, while building new coalitions in the Carter White House, thereby easing potential conflict and threat between the presidential and vice-presidential staffs. "No one had to wear nametags," a Mondale assistant argued. "By the end of the second year, we were pretty well merged. We retained our identity and they kept theirs, but we had good working relationships." Mondale's feat was topped only by Reagan's appointment of James Baker III as his chief of staff. As a close associate of Bush, Baker acted as a "superconduit" to the Vice-President in the first two years. Indeed, the three key offices in the southwest corner of the Reagan White House were eventually occupied by Bush people: Baker as chief of staff, David Gergen as communications director, and George Bush as Vice-President. As one of the triumvirate of aides supervising the flow of policy, Baker could help Bush make the transition from a ceremonial Vice-President to a senior adviser. Moreover, like Carp and Aaron, Baker also increased the potential for hidden-hand influence. Thus, perhaps the most effective way for increasing goal compatibility with the President's staff is to make some of those staffers your own people.

Presidential Staffs versus Vice-Presidential Staffs

If the presidential staffs rarely reach agreement with the Vice-President, the relationships with the vice-presidential staffs are often worse. From the Vice-President's standpoint, the lack of goal compatibility between the two staffs is a serious problem. As noted earlier, the integration of the two staffs can serve as a powerful conduit for vice-presidential advice and influence. Unfortunately, since both staffs are highly protective, there is generally more conflict than consensus. Among recent staffs, again only the Carter-Mondale pair reached any accommodation. As we will note later in Chapter 6, much of the compromise was based on the merging of the two staffs during the 1976 campaign. Instead of setting up the vice-presidential headquarters in a separate location, Mondale opted for a central campaign organization in Atlanta. From the very beginning, the Mondale staff worked side-by-side with the Carter staff. Friendships were made, working relationships were established. Short of having worked together for years, the arrangement provided the greatest opportunity for the two staffs to form cooperative ties. The decision to merge the staffs, a departure from previous campaign procedure, contributed to greater goal compatibility. "We got the idea that we were all in it together," a Mondale assistant remembered. "We were all mixed in without much attention to who we worked for. It was the Carter-Mondale campaign and we worked for it. It was the first chance we had to prove to the Carter people that we weren't all bad. At least it gave us the chance to get to know one another before being in the pressure cooker."

Moreover, though many observers have criticized the informality of the Carter White House, the atmosphere contributed to an integrated working style. The disregard for the traditional symbols of power, whether office space or limousines, helped Mondale's staff gain greater access. Unlike those in previous administrations, White House mess privileges were easy to get and contact between the two staffs was frequent. This lack of open conflict, if not friendship, contributed to Mondale's policy impact. It was particularly valuable in the agenda-setting process. Since the Mondale staff was responsible for canvassing the agencies and White House for ideas, as well as making initial cuts on priorities, the high level of goal compatibility averted unnecessary fights over issues. "Some of those decisions were painful," a Mondale aide recalled. "They did strain the relationships with some departments and policy staffs. Had we not had some decent working relationships, it would have been enough to create a backlash against Mondale and his 'power-hungry' staff. As it was, we were able to make some tough choices and ride out the fights."

CHANGING INCENTIVES

Whatever the staff or vice-presidential goals, the job description remains highly dependent on the President. The Vice-President's work is still largely whatever the President makes it. Yet, Vice-Presidents are no longer completely dependent on the President. Though Presidents determine the extent of participation, Vice-Presidents can make their involvement more attractive, particularly in the current political environment. As Presidents and their staffs assess the chances for reelection and congressional success, Vice-Presidents look much more valuable today than in the 1950s.

The decline of the national parties, for instance, increased the Vice-President's value as a campaigner, spokesman, and public liaison officer. Both 1976 and 1980 reinforced the President's interest in building a continuing campaign operation once in office. Ford and Carter were both challenged from within their own parties. Ford was the first incumbent President to be defeated for election since Herbert Hoover; Carter was the second. As a Mondale aide remarked: "With the parties now unable to backstop the President, the White House has had to take over most of the job. It's now the President's responsibility to set up the reelection committee. It's now the President's responsibility to monitor the fund-raising and media campaigns. It's now the President's responsibility to keep track of the delegates. All of those demands give the Vice-President some additional responsibilities." The separation of the presidential campaigns from the congressional campaigns also heightened the Vice-President's role as a surrogate for the President.

The longer primary season also raised the Vice-President's value as a campaigner. Once Presidents had to choose between campaigning and tending to the business of government, and once Vice-Presidents had the political credentials to act as substitutes, the campaigning role became the most pronounced feature of the job description in the second and fourth years of the term. The incentives were highlighted in the Carter administration. With Carter's immersion in the details of policy, Mondale spent at least six months campaigning in 1978 and another ten months in 1980. Once Carter adopted the rose garden strategy, Mondale was the most visible representative of the administration. According to a Carter aide: "There were any number of reasons for bringing Mondale on so hard in 1980. He was a strong speaker, a good contact man in the party, a good campaigner. He was the best person we had short of Jimmy Carter." Moreover, once Carter fired Califano in the midsummer crisis of 1979, Mondale became one of the few ties to the liberal wing of the Democratic party.

Problems with declining public approval of Presidents over the term also increased the Vice-President's stock as a visible national spokesman. If the trends of the past twenty years hold constant in the future—and they have held in the Reagan administration—Presidents can expect a rapid drop in their public support from the first day of the term. Ford's thirty-point drop following the pardon of Nixon reinforced his hope that Rockefeller could help in the coming year. As one assistant argued: "Ford wanted Rockefeller on board as fast as possible. He still believed in the pardon, but needed some help with the polls. Rockefeller was just the kind of national spokesman who could help build up Ford's image." As the decline continues in an administration, Presidents often counter with frequent public appearances by the Vice-President. "One reason we wanted the Vice-President on the circuit," a Nixon aide reported, "was that we saw the President's support falling so fast. We believed that we had to have some kind of counterattack. Agnew seemed at the time to be the next best thing to the President. He could say things that Nixon couldn't. He took some of the heat off for a while." The Vice-President's role as a spokesman-defender-hitman generally increases as public approval falls. As an observer noted:

> There comes a time in administration when the public opinion polls start to go sour. You see the President slipping each month, regardless of what you do. The natural reaction is to use all of the tools you have to raise the President's stock. Send out a cabinet member, go to a town meeing, have more press conferences, give a major address on foreign policy, beef up the public liaison operation, project a positive image as you slash the budget. At least in the Carter administration, you also sent out your Vice-President. Mondale had a good pulling power and got press coverage. He was passable as a speaker and raised Carter's flag. He was never as hot a draw as Agnew, but he held his own. Instead of just having him sit around, Carter sent him out every other week and had him selling the good deeds of the administration. He was just as good as any cabinet member and was a better salesman with the liberals.

A decade of change in Congress contributed to the Vice-President's political role, too. As congressional power shifted away from the committees to the subcommittees, the Vice-President's role as a lobbyist gained more importance. The first step toward an expanded role came in 1969 when the Nixon White House appointed Agnew's liaison team. By 1974, the Vice-President's Capitol Hill office had become a resource for lobbying on most presidential legislation. Though the White House liaison office remained in charge of strategy and lobbying, the Vice-President's role increased. From the standpoint of providing information, the Vice-President and his liaison staff became firmly established in the head-counting business. As one Ford aide noted: "We still wanted to have a couple of different counts, but Rockefeller's people did help us keep track of a number of bills. If they were willing to do some of the head counts, we could save time for other problems, like twisting arms and making trades." From the standpoint of lobbying, Mondale was quite active on several high priority bills. Since Mondale had considerable Washington experience and a long list of former Capitol Hill aides, he was particularly valuable in the close fights—civil service, Panama Canal. Moreover, because Carter had only limited contact with Congress as governor of Georgia—not knowing even his own state delegation well—Mondale also served as a conduit for complaints.

Yet, Mondale's role flowed from a number of specific changes in Congress. The increase in the number of subcommittees meant that Presidents had to devote more time to simply tracking legislation. The dispersion of power to individual entrepreneurs meant that there were many more obstacles on the road to passage. Though the Speaker of the House finally gained the power to split bills for referral to the different committees involved, that also meant more work bringing the bills back together for a final decision. In all, the broad reforms in the House and Senate gave more incentives to the Vice-President's own lobbying activities. According to an observer: "It would have been a waste not to use Mondale. He had so much to lend to Carter in terms of his background and skills. But, more than that, the legislative process has changed to the point that the President can't waste any leverage he has. Whatever else the Vice-President is, he is one more weapon to use in Congress. He can break an occasional tie, but can also gavel down debate, work the floor, and talk to old friends. He's more an asset than at any other time because Congress is much more involved in the President's program."

Changes in the pool of policy issues also increased the value of the Vice-President's policy role. With ever-tightening federal budgets and seemingly intractable economic problems, recent Presidents have been faced with a new set of highly divisive policy issues. Unlike the issues of the 1960s, the new issues have few active constituents. Carter's energy plans, welfare reform, and hospital cost containment all failed to fit the traditional political framework, only to be followed by Reagan's social security proposals and budget cuts. The rise of this new set of "constituentless" issues raises the political cost of legislative success, while presenting difficult choices in the advisory process. The changes in the pool of issues may reflect an increase in what British political scientist Anthony King calls "the atomization of politics." As King argues, political coalitions have become fragmented, fleeting, and unstable (1978, p. 390).

Part of the Vice-President's role in dealing with such atomization is political: increased public liaison, speaking, campaigning, and lobbying. Another part of the response is based on the Vice-President's policy role. Once Presidents decided to centralize their policy agendas in the White House as one way to gain control over the issues, the Vice-President's policy role became more attractive. Basically, as power shifted away from the executive branch toward the Oval Office, Vice-Presidents were able to capitalize on the need for more advisers and alternatives. There are two simple reasons for the pattern. First, at the same time Presidents pushed for more centralization of the policy machinery, they also vowed to reduce and contain the White House staff. As a backlash against Watergate, both Ford and Carter promised to reduce what Thomas Cronin once called "the swelling of the Presidency" (1975). The apparently contradictory goals of centralization and staff reduction heightened the incentives for using *all* of the President's staff, including the Vice-President and his sizable office. Second, as presidential doubts about executive branch loyalty grew, the Vice-President's stock also increased." At least we knew that Mondale wouldn't carp to the press," a Carter aide argued. "His future was at least temporarily tied to ours. He was sure as hell more loyal than some members of the cabinet, and he proved that he could be trusted." Such perceptions may come from the increased freedom of Presidents to select their Vice-Presidents at the convention or from Vice-Presidents' own strategies in playing the policy role. Yet, whatever the political or policy problem—whether a decline in the parties, longer campaigns, or more complex issues—the Vice-President's substantive role is strengthened whenever the President must turn in toward the White House for basic electoral and advisory support. Once again, though centralization may have negative consequences for good policy, it had some positive rewards for Vice-Presidents.

In this sense, the White House is a highly adaptive political institution. As the primaries increased from fifteen in 1960 to twenty-two in 1972 to thirty-seven in 1980, the White House needed new tools to mold delegate support. A public liaison office was added under Nixon, consolidated under Ford, and expanded under Carter; new units for constituent relations were added during the 1970s; polling became a standard feature of the presidential policy process; a media office arrived early in the decade. Part of this overall effort to centralize political support in the White House involved the Vice-President. Since the Vice-President's office was well staffed to support an expanded political role, it was natural that Presidents would see the value of the assignment. Vice-Presidents could travel, speak, campaign, and lobby without absorbing any of the President's staff support. "If you were fighting a war and had this weapon lying there, wouldn't you use it?" an observer asked. "That's what happened to Vice-Presidents. As long as they were available, why not use them?"

CONCLUSION

Once there is minimal agreement on the Vice-President's role, a second set of problems arises. In order to perform an advisory duty, the Vice-President, or any adviser, must have a store of certain resources. Even if the President, Vice-President, and the two staffs reach some consensus on the advisory role, there are limits to the Vice-President's advisory capacity. These limits arise from time, information, expertise, energy, proximity, and the President's willingness to listen. These resources fit into an outline of Vice-Presidents as advisers, and will be tackled in the next chapter.

5.

Vice-Presidents as Advisers

Whatever the impact of precedent, Watergate, individual Vice-Presidents, staffs, or goals, the advisory role is often determined by the simple mix of interests that occurs in the heat of a national party convention. Vice-Presidents are rarely "hired" for their policy skills. Nor are they hired for their administrative abilities. Yet, it is not always clear just what Vice-Presidents are hired for. Nixon, for instance, may have selected Agnew because he was the *least* qualified and, therefore, the least threatening of all the candidates, preferring to run with Agnew if he had to run with anyone.

In the twentieth century, the main criteria for hiring Vice-Presidents have been geographical balance first, and ideological balance second. As Theodore Sorensen, Kennedy's campaign chief, remembers the selection of Lyndon Johnson:

> The selection of a vice-president is not the writing on the clean slate that one thinks it is. After a while, you get down to the choice of who is going to hurt you the least. So the list narrows down by itself rather quickly. In the 1960 case it was particularly important that the vice-presidential candidate be a Protestant and not be from the Northeast. Of those ending up on my list as viable possibilities, I ranked Johnson at the top. . . .
>
> I think it is true to say that Kennedy did not expect Johnson to say yes, and it would be inaccurate to say that he was hoping Johnson would say no. Johnson was the logical person to ask. He was the runner-up at the convention. He was the leader of that segment of the party where Kennedy had very little strength—the South, and to some extent the West. He was the leader of the party in the Senate. He was a man with whom Kennedy had worked and knew he could

work. Compatible. And he was a man whom Kennedy admired. Had the great-
ness, the stature.

So for all these reasons, it was logical to go first to Lyndon Johnson and ask
him if he would be vice-president (Miller 1980, p. 254-55).

Carter's choice of Mondale reflected a similar blend of needs. According
to Hamilton Jordan:

> Two months before the 1976 Democratic convention, I wrote the first memo to
> nominee Jimmy Carter that urged Mondale's selection as Vice President. Despite
> the antiestablishment rhetoric of the primary campaign, I knew, and Jimmy Carter
> knew, that he needed an experienced Senator as his running mate and as his Vice
> President. Fritz Mondale had a good relationship with the political and press com-
> munities, and, most important, a perspective that was different than Carter and
> most of us around him. Mondale was chosen to run precisely *because* he was a
> product of the Washington establishment, was from a different area of the country,
> and represented the other wing of the Democratic party (*New Republic,* 6 June
> 1983).

Though geography and party support are important in the nomination of
Vice-Presidents, they have little to do with the advisory role. Two very
different aspects of the electoral connection affect the Vice-President's role
in office. First, if Presidents have control over the choice of their running
mates, the prospects for a successful Vice-Presidency increase. Prior to the
1950s, presidential candidates generally left the selection of their running
mates to conventions. Though Roosevelt retained a veto over the choice in
1940 and threatened not to run if Wallace was not nominated, he did not
exercise carte blanche over the final decision. The same held true for
Truman and Dewey in 1948. Both threw the vice-presidential nomination
to the convention. Eisenhower dictated the nomination of Nixon in 1952,
but Adlai Stevenson watched passively as Estes Kefauver and John Kennedy
battled for the Vice-Presidency in 1956. According to Barbara Hinckley,
one of the few authors of political science textbooks to include a separate
chapter on the Vice-Presidency:

> It is commonly held at convention time that "the presidential candidate always
> selects the vice presidential nominee." We can identify this as myth number
> one. It appears, in fact, to be a very recent precedent developing only since the
> 1960s. In earlier conventions a presidential candidate might have an effective
> veto on a proposed vice presidential candidate, as would to a lesser extent other
> individuals and factions within the party. But the positive decision—within
> some pool of nonvetoed candidates—was made by the convention delegates as-
> sembled following the procedure of presidential nominations. Indeed, in al-
> most half of the conventions from the beginning of the twentieth century
> through 1956 where a new vice presidential candidate was to be nominated there
> was a contest in the delegate balloting over the choice. Even in some of those

conventions where no contests in the balloting appeared, the delegates were
deciding among some reputedly "eligible" candidates—for example "favorite
sons" in the presidential nomination and others whose names may have been
mentioned—and emerging with a consensus choice (1981, p. 137).

The change in the 1960s gave Presidents more say in the hiring of their
Vice-Presidents and produced some notable successes and failures—Eagle-
ton and Agnew to name but two problems. If the presidential nominee is
insecure, the vice-presidential candidate will probably be nonthreatening
and passive. If, however, the presidential nominee takes the choice seriously,
the result can be a stronger advisory relationship. In 1976, for instance,
Carter brought several potential nominees to his home in Plains for preconvention interviews. He spent a day with each candidate, talking about
political issues and perceptions of the Vice-President's role. Carter's eventual
choice narrowed down to Mondale, Humphrey's protégé from Minnesota,
and Edmund Muskie, Humphrey's running mate in 1968. As a Mondale
aide suggested: "We think the decision went to Mondale on the basis of his
personal rapport with Charles Kirbo and the interview with Carter. Carter
seemed to genuinely like Mondale and once the political questions could be
answered, the nod went to the one that Carter could work with easiest." In
many respects, Carter's choice of Mondale was the forerunner of his transition talent search for cabinet and White House appointees. Carter considered
a number of criteria in making his decision: politics, ability, connections,
background. Once Mondale cleared the regional and political hurdles, he
was hired like many of Carter's other aides. That made a difference as
Mondale sought a policy role in the White House. According to an aide:

> Mondale wasn't there just because he met some criteria for the Vice-Presidency.
> And he wasn't there just because he happened to be from the North. He was
> there because Carter made a very deliberative choice, using the interviews as
> a screening process. Obviously, Carter knew Mondale could help in the cam-
> paign, but it was more than that. Muskie could have helped, too. And, in terms
> of campaign experience, Muskie was the better choice, But Carter wasn't just
> thinking about the short term. He wanted to make a good hire because he
> wanted a good officer in the Vice-Presidency.

A Carter assistant agreed. "It's always better to be able to choose your own
people. Most arranged marriages end up with both partners unhappy. If
you can pick your running mate, there's always more potential for an easy
relationship."

The second aspect of the electoral connection that affects the advisory
role is the match of presidential and vice-presidential experience. The
President's inexperience creates vacuums for advice. Presidential *outsiders*
—candidates with little Washington experience—have more use for active
Vice-Presidents than presidential *insiders*. The recent outsiders—Eisen-

hower, Carter, and Reagan—were attracted to insiders as their vice-presidential nominees, while the insiders—Roosevelt, Truman, Kennedy, Johnson, and Ford—paid less attention to the experience of their running mates. Thus, the best combination for an advisory role is an outsider President with an insider Vice-President. That situation has occurred in three modern Vice-Presidencies: Eisenhower-Nixon, Carter-Mondale, and Reagan-Bush. In the first instance, Nixon was able to expand the job description to include an explicit campaigning role. In the second instance, Mondale was able to build a prominent policy role. The third instance, Reagan-Bush, will be explored in Chapter 8. The outsider/insider combination offers greater opportunity for Vice-Presidents to supplement presidential resources, while creating a number of advisory vacuums. According to a Mondale aide: "One of the nice things about the administration was that we had plenty of chances to put our two bits in. There was a general shortage of information at the start of the term and we were pretty well equipped to fill in." Over the course of the term, the outsider/insider advantage closes. Presidents and their staff catch up and fill the vacuums themselves. Yet, if Vice-Presidents can demonstrate the value of their advice during the early days of the administration, Presidents can easily develop the habit of asking for opinions.

The worst combination for the advisory role is an insider President with an outsider Vice-President. That situation existed in its purest form only once in the contemporary period: Nixon-Agnew. Though Agnew was originally given significant political duties, he was not included in substantive policy. Nixon did not seek Agnew's advice on foreign or economic policy, listening to Agnew only on domestic policy and then only in the first year. Most other Vice-Presidencies have involved the insider/insider combination: Roosevelt-Wallace, Roosevelt-Truman, Truman-Barkley, Kennedy-Johnson, and Nixon-Ford. In only one of these six cases did the President give the Vice-President substantive policy assignments, and that was at the very start of the list with Roosevelt-Wallace. Three of six insider/insider Vice-Presidencies involved very unusual circumstances: the start of a war (Roosevelt-Wallace), a three-month term (Roosevelt-Truman), and a presidential resignation (Nixon-Ford). However, the Kennedy and Johnson cases illustrate the tendency of insider Presidents to discount vice-presidential advice. Neither President viewed his Vice-President as a source of information or expertise. Nor did the presidential staffs seem particularly interested in the Vice-President's participation. Since insider Presidents generally bring insider staffs, goal compatibility with the Vice-President is frequently low. Unlike outsider Presidents who may actually accept staff members from insider Vice-Presidents, insiders are often closed to the concept of an advisory role. As one observer noted: "Kennedy had become quite accustomed to working with a fairly small group of aides, many of whom had been with Kennedy under Johnson as majority leader. It was a pretty finely tuned staff to begin with and didn't have much room for new-comers, especially for someone who had once been so strong."

The one Vice-Presidency that defies easy description here is Ford-Rocke-feller. Was Rockefeller an outsider? Not in the sense of his strong staff and his own ambition for the Presidency in at least two previous elections. Not in the sense that he had considerable contact with the federal establishment through his Commission on Critical Choices. Was Ford an insider? Not in the sense of having pursued the Presidency in his own right. Not in the sense of having been a legislative activist in the House. Since the insider-outsider connection is actually a continuum, ranging from limited Washing-ton experience to extensive experience, Ford and Rockefeller could both be viewed as insiders, with Ford just ahead of his Vice-President on legislative matters and Rockefeller just ahead of the President on campaign politics. Yet, the conditions surrounding Rockefeller's appointment resembled the problems that outsider Presidents have upon entering office. Ford did not have the staff to cover many positions and did not have a firm legislative agenda. Ford did not have much administrative experience and had only limited background in foreign policy. Indeed, the first months of the Ford Presidency were characterized by many of the same resource shortages that outsiders face. At least at the start, Ford needed Rockefeller's political and policy resources.

RESOURCES AND ADVICE

All of the explanations for the new Vice-Presidency point toward *resources* as the key to change. Watergate gave Vice-Presidents more bargaining lev-erage for staff and access; institutionalization gave Vice-Presidents more information and expertise; changing incentives in the American political system gave Presidents more reasons to listen to their running-mates; and, at least in 1976 and 1980, the election of outsider Presidents meant that the Vice-President's own store of resources would look even more inviting.

Just like other White House and Cabinet advisers, Vice-Presidents need certain resources to perform the advisory role. Over the past twenty years, they have finally secured most of the resources to become institutionalized advisers to the President. This notion that advisers need resources fits with Mondale's view of the keys to his success.

> An adviser must be ready to advise. He must have a capable staff preparing him to do so. The President and I directed our staffs to work as a team and, in fact, they did. An adviser must have a grasp of the background and details of all cru-cial issues, and for four years, I had access to all the papers, classified and other-wise, that the President saw.
>
> That might sound like a little matter, but you cannot possibly imagine the tre-

mendous volume of paper that flows into and from the President's personal office. You cannot possibly imagine, unless you have been part of it, the tremendous flow of secret classified information on defense, the political situation
in other nations, on assessments and appraisals by our intelligence communities.
I think I was the first Vice President in American history who was privy to
those materials, including the most highly classified of all documents, the
Morning Presidential Daily Brief[ing].

An adviser must also participate in those meetings which prepare recommendations for the President. And I was a member of every established and
ad hoc group that prepared recommendations for the President.

An adviser must have access to the President. He must be able to give his
advice directly, and I had that access. As a matter of fact, when we first began,
the President said, "You're invited to every meeting that I've scheduled," and I
could pick and choose, and did throughout those four years, those meetings I
chose to attend.

We had an institution called the weekly luncheon where, once a week, we
would have a private luncheon to discuss any matters either of us wished to
bring up. What we said was confidential and will remain so, but what I was trying to achieve was not (remarks, 18 Feb. 1981).

Once again, it is important to distinguish between advice and influence.
Advice involves an actor's view of what should be done, while influence
involves the impact of that advice on actual decisions. The bridge between
the two is the advisory role. Unless an actor has an opportunity to present
advice, there is no chance for influence. There is little doubt that most Vice-
Presidents have plenty of advice to give to the President. Wallace, Barkley,
Nixon, Johnson, Humphrey, Ford, Rockefeller, and Mondale all had
opinions on policy issues. However, until recently, Vice-Presidents were
not given an advisory role in the White House. They did not have regular
access to the President or the policy process. Whatever their potential contribution to presidential decisions, they were rarely given the chance to
participate. Moreover, even with an advisory role, there is no guarantee of
influence. Rockefeller had frequent input to Ford, but little influence. Thus,
we must first ask what is needed for advice, then what produces influence.
In the following pages, I look at six resources that are critical for the
advisory role: time, energy, information, expertise, proximity, and the
President's willingness to listen.

Time

Time is the most basic resource in the advisory role. Vice-Presidents need
time to digest information, time to talk with the President, time to sculpture
arguments, time to build advisory networks, time to direct the staff, and
time to answer policy questions. Before Rockefeller and Mondale, time was
an abundant vice-presidential resource. "If anything, we had too much
time," a Humphrey aide remarked. "Humphrey was always occupied with
some issue, but we had a lot of time to kill. It wasn't until 1968 and Johnson's

withdrawal from the campaign that we had too little time." With the rise of the political and policy roles in the post-Watergate era, time has actually become a scarce vice-presidential resource.

The most serious threat to a Vice-President's time is a line assignment. Unlike the political roles which ebb and flow with the electoral cycle, a line assignment can absorb massive amounts of time over the entire term. Rockefeller's decision to occupy the Domestic Council committed his time to administrative duties at the very moment he wanted to shape the President's agenda. As an assistant argued: "He wasn't aware of just how much time you have to have just to push the paper around. Being an administrator at that level can involve so much trivial work that you never have the time to look at long-range issues. When Rockefeller took over, all he wanted to do was work on long-range planning. By the end of the first few months, all he was really doing was administrative work." Mondale avoided those kinds of line assignments as part of his overall strategy as an adviser. He did not want to make any long-term commitments to any single assignment, preferring to reserve his time for important short-term issues. According to a Mondale aide: "He wanted to be able to move to the hot issues without having to keep an eye on some administrative chore. He wanted maximum flexibility in his scheduling and tried to keep much of his calendar open. A lot of White House staffers point to their calendars and say 'Look how busy I am. I haven't got a block of time open for a month.' Mondale didn't do that. He kept roughly one-quarter of his schedule open for last-minute problems." As noted earlier, Mondale kept track of his time through a regular computer summary. Mondale's personal secretary recorded his time in ten-minute increments on a desk-top computer. Every three or four months, Mondale's top aides would sit down with the time analysis and make suggestions on strategy. Perhaps Mondale was spending too much time in meetings with lower-level aides and needed more time with the President; perhaps Mondale was spending too much time on issue briefings and needed more on Capitol Hill. The analysis reflected a concern with time as a critical resource.

The amount of time available for the advisory role changes over the term. In the first year, there is simply more time available for the policy Vice-Presidency. Presidents, Vice-Presidents, and their assorted staffs have more time to deal with the agenda-setting process. In the second year, the Vice-President's time is divided between the midterm elections and the policy role. The third year involves another round of policy activities, but with the lengthening nomination campaigns, Vice-Presidents must return to the political role early in the fourth year. Further, the President's available time for the Vice-President changes over the term. The first year is the best opportunity for presidential access. As an Agnew aide said: "Those first few months aren't just a honeymoon with Congress. They're a honeymoon with the Vice-President, too. Nixon was much more willing to see Agnew in those first few months than at any other time in the term. Everyone was pulling together at the start, but by the summer, Nixon was tired of all the bullshit and closed the door on Agnew and the cabinet."

Yet, if the first months are the time for honeymoons, they are also the time of the greatest unfamiliarity. Though Presidents and Vice-Presidents often know each other from previous careers—Johnson and Kennedy had worked together in the Senate, but with Johnson as the leader and Kennedy as the subordinate—they rarely have much opportunity to build a working relationship before the transition into office. And if Presidents and Vice-Presidents are on awkward terms, the staff relationships are often strained. Thus, Vice-Presidents need time to explore their roles, time to build advisory networks, time to generate internal capital, time to forge a working relationship with the President, all preferably long before the next presidential election. As we will see later, the Vice-President's need for time conflicts with the President's need to set the agenda quickly. Vice-Presidents usually do not have the kind of working relationship to affect the policy agenda early in the term. Unfortunately, that is precisely when the agenda is generally set. Among recent Vice-Presidents, Ford had the least time to build an advisory role, followed by Rockefeller. With the election looming so soon in the future, neither Ford nor Rockefeller had much time to establish working relationships in a postelection euphoria.

Energy

Like time, energy is a basic resource for advice. Vice-Presidents are just like other human beings. They have a certain level of stamina and a certain level of emotional strength. Though Vice-Presidents do not have the stress of making final decisions, they do expend considerable energy in the political and policy roles. As Mondale discovered in his brief campaign for the Presidency in 1974, sleeping in hotels night after night can be a remarkably draining experience. As Rockefeller discovered in his work on the Domestic Council, routine administrative duties can also be exhausting. Regardless of the age and stamina of the Vice-President at the start of the term, changes in the political and policy roles place limits on energy as an advisory resource.

The greatest threat to vice-presidential energy is the political role. Traveling on the campaign road can be the most tiring of all vice-presidential duties. The exhaustion affects both the Vice-President and his staff. As one advance aide noted in 1981: "I used to wake up in the middle of the night not knowing whether I was in Kansas City or Miami. I usually worked on four hours of sleep a night and stayed out on the road for three months straight. I'm still not recovered and the election was over a year ago." One of the advantages of the institutionalization of the Vice-President's office was that the staff traveling with the candidate was not always the staff that worked on policy issues. Before 1974, however, the Vice-President's staff had to cover a number of different support roles. Humphrey's policy people doubled as campaign aides, schedulers, speechwriters, and advance workers. That multiplication of duties led to some confusion among the staff. As one Humphrey aide remembered, "I had so many hats to wear that I lost count, but since the campaign thing had to come first, I usually took off my other hats for later." Now, the Vice-President has room for a substantive policy staff *and* a campaign organization. That means there is a store of energy for the advisory role even in the midst of an election year. That store may be most valuable during the midterm campaigns. As one Mondale assistant said: "Very few of the policy staffers actually traveled with Mondale during the campaigns. That was left to advance and scheduling. Most of us stayed home and continued working on programs. That was especially true during the 1978 midterm elections. Even with Mondale on the road half that year, he never broke stride when he came back to town."

Like time, the amount of energy for the advisory role ebbs over the term. Whatever the Vice-President's role—whether as an active adviser and campaigner like Mondale or a ceremonial fixture like Johnson—energy drops over time. Mondale and his staff lost energy at the very time they needed the stamina to fight budget cuts and cabinet firings. Vice-Presidents and their staffs have several tools for dealing with this natural fatigue. Mondale liked to have regular office hours and semiannual vacations, while his staff used overseas trips as vacations of a sort. Sometimes, however, the Vice-President and the staff run on pure adrenalin. Their ability to generate energy can make the difference between policy success or failure.

Information

Among contemporary Vice-Presidents, perhaps Humphrey had the greatest store of personal energy. Yet, Humphrey filled his time with ceremonial activities, becoming the quintessential commissioner. Humphrey's problem came from lack of information on presidential policy decisions. Though Humphrey had considerable knowledge on a wide range of issues, he lacked the information needed to apply that knowledge to Johnson's choices. The problems began soon after his inauguration. Three days after the inauguration, Johnson was taken to Bethesda Naval Hospital suffering from chest pains. As Humphrey remembered, "At first they were thought to be signs of a heart attack, particularly frightening because Lyndon had suffered a serious one ten years before. Johnson, for some bizarre reason, refused to let any medical facts be given to me immediately. Instead, the orders came that he wanted me to fulfill my scheduled weekend commitments so that no one would think his illness was serious" (1976, p. 314). Humphrey was not the last Vice-President to be denied information on the President's health.

Ford, for instance, was not told of Nixon's problem with phlebitis. As Ford remarked about the incident, "Questions have been asked about it. That was a very tightly held secret, and I think rightly so. It was so important for his mission, or missions, that the slightest hint of that illness, I think would have handicapped the success. So I don't think he told more than four or five people. He may have told Al Haig, I don't know, but that was of such serious magnitude, I don't see anything wrong with him not telling me" (*National Journal,* 10 Aug. 1974). Ford's explanation conflicts with the seriousness of Nixon's physical problem. As a Ford aide admitted: "He should have been told. It affected his future just as much as it affected Nixon's. He should have been informed."

There are three types of information that are important for the Vice-President's advisory role: information about the policy problems, information about the meetings, and information about the opposition. All of it must be *timely.* If Vice-Presidents, or any policy advisers, are to be involved in the decision-making process, they must have information in time to use it.

The first kind of information necessary for an advisory role is raw knowledge about the *policy problem itself.* In order to compete within the policy process, the Vice-President needs the same information as other players. Though several recent Vice-Presidents—Humphrey, Ford, Rockefeller, and Mondale in particular—had substantial knowledge in domestic affairs, few Vice-Presidents have independent sources of information on foreign policy. How could Agnew advise Nixon on détente with China, for instance, if he was never told that the issue was being discussed? According to one report, when asked whether he had told Agnew about China, Nixon replied: "Agnew? Agnew? Oh, of course not" (*Washington Star-News,* 16 May 1974). Perhaps the most important source of foreign policy information is the Presidential Daily Briefing (PDB). Among recent Vice-Presidents, only Mondale and Bush were given firsthand access to the PDB. Other Vice-Presidents settled for briefings summarizing the PDB. As one Agnew aide noted: "Agnew's access to information was selective. He had an intelligence officer who kept him briefed, but he wasn't given the PDB. He didn't know about the China initiative until it was announced publicly." How could Rockefeller advise Ford on the Mayaguez rescue attempt if he was never told that the raid was in progress? As an assistant remembered: "We knew we weren't involved on the major decisions. We often had to rely on the *New York Times* for our information. We read about Mayaguez in the papers."

Whatever the type of information—whether on domestic, economic, or foreign policy—Vice-Presidents must be included in the paper loop to succeed as advisers. But being in the loop is not quite enough. The Vice-President must be in the loop at the same time as other entrepreneurs. According to a Rockefeller assistant: "Yes, Rockefeller was in the 'loop.' He was one of nine or ten to receive the paper, but he always got it late and over in the EOB. Even with the Domestic Council, we didn't see the 1976 budget figures until it was too late to challenge OMB. Yes, we saw them. But it was too late." A second Rockefeller staff member concurred. "We were just not in the paper flow. We received timely information mainly by accident. We sometimes didn't get the information at all; sometimes we got it only after the President had already decided; sometimes we got it a day or two before the meeting. The timeliness was the problem. It was up to Rumsfeld to see to it that we got the information, but he didn't want us involved. Ford couldn't spend his time hand-delivering documents, so we were usually surprised." Thus, Mondale's position in the paper flow cannot be minimized as an advisory resource. He received virtually the same documents as other advisers and even occasionally called Cabinet members over for additional briefings. As an administrative officer noted: "There was a different kind of paper moving into the Vice-President's office under Carter. It was more detailed and more timely. We used to see papers go in to Rockefeller that were two or three weeks old. In the White House, that can be forever." As a national security aide remarked:

> Mondale started each day with the same intelligence information that Carter got. He was also briefed during the day for updates. He was very well informed. I had worked under Nixon and Ford and, by God, their Vice-Presidents did not get that kind of information. It was always an afterthought or an accident. Kissinger might say "Maybe we ought to brief what's his name." Agnew, Ford, and Rockefeller were compartmentalized. They were out of the flow. *They didn't even know what the problems were,* let alone being able to say something about them to the President.

The second kind of information necessary for an advisory role is knowledge about the *decision-making process.* Even if the Vice-President knows something about the policy issues—which is more likely in domestic policy than in foreign affairs—he must know where the decisions will be made. The "who," "where," "when," and "how" of a decision may be just as important as the "what." According to a Rockefeller staffer: "Hell, we didn't even know the office numbers and participants in the key meetings. We knew that the budget problems would include Jim Lynn at OMB and Alan Greenspan at CEA, but we didn't know when they were going to meet or where. Maybe at lunch at the Sans Souci. Maybe in a conference room in the West Wing." In contrast, Mondale had access to the President's daily schedule. He could spot the critical meetings and had an open invitation to attend. Moreover, with Bert Carp and David Aaron in top positions on the Domestic Policy Staff and the National Security Council, it was almost impossible to schedule a meeting without Mondale knowing. The Monday lunch, the intelligence briefings with CIA Director Stansfield Turner and Brzezinski, the Friday foreign policy breakfast, the cabinet meetings, all gave Mondale advance warning on major decisions.

This kind of information is important for both advancing ideas and stopping competitors. Rockefeller was unaware that Ford was moving toward a "no new spending" rule in the 1975 State of the Union message or a budget ceiling in 1976. Rockefeller was not included in the key meetings and had no information that the ideas were being discussed. Had Rockefeller known about the ideas, he might have prevented or modified the final decisions. According to a Rockefeller Domestic Council assistant: "If there was one thing Rockefeller could do, it was bend a decision around. He could change a few words and win a major victory. The no new spending rule was so clear that there was very little Rockefeller could do to get around it. Had Ford just said 'until the need arises, there will be no new spending in domestic policy,' Rockefeller would have found the need." A second Rockefeller aide agreed. "In this town, even a comma can make a difference. The reason Rockefeller wasn't included in the budget meetings was because OMB and CEA were scared of him. He could charm you out of your socks and could make policy in the flick of his wrist."

When asked why the budget meetings were hidden from Rockefeller, a Ford economic adviser admitted that "the main reason was convenience. We just didn't have time to bring him in. We knew pretty much where we were going and didn't want to get involved in a long battle with Rockefeller or Cannon. It was an economic issue, not a domestic policy issue anyway." Even though Rockefeller should have been involved in the budget decisions given his position on the Domestic Council, the lack of information on meetings and forums kept him effectively isolated from the process. Mondale simply did not face that kind of subterfuge. As Mondale noted at the end of the term, "Although I did not agree with every decision the President made, not once in four years was I surprised by what the Administration did, for I took part in every one of his major decisions" (remarks, 18 Feb. 1981). Moreover, because Mondale was involved in the agenda-setting process, he was often involved in scheduling the meetings themselves.

The third kind of information necessary for the advisory role is knowledge about the *opposition*. It is a valuable tool for tailoring the Vice-President's arguments, but is often a luxury in the White House. Perhaps the best way to learn about an opponent's ideas is to watch the paper flow. By reading the paper going into the Oval Office, an adviser can shape an argument to reflect the weakness of the opposition. Since Presidents rarely have the time to read the hundreds of pages in a briefing book, they tend to concentrate on the summary pieces. In the Carter administration, for instance, the final summary in domestic policy was usually drafted by Stuart Eizenstat, Domestic Policy Staff director; the final summary in foreign policy was usually written by Zbigniew Brzezinski, NSC staff director. Though Mondale rarely signed the decision memos, he always saw all the paper before it moved in to Carter, including the final wrap-up memorandum. That made a difference in building advice in Mondale's private meetings with Carter. "After reading through the material," an aide remarked, "he could pinpoint the problems and advantages. When Carter would call him in and ask what he thought, he might say 'Well, I agree with Stu [Eizenstat] on this' or 'I think this program has a couple of flaws.' He often used other people's arguments to make his own advice seem a little softer."

Another way to learn about the opposition is to attend the major meetings. Both Mondale and Bush placed a priority on sitting in on high-level briefings; both built their schedules around the President's. As Bush told the *Washington Post*: "That is my first priority . . . because you've got to establish a relationship, build it and strengthen it. You've got to know enough about what (the president) is exposed to so you can give advice" (30 Mar. 1981). Still another technique for intelligence gathering is to have friends on the White House staff. Though Carp and Aaron could not be called spies, they did keep their former boss posted on the progress of debate.

Information, of course, is never neutral. It enters the White House with political and technical biases. The closer the Vice-President can move to the original sources of information, the more the biases are controlled. Second- and thirdhand information is of questionable value to an adviser. If the Vice-President must wait for his own briefing on the President's briefing, he loses both time and information. In the White House, the best information generally circulates in the paper loop. Though the President's information has its own problems and distortions, Vice-Presidents need access to first-hand information to play the adviser's role. Once the information is received, the Vice-President must have the expertise to convert it into an argument.

Expertise

An adviser's expertise starts with intelligence. Some advisers are smarter than others. In the Carter administration, Eizenstat won a number of victories just on the basis of his preparation and the force of his argument. Though it is always risky to compare the intelligence of past advisers, at least one media observer was willing to take a stab with Vice-Presidents.

> Lyndon Johnson was much smarter on politics than on any issues. He didn't care too much for the details of policy, just the art of getting them passed through Congress. Humphrey was much smarter in the issue sense. He had a good feel for the issues and what needed to be done; good intellect for making choices. Spiro Agnew may have been the cleverest recent Vice-President, but spent most of his time thinking about how to build his bank account. He didn't have the interest in policy. Jerry Ford worked better on budget matters than on anything else, but he was strong on domestic affairs, too. His image as a football

player without a helmet was all wrong. Nelson Rockefeller was smarter than any
of the group at building empires, but wasn't too good on the specific issues.
Walter Mondale was good on the issues, but not as savvy on the campaign road.
The question is, if all these guys were so smart, how come they ended up as
Vice-Presidents? All but Mondale wound up as pretty unhappy men.

Whatever the individual differences in intelligence — Ehrlichman, for instance, accuses Agnew of "mental constipation" (1982, p. 147) — Vice-Presidents must have at least some level of expertise to perform the advisory
role. As a Carter assistant noted: "Obviously, the Vice-President has to have
something upstairs. He's got to have something to say and be able to say it
well." At least for the advisory role, there seem to be three kinds of expertise.

First, Vice-Presidents need some expertise with the *policy issues*. Ford, for
instance, was quite skilled with the budget, having made it a specialty in his
long House career. Humphrey had considerable background in social
policy, having sponsored a number of civil rights and poverty programs in
the Senate. Mondale shared Humphrey's interest in civil rights and open
housing in his early days in the Senate, but moved to the Senate Finance
Committee in 1975. Mondale joined the newly created Budget Committee
in the same year, an assignment that helped him in the White House. "He
understood the importance of the budget," an aide remarked, "and knew
that money was policy. His experience on the Budget Committee taught
him some valuable tactics that he used later." As Mondale learned, a simple
change in language could save millions of dollars, while a shift in a formula
could obligate the government for extra spending. In fighting against
proposed social service cuts inside the Carter administration, Mondale's
background was an advantage. It sensitized him to the importance of the
issue and taught him how to use the budget as an instrument of change.
Among recent Vice-Presidents, Agnew had the least contact with national
policy issues upon entering office. His experience as Baltimore County
executive (1962-66) and governor of Maryland (1966-68) gave him little
opportunity to study federal policy. Nor did Agnew seem particularly interested in such issues as governor, preferring to study problems with the
federal income tax system instead. Though Rockefeller was also a governor
before entering the Vice-Presidency, he was remarkably familiar with policy
issues. He had served in the federal government — as coordinator of Inter-
American Affairs under Roosevelt, as assistant secretary of state, as under
secretary of HEW under Eisenhower, and as chairman of the National
Commission on Water Quality under Nixon. After leaving the governorship
of New York (1958-73), he created the Commission on Critical Choices for
America. The commission was designed to front a third possible bid for the
Presidency in 1976, but also exposed Rockefeller to a variety of issues and
alternatives.

The second kind of expertise involves *advisory skills*. The Vice-President's speaking, campaigning, lobbying and liaison skills also work for building internal networks. According to a Ford aide: "Those are exactly the kinds of skills that an adviser can put to use in the White House. Most of the policy decisions shape up as political battles anyway. If an adviser has some experience with politics, it's got to help." Moreover, long-term political service may sensitize the Vice-President to the kinds of judgments that are often valued in the policy process. As Presidents select issues for the policy agenda, they generally search for benefits (Light 1982b). At least in domestic affairs, Presidents select issues on the basis of the electoral rewards, good policy, or historical merit. In making choices among competing issues, the Vice-President may be able to highlight the political, policy, or historical impact of one issue over another. These judgments may be much more highly valued if the Vice-President has political experience. Mondale, for instance, was perceived as qualified to comment on the impact of certain issues on liberal support in the Democratic party. His views on the budget carried somewhat more weight simply because he had enough political experience to assess the impact of cuts on the Kennedy candidacy.

The third kind of expertise involves *bureaucratic skills.* Rockefeller, for example, did not understand the nature of administrative politics and coalitions as well as other Vice-Presidents. As a governor, Rockefeller had always been in command. He did not have to fight for information or staff. When he issued an order, it was generally followed. Upon joining the Ford administration, Rockefeller was surprised by the bureaucratic infighting. According to an aide, "Rockefeller wanted to be treated like he thought he had treated his staff. He had never seen how tough it could get at the staff level. He never understood the need to build bridges and the need to get written guarantees. Since he had never been a staffer before, he couldn't possibly know what it took to succeed." A second assistant agreed. "Rockefeller never saw the one that hit him. He was so naive about staff politics. He thought everything could be solved by a handshake or a smile. When Rumsfeld started to seal him off, he thought all he had to do was go in and ask Ford for some help. He never thought to clean up after he had won the Domestic Council. He didn't think it was necessary to fire the Nixon holdovers right away. 'Wait a while,' he said. By the time he came back to earth and saw what needed to be done, it was too late."

As Hartmann remembers, Rumsfeld's "disemboweling" of the Domestic Council was a "pitifully easy exercise." The first phase was "the pretense of complete acceptance of the President's decision and utmost cooperation in the new order." The second phase involved the rise of several Rumsfeld allies within the council and Rockefeller's own acquiescence in a novel paper flow:

In his lofty disdain for "paper-pushing," Rockefeller readily accepted Ford's insistence that the Domestic Council's paperwork continue to flow through the White House secretariat, which Rumsfeld controlled. The President himself grossly underestimated the importance of paper-pushers, since he had never before in his life had to depend on them. Actually, it was not a compromise but a contradiction to say that Rockefeller would be in charge but the paper would flow through Rumsfeld (Hartmann 1980, p. 313).

With minimal bureaucratic expertise, Rockefeller would have noticed the impact of such seemingly trivial matters. Though he had served in several administrative posts early in his career, Rockefeller was used to being at the top and had little experience in bureaucratic maneuvering. With his Senate training, Mondale recognized the value of merging the two campaign staffs in 1976. That simple maneuver ensured maximum contact and coalition building long before the move to the White House.

Proximity

Once the Vice-President has the time, energy, information, and expertise to form an opinion on some particular policy, proximity becomes the next obstacle. Johnson, Humphrey, Ford, Rockefeller, and Mondale all had reasonable levels of the first four resources, but only Rockefeller and Mondale had access to the policy process. Whatever Johnson could contribute to legislative strategy, whatever Humphrey could lend to domestic policy formulation, and whatever Ford could add to budgetary decisions, none had the access to offer advice.

Proximity can actually be measured by distance. The Executive Office Building is one hundred yards from the Oval Office; Mondale's West Wing office was less than fifty feet. Proximity also involves access. Agnew once had a West Wing office. At the start of the term, Agnew was physically closer to the President than Johnson, Humphrey, Ford, or Rockefeller. However, because Agnew had difficulty getting in to see Nixon, he was actually just as distant as his EOB colleagues. Moreover, because Agnew's staff did not have White House passes, Agnew's proximity to his own advisory support was limited. Thus, proximity involves *distance plus access.* Vice-Presidents need at least four kinds of proximity: (a) to the President, (b) to the President's top staff, (c) to decisions, and (d) to the Vice-President's own staff.

Proximity to the *President* is the most important of these. If the Vice-President cannot gain access to the President, advice must flow through other channels. Though past Vice-Presidents have used alternative paths to the Oval Office—e.g., Mondale through Eizenstat, Carp, and Aaron—direct access offers the greatest opportunity for advice giving. First, as noted earlier, visibility is a risk in the advisory role. The more the Vice-President exposes his recommendations to competitors, the more opponents can measure influence. One-on-one meetings with the President provide an opportunity for discreet advice. Second, in the bureaucratic jungle surrounding the President, a range of problems arise that may distort the Vice-President's opinions. Even if the Vice-President's White House allies are trustworthy, as with Carp and Aaron, messages often suffer in translation. Since the President's people are often unwilling to transmit conflicting advice, the Vice-President is better served delivering the messages himself. According to both Mondale and Bush, proximity to the President is best served by two specific devices: the West Wing office and an open invitation to all meetings. Though neither Vice-President reports having stopped in unannounced very often, the West Wing office provides the ideal combination of distance and access. "People see that the Vice-President is located in the West Wing," a Mondale aide argued, "and take it as a powerful signal that he is going to be involved. It's more convenient for the President to call him in for advice. There's no fanfare and no need to clear a bunch of people over." The open invitation to meetings also serves as a signal, providing additional access to information as well. These two devices are complemented by some kind of regularized private contact with the President. Regardless of the content of these meetings, they give the Vice-President a chance to offer advice and to create the image of influence. These meetings served as Rockefeller's only opportunity for advice later in the term. Whether Ford continued them out of guilt or real interest, Rockefeller was able to retain some access to the policy agenda.

Proximity to the President's *own staff* is also important, particularly for hidden-hand advice and influence. Once again, the West Wing office is one source of proximity. "Mondale met regularly with Carp, Aaron, Eizenstat, and Wexler," an assistant remembered. "I don't think there would have been that kind of contact over in the EOB. In the West Wing, you see the people walk by and call them in. You walk down the hall to steal a cigar. Your staff bumps into their staff. The EOB is a nice building, but the West Wing is where the decisions are made." In Mondale's case, contact with Carter aides was critical for coalition building. Because Mondale often relied on other aides to represent his opinions, he needed proximity to the staff operation. Rockefeller also had some level of contact with the White House staff, primarily through James Cannon, Assistant to the President for Domestic Affairs. However, Rockefeller was forced to depend on his once-a-week private meetings with Ford as his clear channel for advice and influence. His EOB office and personality conflicts kept him from developing any kind of an operating relationship with the Ford staff. That absence of proximity became critical when decisions were made at the staff level.

Though all Presidents retain discretion over final decisions, the White House staff is usually given responsibilities for framing those choices. Since Rockefeller had few friends and little access to the White House staff—he had difficulty moving back and forth from the EOB to the West Wing, for instance—he had few avenues for advice giving outside the Oval Office. Moreover, because Rockefeller opted out of administrative meetings, he lost additional opportunities for coalition building.

Proximity to *decisions* is a third requirement in the advisory role. As noted above, Vice-Presidents must have information on the movement of issues in the policy process. One way to get such information is to attend the critical meetings. One way to give advice is to be present when the President canvasses his advisers for opinions. Though past Vice-Presidents have been allowed to attend cabinet meetings, most decisions occur in much smaller forums, whether organized or ad hoc. As policy-making responsibility flows in toward the White House and away from the executive branch, the Vice-President's attendance at cabinet gatherings becomes almost as ceremonial as the meetings themselves. Thus, proximity to decisions involves the Vice-President's ability to slip in and out of the policy flow. It may involve access to the spur-of-the-moment meetings or a position in the paper flow; it may include a staff member's attendance at the senior meetings and deputies meetings. It may involve White House mess privileges for the Vice-President's top aides or representation on policy task forces. Haldeman never invited an Agnew staffer to the 8:15 senior staff meetings during the Nixon administration; Haig never invited a Ford aide to the senior meetings during the final months of Nixon's term; Rumsfeld would not include a Rockefeller representative in the morning meetings during the Ford years, though he did invite James Cannon from the Domestic Council. It was not until the Carter administration that a vice-presidential staffer was permitted to attend the senior meetings. That innovation was followed by vice-presidential representation at the deputies meetings, started in Carter's second year. Access to decisions at the staff level was particularly important given Mondale's reluctance to speak out in large meetings himself. If Mondale preferred a low profile, his staff was quite willing to voice opinions and complaints at the senior and deputies meetings.

The final kind of proximity involves access to the *Vice-President's own staff.* Though such access would appear automatic, Agnew found it difficult to see his staff during his brief tenure in the West Wing. The lack of White House passes for his staff prevented easy movement back and forth from the EOB. Eventually, Agnew was moved back to the EOB, where he was reunited with his staff. The problem of staff access is not completely resolved with White House passes. Since the Vice-President's West Wing suite has room for only three people—the Vice-President, his personal secretary, and a personal assistant—the rest of the seventy-member staff must remain in the

EOB. Though Mondale had a number of passes for his top aides—Moe, Berman, Harrison (domestic issues), Eisele (press), McGowan (scheduling), Clift (national security)—he rarely saw the bulk of his staff. Mondale preferred it that way, in part because he did not deal well with personal relationships at the staff level. His successor, Bush, however, found the distance from his personal staff to be a source of frustration. As a compromise in the first year, Bush spent roughly half of his time in the EOB and the other half in the West Wing. He met early in the morning with his EOB staff, walked to the West Wing for a morning of work, then returned for the afternoon in the EOB.

In terms of proximity to the President, the President's staff, or decisions, a West Wing office is critical. As I note shortly, the West Wing office is an important source of leverage inside the White House. In combination with other resources, it can be the key to an advisory role. As one Humphrey aide said: "The geography of power has changed in the Presidency. The course of the Vietnam war might have been different had Humphrey been in the West Wing. The EOB isn't far in linear feet, but it is miles psychologically." A second Humphrey aide concurred. "If Humphrey had just had the chance to buttonhole Rusk or McNamara, or Ball, he might have had an impact. But the EOB is a long walk from the President's office. No one had the time to stop by. You can bet Hubert would have been out in the hall arguing if he'd had a West Wing office. As it was, the best he could do was leave a message and wait for a phone call." Humphrey would have done much better, of course, had Johnson been interested in his opinions.

Proximity can be wasted with overuse. Though Mondale and Bush both had open invitations to any meetings, neither felt free to use them. Nor did Mondale or Bush drop in on the President. Mondale recognized that Carter liked to work on paper or in tightly scheduled time-blocks. Carter was not the kind of President who sat around "shooting the breeze." Bush also sensed the need to curtail surprise visits. As Bush remarked in mid-1981:

> Well, it's not [a matter of] just going in unannounced. I feel free to, but when I've had occasions to see him and tell him something, it is a totally uninhibited relationship. But I don't want to give the impression that I'm in and out of there three or four times a day. . . . That's not the way it works.
>
> But the atmosphere is such that I can go down there and say, "Look, after this next meeting, I'd love to stick my head in for two seconds to tell him something." I don't think I've ever done that and anyone [has] ever said, "Don't do that," or "What do you want to talk about?" He has an openness about him in that relationship that makes me feel inclined, anytime I want to, to do that—and, secondly, it makes me disinclined to overdo it. But I don't quake about it, I don't say, "Oh gosh, should I do this or not?" (*National Journal*, 20 June 1981).

The President's Willingness to Listen

After all else is considered—time, energy, information, expertise, and proximity—the Vice-President's advisory role rests on the President's willingness to listen. As Ehrlichman reports, Nixon eventually denied Agnew's requests for meetings. "Nixon found early that personal meetings with Agnew were invariably unpleasant. The President came out of them amazed at Agnew's self-aggrandizement. Nixon recalled that as Vice-President he had seldom made a request of any kind of Dwight Eisenhower. But Agnew's visits always included demands for more staff, better facilities, more prerogatives and perquisites. It was predictable that as Agnew complained and requested more and more, Nixon would agree to see him less frequently" (1982, p. 145). Whatever Agnew's other resources—which were also highly limited—Nixon's unwillingness to listen negated the advisory role.

There are a number of reasons why a President might want to listen to advice. Alexander George offers a list of motives in foreign policy.

> First, the President may turn to advisers for information and advice; hence, they may help him to satisfy his *cognitive needs* prior to making decisions. Second, the chief executive may interact with advisers in order to obtain the *emotional support* needed to cope with strains of making difficult, possibly fateful, decisions. Third, consultation with leading foreign policy officials of his administration may be useful to the President for gaining their *understanding and support* for whatever decision he makes, since his advisers then at least have the satisfaction of knowing that their views were solicited and considered. Finally, since it is expected that a President will consult and take advice from properly constituted officials who share responsibility in foreign-policy and national security matters, he will want to do so in order to gain greater *political legitimacy* in the eyes of Congress and the public for his policies and decisions. Of course, a President's incentives for consulting may include more than one of these objectives, and his purposes in doing so may vary from one situation to another (1980, p. 81).

The President's interest in the Vice-President's advice can flow from any one of the four needs. As decisionmakers, Presidents have the same demands for time, energy, information, and expertise as their own advisers. Depending upon the experience of the President and his staff, there may be serious shortages of certain resources at the start of the term. In the Carter administration, the lack of Washington experience created shortages of both information and expertise, leading to interest in Mondale's cache of resources. Since Mondale and his staff had considerable federal experience and substantive knowledge, there was cognitive need for listening. As one Mondale aide argued:

> The bottom line was that without Carter's cooperation, it wouldn't have worked. But Mondale brought his own assets with him. It wasn't just because Mondale was a nice guy, which wasn't always true if you worked for him. He had plenty to give Carter in return for a decent role in the administration. The relationship wasn't all one-sided. Mondale had his own capital, but didn't want to come on too strong. He couldn't say, "Look you son of a bitch, either take my advice or

I'm gone." But he could say, "I have some experience in this kind of thing and I think you ought to do this."

Mondale was also able to provide emotional support for presidential decisions, if only because he recognized the burden of making difficult choices. Mondale certainly provided understanding and support for many of Carter's decisions, in part because he was so often included in the critical choices. As a Carter assistant noted: "All of us were involved in one way or another on the major decisions. It was Carter's way of getting the best information and making sure everyone had at least some connection to the final outcome. Nobody could support every decision, but I didn't hear too many complaints about fairness." Finally, Mondale was a source of constituent links in the Democratic party. One way to build legitimacy for Carter's ever-growing budget conservatism was to include administration liberals in the process.

Though these four reasons are important, there is a fifth incentive for listening: the President may listen because that is how he thinks decisions ought to be made. Whether consciously or subconsciously, a President may structure the decision-making process to create maximum input. Some Presidents design the decision making process to conserve their own time and energy, while others provide maximum opportunities for advice. Carter, for instance, may have been more concerned about the process of decision making than the specifics of the choice; more concerned about how a good decision could be made than the final product itself. His structure for domestic policy making included a detailed chain of decision papers; memos on issues, memos on alternatives, and even final decision memos. Carter's system, with its detailed paper flow and lack of face-to-face debate, allowed maximum access for satellite players. Moreover, since there was so little in-person debate, advisers who could get into the Oval Office had that much more advantage.

For Mondale, the system provided at least two stages for input. First, Mondale and his staff had a chance to work at the memoranda stage. As the paper flowed through the administration, Mondale had a chance to see what was happening with regard to specific choices. Second, and more important, Mondale was one of the very few White House aides who had private one-on-one meetings with Carter. Carter did not like one-on-ones because he felt they were a waste of resources: why not read the material instead? His decision to give Mondale at least one hour a week alone constituted a rare advantage inside the administration. During the weeks of 4 April and 11 April, 1977, Carter spent a total of 70 minutes alone with Brzezinski, 45 with Charles Schultze (CEA chairman), 30 with Jody Powell (press), 25 with Frank Moore (legislative liaison), 10 with Hamilton Jordan (chief of staff), 5 with James Fallows (speechwriter), 5 with Robert Strauss (trade representative), 5 with Jack Watson (intergovernmental affairs), and 190 with Mondale (see Shull 1979, pp. 50-51, for the original logs). Though

Brzezinski met more often with Carter—15 meetings for Brzezinski compared to three for Mondale—the Vice-President had the kind of long contacts most likely to cover a broad range of issues. Noting that this was the period in time when major decisions were made on the $50 tax rebate, electoral reform, welfare reform, and hospital cost containment, Mondale's long meetings with Carter became even more significant.

As stated earlier, the way Presidents structure their search for good policy has a major impact on the Vice-President's advisory role. Vice-Presidents have the most difficulty in formalistic or hierarchical systems. The more people the Vice-President must go through to reach the President, the less the opportunity for advice. The more gatekeepers, the more obstacles to the President. Vice-Presidents have the best chances for advice in the collegial or spokes-of-the-wheel system. The more people the President consults at the hub of the wheel, the more opportunity for vice-presidential input. Though it is difficult for Vice-Presidents to crack the collegial network of old friends surrounding the President, the spokes-of-the-wheel approach reflects the President's own commitment to generating maximum sources of advice. Vice-Presidents face the greatest risks in the competitive system. In pitting one adviser against another, Presidents may be able to find the "best" answers to policy questions. In pitting one adviser against the Vice-President, Presidents may soon discover that their running mates have disappeared. Though Vice-Presidents now have more *advisory* resources, they still face considerable limits in *bureaucratic* resources. They do not have the long-term loyalty or service to compete against the President's own staff. Nor do they have any of the tools of power. They do not command White House resources, have no troops for implementation, and cannot order any action from staffers beyond their own people.

The willingness to listen to advice is also shaped by distinct cycles in the President's own decision-making resources. As time and energy dwindle over the term, there is a natural reflex inside the White House. Presidents will have less tolerance for extended debate and less interest in seeing multiple advisers. Kennedy, Johnson, Nixon, Ford, and Carter all moved toward a tighter staffing system as one way of controlling their limited decision-making resources. In Carter's case, the consolidation involved the adoption of an agenda-setting mechanism (which Mondale chaired) and a centralization of the advisory process. As Jody Powell argued:

We found that we needed a greater degree of centralization than we thought at the outset. . . . No system works perfectly all the time, but to the extent that you can have one that works pretty well in most cases, I think we had arrived at one in which there was enough centralization to keep things from slipping through the cracks . . . to impose a sufficient degree of order in terms of the way you consider matters . . . , but which did not block access to the President by key staffers in a way that impeded good decisionmaking at his level . . . (Kessel 1982, p. 29).

In the consolidation, Presidents may decide to close certain advisory channels. In the past, the first group of advisers to lose access has been the cabinet secretaries. As the term progresses, Presidents allocate less time for extended cabinet contact and often find that full cabinet meetings have little practical value for policy making. The second group of advisers to lose access is the White House outsiders, including Vice-Presidents. Advisers who have not proved themselves in the long campaigns may find themselves frozen out of the policy process. Presidents are less willing to continue advisory relationships that are either symbolic or unproductive. In the Nixon administration, for instance, the meetings with Agnew were expendable. Had Agnew contributed to the administration's store of information or expertise, Nixon might have continued his private meetings with the Vice-President somewhat longer. However, as Haldeman and Ehrlichman tightened the noose on the policy process, Agnew was but one of many advisers to lose their access. Cabinet members, liaison officers, CEA chairmen, OMB directors, all found themselves unable to penetrate the inner circle. Thus, over the term, Vice-Presidents find it harder to stay inside of the ever-tightening circle of advisers.

Personality clearly has some bearing on the President's willingness to listen. However, when compared to the impact of resources and goals, personality may have only a marginal impact on the advisory role. Yet, the President's personality does have a bearing on management style. Vice-Presidents have more advisory openings under a collegial system than either the formalistic or competitive style. According to George, at least three traits have some relationship to management approaches: (1) cognitive style, or the way Presidents store, retrieve, and use information, (2) sense of efficacy and competence, or the President's willingness to engage in management and decision making, and (3) orientation toward political conflict, or the President's willingness to immerse himself in the bureaucratic infighting of most policy choices (1980, pp. 147-48). Presidents who are unwilling to engage in policy debates may prefer the relative isolation of the formalistic system, while Presidents who enjoy the give-and-take of internal politics may prefer the action of the competitive system. George illustrates the impact of these three traits in Franklin Roosevelt's competitive approach:

> A dominant feature of FDR's personality was his strong sense of political efficacy. He felt entirely at home in the presidency, acting in the belief that there was close to perfect fit between his competence and skills and some of the most demanding role requirements of the office. Then, too, FDR viewed politics and the games that go with it as a useful and enjoyable game and not, as others before him (for example, Taft and Hoover) as an unsavory, distasteful business to be discouraged or avoided. FDR not only felt comfortable in the presence of conflict and disagreement around him; he saw that, properly managed, it could

serve his informational and political needs. . . . For Roosevelt, exposure to conflict among advisers and cabinet heads did not stir up anxiety or depression; nor did he perceive it as threatening in a personal or political sense. Not only did he live comfortably with the political conflict and, at times, near-chaos around him, he manipulated the structure of relationships among subordinates in order to control and profit from their competition (1980, pp. 149-50).

Thus, Roosevelt felt reasonably comfortable placing Henry Wallace in a position in direct conflict with his secretary of commerce, Jesse Jones.

Though personality does have a bearing on management styles and, in turn, on the Vice-President's advisory role, we may not need to understand the deep-seated psychological drives that lead to the formalistic, competitive, or collegial system. Rather, we need to answer at least three questions in predicting the President's willingness to listen. *First,* what resources are available inside the White House? Does the President need more information and expertise? How much time is left in the term? Is there enough energy and expertise for a larger inner circle? *Second,* what is the level of goal compatibility between the President and Vice-President? Does the President want reelection? good policy? resource management? *Third,* what is the dominant management style? Is the advisory process open to outsiders or closed? Is there room for vice-presidential input? Can the Vice-President get into the Oval Office on a regular basis? Though the answers to the questions may be shaped by psychological drives—particularly the President's goals—we are still a long way from any usable models of presidential personality. At least for the time being, the context of decisions must suffice in predicting the rise and fall of the Vice-President's advisory role. Moreover, even if we could understand the President's psyche, it might provide very little payoff in explaining actual decisions.

Some Comparisons among Vice-Presidents

The six resources—time, energy, information, expertise, proximity, and presidential willingness to listen—are arrayed in the rough order of increasing importance to the advisory role. Time and energy have less impact on advice than proximity or the President's willingness to listen. Though the six resources are related—expertise may lead to greater proximity, etc.—they fall on a continuum of importance. One way to understand the importance of the six resources and the order of importance is to compare recent Vice-Presidents. A comparison of Johnson, Humphrey, Agnew, Ford, Rockefeller, and Mondale should also highlight recent changes in the American Vice-Presidency.

Of the six Vice-Presidents, only two, Ford and Rockefeller, had significant limits on time. Because Ford and Rockefeller took office with less than a full term ahead, they had less time to build the kinds of advisory networks that helped Mondale. Moreover, because Ford and Rockefeller did not participate in any election campaign with their President, they did not have the initial period of grace that follows a victory. They certainly did not have as much time to learn the advisory role. The time limits, however, were most severe for Ford. Following a two-month confirmation proceeding, Ford had just over nine months in office before Nixon's resignation. As one assistant argued: "We had barely enough time to hire the staff and work through our own problems before Nixon left. It was a very fast shakedown with no margin for error. We were just adjusting to the Vice-Presidency when it was time to move to the White House."

Of the six Vice-Presidents, only two, Johnson and Agnew, had any problems with energy. Johnson seemed to tire quickly over the first three years of his term, in part because he simply did not enjoy the job of being Vice-President. Had Johnson been allowed to participate in major decisions, he might have found the energy to do so. Agnew had similar problems engaging in the day-to-day activities of the Vice-Presidency, preferring to play golf and see old friends instead. In that sense, Agnew had plenty of energy, but little motivation to apply it to the policy process. When given an assignment, Agnew found it difficult to immerse himself for long in the details of a problem, leading one observer to quip that "Agnew wasn't lazy, but he wanted to work on his long woods instead of health insurance."

On information, Agnew was also behind his counterparts. Agnew did not bring much raw knowledge about policy problems into office with him and was not given access to the daily paper flow. He did not receive Nixon's schedule and was not privy to information on the progress of decisions. Four other Vice-Presidents—Johnson, Humphrey, Ford, and Rockefeller—had moderate information resources. All four had reasonable contact with policy issues before entering office and some access to cabinet and NSC meetings. Even with moderate information, Humphrey provides the most obvious case of a shortage created by the Vice-President's own hand. At one of the first National Security Council meetings of the new administration, Humphrey spoke against "Rolling Thunder," Johnson's plan to bomb North Vietnam for the first time. According to his staff, Humphrey believed other members of the NSC would join in his dissent, but soon realized that his was the only voice with Johnson present. Though the estimates vary, Johnson refused to hold NSC meetings for a year to eighteen months just to keep Humphrey from participating in his statutory role as a member of the council. By speaking against the President's policy, Humphrey lost his opportunity to collect information and track foreign decisions. Johnson continued to meet with the NSC, but never called the meetings formally. It was all simply to silence a dissenter.

Whereas Johnson and Humphrey had to rely on their own limited sources of information, Ford and Rockefeller had at least some access to the paper flow. Johnson, for instance, was always thankful when Walter Heller,

Kennedy's chairman of the Council of Economic Advisers, sent him copies of memoranda as a courtesy. Ford and Rockefeller did not need to rely so much on the kindness of White House advisers. The Vice-President's office had grown to include an information-gathering apparatus and Rockefeller did see most of the paper moving into the Oval Office—albeit late. The institutionalization of the Vice-President's office ensured that occupants would have at least minimal and independent sources of information. Of the six Vice-Presidents, of course, Mondale had the best information resources, securing access to the paper flow and the critical decision meetings. Mondale had ample advance warning on most decisions through Carp and Aaron, while becoming the first Vice-President with regular access to the PDB. This level of access continued under Bush, suggesting an institutionalization of the information base.

On expertise, five out of the six Vice-Presidents scored high. Johnson, Humphrey, Ford, Rockefeller, and Mondale all had strong political experience before entering office. Of the five, perhaps Rockefeller was the weakest on bureaucratic expertise, with Ford weakest on policy expertise. However, it would be a mistake to conclude that any of these five had problems as politicians. All had reached the Vice-Presidency after long and successful service in other political offices. Together, the five had 87 years of elective experience before entering the Vice-Presidency: Johnson with 23, Humphrey with 16, Ford with 16, Rockefeller with 16, and Mondale with 16. As with information, Agnew's lack of service restricted his political, policy, and bureaucratic expertise, leaving him with little to offer Nixon in terms of advisory resources. Moreover, Agnew's brief service in the Maryland governorship restricted his access to staff. Though Agnew had several qualified aides, his staff was unable to counterbalance his own inexperience.

Proximity to the policy process is a very recent phenomenon in the Vice-Presidency, giving the pre-Rockefeller Vice-Presidents low scores on access and distance. Only one of the four pre-1974 Vice-Presidents, Agnew, had even minimal proximity, and he lost that proximity within three months of entering office. Rockefeller's access came from his weekly meetings with Ford and his initial control of the domestic policy machinery. Rockefeller's access, however, was partially undermined by his distance from the Oval Office. Since Rockefeller did not occupy a West Wing office, he remained relatively distant from Ford's policy process during most of the term. According to an aide: "He stayed up in the EOB office and never saw what was going on in the West Wing, never knew who was meeting with who, what was being planned. He never saw what was being done to his paper and never fit in with the Ford staff." A second assistant agreed: "Every time he went over to the White House, it was a big event. He was never allowed to move around like one of the staff. He always moved with an entourage. He couldn't stop in and say 'I was out to stretch my legs and wanted to check in on the decision on the budget.'" Yet, for all his frustration, Rockefeller did institutionalize the regular meetings with the President, which both Mondale and Bush continued. With Mondale's move into the West Wing, he was able to combine the weekly meetings with a new position in the traffic pattern.

Among recent Presidents, only two, Ford and Carter, showed a lasting willingness to listen to vice-presidential advice. Much of Ford's willingness came from the circumstances surrounding Watergate. Rockefeller had a considerable store of political and policy resources, but he also brought legitimacy to an administration already weakened by the Nixon pardon. Much of Carter's willingness to listen came from resource shortages and his view of how decisions should be made. Mondale's experience and knowledge may not have been greater than Johnson's or Humphrey's, but Carter's lack of experience and knowledge was certainly greater than Kennedy's. Carter also saw Mondale as another officer of the administration, to be used in substantive assignments. "He didn't want to waste anyone," a Carter assistant remarked. "He didn't want to miss any detail and didn't want to see any staff member not working for the common cause. He was a lot like Eisenhower in his training. He had that engineer's mind and had a very mechanical view of how the staffing system should work."

Adding the six resources together over the past twenty years, we can see a steady rise in the Vice-President's advisory support. Johnson, Humphrey, Agnew, and Ford often lacked the information, proximity, or presidential willingness to listen needed to engage in advice giving. Rockefeller and Mondale did not face the same shortages. Part of the rise can be explained by the pressures of Watergate. Nixon was willing to make compromises in institutional support for his Vice-Presidents that he might not have made in normal circumstances. Part of the rise can be explained by changing incentives in the political and policy environment. Presidents began to see the value of active Vice-Presidents. Regardless of the cause, the past two decades have given the Vice-Presidency ample stores of advisory resources. Though Vice-Presidents still need to bring their own information and expertise into office with them, the office is now equipped to sustain an advisory presence across the term. If Vice-Presidents can retain the West Wing office, they will also retain a position in the policy process.

THE WEST WING OFFICE

Was the West Wing office important in the rise of the advisory role? According to a Mondale aide: "If you don't look like an adviser and don't have the same perks as other staff members, then I'd say it's safe to say that you're not going to be an adviser. So much of the White House turns on image. Nobody is going to talk to the Vice-President unless he looks like he's got some clout. Why waste the time?" Whether that image is accurate or not, it is critical for information and access. If other advisers see the Vice-President as an important player, there will be fewer attempts at isolation. As a second Mondale assistant noted: "Part of Mondale's influence was in the perception that he was someone important. The rest of the White House thought he was involved and that he was protected by the President. The perception created an impetus. In that sense, Mondale's discretion about what went on in his private meetings was the better part of the influence. The staff believed he was having an impact on Carter and started going to him first." A third aide agreed, arguing that Mondale's advisory style was well suited to the Carter system.

> Did Mondale have influence? More telling evidence was the perception that he had influence. Over the term, more and more people were coming to Mondale to ask him to help lobby for an idea. Honestly, I can't tell Mondale's success score. Maybe it was 50 percent, maybe 25, maybe less. But Mondale had all the trappings of influence. He looked like a player. That meant that other aides saw him as someone to be included. There were few efforts to ice him out. He had the West Wing office and the perks. He looked strong, even if he didn't win all of his arguments. Mondale wanted to have input and he did. But he was more effective in shaping ideas than in winning or losing on a program outright. The Carter system was set up to give everyone a shot at a program. Most outcomes were the product of compromise among a lot of different options. So we reserved ourselves for trimming and modifying rather than for fighting it out on one or two programs like Rockefeller. I think it was more successful. Of all the programs Carter announced, at least seventy-five percent were shaped at one stage or another by Mondale. Of course, that goes for all of the staff. Everybody had a chance to say something.

Over the past twenty years, the most important changes in the Vice-President's internal reputation came with the West Wing office and the perquisites that went with it. Not only did the office signal the rise of the Vice-President within the inner circle, it also brought White House privileges for the staff. According to Victor Gold, Agnew's press secretary: "When I was with Agnew, I never had a White House pass. I didn't get into the White House more than five times in the thirty months I worked there. When Agnew made a speech, we flew in a plane with no windows. That's where we stood" (*Washington Post*, 30 Mar. 1981). Mondale's staff did not have those kinds of problems. That is not to say they won every battle. Rather, they simply did not have to spend scarce resources fighting to get into the West Wing. Nor did they suffer from claustrophobia on foreign trips. Yet, the West Wing office and the associated perks were important for more than just psychological comfort.

First, the office and perks served as a powerful signal to the rest of the White House staff. According to a Mondale aide: "Perks are a signal. People read the tea leaves very carefully. We had all the right kinds of planes, phones, passes. We also had the official residence. Humphrey had lived in Southwest Washington, LBJ in Spring Valley. Mondale was the first Vice-President who lived in the new residence. It made a difference when he entertained. He had the image of influence." The West Wing office was one of several important signs of Mondale's involvement. As a Carter assistant noted: "Subtle, symbolic actions permeate the White House. Signals from Carter let us know what to do and when to do it. His notion that a Vice-President could have impact was unique and came with the West Wing office. It told all of us to include him, even if we didn't want to. It was the most visible sign of Mondale's role." Carter's decision to give Mondale the West Wing office involved several factors. As noted above, Carter simply believed that the Vice-President should be involved in the administration. He had given some thought to the arrangement long before he arrived in Washington. Carter also had little appreciation for the role of perks inside the White House. As a Mondale assistant argued: "The Carter administration was the least perquisite conscious of any recent administration—sure as hell less than Reagan. Mondale had enough of everything—parking spaces, White House passes, cars, planes, etc. Here was a President who liked barbecue and bluegrass. What did he care about perquisites?" Thus, the West Wing office was a coup for Mondale. It was a critical first symbol of how he was to be treated by the President's staff and cabinet. When Carter gave Mondale the pick of the West Wing offices, he was also giving Mondale a powerful boost in internal reputation.

Second, and more important, the West Wing office placed Mondale firmly in the policy traffic. As a Ford official said: "Anyone who is not in the West Wing is nowhere. Unless you have an office where you can see who's coming and going, you don't know where the action is." Mondale said as much when he first arrived in the West Wing and concluded that it had "a sort of staff smell to it." Though other Vice-Presidents had information and expertise, Mondale was able to add a critical combination to his advisory resources: *proximity plus willingness.* He could see when decisions were going to be made; he could find out where the meetings were going to be held; he could "soak and poke" around the White House to track the progress of his pet programs. Indeed, as Griffin Bell, Carter's attorney general and a frequent Mondale opponent, has argued, the West Wing office was a major Carter blunder, giving the Vice-President far too much input on decisions. As Bell suggests:

> Moving the Vice President into the White House had a profound and adverse impact on the Carter Presidency. I know that President Carter repeatedly praised Mondale as the most effective Vice President in the nation's history and said, in the week following the 1980 election, that he and Mondale were as close as brothers. But Mondale's and Carter's views were not the same . . . whatever

pigeonhole Carter belongs in, it is well to the right of Vice President Mondale's.

But the Vice President tried to shape administration policy to his way of thinking in important areas, and in some instances he succeeded. He managed to do this because of his physical location in the west wing of the White House and because of placing some close aides in crucial posts in the presidential policy-making apparatus (1982, p. 23).

As a Mondale aide remarked: "Policy is the product of osmosis. If you're out of the loop, you're not able to affect policy. You can't pop into the President's office if it takes five minutes to walk across from the EOB. If Mondale spent more than ten hours in his EOB office in the four years, I'd be very surprised."

For Mondale, the West Wing office provided the very kind of information that is most valuable in converting raw knowledge into advice. Mondale was able to ferret out information on decisions and on his opposition. He was able to track the flow of meetings and was always available for ad hoc decisions. Though Mondale preferred to withhold his advice for private meetings with Carter, he was rarely without the basic information on the whereabouts of ideas inside the policy process. Nor was his staff kept out of the White House mess, the site of many important decisions. Because Mondale and his staff had eyes inside the West Wing, they could follow the policy process. Instead of just leaning over the balcony of the Vice-President's palatial EOB office, Mondale and his staff could see the decision-making process firsthand. And instead of calling out to a cabinet member from the second floor of the EOB, Mondale could reach out and pull one in for his own brand of intelligence gathering.

Although the office could be easily denied by a hostile President, that is not likely in the near future. The Vice-President's office has taken on a certain permanence. Had Reagan attempted to reduce the Vice-President's staff or move Bush back to the EOB there would have been inevitable and unfavorable comparisons to his predecessor. As one observer suggested: "The press would have had a field day saying Reagan was not as confident as Carter or that Reagan was not open to criticism. There's some room for precedent here. It would have been almost impossible for Reagan to boot Bush out of the West Wing, if only because Carter had let Mondale in."

JOB CONFLICT IN THE VICE-PRESIDENCY

Though the Vice-President's resources have grown over the past decade, there is still considerable conflict in the job description. Time spent on the campaign trail is time *not* spent in the advisory role; energy expended in public liaison is energy *not* expended in the policy process. Like Presidents, Vice-Presidents must make choices on how to allocate their resources. Vice-

Presidents must distribute their scarce resources across a variety of duties and policy areas. If Vice-Presidents want an advisory role, they must develop strategies for reducing the inevitable role conflict.

There are at least four sources of job conflict in the contemporary Vice-Presidency. First, conflict arises from the competition between the *political and policy roles*. It is almost impossible for the Vice-President to perform both duties simultaneously. Since the political role often involves travel away from Washington, the Vice-President loses time, energy, and proximity in the policy role. As Mike Berman, Mondale's chief counsel, argues:

> The question of how much traveling to do is a difficult one to answer. While you can receive information all over the world, you can't be directly involved in decision-making when you are not with the President participating fully in the meetings. On the other hand, we all quickly learned that you get isolated and insulated in the White House. Mondale felt a need to regularly get out around the country and the world to get a first hand picture of what people were thinking and doing (remarks, 21 Feb. 1981).

Though Mondale's travel record was impressive—36 countries, 586,000 miles, 614 days outside of Washington—it limited his access to the policy process. Mondale could not send a substitute to his regular Monday lunches with Carter nor could he move a senior staff into his West Wing office. As a Mondale aide concluded: "In Washington, 95 percent of our time involved policy questions, while only five percent was ceremonial. On the road, at least 75 percent was ceremonial, while less than 25 percent was policy." Mondale was on the road when Carter fired Califano at Health and Human Services, Blumenthal at Treasury, and Adams at Transportation. According to a Mondale assistant:

> Mondale had just started a five-day swing to the South for SALT II. Those cabinet resignations really hurt Carter and he came off looking like Nixon. The "malaise" speech worked OK, but the firings wiped out any gains Carter had made. Had Mondale been in town, I don't think he could have stopped it. Things were just moving too fast and, since it was so out of character for Carter anyway, I don't think Mondale would have anticipated the decision. It was only announced five minutes before the Cabinet meeting. Mondale was extremely angry about the Califano firing. Califano had been a pain in the ass and had caused all sorts of problems for the White House, but he was still a good secretary. What a wild week anyway. We'll never know if Mondale could have changed anything if he'd been home.

Travel is often incompatible with an active policy role. Johnson learned the lesson when he heard about the Bay of Pigs fiasco in Africa; Mondale learned it when he heard about Califano somewhere in the Southeast United States. Yet, even if travel is incompatible in the short term, it may be the key to long-term influence. As a Mondale aide argued: "If the Vice-President wants any influence, he can't be chasing around town worrying about the Midwestern governors or his former constituents in Saint Paul. But if the Vice-President is going to earn his spurs, he has got to do some of the legwork, to show the President he means to be involved at all levels. Mondale was a stranger to Carter at the start of the term. Others earned their positions through the campaign and loyal service. Mondale had to do it through patience and political groundwork."

The second source of job conflict arises from the competition between *line assignments and the advisory role*. Most line assignments involve so much administrative overhead that Vice-Presidents have little time and energy left for the policy role. "Humphrey's impact was minimal," a Humphrey aide said. "We did some useful things, like being the ombudsman for mayors on the poverty program. Humphrey liked his line responsibilities, but knew they were killing his chances for any kind of input on substantive policy." Rockefeller experienced this job conflict in the extreme. Though he won the initial battle, he was eventually defeated by administrative headaches. For several reasons, Rockefeller was willing to tackle line assignments that reduced his policy role. As noted earlier, Rockefeller may have misunderstood what the Domestic Council involved. He saw the assignment as a policy role, while most of the Ford staff saw it as an administrative chore. Rockefeller may also have viewed the assignment as equivalent to the National Security Council staff under his old friend Henry Kissinger. "If Henry had been able to do all that at NSC," an aide noted, "Rockefeller thought he would be king at the Domestic Council. He had always enjoyed the domestic side of government anyway and saw the council as a chance to become the Henry Kissinger of domestic policy." Unfortunately, Rockefeller also accepted the chairmanship of the President's commission on CIA activities. The commission turned out to be both time-consuming and politically dangerous. As one Rockefeller assistant commented: "The CIA job took more and more time away from Domestic Council at exactly the time Rockefeller should have been consolidating his control. Rockefeller should never have accepted the CIA responsibility. It was too hot to handle." Thus, as Mondale sat down to talk with Humphrey and Rockefeller before his inauguration, one of the major rules that flowed out of the conversations was to avoid line assignments. Line assignments have high administrative overhead and expose the Vice-President to intense pressure. "Being operational means that the President has to choose between the Vice-President and someone else," a Mondale aide noted. "It creates natural conflict that the Vice-President can't normally win."

The third source of job conflict arises in the competition among *policy issues*. Vice-Presidents often have to choose between domestic, economic, and foreign policy. Since the three policy arenas involve different sources of information and different kinds of expertise, there is some potential for conflict between the three. In general, Vice-Presidents are given the greatest leeway in domestic affairs. Since Presidents often allocate their greatest energies to foreign affairs, Vice-Presidents have more opportunity in the domestic field. As a Ford aide remarked: "Nixon had abandoned domestic policy back in 1969. His view was that anyone could run the country domestically. That left some room for the Vice-President. Had either Ford or Agnew tried to meddle in foreign policy, Nixon would have been quick to the throat, with Kissinger close behind." Yet, like Presidents, Vice-Presidents have considerable interest in foreign policy. It seems important and is certainly glamorous. For future candidates, it is an important area to conquer. "You see the President working hard on foreign affairs and you want to be involved, too," a Mondale aide noted. "Domestic policy is important, but it just doesn't compare to foreign policy. Once you get into the White House, it seems to take precedence. All of a sudden, you're in charge of the future of the nation. Small flare-ups around the world take on crisis proportions." Though Mondale was involved in foreign policy—Carter asked him to take over Africa policy, but he refused—there were more vacuums in the domestic field. Since Vice-Presidents must divide their time between the political and policy roles, they may find it expedient to devote their policy energies to just one area.

These three sources of job conflict are complicated by a fourth problem in the Vice-Presidency. Vice-Presidents must often choose between being *national figures or being involved in the policy process.* As a Ford presidential aide complained: "Nelson Rockefeller didn't know whether he wanted to be an inside player or a national power broker. If he wanted to be on the inside, he had to give up the speaker's tour and the weekends back in New York. He couldn't announce every program as his own and had to stop publicizing his victories." Though some White House staff members lose their passion for anonymity over time, most aides accept the relative obscurity of their positions. That anonymity is much more difficult for Vice-Presidents. Since most have spent their political careers in the public spotlight, it is often difficult to accept the role of the invisible staff member. In order to reduce their threat to the President and the White House staffs, Vice-Presidents may have to renounce their public ambitions, submerging their political goals for the four or eight years. That can be extremely unpleasant for some politicians, particularly those who are close to the end of their careers. For Rockefeller, it was almost impossible. He had little time left to pursue his place in history. For Mondale, it was easier. He was young and willing to wait for his own turn in 1984. As a White House observer concluded:

Mondale chose the advisory role and was willing to make the sacrifices to achieve some level of influence. He gave up his own identity to become the President's spokesman. He gave up taking credit for his own ideas to get more accomplished over the term. He even gave up some of his best friends—Ted Kennedy is the best example—to be the point man in the reelection campaign. Mondale made some difficult trade-offs to become an insider. Others, like Rockefeller, weren't willing to give up the national image for more inside power.

Three Solutions

There are several solutions to job conflict in the Vice-Presidency. Though job conflict cannot be completely eliminated, Vice-Presidents have several options in dividing their resources.

The first response to job conflict is to spend as much time in Washington as possible. Though Vice-Presidents have to travel, when possible, they must stay at home. That was particularly important for Rockefeller. According to most accounts, Rockefeller did not like spending time in Washington. He generally left Washington on Friday to spend the weekend with his two teenage sons at his estate in New York. As an aide reported: "He had to watch Kojak on TV on Sunday nights with his kids. Nothing short of nuclear war would stop him. That meant that from Friday noon until Tuesday morning, he was absent. It wasn't great for keeping in the loop." If Rockefeller was out of the loop and unable to secure timely information, he was also unable to influence policy. Indeed, at least one Ford aide was willing to admit that "the weekend was generally the best time to end-run Rocky. He was never in Washington and wasn't going to see what was happening. If you wanted to keep something away from him, you'd just schedule a meeting for late Friday, the weekend, or early Monday." Thus, as a second Ford assistant concluded, the Vice-President must try to remain close to his advisory base:

> If you're operating a complex mechanism like the White House, a person has to be physically present. You can't drift in and out. If you want to be engaged, you've got to be there. You can't be an occasional adviser. It was difficult for Rockefeller to be both Vice-President and still be present for staff meetings. It was also difficult for him to be a Rockefeller and still be willing to stay around town. He didn't like the nitty-gritty and preferred to return to New York and Pocantico Hills rather than fight it out. He'd keep the gloves on until the long weekends.

A second response to job conflict is to spend as much time as possible in Washington during the critical periods. If the agenda is normally set in the first and third years, it is important to be physically present during those years. Since the Vice-President has little impact on implementation, agenda setting may be the most important opportunity for advice and influence. According to an observer,

> The Vice-President has got to be in town when it comes down to setting the agenda. That's probably the most important step anyway. Mondale was gone most of 1980 on the campaign, but he did his share in the earlier years. During the formative period in 1977, Mondale was there and made sure he was in on the early decisions. He pushed hard for electoral reform, the appointment of Califano and Bergland, and had his say on most issues. Then, as the agenda moved up to Congress in 1978, he was out on the road again, leaving the lobbying to Carter's staff.

The Vice-President also needs to be physically present during specific times in each year. Regardless of the year in the term, most major agenda and budgeting decisions are made in the early months—January, February, and March. If the Vice-President wants to affect those decisions, it is important to winter in Washington. As the presidential policy process relaxes during the summer, travel may be less costly to the Vice-President's advisory role.

The third solution to job conflict is to build networks for hidden-hand advice. If the Vice-President has to leave Washington or spend time in political or ceremonial duties, there are still opportunities for advice giving through the staff. The role of the Vice-President's staff in these circumstances rests on the development of ties to the White House. If the Vice-President's staff can build working relationships with the President's staff, they may be able to represent the Vice-President when he is absent. That was the case in the Mondale term. His staff was tightly integrated into the advisory process; his senior aides attended the senior staff meetings, while his deputies attended the deputies meetings. When Mondale traveled, he did not have to uproot his policy staff. Instead, Mondale took a team of political specialists—speechwriters, advance aides, military support, personal assistants. The degree to which the Vice-President's staff understands and articulates his positions has an important bearing on job conflict. "The fact was that even when Mondale was gone, we kept right at our jobs," a Mondale assistant argued. "We didn't break a step. We kept on talking with our contacts, kept on reading and writing, kept on arguing for Mondale's programs. He'd come back to town and start up with his Monday lunches, but we kept on working." Here, the institutional Vice-Presidency can be a critical factor in balancing the Vice-President's competing interests. If the Vice-President has to travel, at least the institutional apparatus can keep him informed and involved, albeit indirectly. If the Vice-President has to choose between foreign and domestic policy, the institutional apparatus can keep him active in both. Mondale's domestic issues staff was involved in policy making throughout the term, even when Mondale was at Camp David trying to interpret Menachem Begin to Carter and the Egyptians. The staff gave him ongoing input, if not proximity, to the White House policy process.

Ultimately, much of the job conflict cannot be easily resolved. Like Presidents, Vice-Presidents simply have to make choices based on their goals and the political context. The key rule is to remain as close to the policy process as possible, particularly during the early months of the first and third years. Of the six resources, time, energy, and proximity seem most susceptible to job conflict. At least some of the loss in time, energy, and proximity can be minimized by maintaining a strong institutional base in the Vice-President's office. However, because the President's willingness to listen may depend on precisely those activities that erode time, energy, and proximity, Vice-Presidents will continue to face job conflict in the future. Travel and other political duties seem to be necessary for building the Vice-President's internal capital and reinforcing the President's willingness to listen. The best solution may rest on remaining physically proximate during peak policy-making periods and traveling during the summers and falls.

CONCLUSION

In searching for explanations of the change in the contemporary Vice-Presidency, we must look both to unique events (Watergate, Nixon's resignation) and to new incentives (decline in the parties, changes in Congress, new issues). It is clear that the Vice-Presidency has more capacity for supporting a policy role today than during the 1950s and 1960s. The past two decades have produced a step increase in policy-making resources, whether time, energy, information, expertise, proximity, or the President's willingness to listen. Moreover, among the many changes during the Ford, Rockefeller, and Mondale years, perhaps the most important was the acquisition of the West Wing office. That office finally gave Vice-Presidents the proximity to the policy process needed for an advisory role.

All of these resources—time, energy, information, expertise, proximity, and willingness to listen—are important to the advisory role. They are valuable for both formulating and giving advice. However, they are not sufficient for influence. Though Vice-Presidents need these resources to give advice, they need a very different set of resources for influence. The resources that created an advisory role for Rockefeller, Mondale, and Bush were not the same resources that created influence for Mondale.

PART TWO

Influence

6.

Rockefeller and Mondale

his chapter is about two senior advisers to the President: Rockefeller and Mondale. Both had access to the policy process; both had their President's willingness to listen; both had the necessary resources. And though their styles differed sharply, both had the chance to offer detailed advice on politics and policy. Though other Vice-Presidents had opportunities to give advice, particularly at the start of their administrations, Rockefeller and Mondale sustained their advisory roles throughout their terms. The major difference was that Mondale had more influence than Rockefeller. Though Mondale had a number of defeats, his record of success outdistanced that of his predecessor. He was involved in the appointments of at least six members of the Carter cabinet, the cancellation of the B-1 bomber program, the establishment of the Department of Education, the revision of the Bakke brief to the Supreme Court, the tax reform proposal, and restoration of social service cuts.

MEASURES OF INFLUENCE

It is almost impossible to give exact measures of influence inside the White House. There are no box scores of internal success and few objective indicators of influence. The problem is that Vice-Presidents and other White House advisers are reluctant to provide any measuring posts for influence. Indeed, according to Mondale: "The only reason to state publicly what you have told the President is to take credit for his success and try to escape blame for failure. Either way there is no quicker way to undermine your relationship with the President and lose your effectiveness" (remarks,

18 Feb. 1981). Faced with this kind of internal discretion, how can we estimate influence inside the presidential policy process?

One solution is to compare the Vice-President's policy positions *before* entering office with the President's agenda *after.* If there are no matches, we can safely assume that the Vice-President was not influential. Looking across Ford's domestic program, for example, one sees that only three decisions bear Rockefeller's imprint: the Energy Independence Authority (often viewed as a simple gesture to a defeated Vice-President by the staffs), several pieces of regulatory reform, and a drug control proposal. Ford's tight domestic budget did not fit with Rockefeller's expansionary agenda. Moreover, Rockefeller was effectively frozen out of the economic and foreign policy arenas. His old friend and protégé, Henry Kissinger, could not tolerate competition, even from Nelson Rockefeller. In contrast, Mondale was involved in a number of Carter decisions: the $50 tax rebate (which Carter eventually withdrew), the establishment of a Department of Education, welfare reform, expanded jobs funding, movement toward a Camp David summit between Begin and Sadat, the Vietnamese boat-people rescue, full legislative passage of the Panama Canal treaties, cancellation of the B-1 bomber program, expansion of the SALT II treaties beyond the Ford outline, normalization of relations with China, admission of the Shah of Iran to the U.S. for cancer treatment, the Iranian hostage rescue attempt, softening of Brzezinski's hard line toward the Soviet Union, hospital cost containment, a harsh approach toward Israel in 1977 but a soft approach in 1978, and pursuit of an urban package. Mondale also persuaded Carter on a number of cabinet appointments, including Bergland (Agriculture), Califano (Health and Human Services), Vance (State), Blumenthal (Treasury), Schultze (Council of Economic Advisers), Landrieu (Housing and Urban Development), and Goldschmidt (Transportation).

Whether Mondale was the "swing" vote on the $50 tax rebate, welfare reform, urban assistance, Soviet policy, or SALT is doubtful. Moreover, it is highly unlikely that Mondale merely supported policies Carter already favored. Indeed, Mondale opposed a number of Carter initiatives, including the "racetrack" MX missile plan, the 1979 cabinet purge, Paul Volcker's appointment to the Federal Reserve, the Soviet grain embargo, the sale of F-15 fighters to Saudi Arabia, and Carter's rose garden strategy in 1980. However, because Carter preferred to be pulled and pushed on most decisions, he left ample room for persuasion. Mondale also fought for influence with the departments. According to Carter's attorney general, Bell, Mondale intervened with the Justice Department to change the Bakke brief to support affirmative action. Mondale also worked to prohibit the use of Comprehensive Employment and Training Act (CETA) funds in parochial schools, and to force the department to press federal civil rights charges against a Dallas policeman convicted in the murder of a young Hispanic, but only sentenced to a twelve-year prison term. Though Mondale later argued that he was only acting on Carter's orders, all three positions reflected his own beliefs about the Justice Department's agenda. Thus, on this first measure of influence, there is considerable evidence that Mondale was more influential than Rockefeller.

A second measure is simply to ask the various staffs about the Vice-President's influence. Did Rockefeller have any influence over the Ford agenda? Only 33 percent of the Rockefeller staff said yes. Only 14 percent of the Ford staff said yes. Did Mondale have any influence over the Carter agenda? One hundred percent of the Mondale staff said yes. Over 80 percent of the Carter staff said yes. Moreover, when asked to estimate how much influence the respective Vice-Presidents had, 82 percent of the Mondale staff answered "a great deal," while not one of the Rockefeller aides selected that category.* Thus, if staff perceptions are accepted as an indicator of influence, Mondale emerges as an important player in the White House policy process.

One last measure is to ask whether the conditions of influence were met by the two Vice-Presidents. As noted earlier, in searching for tracks of influence, several questions must be answered: Were Mondale and Rockefeller physically present in the major policy meetings? Had they met with the President shortly before the final meetings? If they were absent, were members of their staffs physically present? Had they shaped decisions earlier in the process? Using these criteria, Mondale once again emerges as more influential than Rockefeller. Mondale met all criteria consistently, while Rockefeller generally succeeded only in his private meetings with Ford. Mondale was usually present at the major policy meetings—including discussions on the budget, foreign policy, and domestic affairs—and had ample representation when he was physically absent. Rockefeller, however, was generally excluded from the major meetings and had virtually no representation when he was gone. Whereas Mondale's tracks run across most chronologies of domestic and foreign policy making in the Carter administration, Rockefeller's tracks are often missing. Rockefeller was consistently frozen away from major policy meetings, most importantly the gatherings leading to Ford's spending freeze on domestic policy in late 1975. Thus, if Rockefeller was to have influence, it had to come in one forum: the private weekly meeting with Ford. If Mondale was to have influence, it could

---

*It is my belief that these responses can be trusted; that the answers are valid indicators of influence. After conducting over one hundred interviews for this book, and over two hundred for other research, I am convinced that the White House staffs are generally honest, particularly when they are given absolute assurances of confidentiality. Once the staff members feel they are protected, interviews become an excellent tool for uncovering patterns of White House activity. After a year of interviewing for this book, I still could not detect any significant bias in the staff responses. Though there was predictable aggrandizement among the staffs, the interviews remain the clearest guide to Rockefeller's and Mondale's influence inside the White House.

come in any number of forums: the weekly lunch, the Friday foreign policy breakfast, the deputies meetings, the senior staff meetings, the ad hoc discussions.

None of this is to suggest that Rockefeller failed as an adviser. He performed that role well. He had access to the Ford agenda through private meetings with the President. He had information and policy expertise. According to his staff, he rarely went to see Ford without some new idea or program. As one Rockefeller aide remarked: "The briefing books for the meetings were based on whatever was hot—inflation, defense, Reagan, cruise missiles, SALT II. We would set a time for the meeting, ask the Vice-President what he wanted to talk about, and prepare some talking points. One briefing book went to Ford and the other stayed with the Vice-President. None went to Rumsfeld." Yet, whatever the agenda, Rockefeller was not as successful in gaining Ford's interest in his ideas as Mondale was with Carter. Rockefeller was a senior adviser in the White House, but not particularly influential. According to a Ford presidential aide, Rockefeller had input, but little influence.

> Was Rockefeller a failure? Not to my mind. What I know is that we met with the President frequently. Rockefeller and his deputy, Jim Cannon, would sit on one side of the President's desk and I would sit with my deputy on the other. Rockefeller would put his cup of coffee on the edge of the desk and weigh in with whatever he considered important. And the President listened. Ford didn't usually take Rockefeller's advice, particularly on the budget side, but he did listen and did ask questions. And Rockefeller would sit there and stir his coffee with the bow of his glasses and answer. Ford valued the advice. He wouldn't have met with Rockefeller if he didn't.

Compare that assessment with Jordan's view of Mondale:

> Mondale's role as Vice President was real. He was the only person in the White House other than the President who saw the "PDB"—the President's Daily Briefing. This document, which contained the country's most secret information, was compiled overnight, hand delivered to the White House, and carried by the President's secretary every morning in a red folder from the Oval Office down the hall to Mondale's office. Mondale got a copy of every domestic and foreign policy memo given to the President, and was automatically included in all substantive meetings and discussions. He saw, read, heard, and was privy to virtually everything that was available to the President. Carter made it plain from the very first day that everyone who worked in the White House had two bosses, the President and the Vice President. That admonition was heeded (*New Republic*, 6 June 1983).

In the following pages, I explore the Rockefeller and Mondale Vice-Presidencies in more detail, looking for answers that might explain the contrasts in influence. As we shall see, Rockefeller had most of the basic advisory resources, but faced severe shortages in his influence resources, particularly internal capital and Ford's own persuadability.

ROCKEFELLER

Upon accepting the vice-presidential nomination in August 1974, Rockefeller had a number of reasons to expect substantive responsibilities and impact. First, he had Ford's own assurances that he would be given a major role in domestic policy. Though Rockefeller later had problems remembering whether Ford had promised him the Domestic Council in those early meetings, he did have the President's agreement that the Vice-President would be a key player in the domestic policy process. Second, Rockefeller had the self-confidence of a four-time governor of New York. As James Richley, a Ford assistant and historian, argues:

> When Ford offered him the vice-presidency, it seemed to Rockefeller that he might after all have the opportunity to apply his vision and resources at the summit of national authority, even if not as president. (And if he were the incumbent vice-president, who could be sure what 1976 would bring?) He liked and respected Ford—"loved the guy"—but he probably shared Nixon's view that Ford was not likely to be a dynamic national leader. Rockefeller saw that the staff Ford was bringing to the White House would need a great deal of help in managing the executive branch. He anticipated a good working relationship with Hartmann, whom he had first known as a journalist, and who he assumed would remain Ford's closest personal adviser. Buchen and Seidman were members of the Grand Rapids affiliate of the eastern establishment that had always formed part of his constituency. He had also formed a friendly association with Haig, who he thought might be staying on as chief of staff (1981, p. 299).

Third, though Ford had generally been conservative on most policy issues, there were signs that he was drifting toward a more liberal position. Who better than Rockefeller to anchor the liberal wing of a new Republican coalition? As one observer noted: "There was no reason for him to suspect that he would be thrown off the ticket in less than a year. The whole future looked good. Ford seemed to be willing to give him a major role and Rockefeller was more than willing to take one. Given the Mondale and Rockefeller Vice-Presidencies, anyone would have picked Rockefeller's as the most likely to succeed."

During the first few months, Rockefeller did succeed. He won control of the Domestic Council after a bitter contest with Donald Rumsfeld. He won Ford's signature on the Energy Independence Authority, which would have provided over $100 billion in federal loan guarantees for energy development. He also persuaded Ford to reestablish the office of White House Science and Technology and was involved in the denial of New York City's request for emergency funds. In the first three months following

Rockefeller's confirmation, the new Vice-President was an active participant inside the administration. Yet, almost as quickly as he had risen, Rockefeller was frozen out of the policy process. As one Rockefeller aide argued:

> There were really two periods in the Rockefeller Vice-Presidency. The first ran only a couple of months and was one of influence. Rockefeller took over the Domestic Council and started producing some interesting programs. The second started in March 1975 and lasted the rest of the term. The political staff was able to cut Rockefeller out and persuade Ford that he couldn't win in 1976 with Rockefeller on the ticket. After Rockefeller was defeated inside the White House, he spent the rest of his time on his policy forums. He'd get a few cabinet members together and go out around the country on a "dog-and-pony" show.

Though Rockefeller continued to meet frequently with Ford, he lost whatever influence he once had. He was still a senior adviser, but he had no impact.

There are at least seven reasons why Rockefeller's influence dropped inside the Ford administration: (1) the long delay in his confirmation, (2) his problems securing policy information, (3) his acceptance of line assignments, (4) the rise of strong opponents, (5) Rockefeller's personal style, (6) the political problems outside the Ford White House, and (7) Ford's own management style and policy goals.

The Long Delay

Of the Ford and Rockefeller aides interviewed, 83 percent mentioned the long delay in Rockefeller's confirmation as a cause of his later frustration in shaping policy. Rockefeller had been nominated to the Vice-Presidency on 20 August 1974, but was not confirmed until 19 December. According to Reichley:

> Looking back, Rockefeller believed that if Congress had moved quickly to confirm him as vice-president, his relationship with the Ford White House, and perhaps the nature of the Ford presidency, might have been different. But Congress did not move quickly. Democratic liberals and some of Rockefeller's old enemies among Republican conservatives on the congressional committees reviewing the nomination took full advantage of the unprecedented opportunity to probe the size and reach of the Rockefeller fortune — not only Nelson Rockefeller's personal holdings, but also those of his brothers and other members of the Rockefeller family (1981, pp. 300-301).

Several aides who worked on the confirmation hearings reported that Rockefeller came close to withdrawing when the hearings turned to other members of his family. Whatever the reasons for the delay — whether congressional curiosity about the family fortune or a Democratic plot to keep Rockefeller from campaigning for Republicans in the 1974 midterm elections — the delay hurt the new Vice-President on a number of fronts.

First, the unexpected problems with Congress cost Rockefeller some internal capital in the Ford White House. As one Ford assistant noted: "We did not expect him to have any troubles and all of a sudden he was embroiled in controversy. There were rumors about his family, rumors about books written by former aides to discredit opponents, rumors about his manipulation of Ford, rumors about his withdrawal. We had hoped for a clean confirmation, but ended up spending some capital rescuing him from Congress." Some of the Ford staff blamed the problems on Rockefeller's national reputation, while others accepted the delay as an aftereffect of Watergate. However, many suggested that it was an unnecessary waste of political capital at the very time the Ford administration was in deepest trouble. "After the pardon," a Ford aide said, "the last thing we needed was to have to bail Nelson Rockefeller out of trouble. We needed him to be on the road helping us."

Second, the delay effectively froze Rockefeller out of the domestic policy process during the first four months of the administration. During the hearings, Rockefeller did not engage in any policy planning nor did he have contact with the Ford staff. Though Ford offered him an office in the EOB, Rockefeller did not accept, and Ford eventually withdrew the idea. As a Rockefeller aide noted:

> We studiously avoided working on policy during the confirmation hearings. We agreed that the Vice-President shouldn't be connected to the administration until the hearings were over. It was during the confirmation that the chief-of-staff system was developed under Rumsfeld and the paper flow established. We weren't involved in that nor did we get involved in any of the early discussions on policy. We had nothing to do with the decision to drop national health insurance from the 1975 agenda. We had nothing to do with the pardon or the amnesty.

A second Rockefeller aide agreed. "You have no idea just how time-consuming those hearings were. We had to account for every penny in the governor's accounts. We had to produce every piece of correspondence with the federal government over the past thirty years. We had to explain every possible problem. We had no time left to think about policy or how the Ford administration ought to be run." Moreover, because Rockefeller was already behind in experience with the federal government, he lost four months on his learning curve. Since all of the Rockefeller staff remained in New York until December, the new Vice-President did not benefit from staff learning either. "Rockefeller went through the confirmation with very little contact with the Ford people," an aide reported. "He was four months behind at the start and wasn't receiving any briefings to note during the period. The only source for any advance work was the Commission on Critical Choices, but most of that material was already a couple of years old." As one Ford aide concluded: "Given more time, I think Rocky would have come up with some new ideas that would have fit within the budgetary constraints. The fact was that he didn't have the time."

Third, the delay meant that Rockefeller was absent from the White House during the critical time when working relationships and networks were formed within the President's staff. It is during the first few months of an administration that lasting coalitions are often built. As aides scurry about looking for desks and phones, they also develop policy contacts. Unfortunately, Rockefeller was gone during that formative period in the Ford White House. According to a Ford aide: "A lot of things happened over the first four months. The White House was frozen in place by December. Rockefeller missed the opportunity to build from the ground up. The people who eventually gained the power to cut him off might not have been so successful with Rockefeller in place. Or, better still, they might have owed their jobs to him." A Rockefeller assistant concurred. "The whole context of the Ford Presidency worked against Rockefeller. There was no campaign where the two staffs could work together, no time to become acquainted. We were thrown into the caldron together and had to work it out as best we could. We got along OK, but never had a chance to prove our loyalty and trust during a campaign."

By the time Rockefeller arrived in December, Ford had changed policy directions from a liberal drift back to the right. According to James Cannon: "Rockefeller really thought he was going to make decisions and indeed hoped he was. But the fact is, between the time that Rockefeller was nominated and the time he was confirmed, Ford became a very different person as President. I recognized that, because I had seen this through the eyes of Jack Marsh and various other people I was working with at the White House. I had seen this change, but I don't think Rockefeller did" (Turner 1978, p. 270). Many Rockefeller staff members suggest that the change might not have occurred had the Vice-President been in place in September or November. As Reichley concludes:

> While confirmation of the nomination hung fire, Rockefeller felt it would not be appropriate for him to play an active role within the White House. When he finally took office at the end of December, it seemed to him that the outlook and direction of the administration had changed significantly since Ford had offered him the vice-presidency four months before. "When I was appointed," he later said, "Al Haig was still chief of staff. By the time I was confirmed, there had been a change of personnel in the White House. Don Rumsfeld had come in" (1981, p. 302).

Yet, it is not clear that Rockefeller would have moved against Rumsfeld and the growing political opposition inside the White House even had he been confirmed quickly. "He didn't have much against Rummy at the start," a Ford aide argued, "and never suspected that Rummy was gunning for him.

Had Rocky been confirmed early, I don't think he would have seen the danger early enough. He didn't suspect anything until it was too late." However, Rockefeller certainly would have been in place and better prepared when Rumsfeld made his move.

Information

Whatever the cost of the delay in terms of capital or coalition building, Rockefeller was also hurt by his lack of information and his acceptance of time-consuming line assignments. Both affected his ability to compete for influence within the policy process. Since internal influence is often based on the simple force of argument, Rockefeller's gubernatorial experience may have cost him valuable contact with national issues and players. As a Ford OMB assistant noted: "Neither Rockefeller nor his staff knew who the critical players were. They knew the people at the top, but not lower down. There was a need for learning, for time to become accustomed, but the delay in confirmation meant they all had to hit the ground running. It slowed their ability to come up with useful recommendations for the President. And, since we had become accustomed to working without them, there was no incentive to wait."

Rockefeller's problems with information came at two levels. First, he was often denied information on the progress of issues in the presidential policy process. Though this information is important to the advisory role, it is also necessary for influence. Rockefeller did not have the information needed to block opponents or move his own ideas forward. Since he often did not know where decisions were being made, he had no opportunity to either give advice or press for influence. The appointment of Bo Callaway as the Ford campaign manager in mid-1975, for instance, caught Rockefeller unaware. Callaway had been a historical political enemy of Rockefeller and immediately announced that the Vice-President should be dropped from the ticket. According to the Rockefeller staff, the Vice-President was not notified of the Callaway appointment until it was too late. "Nobody asked Rockefeller," an assistant reported, "because they probably knew what he would say. Ford called Rockefeller the day of the announcement and told him about Callaway. Rockefeller was completely surprised. And I don't think Ford even realized what had happened." The same problem occurred with the 1975 budget decisions. As noted earlier, Rockefeller was never told that Ford was considering a freeze on domestic spending, a decision that would profoundly shape Rockefeller's Domestic Council duties. Without that information, Rockefeller was unable to advise Ford against the option or to cut off the decision at the preliminary stages. As a Ford assistant suggested:

The spending freeze was thought up by Jim Lynn at OMB and Alan Greenspan at CEA. They thought it was a great idea and sold it to Ford without Rockefeller ever suspecting a thing. It was a classic way to freeze the Vice-President. I don't think either Lynn or Greenspan had anything against Rockefeller personally, but they didn't like his style of governing. I honestly believe that they were frightened of his persuasive skills and didn't want him knowing about anything until it was a *fait accompli.* The freeze has to be a classic end run of the domestic policy machinery.

Though the Ford advisory system was technically designed to include input from all major actors, Rockefeller was easily excluded toward the end of his first year in office.

Rockefeller's second information shortage came with regard to specific policy issues. Rockefeller and his staff were simply unable to keep pace with the flow of issues in the first months of their term. Already behind in the learning curve because of the delay, Rockefeller and his staff were frustrated in their effort to build an information base quickly. As a Ford officer suggested:

Nelson came in with the feeling that he was going to have a major role in domestic policy. The people he brought with him were his basis for playing a major role in domestic policy. I don't know what the understanding was between Ford and Rockefeller, but it was clear that, in spite of considerable governmental experience, they were pretty far back on the learning curve. They were the latecomers. Their work experience was in state government and their perspectives on welfare, health, energy, etc., were much narrower. They had very limited policy experience and, as a result, there was a need for a lot of information building. They had good political skills, but not at the federal level.

Whether the staff was quite as far behind as the Ford aide argued, there were problems catching up during the first few months. Because Rockefeller had not been briefed during the confirmation period, and because his staff had remained in New York, there was a significant gap between the vice-presidential and presidential staffs on information. "We could not communicate with them as easily," a Rockefeller Domestic Council aide acknowledged. "They had already developed a code and had some common background. We found it difficult at times to break into their system, to speak the same language on the issues. Sometimes they would refer to briefing papers that had been circulated a month or two before we came on board. It was more of a problem because they didn't really want us involved to start with, but we could have used some more backgrounding."

Line Assignments

Rockefeller's information problems were complicated by his acceptance of the two major line assignments: (1) the Domestic Council and (2) the chairmanship of the commission on CIA activities. Both assignments involved significant commitments of time and energy that might have been better spent in the advisory process. Both involved internal conflict and placed Rockefeller in the middle of bureaucratic disputes. The CIA investigation, for instance, squeezed Rockefeller between liberals in Congress and conservatives in the Republican party. On one hand, Rockefeller did not want to whitewash allegations of CIA misconduct during Watergate and the Vietnam war. On the other hand, Rockefeller did not want to further alienate conservatives with a harsh indictment of the agency. In the end, Rockefeller failed with both. Congressional investigators branded his report as a cover-up and enacted a much stricter accounting of the CIA through the intelligence committees; conservatives attacked his report as a framework for the destruction of the agency and as the starting point for the congressional effort. Little wonder that one Rockefeller aide saw the CIA commission as part of an overall plot to discredit the Rockefeller Vice-Presidency. "Rumsfeld finally wrapped Rockefeller up in the CIA review, a real hot potato, destined for conflict. It was a no-win issue and Rockefeller took the bait."

If Rockefeller was tricked into the CIA commission—which is highly doubtful—he pursued the Domestic Council with a characteristic fervor. From his very first conversation with Ford in August 1974, Rockefeller pressed for the domestic policy assignment. According to several aides, Rockefeller believed that White House power flowed from formal positions; that Kissinger had risen to his heights by using the National Security Council post as a power base. Rockefeller was not comfortable being a free-floater. "He wanted a title beyond being Vice-President," an assistant remarked. "He didn't think there was much power in just being Vice-President. He wanted to be chairman of the Domestic Council or chief of staff. He was one who believed that his influence came from a specific duty. That makes some sense when you look back over his career." Indeed, being an assistant secretary of state (1944) or an under secretary of HEW (1953) or governor of the State of New York might well lead a politician to see influence as a product of position. Being a United States senator or representative might lead a politician to a very different conclusion. As a Ford presidential assistant argued: "If you've been in the U.S. House for twenty years, you sooner or later learn that power is fluid. It doesn't belong to the speakership, but to the Speaker. Ford learned that when he beat Charlie Halleck for the minority leadership. It's something that Nelson Rockefeller never learned. He thought that being vice chairman of the Domestic Council would be enough. He was wrong about that. Power doesn't belong to anyone in the White House for very long."

Among the Ford staff, there were at least three arguments used against the Rockefeller assignment. One was organizational. According to one aide: "It takes a new man on the Domestic Council staff almost a year just to acquire the minimum knowledge and information to deal with the issues. You can't find people off the street to do this kind of work; it would be six months before they found their way to the bathroom." A second was the fear that the Vice-President would take over domestic policy just like his protégé, Kissinger, had taken over foreign policy. According to the same aide: "If I were coming on new, I would want to know how things get done, what button to push. Basically, the council is people oriented. There are an awful lot of subtleties to get the work done properly. The new guy should make the best use of the people who are here and who have shown their loyalty to the President." A third argument was the notion that Ford people should be making Ford policy. As the aide concluded: "Over a period of time there will ultimately be changes, the qualities of the present staff will be reassessed but that will be resolved on the basis of chemistry between the old members and the new people. I wouldn't rush in and make a clean break. That would result in a complete slowdown" (*National Journal*, 25 Jan. 1975). All of these arguments carried some weight, particularly since Rockefeller did not take control of the council until the Ford administration was seven months old. But perhaps the most persuasive argument against Rockefeller came from the Vice-President's own status. According to a Ford aide: "You can't make a Vice-President a line assistant. He carries too much damn weight. You can't put a Vice-President in between staffers. Either the staffers won't talk in the presence of the veep or they'll cut him to ribbons."

The Domestic Council assignment, of course, became the most bitter episode of the Rockefeller Vice-Presidency. It was mentioned as the primary cause of the Vice-President's loss of influence by 77 percent of the Ford and Rockefeller staffs. From the start, members of the Ford staff viewed Rockefeller's assignment as sure evidence of his presidential ambitions; members of the conservative wing of the Republican party viewed Ford's acquiescence as a test of his purity for future election; Rockefeller himself saw the Domestic Council as guaranteed access to the Ford legislative agenda. All three were wrong. For Rockefeller, the assignment became an albatross, absorbing vast quantities of administrative energy, creating conflicts within the White House staff, and providing little real value in shaping the increasingly conservative Ford program. Whatever the cause of the problem—whether Nixon holdovers on the Domestic Council staff (Hartmann's explanation), Rockefeller's own bureaucratic naiveté (the staff's explanation), or deliberate sabotage by Rumsfeld (Rockefeller's explanation)—the Domestic Council became a source of frustration instead of influence.

By the end of 1975, Rockefeller asked to be relieved of the assignment he had worked so hard to achieve. Rockefeller's theory that internal power derived from formal authority was disproved. All of the mandates for long-range planning, policy coordination, forecasting, evaluation, legislative clearance, etc., given in Ford's original February memorandum appointing Rockefeller as vice-chairman of the council were useless in actually performing those roles in the White House policy process. Indeed, as one

Rockefeller aide complained: "Those mandates were so far off target, it's hard to guess what Ford had in mind when he wrote them. But Rockefeller had the paper and assumed that was it." A second Rockefeller aide concurred. "Rockefeller's line assignments were what destroyed his base. First, his CIA recommendations were widely received as being too weak. Then his proposals for a change in federal pay rates were cut down. Then the Domestic Council wasn't able to get a single new program placed in the 1976 State of the Union address. Rockefeller subjected himself to all that criticism and was a sitting duck for any conservative who wanted to score some points back home." A Ford Domestic Council assistant offered a final observation on the line assignment. "Ford and Rockefeller didn't know what they were getting into. Even Rockefeller came to recognize the mistake. He shouldn't have taken the entire Domestic Council apparatus. It tied his hands. Had he not been running everything, he might have been a stronger advocate. He came to realize that he needed to be free of that kind of long-term baggage."

Opponents

Rockefeller also faced stiff competition inside the White House. Part of the competition came from a single player: Donald Rumsfeld. Part came from fiscal conservatives at OMB and CEA. Both constituted strong opposition to Rockefeller's domestic agenda. It is important to note, however, that Rockefeller was not singled out for special attention. Though Ford sought to project an image of calm, his White House staff was beset by territorial infighting long before Rockefeller arrived. One of Ford's first decisions as President was to keep most of the Nixon staff on board. As Ford told Reichley: "I felt . . . when I came into office that it would be wrong to clean out the Nixon appointees on a wholesale basis. Everyone, I felt, should have four or five months to give them a reasonable chance to find other jobs." Yet, as Reichley concludes:

> Besides humanitarian concern, Ford's slowness to remove Nixon's people grew out of his realization that in many cases qualified replacements were not quickly available. During his career in Congress, Ford had operated with a surprisingly thin staff. For advice and legwork he had largely relied on trusted colleagues like Laird, Goodell, and Rumsfeld. After 1969 he drew on the assistance of the White House congressional liaison staff. As a result, he had no extensive entourage of experienced political and governmental technicians to take with him to the executive branch (1981, p. 293).

As Donald Rumsfeld argued, the decision to retain many of Nixon's people created inevitable tension with the new Ford staff.

> The president . . . was subject to two tugs. On the one hand, he recognized that these people [Nixon appointees] were overwhelmingly fine, decent human beings. Most of them had never thought of doing anything wrong. To fire them

immediately would give the impression that he thought they were in some way connected with Watergate. In addition, they were skilled people. He needed them to operate the institutions of government. On the other hand, executive authority under Nixon had come to appear, both externally and internally, illegitimate. Things had reached a state in the government where if someone would say, "Good morning," others would think, "What does he really mean by that?" This attitude had developed momentum, inertia, and had spread to the entire country. . . . So the first thing the president had to do was to restore a sense of legitimacy to the executive branch. There was a need for continuity, but also there was a need for change—or for a sense of change. The solution, Ford decided, was to make the minimal number of changes that would be needed to allow the critical mass that remained to become once more legitimate. His aim was to create a Ford presidency, rather than a Nixon presidency over which Ford was now presiding (in Reichley 1981, p. 295).

Ford eventually fired Alexander Haig, Nixon's former chief of staff (and former secretary of state under Reagan), and hired Rumsfeld, a congressional colleague, then United States ambassador to NATO. Rumsfeld had participated in Ford's August transition, but had returned to NATO. He came back to the United States in late September for his father's funeral and was invited to become Ford's chief of staff.

When Rumsfeld arrived at the White House, he faced a severely divided staff. Robert Hartmann, Ford's vice-presidential chief of staff, had been moved to a counselor's spot, but refused to yield his old turf without a fight. Nixon holdovers fought with new Ford appointees, Cabinet members fought with the White House and Ford shifted away from his initial spokes of a wheel system to a more hierarchical framework. It is not surprising that Rumsfeld tried to consolidate his power as quickly as possible. Rumsfeld designed a new paper flow that started and ended in his office, while trying to reduce the number of old friends with access to the President. However, though Hartmann had been moved, he still retained his friendship with Ford. He continued to advise the President through back-channels. Philip Buchen and William Seidman, Ford's former Michigan law partners, also continued to operate as semifree agents.

Thus, when Rockefeller arrived with his planeload of staff in December, Rumsfeld faced his greatest challenge. If Rockefeller could succeed in breaking the Rumsfeld system, the rest of the White House staff might follow suit. In an administration filled with latent conflict, Rumsfeld saw Rockefeller as a threat, both administratively and politically. Had Rockefeller arrived first, Rumsfeld might never have been hired. But by the time Rockefeller was confirmed, Rumsfeld was already entrenched. As one Ford aide remarked: "Rockefeller thought he would be working directly with Ford, for whom he had a genuine liking. He also thought he would be working with Alexander Haig. He sensed he could work with most of the staff. I don't think he had ever heard of Donald Rumsfeld before he became Vice-President." Indeed, in what may have been an apocryphal story, Reichley reports that

> actually, Rockefeller and Rumsfeld had met. In 1971 Nixon had sent Rumsfeld to a meeting on revenue sharing in Albany. Rockefeller repeatedly referred to Rumsfeld as "Ruckelshaus," apparently confusing him with William Ruckelshaus, Nixon's appointee as director of the Environmental Protection Agency. After Rockefeller had made this error for about the fifth time, Rumsfeld stepped forward and said: "Governor, my name is Donald Rumsfeld, and I think you should remember that." Rockefeller, evidently, did not remember (1981, p. 309).

In all, 53 percent of the Ford and Rockefeller staffs blamed Rumsfeld for the Vice-President's drop inside the administration. Some argued that Rumsfeld was acting out of frustration in dealing with administrative headaches. As the chief of staff, Rumsfeld naturally wanted all of the paper to flow through him. In the initial arguments over the Domestic Council, however, Rockefeller had proposed direct access to the President. Paper would first move to Ford, then to Rumsfeld. As Ford notes:

> I could see both sides of the argument. Nelson felt that he knew more about domestic policy and politics than Don, and he was probably right. On the other hand, Don was the man responsible for organizing and managing the West Wing. To do so effectively, he had to have control. Finally, after three of four unhappy meetings, I made the decision to go along with Nelson. The paper would have to flow through Don as chief of staff, but Nelson would be in charge of domestic policy. To his credit, Don didn't complain. I'm sure he was disappointed, but the only comment he made was: "Fine, we'll try to make it work" (1979, p. 234).

According to most of the staff, Ford solved the Domestic Council question by taking the worst of both worlds. He gave Rockefeller the top spot, as well as authority to hire the staff director, James Cannon, and one deputy, Richard Dunham. However, Ford reserved a second deputy's position for James Cavanaugh, a Nixon appointee and a Rumsfeld ally, and kept many of the Nixon Domestic Council aides. As one Rockefeller assistant remarked: "Rockefeller only got the top of the cake. Cavanaugh was moved to a smaller office, but Rockefeller wasn't able to get all of the positions he needed." By the end of the first three months of the experiment, Dunham resigned and Cavanaugh became the sole deputy.

Though there were administrative problems, 57 percent of the staff saw Rumsfeld's own political ambitions as a source of conflict. As one Ford aide argued: "From everything I saw, Rumsfeld wanted the nomination for himself in 1976. From the first day, he was at Rockefeller's throat. He headed the group to dump Rockefeller and worked behind the scenes to embarrass and humiliate the Vice-President, using all of the old stereotypes about Vice-Presidents to Rockefeller's detriment." A second Ford assistant agreed. "I believe that Rumsfeld always wanted the Vice-Presidency for himself. He was angry that he didn't get it when Ford appointed Rockefeller and wanted to push Rockefeller off the ticket." Whatever Rumsfeld's ambition, the conflict involved more than just administrative order. To the end of the term, Rockefeller blamed Rumsfeld for most of the problems, accusing him of sabotage. According to one outside observer: "There was no love lost between those two. Some was due to the organizational struggle over the Domestic Council, but most was a very personal matter. They were both savvy old politicians, but Rumsfeld was a little bit stronger. A great deal of ambition got mixed up in there. There are always many reasons why politicians act the way they do, but Rockefeller and Rumsfeld may have simply hated each other."

Given the lack of administrative or personal rapport, Rumsfeld still possessed more bureaucratic weapons. He had been in the administration longer; he controlled the paper flow; he had more allies in the Republican right wing. As a Rockefeller Domestic Council aide argued:

> If there was a major decision in the works, Rockefeller had to hear about it from a reporter. That was Rumsfeld's way of making sure Rocky never had any impact. He would leak embarrassing material to the press, ignore Rockefeller's requests for meetings, make the Vice-President's staff rewrite Rockefeller's memos. He was a real hardballer and made sure Rockefeller felt the cold. And when he was done establishing himself and removing Rockefeller from any future on the ticket, he accepted Ford's nomination to the Department of Defense, becoming a very visible candidate for the Vice-Presidency in 1976.

Although Rumsfeld had a great deal of impact on Rockefeller's role, at least one Ford assistant noted that "people liked to blame Rumsfeld for everything that went wrong. Most of the people who complained were people who lost to him. I'm not sure about his grand designs, but I'll agree that Rumsfeld was a very ambitious individual who didn't let too many people get in his way."

Beyond Rockefeller's troubles with Rumsfeld, he found few other allies on the Ford staff. In a White House of many power centers, Rockefeller was unable to build any policy coalitions. Only Rumsfeld succeeded in forming a powerful internal coalition, drawing on James Lynn and Paul O'Neill at OMB. It was this group that effectively worked for the spending freeze on domestic policy in 1975. At times, the Rumsfeld/Lynn/O'Neill coalition was augmented by Alan Greenspan, chairman of the CEA. Together, this group pushed Ford toward a much more conservative fiscal policy in 1976. Though the economy was in a recession by then, Ford's conservative advisers persuaded him that the budget was the tool for combating unemployment. And though Ford initially proposed a $16 billion dollar tax cut to stimulate the economy, he eventually vetoed the legislation when it passed without a federal spending ceiling. As a Rockefeller assistant remarked: "At exactly the time you would have thought Nelson Rockefeller would have had the advantage, Rumsfeld and Lynn were able to move Ford toward the right. If any economic climate favored Rockefeller, it was a recession, but Rumsfeld had already cornered Ford." Though Greenspan and O'Neill were the key players in the decision, Rumsfeld had an important role. According to Michael Turner:

> ... the case of Ford's decision to hold his 1976 federal budget to a ceiling of $395 billion provides an example of Rumsfeld's less than neutral role behind the scenes. This decision was taken by Ford in an exclusive meeting with Greenspan, Lynn and Cheney. According to William Seidman, the initiative for the meeting was "mutually a Rumsfeld-Greenspan initiative." And when the decision was presented at an EPB [Economic Policy Board] meeting, Seidman further recalled that it was "mainly argued by Rumsfeld" as a "great political boon with a balance of tax cuts and spending cuts" (1978, p. 298).

Together, the triumvirate of Rumsfeld, Lynn, and Greenspan was able to thwart most of Rockefeller's arguments in both economic and domestic policy. Rockefeller's only acknowledged success during that period was the Energy Independence Authority, the $100 billion program to aid research and development in new energy areas. As the forerunner to Jimmy Carter's synfuels program, Rockefeller's proposal generated intense opposition from the conservative coalition. Unable to forestall Ford's decision—which some said was merely a symbolic gift to a beleaguered Vice-President—Lynn and Greenspan refused to support the program on Capitol Hill. Whatever Ford's reasons for giving "one to the Gipper," as an aide remarked, the President never pushed the program in Congress. Rockefeller had succeeded only at the agenda-setting stage, failing to gain passage of his program. Further, even had he won in Congress, Rockefeller's program faced strong opposition in the Federal Energy Agency, which had opposed the program from the start.

Perhaps Rockefeller's greatest frustration came in dealing with his own aides on the Domestic Council. Rockefeller often asked his aides to choose between Rumsfeld or himself. Thus, James Cannon, Rockefeller's long-time New York aide, found himself in the unenviable position of having to pick between his loyalty to the Vice-President and his duty to the President. As Cannon noted:

> I never made any bones (about it). I said that I work for Ford. I came here to work through Ford for the country. I never made any questions about it, my loyalty to Ford. When it came to choice though, I would give (Rockefeller) my best advice—but I worked for the President and not the Vice President. The

Vice President was my friend, my close ally, and I hoped it would (so) continue. But my responsibility was to Ford and what I believed was the right thing to recommend to him.

I (was) going over physically to the White House (to) undertake a very difficult job. And I told Rockefeller that his interest was my interest, that I not fail. (I explained) that every s.o.b. and his brother over there were looking for me to stumble and fail and not, literally not, to be able to keep up with the paperwork (Turner 1978, p. 111).

Much of the conflict between Cannon and Rockefeller surfaced over Cavanaugh, the Domestic Council holdover from the Nixon administration. Rockefeller saw Cavanaugh as Rumsfeld's spy on the Domestic Council and asked Cannon to fire him. Cannon refused. According to a Rockefeller aide, Cannon eventually had to tell the Vice-President to leave him alone, that he was the President's Domestic Council director, not the Vice-President's man. "Rockefeller was pushing Cannon too hard and Cannon blew off by telling the Vice-President to get lost. But Cannon was always a Rockefeller man and couldn't change that. He was still loyal, but worked for the President first." As I note shortly, Mondale viewed his former aides differently. They were no longer *his* staff, but presidential assistants. Mondale's approach was to treat them as informal conduits, not personal aides.

All totaled, Rockefeller's competition in the White House was well organized, generally cohesive, and in place several months before he arrived. Finding few ideological or political allies in an increasingly conservative administration, Rockefeller's opportunities for influence were limited. His competition had been seasoned by Watergate and gave little ground to the new Vice-President.

Rockefeller's Style

Of the presidential and vice-presidential staff members interviewed, 85 percent pointed to Rockefeller's style as a problem in his influence over the term. As noted earlier, Rockefeller worked as an advocate in the Ford policy process, taking highly visible positions on a variety of issues. The Energy Independence Authority, for instance, was clearly identified as a Rockefeller program inside the White House. His staff designed the proposal, argued for its internal adoption, worked for its passage on Capitol Hill, and took both the credit and the blame for the results. Rockefeller's highly visible advocate's position caused a variety of problems in his policy influence. First, by taking open stands on most questions, Rockefeller allowed outsiders to measure his success. Instead of remaining quiet, Rockefeller was willing to tell the media what programs he favored and opposed. In doing so, the media were eventually able to calculate his relative success. Since Rockefeller was not as successful as other, discreet advisers, his failures came to shape his reputation for influence. Second, even though Rockefeller was already opposed by a number of White House senior staffers, his willingness to expose his positions may have created unnecessary opposition. "When Lynn or O'Neill found out that something was a Rockefeller idea," an aide reported, "that really made them jump. Nelson had a reputation as being a good salesman and that made everyone sit up and notice when his ideas came down the line. He might have been more successful by disguising his ideas and lobbying only with Ford. Whenever he circulated one of his proposals, the sharks would come in to feed." Third, Rockefeller's visibility created the kind of threat that released the natural staff hostility. Long before Rockefeller was confirmed, the White House staff was introduced to images of Rockefeller's power in cartoons, editorials, and so forth. Fears of a take-over led to Rumsfeld's attempt to keep Rockefeller off the Domestic Council. In the Vice-President's early maneuvers, Ford aides could see the start of a Rockefeller presidential bid in 1976. Whether or not the image was true, Rockefeller did little to diffuse staff fears. Instead, his efforts on the energy bill seemed to confirm what many Ford staffers already suspected— that Rockefeller would go over and around Ford to get his programs enacted.

Rockefeller's style flowed from his long career as a national figure. He had campaigned for President three times in the 1960s and had a national reputation to equal that of any other Republican, including Jerry Ford. As a Ford assistant acknowledged:

> Both Mondale and Bush were defeated rivals. Remember that Mondale ran for the presidential nomination in 1974 and gave up because he didn't want to spend that much time in Holiday Inns. Bush was much more interested and pushed Reagan in the beginning. The fact that both Vice-Presidents had been defeated or forced out in the primaries made them less of a threat to their Presidents. Rockefeller was not in that class. He was more than Ford's equal. He was actually stooping to take the nomination. Ford was supremely self-confident to even think of Rockefeller as Vice-President.

Moreover, as a former governor, Rockefeller had a normal desire to be first. He had never worked in the House or Senate, had never learned what was involved in bargaining with a staff of equals. According to one of his most frequent opponents inside the White House: "Rockefeller was a leader, not used to being second. Ask an understudy at a Broadway show how they like it sitting there night after night. I had a lot of sympathy for him, but had to oppose him on a number of issues. I tried to scuttle his energy program every time I could." Indeed, even a sampling of quotes from Ford and Rockefeller aides demonstrates the importance of Rockefeller's own background in shaping both his influence and their perceptions:

> When Ford asked Rockefeller to be Vice-President, I told him not to take the job. A Nelson Rockefeller and a major political heavyweight just couldn't adjust (Rockefeller aide).

From time to time, Rockefeller forgot he was Vice-President; sometimes he thought of himself as a chief officer. He had been running a state for fourteen years and it was hard to break the habit. He had never been forced to compete inside any administration (Rockefeller aide).

Rockefeller liked to say "I'm never going to be President so now I'm going to be a loyal staff man." By the nature of his reputation, it was impossible for him to do that. He kept saying: "I'm going to do it. Just be a mouse in the White House." It was bullshit (Ford aide).

Rockefeller had been king so long, he didn't know how to be a courtier (Ford aide).

Rockefeller's problem wasn't just a personality clash with Rumsfeld. The institutional reason was in having a staff of unequals. Rockefeller exceeded his mandate and used the Vice-Presidency and his access to get around the senior staff. He wanted to be a senior staffer, but didn't want to follow the senior staff rules. His frustration was less in the lack of power and more in comparison to his power as governor of New York. New York was his play toy (Ford aide).

He has a totally different role than when he was Governor of New York, but I don't notice any change in his demeanor; he's still Nelson Rockefeller, he's still an executive and still a great force. He's now on a greater stage, although some might say he has a smaller role in affecting policy. As Governor, his voice was supreme. But he's still optimistic and full of energy; I've seldom seen him down or lose his temper (Peter Wallison, personal assistant to Rockefeller, *National Journal*, 18 Oct. 1975).

Rockefeller is incapable at his level of experience of being a staff assistant to anybody. He was an executive. He was a decision maker. For fifteen years he had been a governor, he had been the chief executive. You can't put that genie back in the bottle — where you have to be when you're the staff assistant (James Cannon, in Turner 1978, p. 293).

None of this should suggest that Rockefeller entered office determined to undermine the Ford Presidency. Indeed, many of the Rockefeller and Ford staff members admired the Vice-President's self-restraint in the first months. Faced with obvious insults from Rumsfeld — a memo returned for grammatical corrections, leaks to the press, end runs of the Domestic Council — Rockefeller did not threaten to resign. Nor did he go to the press with his complaints. Instead, he went to Ford and asked the President to resolve the disputes. Though Rockefeller was willing to take highly visible *internal* stands on most issues, it was not until the summer of 1975 that he went outside with his frustrations, attacking Rumsfeld's continuing sabotage, the appointment of Bo Callaway, the refusal of the Ford staff to push the energy plan in Congress.

The problem may have been that Rockefeller could not adapt to his new lack of status fast enough. As Peter Wallison noted above, he was "still an executive" in October 1975, when he might have been more successful

as a "staffer." As another Rockefeller assistant noted, the Vice-President
may have been blinded by old habits and his own self-confidence:

> Nobody should have known better about the Vice-Presidency than Nelson
> Rockefeller. First, he used to play tennis with Henry Wallace up at Pocantico
> Hills. He knew it was a frustrating job. Second, under Eisenhower, he headed a
> study group on what to do with Vice-President Nixon. He concluded back then
> that there was very little for the Vice-President to do. But, when Ford called, he
> had no choice but to accept. In the back of his mind, he understood the limita-
> tions of the office, but he also saw himself as a stronger and more creative leader
> who could somehow make it work. That was always the image he had as gover-
> nor and it was how he deceived himself as Vice-President. I don't think he ac-
> tually admitted the failure until a year or so after he left the office.

The Political Context

Much of Rockefeller's trouble came from his long-term association with
the liberal wing of the Republican party. As a Ford aide argued: "1975
wasn't a good vintage for liberals. We had a very hard fight coming against
Reagan in the primaries and had some tough economic problems. It wasn't
a good year for Rockefeller or any of the liberals in the party." All totaled,
73 percent of the Ford and Rockefeller staffs interviewed pointed to the
Vice-President's liberalism as a problem in his influence over the term.
Though many Rockefeller aides argued that the Vice-President had been
moving toward a more conservative stance long before entering office,
Rockefeller was still widely perceived as a liberal in an administration of
conservatives. "Maybe Rockefeller had changed," an OMB opponent noted,
"but I always believed he was still of a time when money chased problems."

Rockefeller's reputation as a liberal was well deserved. He had campaigned for the Republican presidential nomination as a liberal in 1960,
1964, and 1968. He had even been offered the Democratic party's vice-presidential nomination by Humphrey in 1968. He had attacked Barry Goldwater, the standard-bearer of modern Republican conservatism, on the floor
of the 1964 convention, earning the lasting anger of the right wing of the
party. As four-term governor of New York, he had supported a variety of
liberal programs, including aid to education, urban renewal, civil rights,
and expanded welfare. During his fifteen years as governor, his state budget
quadrupled, while the number of state employees doubled. Yet, by the end
of his third term, Rockefeller had begun to change. He proposed a ceiling
on welfare costs, fought for a tighter state budget, opposed the bailout for
financially troubled New York City, and pushed the toughest law against
the sale and use of narcotics. Though Rockefeller was certainly more liberal
than Ford in 1974, he was much more conservative than he had once been.
His problem inside and outside the Ford administration came from decades
of party conflict, nursed by uncertainty within the party over Vietnam
and urban unrest, heightened by resentment of the Rockefeller fortune.

When Rockefeller became Vice-President, conservatives watched for any signs of his old liberalism. Would Rockefeller continue to attack the conservative wing? Would Rockefeller present some new proposal for government expansion? Rockefeller provided much of the answer in early Senate debates over Rule 22, which regulates cloture on filibusters. As noted in Chapter 2, Vice-Presidents have some impact on cloture by giving opinions from the chair on the permanence of Senate rules from one Congress to the next. In 1975, Rule 22 favored conservatives in the Democratic and Republican parties. At that time, the rule required two-thirds of the Senate to end a filibuster. However, when Senate members asked the new Vice-President for rules for changing the rule, Rockefeller argued that it could be changed by a simple majority, with filibusters subject to cloture by a simple majority. That opinion and subsequent debate convinced conservatives that Rockefeller had not changed. His ruling—whether right or wrong—gave Senate liberals an opportunity to change the cloture rule from two-thirds to three-fifths.

Moreover, Rockefeller's behavior in recognizing liberals in the ensuing debates also confirmed conservative suspicions about the Vice-President. Rockefeller seemed to be unable to spot conservatives who wanted to speak against the change, most importantly Allen of Alabama. Though the incident seems minor in retrospect, it was taken as evidence of Rockefeller's enduring liberalism. As one observer remembered:

> The ruling caused a major battle on the Senate floor between liberal Democrats and conservative Republicans. Rockefeller's decision to throw the cloture decision to a simple majority angered many of the conservative members of his own party who had used filibusters to stall liberal legislation. But Rockefeller's ruling was nondebatable and thereby not subject to a filibuster, just a simple vote. Finally, on February 26, he forced through a critical vote without recognizing Allen, who repeatedly rose for a parliamentary inquiry. It was a classic liberal-conservative fight, with Rockefeller clearly on the liberal side.

Rockefeller's cloture ruling was all the evidence conservatives needed to start a campaign to remove him from the 1976 Republican ticket. However, it would be a mistake to attribute all of the firestorm to that one cloture fight. The resentment caused by the cloture ruling was only a snowflake in an avalanche of criticism directed against Rockefeller. According to a Rockefeller Domestic Council aide,

> The real thing that contributed to the derailment was the tension between the governor and the conservative Republicans. The conservatives threatened Ford daily about Rockefeller's place on the ticket. There were constant innuendos and threats if Rockefeller wasn't pulled off. Ford's political staff was scared that Reagan might run if Rockefeller stayed on. Reagan ran anyway, but it was too late for Rockefeller. Ford thought he could buy Reagan off by dumping Rockefeller, but it didn't work. The first test of Rockefeller was Rule 22. Rockefeller

made a few bad rulings and that was it as far as the conservatives were concerned. Rockefeller was still a red liberal.

Or, as a Ford assistant noted: "For a decade, Rockefeller had been a dirty word to Nixon and the conservatives. Rockefeller was in the White House with only one friend, Jerry Ford. Any conservative worth a grain of salt hated Rockefeller." Rockefeller was eventually forced off the ticket when Ford announced in the fall of 1975 that he would delay naming his vice-presidential running mate until the Republican convention. Rockefeller responded to the decision by withdrawing on his own accord in November.

Reagan was an obvious factor in the political pressure. As the conservative wing of the party continued to threaten Ford, the White House political staff pushed for Rockefeller's separation. As the head of the conservative wing, Reagan was always in the back of the minds of the Ford political team. According to a Ford aide: "You can't blame us for watching Reagan. He was giving all of the signals of a run for the nomination even before Ford was nominated as Vice-President. We weren't running away from him in 1975 and thought it was important to position the campaign to meet the most obvious challenge." Unlike Mondale, who stood between Carter and Kennedy in 1980, Rockefeller stood just to the left of Ford and far to the left of Reagan in 1976. Ford acknowledged the problems in his autobiography:

> In mid September [1975], 55 percent of the respondents to a Harris poll gave him a negative job performance rating. Only 27 percent thought he'd done a good job, and the rest said they weren't sure. Even more ominous, 25 percent of the Republicans polled said they wouldn't vote for me if Rockefeller remained on the ticket. I was sorely disappointed by those results, which were completely unwarranted. I couldn't believe they stemmed from anything he had done as Vice President. Rather, I thought they derived from things he'd said and stands he'd taken earlier in his political career. In his past Presidential campaigns, he'd established a reputation as a liberal, and he had outraged many ultraconservative Republicans. Apparently, their antagonism wasn't going to fade away (1979, p. 327).

As a Rockefeller aide admitted: "He couldn't have been much help in the primaries because Reagan was so far to the right. But [Rockefeller] would have been the margin of victory in the general election. Ford would have won Ohio with Rockefeller as a running mate. It's easy to see in hindsight, but no one anticipated Jimmy Carter winning the Democratic nomination." The decision to remove Rockefeller had reflected a desire to repeat Nixon's 1972 Southern sweep. However, with Carter as the Democratic nominee, the strategy was useless. Unfortunately for Rockefeller, many of the decisions to drop him from the ticket came in mid-1975, when Carter was still discounted as "Jimmy who?"

Rockefeller was also affected by the political context on Capitol Hill.

Following the midterm elections in 1974, the Republicans controlled only 144 seats in the House, the lowest level of support for a sitting President in this century. Moreover, Ford's public approval rating dropped thirty points between his inauguration and Rockefeller's confirmation. As a result, Ford was forced to fashion a veto strategy to maximize his limited political resources in Congress. As one Ford aide argued: "There was no sense in presenting a full legislative agenda. Economic conditions did not permit any increase in federal spending; political conditions did not permit any flexibility in Congress. It was better to wait for Congress to act, and see what we could do with a one-third-plus-one approach" (Light 1982b, p. 26). Though the veto strategy may have produced a number of victories, it restricted Rockefeller's internal influence. Since the Ford administration did not have enough support to pass legislation, Rockefeller had few opportunities to argue for domestic initiatives. The lack of political resources meant that the Ford administration had very little room to innovate. That, in turn, meant that Rockefeller had very little agenda-space. In an administration that had to adopt a veto strategy—vetoing sixty-six bills in the abbreviated term —Rockefeller's support for a full slate of new domestic programs fell on deaf ears both inside and outside of the administration. The Ford liaison staff did not have any time to lobby for new bills while building support against veto overrides. The Ford budget staff did not have any interest in new spending while pushing for strict spending ceilings.

Ford

Throughout Rockefeller's troubles—the fights with Rumsfeld, the policy disputes, the removal from the ticket—he shared a strong personal relationship with Ford. Not one Rockefeller or Ford aide noted any personal problems between the two individuals. "There were problems between Rocky and Rumsfeld, Rocky and Greenspan, Rocky and Lynn," a Ford assistant reflected, "but I can't think of a time when Rocky had any personal problems with Ford. . . . I never heard any bad words between them." Whereas Mondale staff members argue that the warm personal relationship between the Vice-President and Carter was a major factor in Mondale's internal role, there is little doubt that Rockefeller and Ford shared a very close friendship, too. As Ford remembers the first year:

> In the nearly eleven months that he had served as Vice President, he had done an outstanding job, and our personal relationship was a source of great satisfaction. The two of us would get together in the Oval Office at least once a week. He would sit down, stir his coffee with the stem of his horn-rimmed glasses, and fidget in his chair as he leaped from one subject to another. What an active and imaginative mind he had. Our talks would range from the need to redesign the Vice President's official flag all the way to his plan to create a $100 billion Energy Independence Authority. No detail was too small to escape his atten-

tion; nothing was too grandiose for him to propose. And always, after we had covered the substantive matters on his list, we would talk about national politics (1979, p. 327).

Yet, despite Ford's personal liking for Rockefeller, he affected his Vice-President's influence in at least two ways.

First, Ford seemed to be unwilling or unable to discipline his staff once they started to freeze Rockefeller out of the policy process. On several occasions early in the term, Rockefeller asked Ford to issue orders to the staff to include him in the policy flow. Reluctantly, Rockefeller eventually concluded that Ford would not or could not give the signals that he needed for influence. As a Ford aide said: "Ford wasn't exactly the kind of guy who would sit down with Rumsfeld and tell him to toe the line. He wasn't that forceful. And I'm not sure that he wanted Rumsfeld to include Rockefeller." However, as Ford wrote: "Throughout my political career, nothing upset me more than bickering among members of my staff. It was time-consuming, distracting, and unnecessary. I had told my aides that I wouldn't tolerate it. But it continued, even accelerated when I entered the White House and—given the ambitions and personalities of the people involved—there didn't seem any way to put an immediate stop to it" (1979, pp. 184-85). As Hartmann remembered:

> Ford's style worked superbly in his dealings with congressmen. . . . In the White House, it did not work as well. . . . Ford never came down hard on the way he wanted the White House to operate. He did not like a highly structured military kind of staff. He did not want channels. He delegated responsibility, but he did not delegate authority, which caused a great deal of frustration among some of his staff. . . . Ford did not want to have a true chief of staff—someone who could cast his vote except under direct instructions from the president. . . . When clashes developed, Ford used to complain about them. He used to demand that they be straightened out. But he never really did anything to straighten them out himself (Reichley 1981, p. 314).

Initially, Ford's spokes-of-the-wheel system favored Rockefeller. At least during the first months of the Ford term, there was ample access for multiple advisers. Ford still made the bulk of his decisions with in-person debate. By the time Rockefeller arrived, however, Ford had switched to a more hierarchical system, with his old friend Rumsfeld as chief of staff. Perhaps Ford's unwillingness to order Rumsfeld to cooperate stemmed from the fact that Rumsfeld was a former congressional ally and colleague. Perhaps it came from his own personal dislike for mediating staff conflict—"He always believed things would work out on their own," an aide reported. Whatever the reason, Rockefeller found little help from Ford in settling the increasingly bitter staff conflict. According to an outside observer: "Ford never sat Rumsfeld down and said 'Go along or you are fired.' That's the only signal anyone understands on the inside. Ford wouldn't do it. Rumsfeld was too valuable, but Ford never would have done it anyway." Indeed, according to Hartmann, Ford may have actually encouraged the infighting. "He pretends that he doesn't like this bickering. But the fact is that he does try to play off one against the other, which he thinks is administratively sound" (Turner 1978, p. 289).

Second, and more important, Ford adopted a highly restrictive policy agenda, severely limiting Rockefeller's influence. Ford was not interested in the kinds of expansionary domestic programs that Rockefeller produced. Though Rockefeller had been moving toward a more conservative program, the Domestic Council did prepare a variety of new initiatives in welfare reform, health insurance, energy, social security, tax reform, and deregulation. Ford was not interested in any of the ideas beyond deregulation. Because he had adopted a tight budget as one component of his antirecession policy, Ford was not *persuadable* on the Rockefeller agenda. Though he did listen to Rockefeller's proposals, often presented in the form of specific legislative drafts, Ford was not willing to adopt any new spending programs. Facing the largest budget deficits in history, Ford adopted his no new spending rule instead. At least in the domestic arena, economic costs became the first question asked of any new program. As one Ford assistant said: "The spending rule was applied to every new idea. It was used against welfare reform and catastrophic health insurance, public works and emergency housing. It was sure as hell applied to the federal budget." During the two-year Ford term, the first question asked of most programs was: How much does it cost? Since the rule did not apply to defense, it worked mainly against domestic policy innovation. The adoption of a restrictive policy agenda meant that: (a) new ideas would have to pass more obstacles to clearance inside the White House, (b) new programs would face more competition for scarce funds from established programs, and (c) there would be more conflict within the policy process as programs and players fought for position. Further, because the Domestic Council became deeply involved in the business of saying no to the departments, Rockefeller lost valuable opportunities for building alliances with the executive branch.

Summary

Among these seven explanations for Rockefeller's lack of influence, three carry more weight than the others. First, the delay in confirmation affected the Rockefeller Vice-Presidency at all levels. The four-month delay meant that Rockefeller was behind on time and information from the start of his term. It also meant that opponents were able to entrench themselves long before Rockefeller arrived. It meant that the policy process was designed without any vice-presidential input. It meant that a West Wing office was impossible. "What were we supposed to do?" a Ford aide asked. "Wait for

Rockefeller before starting to think about policy? Wait for him before getting on with the budget and the State of the Union address? Were we supposed to hold a West Wing office for him for four months? Hell, he was lucky to get any office space at all." Second, the political context surrounding the Ford administration also shaped the Rockefeller Vice-Presidency in profound ways. Rockefeller's ties to the liberal wing of the party became useless as the conservatives gained strength. Ford's problems on Capitol Hill worked against the Vice-President's domestic policy influence, while the Rule 22 decision confirmed the conservatives' worst suspicions about the Vice-President. We can assume that any domestic policy adviser—Ehrlichman, Eizenstat, Stockman, or Rockefeller—would have had trouble shaping the agenda under those political circumstances. Third, regardless of the delay or the political situation, Ford might have made life much easier for Rockefeller inside the White House by issuing strong signals to the presidential staff. When he did not issue those signals, the White House staff acted out of natural territorial instincts. Moreover, had Ford adopted an expansive policy agenda, Rockefeller would have had more success. That Ford was not persuadable on most issues meant that Rockefeller had little input in building the policy agenda.

MONDALE

Like Rockefeller before him, Mondale had reason to expect substantive responsibilities and impact in the Vice-Presidency. First, Carter had expressed his commitment to having an active Vice-President several weeks before the convention. In talking with Mondale, Carter had agreed that the Vice-President should be involved in the policy-making process, but did not talk about specifics. It was not until after the election that Mondale gave Carter a memorandum on the Vice-President's duties in the coming administration. This transition memo became the basis for the subsequent relationship. As Mondale's chief counsel, Berman, remembers:

> Shortly after the election Mondale met with Senator Humphrey, Vice President Rockefeller, a group of former Humphrey vice presidential staff people and others to seek advice. In early December 1976, he gave to President-elect Carter a memorandum outlining the role in which he thought he would be most effective.
>
> Mondale described the role as being a general adviser and troubleshooter to the President. He suggested that as the only other nationally elected public official, not burdened with the specific institutional demands of the Congress or the Executive Branch and being able to look at the government as a whole, put him in a unique position to advise and represent that President. To do the job he told the President that he needed the following:

—access to all information and briefings, classified and otherwise, available to
the President;
—a relationship with members of the Executive Branch which required them to
respond to his requests for information and help;
—participation in all key policy groups;
—a seasoned independent staff of his own;
—a special relationship with the White House staff;
—access to the President whenever necessary.

Mondale also asked that he not be given line authority assignments. He believed that if the assignment was important, it would cut across the responsibilities of one or more Cabinet officers or other agency heads and involve him in
debilitating bureaucratic fights. If, on the other hand, the assignment was meaningless or trivial, it would undermine the Vice President's reputation and
squander time (remarks, 21 Feb. 1981).

As Mondale notes: "President-elect Carter agreed completely with the
memo. In addition, he told me he wanted my office to be down the hall from
the Oval Office in the West Wing of the White House. . . . That did not seem
too significant to me at the time; but as a matter of fact, it was one of the most
important steps that we took" (remarks, 18 Feb. 1981).

Second, even with the on-paper agreements, Mondale saw a number of
vacuums for vice-presidential impact. Though the Carter staff had considerable experience in electing a President, they had little experience in
operating the federal government. Their lack of background in policy increased Mondale's opportunities for advice and influence. As one Mondale
assistant noted, "We liked the Carter people very much. Most of them were
down-to-earth and easy to work with. It was no secret, however, that they
weren't well prepared for the administration. Very few of the top people
had much understanding of how the federal government worked. That's
where we fit in so well." Mondale also benefited from the transition battle
between Hamilton Jordan and Jack Watson over the White House policy
process. Watson had spent the campaign working on policy issues for the
transition, building a reservoir of material on potential Carter programs
and appointments. Jordan had spent the campaign as Carter's top political
manager, devoting his energy to winning the fall election. After the
November victory, Jordan bested Watson in a struggle for internal power.
Unfortunately for the Carter administration, most of Watson's policy planning was lost in the days that followed. As one observer argues:

The shuffling for position was a delay and a distraction, a period of about ten
days during which, as one transition staffer conceded, "basically nothing was
happening." Even after the original plans had been reordered, an atmosphere
of tension and uncertainty prevailed among those charged with carrying on the
process. It is hard to tell how much more might have been accomplished under
other circumstances, but the bumpy beginning robbed the incoming admin-

istration of some of the early impetus its leaders had hoped to build (Shogan 1977, pp. 80-81).

Though the delay hurt the administration overall, it helped Mondale by enhancing his role as one of the few top advisers with substantive experience. Moreover, because the Mondale staff had allied themselves with Jordan during the fight, they received at least some of the rewards of the victory.

Third, though Carter had been widely perceived as a conservative Democrat in the fall campaigns, there were early signs that he intended to move toward the liberal wing of the party. Indeed, the first three months showed Carter to be very much in the Democratic mainstream. The Department of Education, the $50 tax rebate, expanded job training, a new welfare initiative, and electoral reform all fell within the traditional Democratic program. It was not until the economy began to sour that Carter moved back toward his conservative roots. At least at the start of the term, Carter was persuadable on the kinds of domestic programs that Mondale favored. Mondale took advantage of these early policy "windows" to lobby for a number of liberal policies, building his advisory relationship with the President. According to one Carter assistant: "Carter was pretty willing to consider a whole range of ideas right after the election. He wanted low-cost programs, but didn't restrict himself to any specific ideas. He was willing to listen to practically anything during the first three or four months. That favored anybody who had ideas ready to go." From the beginning of the relationship, Carter had shown a willingness to cooperate with Mondale on issues large and small. Mondale, for example, had argued against inviting Richard Nixon to the inaugural. According to the Mondale staff, Nixon was eventually invited, but only under an arrangement where he would decline to attend.

There are at least six reasons why Mondale became a member of the President's inner circle: (1) the merging of the Carter and Mondale campaign staffs, (2) Mondale's refusal of line assignments, (3) the rise of strong allies, (4) Mondale's personal style, (5) the political context outside the Carter White House, and (6) Carter's own management style and policy goals. In many respects, Mondale's Vice-Presidency was the inverse of Rockefeller's. Indeed, as one White House reporter argued: "Mondale went to school on Rockefeller. He saw the problems of the line assignments, the problems with a high profile. Once you have a line assignment like Rockefeller, you're caught in bureaucratic politics. You're in charge of an office where your opponents can measure your success. And whether you're a Vice-President or a regular adviser, anytime they can measure your success, there's trouble."

The Merging of the Campaign Staffs

Immediately after the 1976 Democratic national convention, Carter gave Mondale the traditional choice of his own campaign headquarters. Some

of the staff suggested Minnesota, Mondale's home state. Others suggested
Washington, near Mondale's Senate base. However, on advice from a
number of his top aides and friends, Mondale moved his campaign operation
to Atlanta, in the same building with the Carter staff. The two staffs slept in
the same hotel and ate in the same restaurants. The merging of the campaign
headquarters allowed the Mondale staff to start building relationships with
their eventual White House contacts long before the transition. Short of
having worked for Carter from the very beginning, the merging gave the
Mondale staff an opportunity to earn the respect and trust of the President's
staff. Of the Carter and Mondale aides interviewed, 63 percent mentioned
the merging as an important factor in the Vice-President's later role in
shaping the policy agenda. As Berman notes: "That decision gave the
Mondale staff people and the principal Carter staff people an opportunity
to get to know one another and work together during the informality of the
campaign. When we got to Washington after the election and the principal
Carter campaign staff workers became the core of the White House staff,
our relationships were established. It was easy to continue the cooperative
working relationships that had been established in Atlanta" (remarks, 21
Feb. 1981). As a second Mondale aide said:

> The White House is a very formal place, a lot of attention to status. In Atlanta,
> all of us worked together, lived in the same hotel and worked in the same build-
> ing next door. There was no way to be formal. Once we moved into the more
> formal atmosphere in the transition, we already had our friendships and work-
> ing ties. The transition allowed the relationships to develop further before we
> moved over to the EOB. We didn't get caught in the Jordan-Watson fight either.
> We had been on the political side during the campaign and, once Jordan won,
> we were actively involved in the transition. Moe was responsible for cooking up
> a list of economic advisers; Mondale worked on cabinet recruitment; Berman
> worked on the staffing system.

The merging of the campaign staffs had three important impacts on the
Mondale Vice-Presidency. First, the Mondale staff was "present at the crea-
tion" of the White House policy process. Since much of the White House
process is the product of habit, the merging allowed Carter people to get in
the practice of calling on Mondale aides, if only out of courtesy. "We didn't
really care why they called," a Mondale aide remarked, "as long as they
called. If it was courtesy or tokenism or a real need for advice, we didn't
care. What we wanted was a chance to have some input. We felt the strength
of our ideas, regardless of why they were sought, would be enough." As the
Carter policy process hardened into place, Mondale and his staff were able
to claim a position in the loop. Unlike Rockefeller and his staff, Mondale
was on the inside from the very start. Even during the transition, Mondale
and his staff were actively consulted on a variety of issues. As noted above,
Mondale was involved in the selection of a number of cabinet officers, in-

cluding Califano, Bergland, and CEA Chairman Schultze—an activity that not only got the Carter staff in the habit of listening to the Vice-President, but also contributed to alliance building with those appointees later in the term.

Second, the merging acted as a critical opportunity for the Mondale staff to size up the Carter team. Even during the intensity of the general election campaign, Mondale aides were able to find the pulse of power in the Carter organization. It was no accident that the Mondale people sided with Jordan in the post-transition battle with Watson. According to one observer: "They were able to see pretty early that Jordan and Powell were the top movers in the campaign. Watson was important, but not as wired to Carter as Jordan or Powell. By working with Jordan instead of Watson, Mondale's staff wound up on the winning team. They were able to store up a little capital in the process." Though several Mondale aides argued that the move toward Jordan involved only simple campaign mechanics—"We were much more interested in getting Mondale elected than talking about the transition," an aide noted—others acknowledged that the move reflected sound political strategy. "It was clear that Jordan and the political types would be running the White House," a Mondale staffer noted. "It made a lot of sense to stick with him in the campaign. It wasn't sinister, just smart politics." Whatever the reason for the move, the campaign allowed the Mondale staff to get in on the ground floor of the Carter White House. As I argue shortly, many Mondale aides point to Jordan's cooperation as one reason for the Vice-President's success. Perhaps Jordan remembered that Mondale and his staff were on his team during the bitter transition fight.

Third, because the Carter staff was initially short on policy experience—particularly after Watson lost—the campaign merging allowed the Mondale staff to demonstrate their own ability. When the transition turned to the difficult process of filling government positions, a number of Mondale aides were moved to the departments. More importantly, Mondale's former campaign aides, Carp and Aaron, were moved to pivotal positions on the Domestic Policy Staff and the National Security Council staff. When asked why Carp and Aaron were appointed, a Carter aide answered that "they were two highly qualified people. They had done a very good job for both Carter and Mondale in the campaign. They came with strong recommendations, but had proved their value in the election and transition." Unlike Rockefeller's aides, who had no opportunity to prove their ability in a campaign, the Mondale staff entered office with at least some acknowledgement of their role in winning the election.

Thus, on an objective basis, Mondale had much more time to build his policy influence than Rockefeller. Compared to Rockefeller's twenty-six months in office, Mondale had forty-eight. Further, Mondale had more time during the critical agenda-setting stage of the term. He was on board during the Carter transition into office and did not start his major travel schedule until late in the first year. He was also present during the third year, as Carter prepared another legislative agenda. All totaled, Mondale had thirty-six months in office before the first Democratic primary in 1980, while Rockefeller had only thirteen months before the first Republican primary in 1976. That meant that Mondale had more time to build his advisory role in a more relaxed political setting. According to a Rockefeller assistant:

> When you look at how bad things were when Rockefeller joined the administration, it's not surprising that things went downhill so fast. Ford's public approval rating was already at the botton. He was in trouble on Capitol Hill. Reagan was raising money hand over foot. It was a very tense place to be. When Mondale became Vice-President, it was after a tight election, but it was still pleasant. Carter was at the top of his public opinion. The honeymoon was on. Every one was looking forward to the future. Mondale was able to begin under the best circumstances. By the time Carter had reached the same point Ford was in, Mondale had already built up some support and had a lot of friends.

As noted earlier, Vice-Presidents have honeymoons both inside and outside of the White House. Because Mondale entered office in the normal manner, following a reasonably normal election, he had more time to work for influence. When Carter did hit his political low in the summer of 1979, Mondale was able to survive on the capital he· had stored during the first three years.

Line Assignments

Mondale also saved considerable time by avoiding line assignments. Indeed, instead of working for a major line role, as Rockefeller had done, Mondale actually reduced the Vice-President's formal assignments. When Carter remarked in an early transition meeting that Mondale would be "my chief staff person," Mondale immediately disclaimed any interest in the position. When Carter asked Mondale to take responsibility for the administration's Africa policy in 1977, Mondale also declined. As Mondale remembered his decision:

> One day the President announced that I was in charge of Africa. I declined. There were sighs of relief all through Africa and it wouldn't work, in my opinion, because, first of all, the personnel, the skills, the experience to handle that were clearly beyond anything a Vice-President could or would want to assemble. In addition, the skills in the State Department and elsewhere are superb and there is absolutely no reason why a Vice-President could not work cooperatively with the existing agencies where he can be helpful in achieving these results—and that's what we did. Another time it was suggested that I was going to be Chief of Staff of the White House. I turned it down on the spot. If I had taken on that assignment, it would have consumed vast amounts of my time with staff work and distracted me from important work (remarks, 18 Feb. 1981).

The only ongoing assignment that Mondale accepted was the agenda-setting operation. However, unlike Rockefeller's Domestic Council duties, the agenda-setting process involved only limited involvement for a very brief period at the end of each year. Mondale avoided line assignments for several reasons. First, as noted above, he didn't want to take any position which would expose him to intense political warfare. "He knew that the hardest thing to do was to say no to a department," an assistant said. "He didn't want to take that kind of political heat. He'd seen what it had done to Rockefeller." Second, he didn't want to make the time commitment to a continuing line duty. Mondale preferred to stay apart from the mechanics of the policy process, floating in and out of areas as the need arose.

Compared to Rockefeller, Mondale had more *quality* time to devote to policy. As a Mondale staffer remarked: "We were up to speed very quickly in the transition. We had the Senate staff ready to plug in and had people down to the clericals who had worked for Mondale at least two years or more. That's not to say we tried to muscle in on the Carter people. We moved cautiously at the start and became more aggressive over the term." Once again, Mondale was in sharp contrast to Rockefeller. Mondale's staff was ready to assume substantive policy responsibilities at the start of the transition. Unlike Rockefeller, the Mondale staff had ample experience with federal policy and knew who the key players were inside the White House. Though Carter also had experienced aides—including Eizenstat, Brzezinski, several cabinet secretaries—his White House staff was far behind at the start of the term. As noted above, at least part of the problem came from the transition fight between Jordan and Watson. The lost time created shortages of raw knowledge at the start of the term, emphasizing the disparities between the Mondale and Carter staffs. According to a Carter aide: "At the beginning, the best way to win an argument was to be better prepared. The President was the kind of man who would make some decision on the basis of information. The people who were prepared and had the facts had an advantage. Eizenstat was awesome in the early meetings. He won some issues on the facts alone. He was always overprepared."

Mondale's West Wing office also shaped his influence over policy. As one Carter assistant remembered: "Carter's idea was for Mondale to be in the White House. Jordan brought Mondale a floor plan during the transition and asked which one Mondale wanted. They were all open, including Haldeman's old corner office. Mondale apparently decided the corner office would be too much and took the middle office instead. Once Mondale was over there, he was in the loop, not just the paper flow, but informal conversation. You know, he could say, 'Hey, Zbig, what's going on in Israel?'" The office became especially valuable for Mondale's coalition-building activities. In trying to recruit sympathetic advisers on specific decisions, the West Wing office provided a combination of status and discretion. "Mondale didn't have to beg anyone to visit him in the West Wing," an assistant commented.

"The West Wing is like a magnet to the big shots. He could casually sit down with a cabinet member and work him or her over on an issue. They would never know what hit them. It all worked to keep his cover." The West Wing office also kept Mondale in close contact with Carp and Aaron. Instead of working by phone, Mondale could walk down the hall and ask Aaron about a specific issue. Instead of calling Carp over to the EOB, he could walk up to the second floor of the West Wing and talk in person. Though the office created some resentment among several Cabinet members, including Carter's Georgia friend Griffin Bell, it was an important tool in Mondale's influence. In all, 73 percent of the Carter and Mondale aides pointed to the office as a factor in the Vice-President's policy impact.

Allies

Unlike Rockefeller, Mondale had a number of allies inside the Carter White House. Though Mondale had strong opponents on policy issues, he did not face the same degree of political hostility or competition as Rockefeller. The Carter White House did have internal battles, particularly as the administration aged, but it remained a relatively collegial place to work. As a Carter assistant maintained: "When we fought, it was over policy. There weren't too many personal grudges on the staff. There was the normal departmental bickering and complaints about the cabinet, but there wasn't much fighting inside the West Wing." During the Carter term, Mondale's closest allies included Hamilton Jordan (chief of staff), Stuart Eizenstat (Domestic Policy Staff director), Bert Carp (Domestic Policy Staff deputy director), David Aaron (deputy to the national security adviser), and, when she arrived later in the term, Anne Wexler (public liaison director).

Of Mondale's early allies, Jordan may have been the most important. Seventy-four percent of the Carter and Mondale staff pointed to Jordan as an important factor in the Vice-President's influence. Though Jordan eventually opposed Mondale as the economy worsened, he ensured continued access to information over the term. As Richard Moe, Mondale's chief of staff, noted in 1978:

> Jordan insisted that we were plugged in. Now the two staffs are almost indistinguishable. We have the same goals and we serve the same President. . . . Previously, Presidents and presidential staffs felt threatened. That's not true in this case. Carter made it clear at the beginning what role he wanted the Vice President to play. Also, the top White House people have a longtime, established relationship with the President and are not likely to feel threatened. There is a total lack of intrigue and back-biting here. For one thing, Carter wouldn't stand for it (*National Journal*, 11 Mar. 1978).

In his role as acting chief of staff, Jordan had considerable control over Mondale's impact. By restricting access to information, Jordan could have easily sabotaged Mondale's advisory role. By isolating the Mondale staff,

Jordan could have prevented any hidden-hand influence. As the gatekeeper to the President, Jordan had a catalytic impact on Mondale's opportunities for policy influence. However, early in the administration, Jordan reported that "I consider I work for Mondale. . . . He's my second boss, the way Carter is my first boss" (Lewis 1980, p. 237). Though Carter threatened to fire any staff members who deliberately attacked Mondale, it is far more likely that Jordan's acquiescence in Mondale's continuing role was voluntary. Jordan was too valuable to sacrifice in guaranteeing a vice-presidential advisory function.

There are several reasons why Jordan cooperated in Mondale's role. As noted above, Mondale and his staff had worked side-by-side with Jordan in the campaign and transition. According to several Mondale aides, Moe and Jordan had become friends and had built a good working relationship. Further, as Moe argued, Jordan was one of a number of Carter aides with very long ties to the President. Jordan had a very relaxed style and did not seem to be threatened by the rise of competitors in the policy process. "No one could have severed his ties to Carter," a Mondale assistant reported, "so why would he feel threatened by Mondale's Monday lunches? He had no need to be uptight about anybody stealing the President away." Unlike Rumsfeld in the early days of the Ford administration, Jordan had no reason to consolidate his power. It had been consolidated long before the Carter administration began. Finally, Jordan seemed to be extremely relaxed in his role as acting chief of staff. The image of Jordan without a tie, in blue jeans and hiking boots, lounging in Haldeman's old office, was an accurate portrait of his administrative style. His "laid-back" image led to considerable criticism and may have hurt the administration, but it certainly helped Mondale gain greater access. As one Mondale aide said,

> I remember being with Mondale one morning when Jordan pulled up to the White House. He got out of his car and hauled out a big bag full of laundry. He didn't have a tie and was typically underdressed. Mondale looked at him and said "Now that's what's wrong with this administration." But it was also what was right with the administration. The whole place was so relaxed. They didn't play much hardball, at least on the domestic side. And Jordan was the king of the hill. He had laundry privileges no less.

Apart from Jordan, Mondale's strongest allies were his two former Senate aides, Carp and Aaron. Sixty-seven percent of the two staffs mentioned Carp and Aaron as significant factors in Mondale's impact. On one level, Carp and Aaron were simply additional conduits for information. As one of the pair noted: "We were helpful in keeping Mondale informed. It was not just a question of knowing things, but people knew we were here. No one felt they could get around him. I saw my role, however, as mainly keeping him posted on the issues." On a second level, Carp and Aaron acted as a powerful signal to other White House players on Mondale's position in the policy process. As Berman noted,

While they were loyal to the President and served him most directly, the President and everyone knew of their strong allegiance to Mondale. Everything that went on in the foreign policy area or the domestic policy area went through those two people.

Every Cabinet secretary, every policy-maker in the Executive Branch knew that these two people would keep Mondale and his staff informed on any issues in which Mondale had or should have an interest. Any Executive Branch policy-maker inclined to exclude Mondale from the process was quick to learn that it wouldn't work (remarks, 21 Feb. 1981).

A second Mondale assistant agreed. "The biggest problem in the past for Vice-Presidents was isolation. Carp and Aaron made it impossible to cut Mondale off. There was no percentage in trying to avoid him. He would just call over to Carp or Aaron and find out, or better yet they would just call over to him." As one of the pair remarked: "We weren't plants in the White House, but were symbols. There is always a tendency to exclude people whenever a strong signal isn't given. The appointment of us was such a signal. We kept Mondale informed, went out and ate together. But it wasn't anything dirty. It was just like any other working relationship." Aaron was also important because Mondale frequently disagreed with Brzezinski. Aaron kept Mondale informed on Brzezinski's proposals, while serving as an informal link between Mondale and the executive branch. On a third level, Carp and Aaron acted as representatives of Mondale even when the Vice-President was not physically present. Especially for Carp, who had served Mondale much longer than Aaron, it was difficult to separate his views from the Vice-President's. "That's not to mean that Carp was a puppet," a Mondale aide argued. "But when you serve with someone as long as most of us did, you just absorb a lot of his thinking. You kind of learn from each other and move to some common positions. Even when Bert was speaking totally for himself, Mondale had some part of the words." Finally, because Carp and Aaron were well respected as policy advisers in their own right, they reflected on the rest of the Mondale staff. If Carp and Aaron were so good, perhaps Moe and Berman were good, too.

Mondale was also able to build strong relationships with Eizenstat and Wexler. Eizenstat often agreed with Mondale on policy issues and Wexler came to share many of the Vice-President's positions on legislative strategy, in part because she was recruited by him. White House coalitions can rest on shared beliefs, personal relationships, overlapping responsibilities, and past favors. Mondale's relationship with Eizenstat rested on all four. The two shared a liberal outlook, a personal rapport, domestic policy responsibilities, and past exchanges of help. They also shared Bert Carp, Eizenstat's deputy and Mondale's former Senate adviser. As Eizenstat's deputy, Carp was able to bring Mondale's arguments into the domestic policy process. However, Eizenstat also had considerable federal experience before joining the Carter White House, and worked with the Vice-President to restore at least part of the deep social spending cuts in the 1978 and 1979 budget fights. Eizenstat also worked with Mondale to head off the midsummer crisis in 1979, agreeing that Patrick Caddell's portrait of public "malaise" was "crazy" (*Boston Globe*, 25 Feb. 1983). Eizenstat and Mondale eventually succeeded in cooling the evangelical flavor of Carter's televised address, effectively removing all references to the word "malaise." Instead of blaming the American people for their problems, Eizenstat and Mondale worked for a more traditional "rally-round-the-President" theme. However, neither was able to stop Carter's subsequent cabinet and White House shakeup. Though Eizenstat and Mondale formed a powerful coalition, they were not strong enough to prevent Califano's firing.

Finally, Mondale was able to recruit some allies from his early service in the Cabinet selection process. As a key participant in the recruitment process, Mondale was able to gauge the strengths and weaknesses of potential allies and opponents, while allowing future colleagues to learn more about him. As one observer notes:

> As Carter's talent scouts began screening and recruiting Cabinet members and other top policy-making officials, Mondale found himself standing near the apex of a selection process, one step below Carter himself. Aspirants for top-echelon jobs discovered that an interview with Mondale meant they were among the finalists. The ultimate decision was usually made when the president-elect and the vice president-elect would meet alone (Lewis 1980, p. 232).

Though these advisers did not owe their jobs to Mondale, his role in their appointments did not hurt his influence. Califano, for instance, was always willing to give Mondale additional briefings on domestic issues, while accepting at least one former Mondale aide as a department officer. When Califano was fired in 1979, Mondale lost a strong ally. The secretary had been an additional conduit for information and, like other Mondale allies, had represented many of the Vice-President's views in the policy process.

Although Mondale had a number of allies in the White House and executive branch, he was not without strong opponents. As the economy worsened in 1978 and 1979, West Wing liberals found themselves in the minority. A powerful coalition of economic conservatives, led by Schultze and James McIntyre (OMB director), argued for a much tighter federal budget. Facing rapidly increasing inflation, Carter agreed. As with the Ford administration, the budget became a critical battleground over priorities. Mondale, Eizenstat, and other White House liberals were able to reduce the depth of the cuts, but were unable to turn Carter away from the restrictive fiscal policy. However, throughout the arguments, there was no effort to push Mondale out of the process. Though there was intense debate over the size and direction of budget cuts, there was no political threat to the Vice-President. Unlike Rockefeller, who faced both policy and political opposition, Mondale never had to defend his position on the presidential ticket. "It was all a policy question," a Carter assistant said. "No one ever thought to say Mondale should go. It was a very difficult time inside the administration, but no one got down to personalities. The budget fight was a question of what was the best approach to managing skyrocketing inflation, not whether Mondale was a decent Vice-President." It was during this period that Mondale switched from an offensive style of influence to a defensive style. Given the rising strength of the administration conservatives, Mondale and other liberals moved to stop or reduce cuts rather than support new programs. Though Mondale continued to work for some form of national health insurance and electoral reform, he spent more time trying to stem the tide of conservative budgeting.

Though Mondale had opponents later in the term, he may have benefited from the resignation of Bert Lance at the start of the administration. As Carter's first OMB director and an old Georgia friend, Lance was Carter's closest policy adviser. He was also one of the few White House staff members in Carter's age range. Remember that the bulk of the Carter staff were in their thirties, with the bulk of their political experience coming from just one campaign in 1976. When Lance was forced to resign following allegations of financial mismanagement in Georgia, he left a vacuum inside the White House. Asked whether Lance's departure made any difference in Mondale's influence, however, only 13 percent of the staff answered yes. As one Mondale domestic policy adviser remarked:

> I don't think it made much difference, not because it wasn't a serious loss for Carter, but because things were already going pretty well before Lance left. First, Mondale never had any trouble with Lance to start with. Second, once he left, there was a loss of ideological balance in the White House. With Carter's strongest conservative gone, it was more difficult for Mondale to support liberal policy without being seen as an advocate. Before Lance left, Mondale was just throwing his two cents' worth. It is true that Lance left a hole for someone like Mondale. Lance and Mondale were the only high-level older politicians in the West Wing. With Lance gone, Carter only had Mondale as a peer adviser, though Charles Kirbo was generally around.

Mondale's Style

Of the Carter and Mondale aides interviewed, 80 percent argued that the Vice-President's discretion and low visibility were critical factors in his influence. Unlike Rockefeller, Mondale preferred to operate through hidden channels, avoiding open advocacy of specific programs. Though Mondale supported specific policies in his frequent closed meetings with Carter, according to most of the staff, Mondale rarely took an open position in policy meetings. "I attended almost every cabinet meeting that Mondale did," a Carter assistant remembered, "but I can't recall more than a dozen times when he spoke up about a decision. He usually waited for Carter to ask what he thought, then he'd defer to the President. If he was influencing Carter, it wasn't in the cabinet meetings." A second Carter aide agreed. "We couldn't tell if Mondale was winning or losing. He didn't tell anyone what he was telling the President. That was sometimes very frustrating—you can't fight what you can't see. But it was a good tactic. If I couldn't figure out whether he was losing, then I had to assume he was winning. He projected the image of being influential. That was enough for most of us. I always tried to cover all of my bases and I think everyone else did too. That meant checking in with Mondale along the way." The decision to pursue a low-profile approach reflected Mondale's understanding of White House politics. He understood that he could not win in any one-on-one fights with the staff. In order to avoid such battles, he decided to keep his positions private. Even Mondale aides profess not to know what went on in the private meetings with Carter. As one aide said: "He didn't want anybody to know what he was telling Carter. He was never the kind of person who would walk out in the hall and tell his staff secrets. He was very much a private man. And that helped build confidence with Carter." Indeed, as Mondale has argued, trust was the basis of the relationship with the President.

> We could have had no relationship at all, of course, if we had not also gotten along well, and liked each other, and become, as we remain today, each other's friend. But the original basis of our relationship was professional—and because of that it was sound and strong. We understood each other's needs. We respected each other's opinions. We kept each other's confidence. Our relationship in the White House held up under the searing pressure of that place because we entered our offices understanding—perhaps for the first time in the history of those offices—that each of us could do a better job if we maintained the trust of the other. And for four years, that trust endured (remarks, 18 Feb. 1981).

Mondale's discretion also affected the President's staff. As one Carter aide argued, "Mondale understood who was President. He made his case, made it once, didn't carp about it, didn't tell what happened to outsiders, and never embarrassed the President. That made us much more willing to talk with him."

Because Mondale had more time to build his relationships than Rockefeller, the low-visibility approach had high payoffs. Most importantly, it added to Mondale's store of internal capital. Unlike external capital which reflects the Vice-President's standing in the public, internal capital involves the Vice-President's standing with the President and the White House staff. Agnew, for example, had strong external capital—he was well liked in the Republican party and was the front-runner for the 1976 nomination. However, Agnew had very little internal capital. Nixon did not trust him, nor did he respect his abilities or seek his opinions. Nixon's staff followed suit.

According to several Mondale aides, the low-profile strategy involved an effort to build the Vice-President's internal capital. "It was not our style to impose our views on the White House nor could we do it. We were fairly new and had to earn our stripes. Carter's staff was very good politically and didn't want to be told what to do. They were from a different culture and politically different from us. We were from a strong party state. They were outsiders. It took a while to convince them we could be trusted, to build up some confidence that we were all right." Both Mondale and his staff had an operating style that emphasized a quiet, "speak only when spoken to" strategy. That allowed the Carter people to get to know them under the best possible circumstances in the honeymoon. By the end of the first year, the Vice-President and his staff were more visible, but they first had to prove their loyalty to the new President. Rockefeller did not have that kind of leisure.

Though Mondale's style added to his internal capital, it also meant that certain issues were off limits. According to one reporter: "Mondale's biggest failure was not pushing for Frank Moore's resignation. Mondale wouldn't intercede to rebuild the legislative operation and wouldn't preempt Moore. Mondale was too damn cautious. I still don't know why he didn't head off the water projects fight. That cost Carter a great deal of support. Mondale wanted to submerge his own opinions to save his capital, but he was sometimes overly protective." Unlike his mentor, Humphrey, who took a highly visible stand against the bombing of North Vietnam, Mondale avoided open conflict. Yet, unlike Humphrey, Mondale retained his access to the President. As a Mondale aide said: "He decided to keep quiet on some things because he felt they were too hot. He never said one word that I know of about Bert Lance either way. He never criticized any members of the Carter staff. He never said anything about the Billy Carter mess. He knew none of those things were any of his business. I never heard that Carter meddled in Mondale's staff either."

Mondale's style may have come from his long service as a second to other politicians. As James Johnson, Mondale's personal assistant, once noted, "On the fundamental question of being the junior partner, he was schooled beyond anyone else in American politics, probably" (Lewis 1980, p. 23). According to other outside observers, Mondale had the perfect training to be Vice-President. He had risen to the top by attaching himself to a series of political benefactors. He had worked for Humphrey in the 1948 Minneapolis mayoral contest and for Orville Freeman in the 1956 Minnesota governor's race, and he was Freeman's campaign manager in 1958. As Mondale's biographer notes:

> At forty-eight, Mondale had certainly been one of the luckiest men in American politics—and also one of the most skilled. He was never out of position. The pattern began in 1960, when Governor Orville Freeman appointed Mondale

from the ranks of Minnesota's Democratic Farmer-Labor (DFL) party to a vacancy as the state's attorney general. It was his first public office. He was then reelected twice in his own right by landslide margins, establishing himself as a power in state politics, second only to Humphrey himself. It happened again in 1964 when President's Kennedy's assassination a year earlier set in motion a chain of events that swept Humphrey to the Vice Presidency. Karl Rolvaag, then the governor, named Mondale to fill the vacant Minnesota seat in the U.S. Senate (Lewis 1980, p. 9).

In each office, Mondale converted his effective service and loyalty into a higher office. As Vice-President, Mondale used his old political style to move himself into the front-runner's spot for 1984. If there was one lesson from Mondale's earlier career, it was that patience would lead to success. Instead of pushing for immediate Carter acceptance of his programs, Mondale decided to move at a slower pace. Whether in negotiating a civil rights plank at the 1964 Democratic convention or working on social service cuts in the 1979 budget, Mondale applied the strategies of a politician trained to compromise. Whereas Rockefeller's motto had once been "I never wanted to be Vice-President of anything," Mondale's motto might have been "Patience is a virtue."

This is not to argue that Mondale was willing to bide his time for four or eight years until his own Presidency. He had a full policy agenda that he wanted to see enacted. Rather, Mondale was willing to use more discreet methods of persuasion that would not threaten the President or his staff. He knew how to build coalitions and was a skilled practitioner of hidden-hand influence. Unlike Rockefeller, who had been trained at the top of the pyramid, Mondale was schooled to negotiate results by working with more powerful actors. As a campaign manager for Freeman, an appointed attorney general, an appointed Senator, and a Vice-President selected by yet another front-runner, Mondale had learned the strategies and tactics of a second player. Mondale had nothing to be ashamed of in his long career—he had been elected to the Senate in his own right twice and had become a member of a powerful liberal coalition on Capitol Hill. However, the skills that Mondale acquired in gaining his major political positions in the first instance were of considerable use to him as Vice-President. Rockefeller's skills as a governor were not as valuable as Mondale's skills as a "junior partner," skills that elevated him to his position as a senior adviser in the Carter administration.

The Political Context

Much of Mondale's internal success came from his connections to liberals outside the White House. In all, 57 percent of the Carter and Mondale staffs mentioned his liberal ties as an advantage in the policy process. As Carter moved toward the left to meet Ted Kennedy's challenge in 1980, Mondale became a critical link to mainstream Democratic constituents. Because Carter had emerged from outside the traditional ranks in 1976, Mondale also served as the "Washington connection" on legislative and political problems during the term. "Mondale and Carter were a good match," a Carter assistant reported. "Mondale had all the contacts in our weak areas: blacks, labor, Jews, liberals. He was a great help to us in both 1976 and 1980 with those groups. He was their interpreter in the West Wing." Whereas Rockefeller's liberal ties became a hindrance to Ford in the 1976 nomination season, Mondale's liberal connections were an advantage to Carter throughout the term.

Though several Mondale aides argue that the Vice-President had been moving in a more conservative direction toward the end of the term, Mondale retained his liberal credentials. From his early work with Humphrey to his support of open housing and migrant labor legislation, Mondale had been a member of the Senate liberal club. However, during the 1978 midterm elections, Mondale made a number of maneuvers in his home state of Minnesota that cost him some support in the liberal coalition. After Mondale was elected Vice-President, then-governor Wendell Anderson arranged to have himself appointed to fill Mondale's term until the next election. Because Humphrey's old Senate seat also fell open in 1978, Minnesotans faced two U.S. Senate contests on the midterm ballot. Though the state had voted Democratic for two decades, the midterm campaigns were particularly divisive.

First, there was a bitter Democratic nomination fight between Donald Fraser, a former congressman, and Robert Short, a self-made millionaire. Though Mondale was a close friend of Fraser's, he could do little to derail Short's anti-abortion candidacy. Immediately following Short's upset victory in the primary, Mondale endorsed the new candidate. Liberals in the party were outraged. Not only did Short defeat the liberal candidate, but Mondale had bestowed a measure of legitimacy on the victory. With Anderson and Short as the two Democratic nominees, the party lost both Senate seats in the midterm elections, as well as the governorship and the state legislature. The loss was the worst in recent Minnesota history and seriously undermined Mondale's position in the state. Second, the defeats in Minnesota were paralleled by a serious erosion of support for liberal candidates nationally. The 1978 midterm elections were merely a harbinger of what was to come in the 1980 campaigns. These trends affected Mondale's standing inside the White House. As an observer noted:

If Mondale couldn't carry his home state, maybe his value to Carter had dropped somewhat. That was a very bad year for Democrats anyway. It was the first sign of 1980. Carter correctly saw the election as a move toward the right. The fact that both Minnesota seats went to the Republicans despite Mondale's best effort had to have some impact in the White House, especially with

SALT II coming up in the Senate. It put some pressure on Mondale to prove he could still bring home the bacon. More than that, it was a sign the nation was changing. You can bet Carter saw what was happening. You might question his skills as President, but not his skills as a politician. He could read the tea leaves.

It is difficult to guess how far Mondale's stock fell inside the White House after the 1978 losses. His ties to liberals were in some jeopardy and his skills as a campaigner were in doubt. Yet, the criticism from liberals was not necessarily bad in an administration that was becoming more conservative. Though Mondale still supported liberal policies, he saw the same polling data as Carter.

Whatever Mondale's position immediately following the 1978 campaign, he benefited from what was clearly the most important event in the Democratic party in 1979: Kennedy's decision to challenge Carter for the presidential nomination. Whatever Mondale's stock before the announcement, Kennedy's decision moved the Vice-President back up. Mondale stood directly between Kennedy and Carter on the Democratic spectrum, providing considerable internal capital. Though Mondale had been under fire from some liberals after 1978, he was able to use his old connections to help Carter in the early primaries. Mondale also benefited from Carter's decision to stay in the rose garden during the first three months of the nomination campaign. However, regardless of Carter's decision to remain "presidential," Mondale's place on the ticket might have been in doubt without Kennedy's candidacy. As it was, Kennedy almost succeeded in unseating both Carter and Mondale.

Beyond Mondale's contributions to Carter's reelection campaign, problems on Capitol Hill also aided the Vice-President. Though Carter had a sizable Democratic majority at the start of his term, his legislative program had stalled in the first year. As noted earlier, Mondale did not want to take a major role in rebuilding the legislative liaison operation, under the control of Frank Moore. However, Mondale's connections to old Senate allies did prove of some value in passing several big-ticket programs. Unlike Rockefeller, who started his term in the Senate with a controversy over Rule 22, Mondale preferred to work behind the scenes. He was generally reluctant to engage in major lobbying, but did use his contacts on the Panama Canal treaty and the Department of Education. As a Carter assistant acknowledged: "Mondale may have been the swing factor on the Canal votes. It was so close that there were two or three people who could have defeated the treaty. He used some of his old networks for us. The surprising thing was that he was more valuable with some of the Democratic conservatives than with the liberals." A second assistant concurred. "Mondale had established himself as a quiet negotiator in the Senate before coming to the Vice-Presidency. He had a number of conversations with several Southern conservatives that were important on the final vote. I think they trusted him to be straightforward with them."

Carter

Like Ford and Rockefeller, Mondale and Carter shared a close personal relationship. As Mondale remembered his talks with Humphrey and Rocke- feller in 1976: "They each said two things. First, they said the personal re- lationship with the President was everything. Secondly, they warned me there'd be no way of getting along with the White House staff. But we haven't had a bit of trouble. I think Carter has brought that about. And being here in the White House has also helped (*National Journal*, 11 Mar. 1978). There were several reasons why Carter and Mondale were able to build a good relationship. Both were small-town boys. Both were from rural areas, though they had grown up in very different cultures. Mondale's father was a minister, as was his wife's father. Mondale had a deep re- ligious background to match his "born again" President. Finally, as a Mondale aide argued, "Mondale had the right kind of personality to go with Carter. He wears well, has a fair sense of humor, and is not the kind of person who is constantly on edge. Carter is not a very open person either." However, whatever Carter and Mondale's relationship, it was neither better nor worse than Ford and Rockefeller's. What is evident is that Carter in- creased Mondale's influence in at least two ways.

First, unlike Ford, Carter gave strong signals to his staff that the Vice- President was to be included in the policy process. According to one report, Carter told his staff during the transition that Mondale was "their boss and we'll try to mold as much as possible our staff to his staff." As the report continued:

> Powell added that the Carter staff looks to Mondale "as boss in virtually the same degree as we do Governor Carter. . . . I certainly would no more question a directive from Senator Mondale than I would from the governor."
> The statement provoked snickers from many of the President-elect's aides, one of whom remarked, "Can you imagine Hamilton Jordan, Jack Watson or Powell himself taking orders from Mondale?" (*National Journal*, 8 Jan. 1977).

Had Carter left the situation at that in 1977, it is unlikely that Mondale would have been any more successful than Rockefeller. However, Carter continued to give strong signals to his staff that he wanted Mondale included. "After that report came out," a Carter assistant remembered, "there was another round of 'Mondale is one of the team' messages. We heard it so many times that we finally got into the habit of calling him over." A second aide agreed: "Carter made a very determined effort to make the relationship work. I heard him say repeatedly that 'If you get a request from Fritz, you are to treat it as if it's from me.' I also heard him say that 'If you criticize or undercut Fritz, you're out.' I don't know that he enforced that second order, but people tested the system and found out that there was no way around Mondale. He had that weekly meeting and would tell Carter if people were cutting him out." Carter's staff eventually acquiesced. Carter had given the signal so many times that the staff may have felt there was no payoff in having another series of messages. According to the Mondale staff, the only rough period in the staff relationship followed the midsummer crisis in 1979 when rumors circulated about Mondale's place on the ticket. But once again, Carter instructed his staff to desist. To a remarkable degree, they cooperated.

As argued earlier, Carter's decision-making system also favored Mondale. Though a number of advisers had access to the President, Carter liked to make most decisions with little verbal argument. As the administration aged, Mondale's weekly meetings with the President became more valuable. Over the term, Carter restricted access to most of his top aides. He closed the inner circle to conserve his own time and energy. More and more decisions were made on paper. During this consolidation, however, Mondale retained his personal access, giving him special status among most White House staffers. Had Carter wanted to end his Monday lunches with Mondale, of course, there would have been no recourse. Carter's decision to continue the meetings ensured Mondale's continued persuasive vantage point.

Second, and more important, Carter adopted an expansive policy agenda that increased Mondale's influence. As Jordan remembers, Carter wanted Mondale to fight for influence: "Jimmy Carter gave Fritz Mondale the opportunity to be the first fully involved Vice President in the history of the country. Mondale took advantage of the opportunity and tried to influence administration policy, and that was just how Carter wanted it. To the extent people blame Mondale for pursuing his own 'agenda,' he was only doing what he had been urged to do from the outset by the President (*New Republic*, 6 June 1983).

At least in the first year, Carter was interested in a number of domestic initiatives. Though critics of the administration argue that Carter was overcommitted on the domestic front, Mondale was able to bring a series of new ideas into the Oval Office. Unlike Ford, who imposed a strict no new spending rule on domestic affairs, Carter was willing to consider some new programs with minimal price tags. Carter was primarily interested in any new programs with zero price tags—whether electoral reform, hospital cost containment, or deregulation. Yet, because Carter wanted to present a full policy agenda, he was *persuadable* on many of Mondale's ideas.

As the administration progressed, however, Carter was less willing to consider new initiatives. In part, Carter's reluctance stemmed from problems with passing the program already on Capitol Hill. Hospital cost containment, welfare reform, energy, electoral reform, urban assistance, tax reform, civil service reform, and the Panama Canal treaties all took longer to reach the floor than originally anticipated. Once they did reach the floor, most needed considerable redrafting to pass. Even with retooling, several remained lodged in the system until the end of the administration. In part, Carter's increasing lack of interest in new initiatives came from the worsening economy. With inflation in the double-digit range, Carter moved to curb federal spending. Though Carter experimented with "real wage insurance," he eventually adopted a traditional fiscal policy, imposing a no new spending rule similar to Ford's. The shift clearly reduced Mondale's impact on behalf of new initiatives. However, unlike Rockefeller, Mondale changed his influence strategy to a defensive posture, working to reduce cuts in domestic programs. Finally, Carter's involvement in the Iranian crisis severely restricted his program interests. That single event dominated the administration in the fourth year, coloring the agenda and the presidential campaigns.

Summary

In contrast to the Ford administration, the Carter Presidency had a reasonably normal first three years. There was an agenda-setting phase in the first year, complete with new programs and fanfare. There was a midterm phase in the second year, with opportunities for agenda setting, but dominated by the congressional campaigns. There was a normal start of the second congressional session. In this relatively stable setting, Mondale had an opportunity to build influence networks, store internal capital, lobby the President for long-term programs, and integrate his staff into the White House policy process. This normalcy allowed the vice-presidential relationship to flourish outside of the pressures of a campaign. It allowed Mondale to demonstrate his value to the Carter White House under the best possible circumstances.

Among the six explanations for Mondale's policy impact, three carry more force than the others. First, the merging of the campaign staffs set the stage for a successful Vice-Presidency. By giving the staffs a chance to build relationships before the more difficult days of the Carter Presidency, the merging added to Mondale's advisory resources and allies on the White House staff. Second, Mondale's style had an important impact on his advisory role. His willingness to remain behind the scenes contributed both to his internal capital and to the lack of noticeable criticism of the Vice-President. Finally, Carter's expansive policy agenda gave Mondale ample early opportunities to influence the direction of administration programs. Moreover, because Carter was willing to give constant signals to his staff, Mondale was able to avoid much of the territorial conflict that plagued past Vice-Presidents.

CONCLUSION

The most visible disagreement between the two groups of respondents involved what many Mondale and Carter staff members called personal chemistry. When asked why Mondale was able to succeed in his advisory role, over 60 percent of the aides answered "personal chemistry." Yet, none of the Ford and Rockefeller staff members mentioned personal chemistry as the source of Rockefeller's failure. As a Rockefeller aide concluded:

> Rockefeller had a very good personal relationship with Ford. They got along well. Who couldn't be charmed by Nelson Rockefeller? Ford felt beholden to Rockefeller for joining the White House. And Rockefeller had sacrificed to come. They were friends all along, although I'm sure each was annoyed by the way the relationship was cut down by the staffs. They both got together often, even up at Rockefeller's estate in New York. Both spoke warmly of each other and tended to blame most of the trouble on the staffs. If they could have gotten along one-tenth as well politically as they did personally, it would have worked.

Personal friendship is obviously important. It is unlikely that a President who cannot bear the sight of his Vice-President will call on him for advice. That much is known from the Nixon-Agnew relationship. However, as the Ford-Rockefeller relationship suggests, personal friendship is only one of a number of necessary, but not *sufficient* resources for vice-presidential influence. Without some personal chemistry, a Vice-President will fail. Even with personal chemistry, a Vice-President will not always succeed. As a Ford assistant said:

> I begin to wonder just how important chemistry really is. Rockefeller and Ford had a pretty good friendship. They got together once or twice a week and seemed to hit it off. In fact, Ford still argues that he made a mistake in dropping Rockefeller from the ticket. He says he still feels guilty. I have no doubt that the two of them had "good chemistry." I don't think it helped Rockefeller much and I doubt that it made a whole lot of difference for Carter and Mondale. The basis of a good presidential-vice-presidential relationship is far more than chemistry. You don't listen to someone's advice because you like him or think he's a fine human being. You listen because he's got something to say.

When one looks for agreements between the various staffs, at least five emerge. First, both the Rockefeller and Mondale respondents agreed that the opportunity to merge the presidential and vice-presidential staffs before entering office is important. Rockefeller simply was not able to build any networks that could survive the pressures of a presidential campaign year. Second, both staffs agreed on the value of allies on the White House staff. The question is why Cannon, Rockefeller's long-time aide, was not as much help to his Vice-President as Carp and Aaron were to Mondale. The answer may rest on Rockefeller's personality and the latent conflict in the Ford

White House. Rockefeller was not content to use Cannon as a source of information or as part of a larger liberal coalition. He pressured Cannon to choose between the President and himself, an unhappy but automatic choice. Third, both staffs agreed on the impact of the Vice-President's advisory style on influence. Most of the Rockefeller aides were willing to acknowledge the dangers of the advocate's position, particularly when played by a Vice-President to a national audience. As I argue shortly, discretion is indeed the better part of vice-presidential influence. Fourth, both staffs agreed on the importance of the political environment in shaping the Vice-President's influence. In a different political climate, Rockefeller might have been much more successful. Finally, though Vice-Presidents can enhance their success by merging their staffs into the White House, building influence networks, keeping a low advisory profile, placing allies in the West Wing, the President's style always has a major impact on internal influence. Without strong signals from the Oval Office, the Vice-President will fall prey to the territorial instincts of the White House staff.

7.

Vice-Presidents as Persuaders

Three factors emerge in the search for explanations of Mondale's success and Rockefeller's frustration. First, just as Vice-Presidents need certain resources to give advice—time, energy, information, expertise, etc.—they also need *resources* for influence. However, the resources needed for an advisory role are not necessarily the resources needed for influence. Second, Vice-Presidents need *opportunities* to persuade the President, whether arising from policy vacuums or the various cycles that shape the policy calendar. Third, Vice-Presidents need *strategies* for influence. As Mondale learned, there are certain strategies that enhance an outsider's influence and other strategies that expose the Vice-President to needless conflict. In part, Mondale's strategy inside the White House was based on his reading of Rockefeller's problems. In part, it rested on Mondale's training as a political second, whether as an appointed attorney general, an appointed senator, or a Vice-President.

Thus, in this theory of influence Mondale's campaign headquarters, his lack of line assignments, and his political ties became resources; the merging, the rise of strong allies, and Carter's goals became his opportunities; and Mondale's lack of line assignments plus his advisory style became part of a successful strategy. For Rockefeller, his acceptance of line assignments and political ties reduced his resources; the delay in confirmation, the rise of strong opponents, and Ford's goals reduced his opportunities; and Rockefeller's acceptance of line assignments plus his advisory style became problems in an unsuccessful strategy.

INFLUENCE RESOURCES

The Rockefeller and Mondale Vice-Presidencies illustrate the importance of influence resources. Rockefeller faced shortages of time and information, as well as of internal support. Though Rockefeller had enough advisory resources to play a policy role, he was severely overextended. He had to divide his time and energy between routine Domestic Council chores and efforts to win Ford's support for specific policies. Moreover, as Ford's agenda shifted with the worsening economic climate, Rockefeller had more trouble persuading the President on his domestic initiatives. Though Rockefeller was one of the most persuasive advisers in recent White House history, Ford was one of the least persuadable Presidents. As one Rockefeller aide argued: "It was a question of two irresistible forces. Rockefeller had to be one of the great charmers of the 1970s. He was clever, intelligent, and a skilled performer. Ford had to be one of the least interested Presidents of the past fifty years. He did not want any innovative programs. He didn't want any new ideas. Rockefeller used every tactic he knew, but couldn't get Ford to budge." In all, the Rockefeller and Mondale Vice-Presidencies illustrate the importance of five influence resources: (1) time, (2) information, (3) persuasive expertise, (4) internal capital, and (5) the President's persuadability.

Time

Just as time and information are important for the advisory role, they have a significant impact on influence. Vice-Presidents need the time to develop influence networks and to build effective strategies. They need time to assure the White House staffs of their loyalty and to take advantage of policy windows. Time remains the most basic resource for both advice and influence. However, even if the Vice-President has enough time for the advisory role, there may be limits on time for influence. As such, time is measured in both quantity and quality. According to a Rockefeller assistant: "The Vice-President was committed on too many issues. He never had the time to settle back and pick his targets. He was so absorbed in the Domestic Council and the CIA investigation that he didn't have the time to see what Rumsfeld was up to." A second Rockefeller aide agreed.

> Rockefeller had barely enough time to handle the administrative assignment on the Domestic Council. It was a tremendous drain on his time. He was involved in shuffling paper and reading reports. It was his choice, but he became convinced later on that it was the wrong choice. He was spending so much time on the trivial things that he couldn't gear up to fight Rumsfeld. That's probably why Rumsfeld wanted to saddle him with the CIA commission. He knew that Rockefeller would get so wrapped up in the problem that he wouldn't be able to stop the freeze.

Moreover, as Joseph Persico, Rockefeller's speechwriter, argues, the Vice-President did not devote enough time to his job. "For all Nelson's hunger for power, he had slighted his job in a way wholly out of character—he had not worked at it hard enough. He had become a commuter Vice President. He flew to Washington on Monday morning and back to Pocantico early Friday afternoon. . . . The White House was a seven-day-a-week operation, and he simply was not on the scene when much of the action took place" (1982, p. 272).

Time becomes particularly important in implementing strategies of influence. Even with the merging of the campaign staffs, the Mondale team needed a year to become fully integrated into the presidential policy process. As one Mondale aide remarked: "That first year had to be spent proving that we could be trusted. We needed that much time to show the Carter people that we were trustworthy. It wasn't something that could happen overnight. There are too many things in the way of an immediate relationship." According to a Carter assistant: "It took many of us several years to become comfortable with each other. We were on the campaign together and had our own friends. Even if the Mondale staffers were the nicest people in the world, it takes time to become convinced of someone's motives. We needed to see [the Mondale staff] in action before most of us were able to trust them." Since much of the Vice-President's influence is based on these personal networks, time becomes an essential ingredient in the merging process. Given the "us-versus-them" attitude toward outsiders, Vice-Presidents must have a minimal amount of time to establish alliances.

Once again, the quality of time also changes over the term. At the start of the term, Vice-Presidents have more time for coalition building than at the end. The simple passage of time leads to a consolidation within the White House staffing system. As the term moves closer to the reelection campaign, Presidents and their staffs are less willing to engage in discussion with outsiders. According to several Mondale aides, a Vice-President has approximately one year to build influence relationships before the inner circle tightens. If the Vice-President has not succeeded in merging the staffs by the end of that first year, he will become only one of many outside advisers to lose their representation inside the Oval Office. As one observer noted: "Presidents set their agendas in the first few months; they make decisions on their staffing arrangements; they do some adjusting of the cabinet; they get used to talking to certain people for help. If you're not able to get inside during that first year, the rest of the term will be wasted." That is not to argue that Presidents are completely set in their advisory patterns at the end of the first year. Anne Wexler, for instance, joined the Carter administration in 1978 and still managed to build an advisory role. However, since the Vice-President is in the administration from the very beginning, the first year remains critical in the development of influence. That is certainly one conclusion from the Rockefeller Vice-Presidency. Absent in the first few months, Rockefeller was unable to recruit allies on the White House staff. Because the advisory process was designed without him, Rockefeller had to expend considerable resources winning access to the President. Since time is a finite resource, Rockefeller's effort to gain an advisory role meant he had less time to build influence networks.

Information

Information is also an important resource for influence. Since influence is sometimes based on the simple force of argument, information can be a source of leverage in the White House. According to John Kessel, there were two ways for advisers to gain influence in the Carter administration. One was respect. The other "was to know what they were talking about."

> This was the case with three staff members: Zbigniew Brzezinski, Charles Schultze, and David Rubenstein. Brzezinski's influence was close to an inversion of the "typical" pattern. Relatively few aides said that he was respected; more said that his opposition was substantial; half of those who mentioned him acknowledged his expertise. Further comments made it clear that his influence was limited to foreign affairs. The reputations of Charles Schultze and David Rubenstein, on the other hand, depended substantially on their knowledge. Another economist said of Schultze, "With Charlie, the professional expertise is always decisive." Stuart Eizenstat said simply: "I think Charlie Schultze is the most informed man in the White House." David Rubenstein was looked to, especially by other junior staff members, as a source of general information. One aide said: "He always seems to have a wealth of knowledge about what's happening in the White House decision-making process, even down to the latest gossip about the White House staff. Rubenstein is always well informed. He and I talk a lot" (1982, p. 19).

Stuart Eizenstat also benefited from influence based on information. As one Carter aide acknowledged: "I never saw him go into any meeting unprepared. Other people would show up and ask questions about this technicality or that problem. It was always Stu who was giving the answers. If you counted the number of times he asked a question to get the basic information and the number of times he answered those questions, the ratio would be one to ten. He was the answer man."

Raw information about the policy issues can be a lever on the presidential policy process, especially if opponents are underprepared. In the Carter White House, Mondale gained some advantage simply from the lack of Washington experience among some members of the President's staff. The relative gaps, however, did not cover all policy areas. Brzezinski in foreign affairs, Schultze in economics, and Eizenstat in domestic policy were all well-seasoned veterans of Washington politics. Mondale's strength became more apparent at lower levels of the White House staff. All of Mondale's policy lieutenants had past experience in Washington, giving them some advantage over their less experienced White House colleagues. Moreover, because Mondale had contacts on the White House staff, he was able to secure information on what opponents were planning. Unlike Rockefeller, who entered office four months behind the learning curve, Mondale was well ahead at the start of the Carter administration.

The Vice-President's greatest information shortages often come in foreign affairs. As Humphrey remembered, Secretary of State Dean Rusk warned the Vice-President to stay out of foreign policy.

> Rusk acknowledged my long interest in foreign affairs, but cautioned that I should not expect to be involved in interagency formulation of policy. He noted that Lyndon Johnson as Vice President had not developed a personal foreign-policy staff, relying instead on information from State, Defense, and the CIA. For constitutional as well as practical reasons, he considered it important that the Vice President, whoever he might be, not intrude himself between the President and the established agencies (1976, pp. 317-18).

Ford, Rockefeller, and Mondale were able to compensate for the information shortages by hiring their own foreign policy advisers. However, it was not until Mondale arrived that the Vice-President received immediate access to the President's Daily Briefing. Without access to the PDB, Vice-Presidents cannot know what the issues are, let alone draft alternatives. With access to the PDB, Mondale was able to increase his foreign policy influence. Mondale also received information through David Aaron, his former Senate aide on the NSC staff. Though Mondale remained stronger in domestic policy than foreign, he did not face the same information problems as his vice-presidential predecessors.

Persuasive Expertise

Once the Vice-President enters the Oval Office for one-on-one meetings with the President, persuasive expertise becomes a critical resource. The degree to which the Vice-President can apply interpersonal skills has a direct bearing on influence. Persuasive skills are important to all senior advisers. In the Nixon administration, for instance, Daniel Patrick Moynihan was able to persuade Nixon of the merits of a costly welfare reform package. According to one of Moynihan's opponents:

> He was one of the very few people on the White House staff who had operated in the Washington bureaucracy and understood it. He had an extensive network of contacts throughout HEW and OEO, many of them Democrats shocked at Humphrey's defeat, who flooded him with research data and other information. And he had great persuasive resources: In the sea of dark gray and blue that surrounded Nixon, Moynihan, in his cream-colored suit and red bow tie, gleamed like a playful porpoise. He was a charming Irish rogue, a delightful dinner companion, a fascinating teller of tales. His presence lighted the gloom

of national policy deliberations, and even his opponents liked to have him around. The President liked to read his memoranda, sometimes even searching through the pile on his desk to find them (Anderson 1978, p. 6).

As a Nixon aide argued: "The President had a weakness for Moynihan's brand of argument. Moynihan kept telling the President that welfare reform would make him a great President; that years from now people would look back and applaud him for the bold ventures. The President bought it." When paired against the reserved, pipe-smoking Arthur Burns, Moynihan had little trouble persuading Nixon of the merits of the ill-fated welfare reform plan.

Among recent Vice-Presidents, two stand out as persuasive artisans: Humphrey and Rockefeller. Both learned the craft of interpersonal influence and perfected their techniques in long political careers. Unfortunately for Humphrey, Lyndon Johnson did not offer many opportunities for persuasion. Only Rockefeller had an opportunity to bring his persuasive skills to bear on the President. Even among his enemies, Rockefeller was respected for his skill. "I never thought Rocky was unpleasant or vindictive," a Ford aide admitted. "In fact, I enjoyed most of my time with him. He was a fine human being and a delight to be with. I never resented him personally, but I did oppose him politically. He wasn't the kind of person you could hate, however." A second Ford aide echoed the impression. "I found it very difficult to get along with some of the old Nixon people. They were hostile and bitter. Not Rockefeller. He was always smiling and a tough competitor. He was a good sport and hard to fight." Precisely because he was such a persuasive individual, many of the Ford staff members were concerned about Rockefeller's one-on-one meetings with the President. That is not to argue that the Ford staff thought the President could be easily tricked. Rather, they saw the private meetings as opportunities for persuasion that few Ford members could control. "There was nobody in that crew who could top Rockefeller," a vice-presidential aide concluded. "He was a remarkable persuader. If you met with him alone, you always came out in agreement. He just wouldn't let you say no. 'Think about it a while,' he would say. That's why the Ford people wanted him in bigger meetings. He could convince anyone if he could get them away from the White House."

It is difficult to pinpoint what made Rockefeller a strong persuader. When asked, Rockefeller aides suggested three factors. First, Rockefeller had a very pleasant demeanor. His charm set him apart from other White House aides. "Ford liked to be with him because he was a likeable person," a White House aide said. "He felt tremendous guilt about [removing him from the ticket] because he liked Rocky so much." Second, Rockefeller framed his arguments around the President's goals. In arguing with Ford, he cast his arguments to match Ford's interests. "If Ford said the program would cost too much," an aide reported, "Rockefeller would point to the long-term cost savings. If Ford said the bill wouldn't pass, Rockefeller would point to a list of sponsors." Indeed, according to several Ford respondents, Rockefeller's energy proposals were developed specifically to meet Ford's budget restrictions. When Ford imposed his no new spending rule, he left room for only one exception: energy. "Rockefeller saw the opening and moved into it," a Ford assistant argued. "He sensed there was some possibility there and got Ford to agree. He had a good sense of what it would take to get Ford to sign off." Third, Rockefeller tried to isolate Ford from his competitors. Instead of relying on large meetings and forums, Rockefeller worked for private contacts. As one Rockefeller assistant noted: "He knew that his best chance for winning was with Ford alone. That's why he would take in memoranda for Ford's signature. He tried to take advantage of his personal ability by getting Ford to initial ideas immediately. He knew that he would lose if he went through the normal staffing system so he went around it." Though Rockefeller's end runs to the President generated considerable staff hostility, he also recognized that the private meetings were the only opportunity for influence.

All this is not to suggest that Mondale was an amateur. According to most Carter and Mondale aides, he had an effective style, was generally liked, and was certainly well prepared. As Jordan argues: "My office in the White House was next to Mondale's, and he would frequently pop in, sleeves rolled up, cigar in his mouth, smiling and quipping. He is a funny man . . . and a shrewd one. In the White House, he played his cards wisely" (*New Republic*, 6 June 1983). Perhaps no other individual in vice-presidential history was so well-trained to play the second position. Mondale had risen to the top by attaching himself to more powerful mentors, riding a series of appointments to national office. Certainly, Mondale had learned how to influence his benefactors, while protecting his own stakes for the future. As one Carter aide argued, "A Vice-President has to be strong, but not too strong; smart, but not too smart; aggressive, well-prepared, and pushy, but without usurping the President's power. That takes a very fine touch that Mondale had. He knew just how to stroke everyone the right way." However, Mondale did not have the same degree of persuasive skill as Rockefeller. He could not rely on his argumentative expertise alone. Though Mondale had a good relationship with Carter, he had a very different persuasive style. Unlike Rockefeller, Mondale did not turn to his charm for influence. Indeed, most reports suggest that Mondale was somewhat distant from the rest of the White House staff. "He was not the kind of person to stand around and chat," an aide remarked. "He didn't get particularly close to anyone, though he was respected. He wasn't a backslapper or storyteller like Humphrey." Mondale's strength rested in his ability to build policy coalitions and influence networks. He did not use the same persuasive strategies as Moynihan or Rockefeller. He did not have that kind of skill. However, Mondale did have the ability to adapt to his own personal limits. If he could not win an argument on the strength of his personality, he could win on the strength of his information. According to one analysis, Mondale's skill rested in his ability to adapt and adjust.

> While he didn't win every battle, he picked his fights carefully and made sure they did not become personal quarrels or confrontations. He helped produce the compromise that quelled an open floor fight at the 1964 convention over the Mississippi credentials challenge. When he sensed that direct legislative efforts on behalf of migrants would lead nowhere, Mondale did not attempt to build the same kind of coalition that had succeeded on open housing. Instead, he broadened his efforts, although his eye was constantly on the goal. . . . When the fight over school busing flared, Mondale took a strong and well-documented stand in support of equal educational opportunity—and then sought the most defensible tactical position he could find. . . . His tenure on the Finance Committee conformed to that same pattern. He shied from a direct battle with Chairman Russell Long—a fight that would have entailed going over Long's head and appealing to a broader constituency within Congress and outside, as well. What he sought was a pragmatic accommodation . . . (Lewis 1980, p. 278).

If there was one theme in Mondale's persuasive style, it was caution. Mondale was unwilling to press for full victories in the short term if they meant a loss of support in the long term. Unlike Rockefeller or Moynihan, who used their access to the President for open advocacy, Mondale reportedly used his meetings for general advice. The fact that Mondale retained that access over his term, while Rockefeller and Moynihan did not, is one indication that persuasive skills are not enough to generate long-term influence.

Internal Capital

Internal capital is based on the Vice-President's image *inside* the White House. It is not based on the Vice-President's status as a front-runner, nor his pomp and perquisites. It is not based on formal statutes or the Senate office. Instead, internal capital is based on the staff's perception of the Vice-President as a team player, on his reputation as an adviser who can be trusted. Though White House staff members may disagree on issues of policy, they expect loyalty to the President. The more the Vice-President can demonstrate his loyalty and support, the greater the internal capital. As Peter Teeley, Bush's press secretary, argued in mid-1981: "During the fall campaign, Bush earned Reagan's respect by working hard, not making mistakes and proving that he was a 100 percent, solid team guy. . . . The first time that Bush went into the Oval Office and the conversation came out in the papers, we'd find ourselves with a job that wouldn't be worth having" (*National Journal*, 20 June 1981).

The notion that Vice-Presidents have both external and internal capital was confirmed in the interviews with the Rockefeller and Mondale staffs. As a Rockefeller aide suggested:

> I don't think there was ever much question about Rockefeller's national image. He was still pretty well received in the electorate, if not the party. He still had problems with his image as a wealthy New Yorker, but he had strong support among the moderates. The problem was inside the White House, where he had all sorts of critics. The White House staff didn't trust Rockefeller. They saw him as trying to take over. They saw Kissinger as his protégé and saw his staff as disloyal. There was a complete lack of support or trust on the inside. That was the real problem.

Rockefeller's problems with internal capital came from several sources. First, Rockefeller had expended a great amount of his internal support on the Domestic Council fight. Instead of taking a low profile in his first months, Rockefeller seemed to confirm all of the worst suspicions of the Ford staff. As Persico remembers:

> What Rockefeller expected to achieve as Vice-President was extraordinary, given his foreknowledge of the job. His protégé, Henry Kissinger, had effectively taken control of U.S. foreign policy in the Ford Administration. Why should Nelson not handle domestic policy? Who was better prepared? Political commentators encouraged the idea, writing of Rockefeller and his staff arriving at the Ford White House as though the New York Yankees were taking over a high-school locker room (1982, p. 261).

Rockefeller was aware of the dangers in taking a visible role in administration policy. As one aide remarked: "He was very publicity-conscious when he first came into office . . . because of all the fuss at the time of his confirmation hearings that he was going to overshadow the President. . . . He didn't want to take any steps that might indicate he was attempting to do that" (*National Journal,* 18 Oct. 1975). Yet, Rockefeller still pushed for policy responsibilities. His Domestic Council victory reduced his already limited internal capital. According to one opponent:

> He had promised that he would not do anything to detract from Ford, but here he was doing just that. I can understand why he wanted the Domestic Council thing. He wanted some formal assurance that he would be involved. Instead, the Domestic Council role was another major victory for Rockefeller in the press. He played it for all it was worth, too. It made Ford and the rest of the White House staff look very bad, like we were being saved from ourselves. I wasn't about to help anyone build that image. He set himself up to be brought down. We had to make some move to show that we were in charge.

Second, Rockefeller's public support weakened over the first year. Though external and internal capital flow from different springs, the two are related. If the Vice-President is under heavy fire from the public, the White House staff will try to minimize damage to the President. It is a natural reflex. It happened when conservatives stepped up their attacks on Rockefeller in 1975. As Rockefeller's public support declined, reflected in negative approval ratings, internal support fell. As a Ford assistant acknowledged: "We might have been more enthusiastic about Rockefeller had he held his own in the polls. He was dropping like a rock in mid-1975. Maybe it was the confirmation hearings or a backlash against liberalism. But Rockefeller was definitely not helping the President in the polls." In some respects, Rockefeller's public problems reinforced his internal isolation, which in turn increased his public problems. It was a circle that was difficult to break. "If he was perceived as a hindrance," an aide admitted, "that meant he was less likely to get any inside help. If he couldn't get any inside help, he would be seen as even more of a hindrance. A lot of the public image was encouraged by certain members of the Ford staff, particularly the political types." As noted above, Mondale's problems in the Minnesota midterm elections may have affected his internal reputation. According to several aides, Mondale had to walk a tight rope between reassuring the Carter staff he was still politically viable and not becoming too visible or threatening. That pressure becomes more intense as the fourth year of the term approaches. Unlike White House staff members, Vice-Presidents must be renominated to retain their policy roles. Renomination, however, is often dependent on public perceptions of the Vice-President's importance, which may work against internal support.

Rockefeller and Mondale both recognized the impact of internal capital on influence. On one level, internal capital affects the flow of information to the Vice-President. Staff members will be more interested in sharing data with trusted White House players. "The minute the Vice-President leaks something to the press," a Carter aide said, "the staff will stop talking to him. If he can't be trusted with sensitive information, he won't get any. His staff won't get any either." On a second level, internal capital is the glue of White House coalitions. Since Vice-Presidents have no sanctions they can use inside the White House, they must rely on their store of capital with the President and the staff. "We had nothing to trade with the President's people except our expertise on a couple of issues and some contacts on Capitol Hill," a Humphrey assistant noted. "If they weren't interested in talking with us, we had no options. We couldn't force them to call and couldn't bribe with anything. Everything depended on their willingness to talk to us. And that depended on their trust." For Humphrey, that trust was undermined by his own gregarious personality. As an aide commented: "They took one look at Humphrey and saw the source of all the leaks. They thought he was talking to the press about the war. They thought he was disloyal. They held all the cards and iced him out."

Unlike public approval, internal capital is extremely difficult to measure. Though Mondale had more internal capital than Rockefeller, it is impossible to say how much more. Since internal capital is based on perceptions among the White House staff, it often varies from year to year. Mondale's internal capital increased over the first two years as he demonstrated his loyalty to Carter. Ford's internal capital decreased over his brief term, hitting bottom when he outlined his hypothetical post-Nixon cabinet to the *New Republic* four months *before* Nixon resigned. However, if it is difficult to estimate internal capital, there do appear to be a number of norms that affect inside support.

According to most staff members, the first rule of internal support is: *Never complain to the press.* If the Vice-President has a complaint, there are several choices. The Vice-President can keep quiet, taking the defeat in stride. He can go to the President, hoping for some internal resolution. Or he can talk to the press, going public with the dispute. The decision to go outside the White House has major consequences for future influence. "Everybody leaks something at some time in the term," a Rockefeller assistant remarked, "but the person who can least afford it is the Vice-President. That can be the final blow for the staff. It is the ultimate sign of disloyalty to go outside."

The second rule is: *Never take credit.* Whatever the policy, whether a vice-presidential victory on the agenda or the budget, the credit always goes to the President. As one Rockefeller aide acknowledged:

> The worst thing Rockefeller did was to take the Energy Independence Authority outside the White House as his program. It had always been a Rockefeller idea, but once Ford signed off, it belonged to the President. Once any idea is adopted in the White House, it belongs to the President. The minute an aide claims credit for a program, he'll be under attack from the rest of the staff. That's not because staffers don't influence the President. A number of Ford programs came from Lynn at OMB or Greenspan, but they never claimed any credit. They never went outside the White House and pointed at a program and said "That's my baby. I got Ford to go along."

Once a Vice-President or any aide claims credit, the doors open for opponents to publicize their cricitism. In Rockefeller's case, the energy bill was lampooned by a string of top Ford officials. In violating the credit norm, Rockefeller exposed his program to intense White House attack. Though that criticism might have gone public anyway, Rockefeller's open position made an easy target.

The third rule for internal capital is: *Fall in line.* As Mondale noted after leaving office, once Carter "made a decision, I wouldn't rag him. I didn't background reporters" on the decisions (*Boston Globe,* 25 Feb. 1983). Though the strategy helped Mondale inside the Carter White House, it may have hurt in his own campaign for President. Because Mondale never made his opposition public, he could easily be tied to all of the Carter decisions. If

Vice-Presidents and other advisers are not to claim credit for victories, they are also not to continue fighting after a decision. After the President makes the choice, aides are expected to support the policy. Though this rule is frequently ignored by White House aides, it is strictly enforced for Vice-Presidents. If the Vice-President wants to protect internal capital, public opposition to presidential programs is far too risky. Vice-Presidents may decide not to lobby or speak on behalf of those programs, but they cannot attack them publicly. "We opposed a number of Carter decisions," a Mondale aide said, "but never told anyone outside of a very small group of people where we stood. No President will tolerate a Vice-President or cabinet secretary who attacks a decision after it has been made. The time for opposition is before the decision, not after." Indeed, as a Carter official argued: "One of the things I came to admire about Mondale was his support for the President's decisions, whatever they were. I knew he was fighting against some of the programs in his private meetings, but I never heard him utter one word outside the White House. That made me more willing to deal with him on other issues. You need those kinds of people to make the process work, so that you don't see all the blood in the newspapers the next day."

The fourth rule of internal support is: *Share the dirty work.* Though campaigning, public liaison, and outside speaking may subtract from the Vice-President's policy role, they are important chores in building internal capital. The Vice-President's willingness to take on political assignments has a direct bearing on staff perceptions of loyalty. Though Mondale was unwilling to speak in support of programs he opposed, he still acted as a frequent public spokesman for many Carter priorities.

All of these rules contribute to the Vice-President's image as a team player. As an outside observer noted of Bush: "His main job his first year was to prove that he was loyal and trustworthy. He had absolutely no internal capital to start with. Nobody trusted him except Baker. Reagan had to get to know him. His trip to Atlanta on the child killings and his reaction during the assassination made a big difference in Bush's stock inside the White House." Unlike long-time presidential associates, Vice-Presidents have to prove their value to the new administration. Part of that testing comes with specific issues. How well does the Vice-President do with electoral reform (Mondale)? health policy (Agnew)? regulatory reform (Bush)? CIA investigations (Rockefeller)? Part of the testing involves the four internal norms. Does the Vice-President go outside with complaints? Does the Vice-President take credit? Does the Vice-President fall in line? Does the Vice-President do his share of the difficult work? All of these questions add to the Vice-President's stock of capital inside the administration.

The President's Persuadability

Even if the Vice-President has ample time and information, strong persuasive skills, and sufficient internal capital, influence ultimately rests on the President's receptivity to advice. Reagan, for instance, was not persuadable on the issue of eliminating the third year of his massive tax cut program. Even with near unanimity among his policy advisers on the need for reducing the size of the tax cut, Reagan remained unwilling to compromise. The closest Reagan would move toward the advice of his senior staff was to delay the third year of the tax cut for ninety days, a compromise that was rejected by House Democrats. As Abraham Lincoln once said to his cabinet, "One Aye, seven Nays. The Ayes have it."

This is not to argue that staffs have no influence on decisions. Rather, the degree to which Presidents are open to persuasion on certain issues affects the impact of advice. Though Reagan was unwilling to budge on his tax cut, he was willing to be persuaded on foreign policy, legislative tactics, and a $98.9 billion tax increase. In some policy areas, Reagan was more persuadable than in others. Even on the economic plan, Reagan was open to influence on specifics, as long as the general ends met his view of government. Once the President and staff agreed that the budget had to be cut, there was room for maneuvering on how and what would be cut. Like Reagan, other Presidents have been more persuadable in certain areas. Ford was not persuadable on new domestic spending programs, having accepted, then rejected, national health insurance in his first months, but he was interested in a new energy policy. Rockefeller took advantage of Ford's persuadability on the issue to win the President's adoption of a sweeping energy plan. Among recent Presidents, perhaps Carter was the most persuadable across the widest range of issues. As James Fallows, Carter's former speechwriter, wrote in 1979:

> During the first year came other indications that Carter did not really know *what* he wanted to do in such crucial areas as taxes, welfare, energy, and the reorganization of the government. In each of these areas, Carter's passionate campaign commitments turned out to be commitments to generalities, not to specific programs or policies. After taking office, he commissioned panels of experts to tell him what to do, usually giving them instructions no more detailed than his repeated exhortation to "Be Bold!" (1979, p. 40).

Carter's openness to advice gave his Vice-President and other senior advisers more room for influence. He gave clear signals that he was willing to be persuaded on policy.

Persuadability rests on several factors. Presidents often vary in their commitment to their political promises. Some relate very different issues to a tightly held common view. When a President reduces every issue to the same black and white choice, there is less opportunity for persuasion. "In Reagan's case," an observer noted, "most issues get cast as a 'big government-little government' problem. There's no way to move Reagan once he sees something as a way to reduce big government. There's no way to move him if he sees a program as somehow increasing the federal role." Other Presidents may be unable to find common themes even among similar issues. Indeed, one of the common criticisms of Carter is that he lacked an overriding philosophy of government, causing him to drift back and forth across a range of issues.

Presidents also vary in the way they solve problems. One style is to break problems down into their separate components and solve each question in order. A second style is to work on different problems simultaneously. As John Kessel notes, the first style "has some advantages; it prevents the lockstep of a too rigid ideology. But it does not provide the intellectual coherence that would allow a president's staff to be serving larger political goals at the same time that they concentrate on their particular assignments" (1982, p. 28). In breaking problems into distinct components, Presidents open themselves to greater influence from the staff. Moreover, because some problems cannot be handled simultaneously, Presidents may often be persuaded despite their intentions.

Presidents also vary in the way they receive advice. Among recent Presidents, Carter and Nixon preferred to work on paper, while Kennedy, Johnson, Ford, and Reagan used in-person channels to gain advice. In theory, the on-paper style restricts influence based on persuasive skills. Nixon, for example, wanted a system that would produce formal options for his isolated decisions. In an on-paper system, individual persuaders like Rockefeller and Moynihan lose considerable advantages. That is one reason why the Ford staff wanted Rockefeller to use the normal staffing system. By reducing his ideas to a set of paper pros and cons, Rockefeller's persuasive powers could be curbed.

A final source of persuadability is the President's personality. As Alexander George suggests:

> Executives who find personal contact with too many advisers inefficient or wearing, or who find exposure to the rough-and-tumble of vigorous debate within the advisory group incompatible with their habitual or preferred mode of decision-making, will seek to limit their direct involvement with others in the search and evaluation phases of policymaking that precede final choice of action. The type of communication network that an executive develops around him will reflect not only his cognitive style but also his conception of the role he should play in the management structure. . . . Some executives prefer to restrict their role to making the final choice of action; others prefer to involve themselves more actively in the search and evaluation activities. . . . But all execu-

tives rely to some extent on a relatively small number of advisers and staff to ferret out information, make suggestions, develop and appraise policy options, and to monitor the implementation of decisions taken (1980, p. 98).

Though it is difficult to pinpoint just what parts of the psyche may be involved, some Presidents may be more willing to be persuaded by certain kinds of advisers. Poverty, unpredictable fathers, overprotective mothers, competitive siblings, and sickness may all have some impact on the President's persuadability. The problem is that there are few models of presidential personality that can tell us how the President's underlying drives might shape advice and influence in the White House. The closest we come is James Barber's (1971) model of presidential character, which argues that the President's style is born in the first political contests and shaped by earlier childhood experience. As Barber analyzed Nixon:

> On the one hand, he is a shrewd, calm, careful, proper, almost fussily conventional man of moderation, a mildly self-deprecating common-sense burgher. On the other hand, he has been a fighter, a rip-snorting indignant, a dramatic contender for his own moral vision. To say that the first theme traces to his mother and the second to his father is but the beginning of an explanation of a pattern in which alternation has substituted for resolution. The temptation for one of his character type is to follow a period of self-sacrificing service with a declaration of independence, a move which is necessary exactly because it breaks through the web of dependencies he feels gathering around him.
>
> Add to this character a style in which intimacy and consultation have never been easy and in which isolated soul-searching is habitual. Add to that an explicit theory and system of decision-making in which the President listens inquiringly to his committees of officials (who have been encouraged in their own independence), then retires to make his personal choice, then emerges to announce that choice. The temptation to surprise them all and, when the issue is defined as critically important, to adhere to it adamantly is exacerbated by the mechanisms of decision (1971, p. 406).

As others have noted, however, Barber's theory is incomplete and lacks clear underpinnings to connect personality and decision making. Moreover, the President's openness to persuasion varies with changes in the political cycles surrounding the White House. Yet, that does not mean personality has no impact on advice and influence, just that we have not yet discovered the links.

OPPORTUNITIES

Regardless of resources, Vice-Presidents (and other advisers) need opportunities to present their advice. There are at least four cycles in the presidential term that shape the opportunities for persuasion: (1) the electoral cycle, (2) the policy cycle, (3) the cycle of increasing effectiveness among White House staff, and (4) the cycle of decreasing influence on Capitol Hill.

The Electoral Cycle

Vice-Presidential influence follows the ebb and flow of seasons in the electoral calendar. Vice-Presidents have fewer opportunities for persuasion when they are on the campaign trail. Because Vice-Presidents now have political duties in the midterm elections and must also campaign for their own renomination, the second and fourth years of the term present less potential for influence activity. Though Vice-Presidents often build alliances and representation with the White House staff, the electoral cycle emphasizes the first and third years of the term as the primary opportunities for influence. As one Carter aide argued: "During most of 1978 and 1980, I didn't see much of Mondale. He was gone on the campaign most of the time. He didn't have much of a presence in the White House, but I did see some of his aides moving around. I'd guess that when he was gone, he had very little to do with any policy making. He wasn't attending any of the major meetings and didn't have much contact with Carter, except on campaign matters. When he was gone, he was out of the loop and there wasn't anyone who could take his place."

Because politics will dominate an administration the closer it moves to reelection, Vice-Presidents have the best opportunities for influence in the very first months of the term. In the natural euphoria following a victorious campaign, Presidents are generally willing to listen to all advisers. They give access to old friends, cabinet secretaries, liberals, conservatives, even Vice-Presidents. The dominant style is congeniality, not hostility. All things are possible in those first few months, and Presidents are open to advice. However, according to a Humphrey assistant:

> Pretty soon after the first six months, people start asking what happened to the Vice-President. That's because it becomes more difficult for the Vice-President to operate either in Congress or the White House. When one of the President's people looks at his calendar, he will finally say "Hell, I don't have time to meet with the Vice-President anymore. Tell him I'm out." At the beginning, we all had White House passes. They took them away by 1966. At the beginning, we even had decent aircraft. They disappeared, sent to another airbase. As things toughen up over the term, the Vice-President is the first to go.

In the first moments after the election, Presidents also suffer some confusion on their agendas. As the President-elect starts to sift through the campaign promises in search of viable programs, there is some opportunity for Vice-Presidents to offer advice. Since most transitions are characterized by a very loose organizational structure, there is also ample opportunity for Vice-Presidents to infiltrate the staff system. As one observer argued: "Carter's transition wasn't any messier than any other, but it was messy enough. There were all sorts of task forces and ad hoc committees at work. There were jobs to fill, reports to write, inaugural festivities to plan. More than at any other time in the term, I think, the President needs extra help." The Vice-President, of course, is one source of that help. At least for Mondale, the transition confusion worked in his favor. As Carter looked for people to fill two thousand White House and executive branch positions, Mondale was able to supply a number of names, including David Aaron and Bert Carp. As Carter looked for people to help organize his first year agenda, Mondale won the position. The first pass at the agenda was presented to the senior staff after Christmas, 1976, on Saint Simons Island, Carter's transition retreat.

> Each guest was given a copy of a twenty-nine page memorandum, ranging broadly over the next half year, along with a more detailed calendar that blocked out on a weekly basis a schedule of Presidential activities through the end of March. The stated purpose of this combined prospectus was to "suggest a strategy for leadership during the crucial first few months of the Carter administration." The Mondale agenda incorporated recommendations from another planning memorandum ordered up by the President-elect, called "An Initial Working Paper on Political Strategy." This sixty-nine page document had been prepared by Patrick Caddell, pollster-in-chief for the Carter campaign (Shogan 1977, p. 109).

Yet, as an administration moves closer to the reelection year, the Vice-President may be unable to retain his image as a senior adviser. Polls are commissioned measuring the Vice-President's contributions to the ticket. Opposition may arise in the party. At the start of the term, the Vice-President may be able to assume a position of anonymity inside the White House. At the end of the term, there is no way to escape the political visibility. It was this aspect of the electoral cycle that hurt Rockefeller. Under normal circumstances, Rockefeller would have had time to work on policy before turning to his electoral survival. However, arriving with only seventeen months to the Republican convention, Rockefeller was forced to defend his position from the very beginning. Unlike Mondale, who benefited from the honeymoon, Rockefeller had to push for renomination only months after his initial nomination.

Mondale may have faced similar problems following the 1978 midterm disaster in Minnesota. Though Mondale remained involved in the policy process, the loss of two Democratic Senate seats left questions for the future. As an observer argued: "The election brought Mondale back to earth and got Carter thinking about him as a politician again. For a while in 1977 and early 1978, he had become a senior staffer. He'd been surprisingly successful at working his way into the White House. The midterm defeats in his home state served to remind everyone that he was still the Vice-President and maybe not so effective as a campaigner." Though Mondale never faced the depth of internal opposition that Rockefeller faced, the electoral cycle made the advisory role more difficult over time, if only because it made the Vice-President more visible inside and outside of the administration. Moreover, as Rockefeller and Mondale approached the fourth-year campaigns, their national reputations became more threatening to the White House. Whether consciously or not, both Vice-Presidents served as potential alternatives to their own Presidents. The fact that Mondale was briefly mentioned as a substitute for Carter in the weeks immediately preceding the 1980 Democratic convention would have had some bearing on his role in a second term. As a Carter aide concluded:

> I have no doubt that Mondale had nothing to do with the "dump Carter" movement. That was all Kennedy's doing. Mondale's name was floated to embarrass the President. But for all its innocence, those couple of weeks hurt Mondale's standing in the Carter group. It reminded everyone that Mondale was a free agent. If Carter lost, Mondale would survive. I didn't feel that way and most of the staff didn't. But it was used by some people against Mondale and it would have been used in the second term. It doesn't take much to plant the seed. And there were plenty of people in the administration who resented Mondale's access to the President who would have helped the suspicions take root.

The electoral cycle may also force Vice-Presidents and other advisers to tailor arguments to changing politics. According to Brzezinski, "Mondale's most important substantive contribution was his political judgement. He was a vital political barometer for the President and . . . had a good sense of political timing. For example, in the early months he was quite keen on pushing hard with our Middle East peace initiatives, even if it meant some transitory conflicts with the Israelis. He was particularly tough-minded after Begin's accession to power." Yet, "by late 1978, with the congressional elections near and the Presidential season gradually beginning, Fritz became an advocate of a rather passive U.S. posture, tilted in favor of the Israelis" (*New Republic,* 4 April 1983).

The Policy Cycle

The policy calendar also presents opportunities for influence. Vice-Presidents have the greatest opportunities for impact at the agenda-setting stage of the policy cycle, with additional chances at the budgeting phase. They face the lowest potentials for influence at the implementation stage. As decisions move away from the White House toward Capitol Hill or the executive branch, Vice-Presidents lose opportunities for impact. They are limited by protocol in congressional lobbying and have no tools for shaping implementation. If Vice-Presidents want policy influence, it must come at the agenda-setting and budgeting steps, both of which occur relatively close to the Oval Office. Vice-Presidents can maintain a low profile at these early stages of the cycle, but take on higher visibility outside the White House. Moreover, as the policy cycle progresses, the costs of success increase. If the Vice-President does not win at the agenda-setting stage, the costs of victory later are staggering. Thus, much of Mondale's impact came from his control of the agenda-setting process, where he could canvass the executive branch for ideas and assign priorities to the President's programs. Rockefeller also tried to control the agenda, hoping the Domestic Council would act as a conduit for the President's domestic priorities. Both Vice-Presidents saw the agenda as the critical stage in the policy process.

The White House policy cycle is the product of two related calendars. As I have argued elsewhere, *"Presidents set their domestic agendas early and repeat them often"* (1982b, p. 41). Whereas Neustadt argues that the first year is a "learning time for the new President who has to learn—or unlearn—many things about his job" (1980, p. 189), most White House staff members say that it is for action. The first year determines outcomes well into the final days of the administration. Because presidential priorities tend to involve more controversy and conflict than routine legislation, they also take more time to enact. Unless the President moves quickly to set the agenda, other entrepreneurs will do it for him. As I have suggested:

> Ultimately, first-year pressure is the result of competition. The President is only one actor among many. As Carter quickly discovered, there is considerable competition for scarce congressional agenda space; there is competition for media coverage; there is even competition on the bureaucratic agendas. If the President is to compete for the scarce space, it is to his advantage to move early. Presidents must also be concerned about opposition. The longer a program must wait for introduction, the greater the potential for organized opposition. . . . The growth of congressional independence has definitely increased this first-year pressure, giving future administrations an even greater stake in the first moments of the term (1982b, p. 43).

The pressure to set the agenda early is often so intense that technical mistakes are accepted as a matter of course. As Stockman acknowledged in his *Atlantic* interview, the need for speed worked against budget coherence in 1981.

> The reason we did it wrong—not wrong, but less than the optimum—was that we said, Hey, we have to get a program out fast. And when you decide to put a program of this breadth and depth out fast, you can only do so much. We were working in a twenty or twenty-five-day time frame, and we didn't think it all the way through. We didn't add up all the numbers. We didn't make all the thorough, comprehensive calculations about where we really needed to come out and how much to put on the plate the first time, and so forth. In other words, we ended up with a list that I'd always been carrying of things to be

done, rather than starting the other way and asking, What is the overall fiscal policy required to reach the target (Greider 1981, p. 54).

This first-year agenda-setting process clearly hurt Rockefeller and helped Mondale. By the time Rockefeller joined the administration four months into the term, the Ford agenda was already set for 1975. Rockefeller had not participated in the planning of Ford's first State of the Union address and had not been involved in discussions of the fiscal program. Because the President's agenda is generally announced at the start of the calendar year in a series of policy speeches, the process was completed before Rockefeller's confirmation; therefore, he had to wait until October 1975 for his first budget action. Had Rockefeller been confirmed even two months earlier, he would have entered office in the midst of the policy debates for Ford's first agenda. Mondale, however, was on the scene from the very beginning and participated in the agenda-setting process. He had access to Carter at the time when choices were being made on the first- and second-year programs. With much of the Carter program stalled in Congress, Mondale's early participation carried impact over the full term.

Presidents have a second opportunity to structure the congressional agenda in the third year of the term, at the start of a new Congress. In most cases, Presidents take the programs that did not pass in the first two years and retool them for reintroduction. As such, the third-year agenda often resembles the earlier program. However, Presidents also have an opportunity to present new ideas. In Mondale's case, the Vice-President's office was fully involved in the third-year agenda process. The agenda-setting mechanism was in full operation and Mondale's staff was actively included in the canvassing process in the executive branch. "We were operating much like legislative clearance in OMB," a Mondale aide noted, "but we were only dealing with the nonroutine programs. OMB handles everything, while we were interested in programs that might be important to Carter. We took each incoming program and made a decision on the level of importance: presidential, White House, or executive branch." Rockefeller, of course, did not have a chance to influence any third-year agenda.

The second policy calendar involves a twelve-month cycle. According to Kessel, Presidents have an annual program cycle that begins sometime "after Labor Day when programs to be proposed to Congress are readied. Fall is probably the time of the heaviest work load for the policy-staffer in the White House, because work is still progressing on Capitol Hill on the present year's program at the same time preparations for the next year are being made." The calendar continues with basic choices on the budget in December, major presentations to Congress in January and February, congressional decision in the spring and early summer, vacations in August, and a return to planning in September and October. As Kessel concludes, "in election years, major bills will be on the floor just before adjournment, following which there will be a rapid shift of focus onto the campaign, so any real attention to the legislative program for the coming year gets deferred until November and December" (1975, p. 9). In the Johnson administration, for instance, the sequence started in the spring.

April/May/June: Idea Gathering: Visits to universities; contacts with outside experts and "idea men" in government;
July: Internal discussions of ideas gathered;
August: Appointment of outside task forces;
Sept/Oct/Nov: Receipt and review of task-force reports, Agency submissions;
December: White House meetings, Final Presidential decisions on the program;
Jan/Feb/Mar: Preparation of messages, Introduction of bills (Thomas and Wolman 1969, p. 132).

For advisers seeking influence, the critical period runs from July through December. Though staff members want to be involved from the "idea gathering" stage until the final messages are drafted, if they have to be absent, the middle months of the year offer the lowest risks. Again, wintering in Washington is a key to influence on the President's policy agenda.

Putting the two calendars together, the greatest opportunities for vice-presidential persuasion are the first two winters of any administration. As one observer noted: "If the Vice-President wants to take a trip or attend a funeral, he should do it in the summer. Everybody else is out of town, so why not him? If the Vice-President has to travel, make it anytime but the fall and winter." The critical difference between Rockefeller and Mondale was their physical presence at the agenda-setting stage of the policy process. Rockefeller's decision to stay away from Washington during the confirmation hearings may have been the proper move, but it cost him considerable opportunities to influence Ford's first-year agenda. Though every President alters the agenda at several points in the term, Rockefeller happened to be in an administration that had only limited agenda space at the beginning. "By the time we got there," a Rockefeller assistant said, "all the decisions had been made for the next six months. Ford asked Rockefeller to do some long-range planning, which meant that decisions wouldn't be made for some time." As Persico reports, Rockefeller acknowledged the problem on the night he was confirmed. "'You know, when this appointment first came,'" Rockefeller said, "'I thought, "Terrific, Maybe I can really be of some help." But after all these months, it's lost much of the meaning'" (1982, p. 258).

The Cycle of Increasing Effectiveness

Vice-Presidents have considerable opportunities for influence if they enter office with more information and expertise than their White House competitors. This advantage only exists until the President and his staff catch up. Because all administrations face a cycle of increasing effectiveness, initial differences in information and expertise eventually disappear. Presidents and their staffs will always learn over time. However, at least in the first year, insider Vice-Presidents in outsider administrations stand a higher chance of success than outsider Vice-Presidents in insider administrations. A major reason is the rise of policy *vacuums* in outsider Presidencies. As a Mondale aide suggested: "Knowledge was power in the Carter administration, especially in the first year. There were so many areas where Carter and his staff had little background that we had a number of vacuums. No one knew too much about electoral reform so Berman got involved. No one knew too much about handling Congress, so Moe got involved." As such, policy vacuums are based on shortages of information and expertise. Depending on the Vice-President's own store of these resources, vacuums create substantial opportunities for influence. "You go where other people aren't," a second Mondale aide argued. "In the first few months, there were a lot of areas that were empty. There was a complete lack of concern for setting priorities.

Policy vacuums have several characteristics that make them attractive to Vice-Presidents. First, because other aides are not actively involved, there is less risk of infighting. When Mondale moved into the agenda-setting area, he did not steal any territory from competitors. Unlike Rockefeller, who moved into the Domestic Council by force, Mondale was drawn into the agenda problem because no one else was there. Second, because other aides are not involved, the Vice-President can stake a claim to the policy area. Though Mondale avoided long-term policy assignments, he was willing to fill the gaps in certain areas. His support of United States involvement in the Indochinese refugee problem was a prime example of moving to a vacuum. Until Mondale became involved, no other agencies were interested. Once these agencies became involved, Mondale stepped out of the area. Mondale also acted as an interpreter for Menachem Begin, a job that few other aides wanted or could perform. Third, policy vacuums have very low resource costs. The Vice-President can enter the policy process for a minimal price, retain a low profile, shape some policy, and exit, all without extensive staff conflict.

Though policy vacuums are important to Vice-Presidents and other senior advisers, they close over time. As the cycle of increasing effectiveness builds White House information and expertise, vacuums are filled. As a Rockefeller aide noted, the delay in confirmation may have had its greatest impact in keeping the Vice-President out of the vacuums. "The delay hurt him because of the short takeoff in the administration. There was a big vacuum at the start of the Ford term. Rockefeller could have filled it, but he came late to the party. The administration had already started to jell by the time Rockefeller was confirmed." A second assistant agreed.

When Ford was in the House he had frequently used other members to do the basic staff work rather than building up his own personal staff. When Rockefeller came to Washington in December, most of the holes had been filled by others. Rumsfeld already had someone to run the Domestic Council, Phillip Areeda, and the last thing Ford needed was another domestic policy aide. Assuming that Rockefeller had been in the administration, say, in October, it would have been Rockefeller, not Rumsfeld, who would have filled the major openings.

Rockefeller was able to take advantage of at least one vacuum during the term. Though Frank Zarb, Ford's energy administrator, was working on legislation, Rockefeller saw an opportunity to build a major program. As a Ford aide suggested: "Rockefeller moved to the energy field entirely because it was the only area where: (a) Ford had said there could be a new program, and (b) no one else was involved. Rockefeller saw the exception to the spending rule and met no competition until he was done with the program."

The greatest number of vacuums in any administration exist at the very beginning. By their very definition, policy vacuums eventually become filled. In the Carter administration, for instance, the legislative liaison operation was in need of a major overhaul by the summer of 1977. Had Mondale wanted to participate, he could have stepped easily into the vacuum. When he refused to enter the vacuum, other players entered the region. New staff members were hired, legislative strategy was modified, and the office was reorganized (see Davis 1979). As an administration ages, the cycle of increasing effectiveness ensures some level of learning. Staff members who enter with no Washington experience cannot fail to learn; staff members who have no knowledge about policy cannot avoid exposure. Thus, if Vice-Presidents are to take advantage of policy vacuums, it is usually at the start of the term. The first year emerges again as the primary target of opportunity for vice-presidential influence.

The Cycle of Decreasing Influence

As the term progresses, Presidents have fewer opportunities to set the policy agenda. The congressional calendar fills, attention turns to the coming presidential elections, inertia sets in. More importantly, Presidents face a cycle of decreasing influence on Capitol Hill. As the President's public approval rating falls over time, Congress becomes more reluctant to pass presidential programs. Moreover, every President since Franklin Roosevelt has lost party seats in the midterm election, ranging from a high of seventy-one seats in 1938 to just three in 1962. This cycle of decreasing influence is not an automatic product of the passage of time. Rather, according to Samuel Kernell (1978), it reflects the impact of a series of chronic national problems over the last four decades: Korea, Vietnam, Watergate, and the seeming presidential inability to solve the economic puzzle.

This cycle of public support is well known inside the White House. As Mondale said in an interview published on Reagan's inauguration day:

"You know, a president, in my opinion starts out with a bank full of good will and slowly checks are drawn on that, and it's very rare that it's replenished. It's a one-time deposit" (*Washington Post,* 23 Jan. 1981). Reagan's budget director, Stockman, also recognized the importance of the cycle of decreasing influence. In a transition memo to the President-elect, Stockman argued that speed was essential in avoiding a "GOP Economic Dunkirk":

> Things could go very badly during the first year, resulting in incalculable erosion of GOP momentum, unity and public confidence. If bold policies are not swiftly, deftly and courageously implemented in the first six months, Washington will quickly become engulfed in political disorder commensurate with the surrounding economic disarray. A golden opportunity for permanent conservative policy revision and political realignment could be thoroughly dissipated before the Reagan administration is even up to speed (*Washington Post,* 14 Dec. 1980).

Once the cycle starts, it has two important impacts on the opportunities for vice-presidential influence. First, because most White House staffs enter office expecting the cycle to occur, a premium is placed on setting the agenda in the first year. Indeed, presidential perceptions of the cycle may have some bearing on actual declines in public support. Reagan aides, for instance, made no secret of their expectations of a public backlash against the budget cuts. James Baker III, Reagan's chief of staff, predicted public dissatisfaction as early as June 1981. "I think you'll see some fairly strong reactions to the budget cuts when they hit the street in October or November," he told one reporter. "The President has said all along that we didn't get into this mess overnight, so don't look for instant gratification or relief as far as inflation is concerned" (*Washington Post,* 19 June 1981). Among recent Presidents, perhaps Johnson was most concerned about the cycle of decreasing influence. As he told his staff in January 1965: "I keep hitting hard because I know this honeymoon won't last. Every day I lose a little more political capital. That's why we have to keep at it, never letting up. One day soon, I don't know when, the critics and the snipers will move in and we will be at stalemate. We have to get all we can, now, before the roof comes down" (Valenti 1975, p. 144). Even if the President remains personally popular, losses in the midterm elections are seemingly inevitable. Even though Eisenhower was still quite popular in 1954, he lost eighteen House seats and one Senate seat in the midterm contests. The pattern repeated itself in 1958, when a still popular President lost forty-nine House seats and thirteen Senate seats.

Second, as Presidents lose their public and congressional leverage, there is a natural tightening inside the White House. As support declines, the number of opportunities for influence also declines. Since there is less room on the congressional calendar for presidential priorities, since there is less chance of passage later in the administration (see Light 1982a), and since first-term Presidents must turn their attention to the next elections, the White House becomes more cautious about policy decisions. As the President's political support dwindles, conflict inside the White House increases. With less room for bargaining, staff members form competing coalitions and fight for dominance. Whereas a spirit of bargaining prevails at the start of the term, there is an inevitable rise in conflict toward the end. The danger for Vice-Presidents is that they will be isolated in an effort to conserve the administration's scarce political capital.

Mondale faced the problem as a conservative coalition gained strength inside the White House. As the economy weakened, producing high interest rates and inflation, conservatives became the dominant coalition in domestic and economic policy. As a Mondale aide remarked:

> Mondale's success decreased over time, but so did the entire administration's. Within the White House, Mondale's influence ebbed along with the rest of the liberals. After McIntyre and the conservatives took over, Mondale had to change tactics. He switched to a stopgap approach. He tried to slow the conservatives down whenever possible. A lot of money was spent on social programs that the conservatives didn't want spent. A lot of things did not take because of Mondale and the rest of the liberals. But there's no question that Mondale was dealing from a position of weakness. The liberals had lost the battle over what direction to take in the coming two years.

Clearly, part of Mondale's trouble came from outside economic conditions. Carter had decided that a conservative fiscal policy was necessary to control inflation. However, Mondale was also caught in the consolidation of power that comes in the final years of an administration. Presidents are often willing to entertain multiple advocates in the first months of the term, but lose patience at the end. As a Johnson assistant suggested: "When the plate is empty, almost everyone can have a choice of dishes. There's space for everything. When the plate is filled to overflowing, you've got to be much more selective." At the start of an administration, agenda setting is a non-zero-sum game—that is, victories on one policy do not necessarily affect victories on another policy. Presidents have the opportunity to make a number of choices. As an administration ages, agenda setting becomes a zero-sum game—Presidents must choose among competing policies, with each victory for one side a defeat for the other.

Policy Windows

These four cycles—electoral, policy, effectiveness, and influence—combine to create a number of policy windows for vice-presidential persuasion at the start of the term. Just as a space launch only has a few moments to pierce the atmosphere into its predetermined orbit, programs have very brief windows for success (see Kingdon 1983). On Capitol Hill, these windows may involve the merging of interests among departments, interest groups, committees, and the President. Such a window opened in the spring of 1974 on national health insurance. Under siege in the House, Nixon finally agreed to a health plan offered by labor, Democrats, and consumer groups. However, the window closed quickly as labor looked to the midterm elections for a veto-proof, liberal Congress. Such a window opened in the summer of 1981 on the tax leasing provisions of the Reagan economic program. Corporate interest groups used the surge of support for tax cutting to win enactment of the controversial leasing package. In the health insurance case, the policy window closed before enactment. In the leasing case, groups jumped through the window just in time.

If policy windows exist on Capitol Hill, they also exist *inside* the White House. There are certain moments in the term when Vice-Presidents have greater opportunities for influence. Looking at the electoral cycle, the policy cycle, the cycle of increasing effectiveness, and the cycle of decreasing influence, the largest windows for success exist at the start of the term. During the first two years, Vice-Presidents will have much more opportunity for policy impact than at any other point in the term. Indeed, for any senior adviser, the first two years are critical. Though Presidents do announce new programs later in the term, particularly at the start of the nomination campaigns, the first two years are critical for policy influence. Within those two years, the winters hold the most windows for success. The problem for Vice-Presidents, however, is that their internal capital is at its lowest point at the very start of the term. White House staff members are most suspicious in these early days. Thus, vice-presidential influence may depend on the ability to build strategies for using the early policy windows, while adapting to lower levels of internal capital.

STRATEGIES

Strategies involve the Vice-President's plan for using resources and opportunities inside the White House. A Vice-President may have numerous advantages in the policy process, but may be unable to convert them into influence. Though Rockefeller faced several obstacles outside his control — the delay in confirmation, the rise of Rumsfeld as a challenger — a more effective influence strategy might have increased his impact. As one aide concluded: "He went about his business in the wrong way. He compromised when he should have fought. He fought when he should have compromised. His whole approach to winning Ford's support was off. He had no understanding of what it was to be a staff man trying to get your boss to agree with some new idea." Mondale gave his own list of strategies to Bush in early 1981:

> One. Advise the president confidentially. . . .
> Secondly, don't wear a President down. He should be bright enough to catch

your meaning the first time. Give your advice once and give it well. You have a right to be heard, not obeyed. A President must decide when the debates must end, this nation must move on, and you must be a part of that decision-making process.

Third, as a spokesman for the Administration, stay on the facts. . . . This office that I have held is important enough not to be demeaned by its occupants delivering obsequious flattery.

Fourth, understand your role as a spokesman. . . .

Fifth, avoid line authority assignments. . . .

Sixth, the Vice President should remember the importance of personal compatibility. He should try to complement the President's skills and, finally and in a real sense the most important of all roles, be ready to assume the Presidency (remarks, 18 Feb. 1981).

Though Vice-Presidents need to shape strategies to fit their own situations, there are at least five general approaches that emerge from the Rockefeller and Mondale experiences: (1) set priorities, (2) build coalitions, (3) accept limited victories, (4) adapt from offense to defense, and (5) use hidden-hand channels.

Priorities

Of the five strategies, priority setting is the most basic. As Vice-Presidents move through the policy process, they are encouraged to save their resources for the issues that they see as most important. Like Presidents, Vice-Presidents must set priorities. Since they cannot possibly win on all issues, they must conserve for specific goals. Rockefeller, for example, wasted a considerable store of his resources on the Domestic Council fight. Instead of holding back for his top policy priorities, Rockefeller spent his limited internal capital winning an administrative assignment. As already suggested, Rockefeller may have confused process with policy, believing the Council guaranteed influence in domestic affairs. In spending so much on the council, Rockefeller was weakened for future policy battles. Though we benefit from hindsight, Rockefeller might have been more successful holding his resources for actual programs. By the time Rockefeller had readied his policy agenda, he had already used a large portion of his capital on the staff contest. Assuming that Rockefeller cared more about policy outcomes than administrative machinery, his Domestic Council effort was a poor investment of his influence resources.

Mondale tried a different strategy, based in part on his reading of Rockefeller's problems. Instead of concentrating on a broad range of policies or on administrative roles, Mondale decided to take a generalist strategy, moving in and out of policy areas at will. In a sense, Mondale operated as a guerrilla adviser. Since he did not have the resources to occupy a policy region for the long term, he adopted a floater position. "He didn't want to stay with any one problem for too long," an aide said, "because he didn't want to be identified as the person with the responsibility for the policy. He wanted to be able to stay out of range of bureaucratic politics because he knew he couldn't win." Basically, Mondale set priorities among the various programs he favored and worked for those at the top of the list. According to his staff and outside observers, Mondale set those priorities on the basis of three criteria. First, Mondale tried to estimate Carter's persuadability on the given issue. On certain policies, Mondale knew that Carter was unbendable. Those were areas to avoid, if only because Mondale did not have the resources to win. Second, Mondale looked at the opposition in the White House. Even though Mondale had considerable expertise in congressional relations, he was reluctant to move against Frank Moore, Carter's long-time friend. Mondale concluded that he did not have enough to win the fight. Further, as an aide reported, "It would have been taken as a bad move by the Carter staff. Even if it was necessary, it wasn't Mondale's place to do it." Nor did Mondale get involved in the plan to bring labor in on the wage-price guidelines in 1978. As one aide noted: "There was no percentage in it for him. If he won, his friends would have said he had betrayed them. If he lost, the White House staff would have said he had no clout with his constituency." Third, though the Carter staff was roundly criticized for its lack of sensitivity to Congress, Mondale set his own agenda with Capitol Hill in mind. He looked at the potentials for passage and public support *outside* the White House, then pressed for Carter's support *inside* the Oval Office. "He wasn't only interested in how Carter would respond," an observer suggested, "but wanted to know whether his programs could pass once Carter signed off."

Coalitions

Rockefeller and Mondale differed significantly in their willingness and success in building policy coalitions inside the White House. Part of the difference was that Mondale simply had more allies to work with. Carp and Aaron provided easy connections between Mondale and other allies. Part of the difference was that Mondale had more attractive positions on major issues. Unlike Rockefeller, who was a liberal awash in a sea of conservatives, Mondale had a number of ideological compatriots. Still another part was Mondale's image as an influential player. Unlike Rockefeller who was defeated on a number of visible policy stands, Mondale never gave his opponents cause to doubt his impact on Carter in the private meetings. Finally, as Rockefeller's stock dropped inside the White House, he became more unattractive as an ally. As Humphrey had learned in 1965, other senior advisers avoid guilt by association. After Humphrey lost on the North Vietnam bombing decision, he was frozen out of the foreign policy process. According to Humphrey:

I desperately needed a high-ranking ally to bolster my views, and I turned to George Ball. He had continued to send memoranda to the President that expounded his dissenting views, and then met with Johnson to expand on them. Knowing that, I [hoped] that some informal liaison could be worked out to continue my education on Vietnam. While [Ball's staff] knew I was an ally, [they] also knew I was a dangerous one. Ball's people clearly wanted to keep a safe distance from me, and they did. I could not blame them. There was the unmistakable possibility that he would have joined me in limbo, his access to the President limited, his counsel unwelcome (1976, p. 327).

Coalition building in the White House depends on political exchange. No one will join a coalition with the Vice-President or any other adviser without some benefit. If the exchange is one-sided, the coalition will not last. There were several components to Mondale's value as a coalition member. First, as Carter tightened his policy process later in the term, Mondale's long one-on-one meetings took on added significance in the White House. Mondale became one of the few players who could lobby the President in person, not on paper. There is no evidence that Mondale ever promised anyone that he would raise an issue with the President, but his continued access meant that he was a valued member of policy coalitions. Second, Mondale had built a store of personal loyalty from his former staff members salted throughout the White House and executive branch. Their respect for the Vice-President meant that he was automatically included and/or represented in most policy debates. Because Mondale had been involved in so many cabinet appointments, he also had calling cards in the departments. Unlike Humphrey, Mondale could ask for special briefings on policy issues without fear of refusal. Third, Mondale did have at least one vantage point to use with other senior advisers: the agenda-setting mechanism. By elevating ideas, Mondale could reward allies. By suppressing others, Mondale could punish enemies. In sum, Mondale was in a much stronger position to make policy exchanges than his vice-presidential predecessors. Unlike Humphrey, Mondale could offer something in return for support.

Though Mondale was a member of the liberal coalition later in the administration, he did not actively recruit allies. On most issues, he was a silent partner. Allies and opponents alike could guess where he stood, but he did not make any visible attempt to build a leadership role. Indeed, there is little evidence on any level that White House policy coalitions spring from specific negotiations. Rather, coalitions arise from informal networks among the staff. As one presidential aide remarked: "You are who you talk with. You spend your time with the domestic policy people, you start to identify with them. You don't like them too much and you switch over to OMB. No one ever sits down and says 'I'll give you this if you give me that.' It's more subtle." That is not to say there were no active coalitions in the Carter White House. Mondale, Eizenstat, and a number of other White House and executive branch liberals joined at several points during the term. However, as Kessel notes in his detailed analysis of policy coalitions in the Carter administration: "To the extent that Carter staff members wanted to promote policies consistent with their own preferences, it would be difficult to predict what they would do. . . . There was nothing as simple as a conservative group opposed by a liberal group. The issue groups were not concentrated in certain units. And there clearly was no consensus that could be called a 'Carter White House point of view'" (1982, p. 9). Instead of two simple liberal and conservative coalitions, the Carter administration was characterized by a number of short-term alliances on specific issues. Whether the shifting coalitions hurt the administration writ large, they helped Mondale conserve his resources for the top priorities.

Limited Victories

Given the Vice-President's internal capital at the start of the term, an important early strategy rests on the acceptance of limited victories. Instead of pushing for full adoption of ideas, Vice-Presidents may have more success with compromise. This approach is easier for some advisers than for others. Mondale had been schooled in the politics of Senate compromise. According to one report:

> Whatever Mondale's disagreements, he kept them private. Despite his un-precedented influences as vice president, Mondale sought only limited victories. His attitude about becoming a "kamikaze pilot" had not changed. He was still the same politician who sat on the Finance Committee to seek modest and pragmatic goals—goals that did not include taking on Russell Long or waging highly visible losing crusades for drastic tax reforms. He worked in the present tense, meaning he was content to go only for goals that were possible. As he had done throughout his career, he sized up the reality of the moment and then devised a strategy that would work—and would not pose undue risks (Lewis 1980, p. 246).

The question is whether Rockefeller—not Mondale—might have been more successful with the same approach. Most Rockefeller and Ford aides argued that the limited strategy would have worked in the short term, but that the political problems would have resurfaced later. "Rumsfeld and the conservatives had no tolerance for Rockefeller whatsoever," an aide replied. "He could have survived a little longer, but it was an inevitable end. He could have slowed Rumsfeld and had some more success, but he would have been out by 1976 anyway." Rockefeller had to balance the benefits of holding back with the personal costs of compromising his policy commitments. It was a trade-off that every White House adviser must make. Perhaps Rockefeller could have won limited adoption of catastrophic health insurance or more support for an energy plan. Perhaps he would have interested Ford in spending increases in domestic policy or a different tax cut to stimulate the economy. We do know that Rockefeller had only one major victory inside the White House—the Energy Independence Authority—compared with a number of limited victories for Mondale. Unlike other advisers, however, Vice-Presidents do not have a choice between exit and loyalty. Whereas other senior advisers can leave to pursue their policy agendas in alternative arenas, Vice-Presidents generally must stay. If they lose their access, they must wait for the next election to exit.

Offense and Defense

As the Vice-President's opportunities decline, a defensive strategy becomes more attractive. If Vice-Presidents cannot win adoption of their agendas, they can work to modify or delay adoption of competing programs. As a Carter foreign policy assistant reported: "If I were to sum up, Mondale was more successful in moderating extreme policies, rather than getting his own programs across. He kept several very bad policies off the agenda, but had trouble getting good things on later in the term. Unless the balance of forces on the staffs are canceled out, it's difficult for the Vice-President to take the initiative." Thus, Mondale was not successful in stopping Carter's midsummer crisis, but was able to tone down the "malaise" speech. He was not successful in stopping a reevaluation of United States policy toward Israel, but was able to moderate Carter's attitudes toward Begin. As the administration aged, Mondale took a defensive position on a number of issues. Because Mondale and his allies were frequently in the minority, defense was the most viable strategy. "We didn't have the edge on the budget after 1978," a Mondale aide argued. "The only choice was to work to keep the cuts from going too deep. We couldn't stop the cuts from happening—and didn't want to stop some of them. The best way to go was to try to keep some of the cuts from happening." Like the minority party in Congress, Mondale and his ideological allies did not have the internal capital to win on most major issues. Their best approach was to modify programs they opposed.

At the beginning of the term, Mondale was far more successful with offense. He worked for adoption of a number of Carter programs, including increases in domestic spending. His offense was the natural by-product of the first-year policy windows. Since there was room on the Carter agenda for competing programs, Mondale was able to win support for the Department of Education, electoral reform, and the tax cut as administration priorities. As the economic climate worsened and the legislative program stalled in Congress, Mondale was forced to change his influence strategy to defense. He could not win support for new programs, but could affect the course of programs he opposed.

In working on defense, Mondale and other senior advisers had three basic choices. First, they tried to *stop* competing programs. If Mondale and his allies could not win on their agenda, perhaps they could stalemate the opposition. That approach was particularly attractive on the budget. Because domestic spending automatically increases with inflation and unemployment, stalemate actually favors proponents of increased funding in social services. Second, failing to stop the opposition, Mondale tried to *modify* competing programs. By amending and adjusting opposition programs, Mondale could still gain a measure of influence. That was the case in Carter's Middle East and China policies. In both areas, Mondale moderated administration policy. He persuaded Carter to relax the pressure on Israel and worked toward a more realistic Middle East timetable. He worked to keep the United States on a steady course with China and helped keep highly sensitive arms negotiations quiet. Third, failing to stop or amend the opposition, Mondale tried to *delay* competing programs. As Mondale had learned in the Senate, delays of weeks or months could mean the difference between legislative success and failure. Though it is difficult to find major examples of Mondale's delaying tactics, at least one Carter aide reported that "Mondale kept a few issues hot longer than necessary. He raised questions and tried to slow things down."

Mondale's switch from offense to defense came after the midterm elections, reflecting changes in the strength of the White House conservatives. Carter had always been concerned about excessive federal spending, but had been willing to adopt a more traditional Democratic program in his first year. During the period, however, Carter continued to press for zero-cost programs. He wanted welfare reform, but with no additional federal spending. He wanted national health insurance, but with the smallest price tag possible. As the economic news changed over the first year, Carter moved back to his conservative fiscal background, leaving Mondale with fewer opportunities for influence. According to Eizenstat, Mondale "tended to favor more money for domestic spending rather than defense, though he was for real defense increases. He was for more money for education, job training, and jobs programs. He was against fighting inflation with austerity, especially the budget cuts of 1980. There was no increase in domestic spending in real terms for all of our four years. Mondale was fighting the trend all the way" (*New Republic*, 4 April 1983). The decision to change to defense involved Mondale's assessment of his chances for success, as well as the rise of the conservative coalitions inside the White House. Unlike Rockefeller, Mondale concluded that defensive influence was an acceptable substitute for no influence at all.

Hidden-Hand Influence

Hidden-hand influence rests on the Vice-President's low profile inside the White House. Though the Vice-President may have considerable influence over policy, credit claiming and posturing are highly threatening to the White House staffs. The Vice-President must generally sacrifice external visibility for internal impact. If the staff and press can measure the Vice-President's influence, isolation may be at hand. This trade-off between visibility and influence applies to most White House advisers, and may apply to Presidents. According to Fred Greenstein's portrait of Eisenhower:

> In his private assertions and actions, Eisenhower consistently preferred results to publicity when strategic and tactical maneuvering was required. He deliberately cultivated the impression that he was not involved even in the most successful of the maneuvers in which he directly participated. Presidents like Kennedy (for example, in the campaign early in his administration to expand the House Rules Committee and his assault on the steel industry) and Johnson (for example, in his highly visible mediation of the railroad strike, early in 1964) deliberately sought to enhance their professional reputations as political operators. Eisenhower seems to have had neither a need nor desire to do so. He employed his skills to achieve his ends by inconspicuous means and was aware that a reputation as a tough political operator could be inconsistent with acquiring and maintaining another source of presidential influence, namely public prestige (1979, pp. 597-98).

For Mondale, hidden-hand influence rested on a number of separate tactics. At all times, Mondale kept his advice to Carter private. He was reluctant to speak at cabinet meetings and did not want his staff taking highly visible stands. As he told one reporter, "I tried to make my views known to the President privately, and sometimes very strongly. Once I made my case, though, and I was sure the President understood it, and I made a thorough argument, I didn't rag him. Once his decision was made, I didn't try to make life miserable for him. I wouldn't want a Vice President of mine to do that, and I didn't try to do it" (*New Republic*, 4 April 1983). Only once during the four years did Mondale leak his position to the press, telling Elizabeth Drew of the *New Yorker* that he thought pollster Patrick Caddell's "malaise" analysis was "crazy." Mondale also preferred to work through his allies. If Mondale could not win in his one-on-one meetings with Carter, he turned to his former aides, Carp and Aaron. Mondale avoided credit for any Carter program—a strategy that helped him retain his access during the term, while avoiding blame for the Carter economic program in his own campaign for the nomination in 1983 and 1984. Mondale's hidden-hand approach allowed him to establish the image of influence. As Mondale argued after the election: "The perception by others that I was close to the President, that I enjoyed his confidence, that he had trust in me . . . this understanding by others made it possible for me to speak for the

President with authority and to act on my own influence. Whether I was working with his staff, with the Cabinet, with the bureaucracy, or with foreign leaders and others, I could make myself heard and get things done because of my standing with the President" (remarks, 18 Feb. 1981). One of Mondale's aides agreed.

> The thing that bothers me now is that some Carter people will say, "I never saw him do anything." He never spoke up at meetings. He didn't say anything until Carter gave him permission. He didn't lobby at the senior staff meetings. He kept his head down and played a backstage role. But none of those people saw what he did in his meetings with Carter. They don't count what Carp and Aaron were doing in domestic policy and foreign policy. They were used to seeing influence at close range and couldn't imagine how Mondale could have any impact.

The advantage of hidden-hand influence for Mondale was that he was rarely drawn into White House fights. Though Mondale did disagree with a number of Carter decisions, he was not involved in the internal conflict. "I never saw him hit by anyone," an economic adviser remarked. "He couldn't be hit because he never made a clean target. He was moving in and out of issue areas, and didn't stay long enough to get hurt. He was a genius at staying out of the line of fire." Even on issues where Mondale took a stand—the Department of Education and electoral reform—he allowed other players to take the lead. According to a veteran reporter: "Mondale didn't care much whether he got the credit for those ideas. The people who knew anything about education or electoral reform knew who was responsible and that was all that mattered. Mondale didn't seem to care about his national reputation like Rockefeller did. He was young enough to wait for his own turn in 1984. He didn't need a list of accomplishments to prove that he was important. That had never been important to him anyway. He was the compromiser, not the show horse." Mondale's willingness to submerge his short-term reputation in favor of more internal influence was a key to his hidden-hand influence. It was a strategy that was almost impossible for Rockefeller. At the end of his long career, Rockefeller did not have the patience to wait.

CONCLUSION

This chapter has focused on the nature of influence inside the White House. In comparing resources, opportunities, and strategies, however, it is important to recognize that the three factors are highly interrelated. Resources shape opportunities; opportunities shape strategies; strategies can conserve resources. Thus, Mondale's influence strategy might have changed under a different political context or in a different policy cycle. Perhaps Mondale would have made Rockefeller's attempt at a major line assignment if he had faced the same lack of opportunities.

Does this theory apply to other White House advisers? The answer is a qualified yes. Though the strategies will vary from one actor to another, all White House advisers have the same need for persuasive expertise, internal capital, and presidential persuadability as Rockefeller and Mondale. Though some White House advisers may not need persuasive skills because of their formal access, all require opportunities and strategies. For Vice-Presidents, the key strategy may remain hidden-hand influence. For others, like Haldeman and Ehrlichman, the key may be forcing competitors out of the White House. The problem for future study, of course, is to start identifying just how the various influence factors interact. What strategies fit with what resources? What opportunities fit with what strategies?

8.

Conclusion

He who giveth can taketh away and often does.

Hubert Humphrey

Mondale's Vice-Presidency offered an attractive example for George Bush. Mondale was involved in the policy process throughout the term, retaining his access to Carter and the Oval Office through the last hours of the administration. He persuaded Carter on a broad range of foreign and domestic issues, while protecting his opportunities with a low-profile strategy. His staff was fully integrated into the White House and had little trouble gaining the perquisites of office. Mondale had a number of allies in the West Wing and executive branch, providing contacts for both information and influence. He remained solidly rooted in his White House office and received all classified material until he left office. However, beyond the Vice-President's staff and the EOB office, few of Mondale's advantages were guaranteed for Bush. As Humphrey said, the President "giveth" and can always "taketh away." Before looking at the first two years of the Bush Vice-Presidency, it is important to review the main findings of this book.

A BRIEF REVIEW

This book has focused on two questions. First, how did Vice-Presidents finally gain an advisory role? Second, why was Mondale more successful in using that role for influence than Rockefeller? The two questions provide an opportunity to examine the nature of advice and influence in the White House. Though Vice-Presidents are certainly different from other senior advisers, there are enough similarities to offer some general conclusions on the presidential advisory process. As Vice-Presidents have moved beyond ceremonial duties into the political and policy arenas, they have come to resemble senior members of the White House staff.

The evolution of the vice-presidential job description occurred in a very brief period. As the President's own job became more complex and demanding, there were greater incentives for an expanded vice-presidential role. The decline of the national parties, the growing fragmentation in Congress, the lengthening campaign season, and the rise of a new set of policy issues all heightened the Vice-President's value as a policy adviser in the White House. These changes had started before Watergate, but were accelerated by Nixon's political problems. Faced with increasing congressional pressure, Nixon was willing to bargain with Ford over the Vice-President's independence. When Nixon resigned, Ford was forced to bargain with Rockefeller. Though Watergate was a unique event in recent American history, it had a major catalytic impact on the Vice-Presidency.

Vice-Presidents also benefited from increasing institutional support. During the early 1970s, the Vice-President's office expanded to include both an administrative and a political core. Though the Vice-President's staff still engaged in political issues, they were free to spend more time and energy on policy. Instead of doubling as administrators and schedulers, they could concentrate on building coalitions inside the White House. As the office grew from twenty in 1960 to seventy-plus in 1977, Vice-Presidents gained increased capacities to act as senior advisers to the President.

The evolutionary process was complemented by changes in the recruitment of Vice-Presidents. Not only did Presidents gain a greater say over their running mates in the past two decades, Vice-Presidents entered office with more experience. Except for Agnew, all recent Vice-Presidents had extensive background in government before their inauguration. Except for Barkley, all recent Vice-Presidents have shown at least some political ambitions for the Presidency. The combination of experience and ambition has made recent Vice-Presidents more sensitive to the ebb and flow of power inside the White House, as well as more prepared to serve as senior advisers. The election of two insider Vice-Presidents, Mondale and Bush, coincided with the recruitment of back-to-back outsider Presidents. The match between Jimmy Carter and Walter Mondale in 1976 provided more opportunity for vice-presidential advice and influence. As an outsider, Carter needed Mondale's experience and skill. As such, Carter and Mondale had compatible views of how the Vice-President could contribute to the administration. Among recent Presidents and Vice-Presidents, Carter and Mondale were relatively high in goal compatibility.

The changing job description reflects an increase in the Vice-President's advisory resources. In order to play the advisory role, Vice-Presidents need at least six basic resources: (1) time to study the issues and engage in bargaining, (2) energy to compete inside the policy process, (3) information on the issues, opponents, and meetings, (4) expertise in policy making and bureaucratic politics, (5) proximity to the President and policy process, and

(6) the President's own willingness to listen to vice-presidential advice. Though recent Vice-Presidents have had ample time and energy, they have often suffered from a lack of information, proximity, and presidential willingness to listen. Humphrey, for instance, was among the most energetic of contemporary Vice-Presidents, but failed to gain access to the policy-making system. Nor was Johnson particularly interested in listening to Humphrey's arguments on the Vietnam war. As the recruitment pattern changed and presidential incentives increased, Vice-Presidents were able to secure more information, access, and presidential willingness to listen. With greater staff support, Vice-Presidents were able to supply alternative sources of advice. With the West Wing office, both Mondale and Bush were much closer to the President. With two consecutive outsider Presidents—Carter and Reagan—Vice-Presidents have been much more successful in gaining the President's ear.

However, as Rockefeller and Mondale learned, the resources needed for advice are not necessarily the resources needed for influence. Defining advice as the Vice-President's act of *giving* opinions and influence as the President's act of *taking* them, at least five resources are needed for policy impact: (1) time, (2) information, (3) internal capital for bargaining, (4) persuasive expertise for one-on-one meetings with the President, and (5) the President's own persuadability on the policy issues. Rockefeller was among the most persuasive of recent vice-presidential advisers, but was unable to move Ford on budget and tax issues. Ford was not persuadable. Beyond these influence resources, Vice-Presidents also need opportunities for persuasion. Most opportunities on the President's agenda come at the start of the term. The electoral cycle, policy cycle, cycle of increasing effectiveness among the White House staff, and cycle of decreasing influence on Capitol Hill all emphasize the first and second years as the primary opportunities for vice-presidential influence. Finally, certain strategies seem to work better for vice-presidential influence than others. Rockefeller's highly visible advocate's style was less successful than Mondale's low-profile hidden-hand approach. Mondale's influence strategy consisted of setting policy priorities, building coalitions inside the White House, accepting limited victories, adapting from offense to defense, and the use of hidden-hand channels.

THE BUSH VICE-PRESIDENCY

By mid-1982, several patterns had emerged from the Bush Vice-Presidency that confirmed the continued presence of a vice-presidential advisory role. Bush retained Mondale's West Wing office and the weekly private meetings with the President. He placed his former campaign manager, James Baker III, as Reagan's own chief of staff, and moved another aide, Richard Bond, to the Republican National Committee as the 1982 congressional campaign director. Though Bush was conspicuously quiet during

Reagan's recovery from the assassination attempt, he lobbied on several presidential programs. Because Reagan adopted a highly restrictive policy agenda, however, Bush did not have the same opportunities for policy influence as Mondale. He was forced to adopt a defensive strategy from the first months of the administration, trying to reduce the size of the tax cut and the direction of the budget cuts. In order to understand the Bush Vice-Presidency, it is important to look at four separate areas: (1) Bush's job description, (2) his institutional support, (3) his advisory resources, and (4) his actual influence.

Bush's Job Description

Bush entered office more willing to take line assignments than Mondale. Upon assuming the Vice-Presidency, Bush was appointed as chairman of Reagan's Task Force on Regulatory Relief. The task force was charged with reviewing over three thousand federal regulations for possible elimination or delay. According to C. Boyden Gray, Bush's counsel, the Vice-President was brought into the regulatory debate on substantive questions:

> According to Gray, the Vice President "has been called upon to make some judgements" with respect to regulatory cutbacks, "although I'm not sure it's appropriate to tell you which ones." He also said that Bush has taken a detailed interest in the "problem of legislative veto" and has been involved in the Administration's attempt to strip the Consumer Product Safety Commission of its status as an independent regulatory agency.
>
> Bush's office helped supervise the preparation of a voluminous regulatory relief progress report released on June 13 [1981] and mailed to about 3,000 reporters and editors (*National Journal*, 20 June 1981).

Bush also accepted responsibility for federal involvement in the Atlanta child murders investigation, taking a visible position as the President's delegate to blacks. In all, the Justice Department funneled four million dollars to the investigation. Bush was also given control of the preparations for Reagan's first economic summit in Ottawa, Canada.

Bush's most important assignment came in early 1981, when he was placed in charge of White House crisis management. The appointment was made as Secretary of State Alexander Haig and National Security Adviser Richard Allen escalated their feud over who would be the "vicar" of foreign policy. As the infighting increased, Reagan asked Bush to move into the middle. Instead of giving Haig or Allen the crisis-management assignment, Reagan compromised with Bush. The assignment was not trivial. When Polish authorities cracked down on the Solidarity Union in December 1981, for instance, Bush was the first to arrive in the situation room and the first to see sensitive intelligence on potential Soviet involvement. Because the assignment placed Bush directly in the line of fire between Haig and Allen, he sought to down play his role. In an interview with the *National Journal*,

Bush argued that the crisis-management "thing is really a standing in for the President . . . in what he defines to be a crisis. If the President is not in the situation room and something is flapping pretty badly, then, you know, it is something I would do. But there is no new staff. That thing got blown very much out of whack, as it were. . . . It's a surrogate thing, a stand-in thing" (20 June 1981). When Bush was appointed to the position in March, he argued that "I'm not competing for something. I want to do what the president wants me to do and I want to do it well . . . but I'm not seeking assignments. I'm not saying, 'Let me do this or that'" (*Washington Post,* 30 Mar. 1981).

Although Bush was more willing to accept such responsibilities than Mondale—recall, for example, that Mondale refused responsibility for Africa policy—he did not see the assignment as a power center. The crisis-manager role only involved Bush during rare moments when other players were absent from Washington. "He was reluctant to take that authority unless there was no one else around," an aide reported. "He didn't want to step on anyone's toes." Yet, the assignment did place Bush directly in the foreign policy traffic pattern, giving him automatic access to intelligence data. The regulatory task force demanded less time. Instead of taking personal charge of the regulatory review, Bush delegated the duty to his counsel, Gray. That placed Gray in a position similar to that of Mondale's chief of staff, Richard Moe, on the Carter hospital cost containment task force. Both had responsibility for coordinating the task force, drawing fire away from the Vice-President. Unlike Rockefeller, Bush did not see a line assignment as a path to internal influence. According to one outside observer: "He had talked with Mondale during the transition and understood the importance of avoiding any long-term duties. He didn't want to get caught between any departments or agencies. He knew the conservatives would accuse him of trying to take over anyway and didn't want to give them any ammunition. He had a long memory and remembered what had happened to Rockefeller."

Bush's job description depended, in part, on his personal and political goals. Given his experience in foreign affairs as United Nations ambassador, CIA director, and United States envoy to mainland China, Bush did not enter office with a deep domestic agenda. Though Bush opposed the size of the budget and tax cuts, he spent the first year proving his loyalty to the Reagan administration. As Bush reported, he attended meetings on the economic plan "only for information purposes so I can better articulate the program to the public or to a congressional group. I'm not trying to direct or guide anything" (*Washington Post,* 30 Mar. 1981). Moreover, as an observer noted: "There was no way Bush could stop Stockman on the budget or Reagan on the tax cut. It would have been wasted effort. The best thing was just to bide his time and show the Reagan people he could be trusted." Other observers have been less kind about Bush's motives. As one suggested:

There's only one thing that matters to George Bush: waiting for 1984. His goal is to show conservatives that he is a Reagan man. It's his one chance to win their hearts before 1984. If Reagan decides not to run, Bush wants to be in a position to win the nomination for himself. That means keeping quiet on the budget, even though he can't believe it's right. He was the one who called it "voodoo economics." If Reagan runs again, Bush will try to hold on for another four years. His biggest challenge will come from someone like Jesse Helms, who is just about as conservative as you can be.

The Vice-President's Office

Bush's office remained essentially similar to Mondale's, with the same functional divisions within the staff. Bush has roughly ten more staff members than Mondale, most of the increase concentrated in the legislative relations operation. The emphasis on legislative operations stemmed from Bush's own interest in the House of Representatives and Reagan's pressure on legislative adoption of the budget and tax cuts. As one report suggests:

> In his capacity as President of the Senate, Bush has a staff of 11 on Capitol Hill, which allows him also to serve as a point man for Reagan's legislative program.
> On most Tuesdays, Bush sits in at the weekly committee chairmen's meeting organized by Majority Leader Howard H. Baker, Jr., R-Tenn., and then attends the Republican Policy Committee luncheon hosted by Sen. John Tower, R-Texas. Before and after those weekly events, he usually meets individually with various Senators. He also makes it a point to keep in contact with his many acquaintances on the House side, some of whom he still confronts periodically on the paddleball courts of the House gymnasium.
> While Bush has so far gone to the Hill primarily as a salesman for the Reagan economic package, his aides say he also does a lot of listening and collects political intelligence of value to the White House. Bush's congressional aides . . . work closely with the White House legislative affairs office in keeping both Bush and Regan abreast of the currents in Congress (*National Journal* 20 June 1981).

Though Bush hired a domestic policy adviser, Thaddeus Garrett, his main interests centered on foreign policy and Congress.* Nor did Bush keep Mondale's agenda-setting mechanism. Unlike Mondale, Bush spent more time acting as an administrative assistant. It was Bush who told Stockman to tender his resignation to Reagan following the *Atlantic* interview, and it was Bush who invited Stockman to visit the President's "woodshed."

In contrast to Mondale, Bush preferred to spend more time in his EOB office. Though Bush retained the West Wing quarters, he enjoyed the splendor of the EOB suite. Early in the administration, Bush had the parquet

---

*However, as one of the few blacks in the administration, Garrett achieved some impact in the aftermath of Reagan's decision to grant tax exemptions to segregated schools. Garrett acted to sensitize Reagan to the backlash against the decision and to soften administration policy toward minorities, but left his position by 1983.

floors refinished and the office redecorated. As an observer suggested: "Bush is more into the elegance thing. He wanted to be closer to his staff and have the bigger office. He's really got the best of both worlds. He spends half of his day over in the White House and half in the EOB." A second outsider agreed. "I'm not sure where Bush fits in the equation. He doesn't have a very firm agenda and has never shown much interest in domestic affairs. He doesn't seem comfortable with White House power politics. He loves that office over in the EOB. It may be like being in Baltimore, as Mondale used to say, but Bush likes it anyway. He wanted to redo the floors, bring in his Oriental carpets and make it a home." However, as Bush explained: "I think when I bring interesting people over there [to the EOB], just by osmosis it makes my staff feel a part of things more. . . . And I don't feel threatened by being away from the White House for a few hours. I don't feel that anyone is trying to get me. . . . So I don't feel I have to wait on the edge of my chair for someone to come in and clue me in on something" (*Washington Post*, 30 Mar. 1981). Part of Bush's security, of course, came from James Baker. As one of Reagan's triumvirate of policy advisers, Baker acted as a key conduit for information to and from the Vice-President in the first year. Though Bush's own staff was not as tightly integrated into the White House as Mondale's staff, Baker was particularly valuable to Bush's advisory role. Moreover, as a Bush assistant remarked: "The West Wing office is important—it's nice sitting there and it's politically prestigious. But Mondale's staff was somewhat isolated in the EOB, cut off from Mondale. They spent a lot of time camping out in the West Wing. Bush likes to spend more time over in the EOB for that reason. Mondale felt that once he got that office, it was 'use it or lose it.' It is vastly overrated."

Bush's office was not designed to provide extensive policy networks inside the White House. Though the staff certainly had more contact with the Reagan operation than the Rockefeller staff had with the Ford team, the Bush office was more of a distinct unit than Mondale's office had been. The loss of the agenda-setting process was a major step in reducing vice-presidential staff access to the policy process. Unlike the Mondale staff, Bush's office was not engaged in administration-wide contact on a policy level. They were not involved in canvassing for ideas nor were they involved in the assignment of priorities to presidential programs. Beyond Baker, there were few contacts at the staff level. Bush's domestic policy staff, for example, was limited by David Stockman's early take-over of Reagan's domestic policy process. Martin Anderson, Reagan's early domestic adviser, was never fully integrated into the policy system, having lost his territory to the more aggressive OMB director. With Anderson's own access in doubt, Bush's domestic policy staff had few channels for input. Unlike Eizenstat's system, which gave ample opportunity to the Mondale staff, Stockman's process worked against the Vice-President's office. Stockman had little patience for talking to cabinet members, let alone vice-presidential aides.

This is not to argue that Bush was effectively isolated. Bush had considerable support in the southeast corner of the West Wing. Both Baker and David Gergen, director of White House communications, were allies. However, at the staff level, Bush did not have the same degree of integration as Mondale. Though the Reagan and Bush campaign staffs shared the same headquarters in Arlington, Virginia, there was a residue of past conflict between the two teams. "Bush and his staff made some pretty nasty comments about Reagan and the overall intelligence of his people during the primaries," a reporter suggested. "Sure they try to forget, but this city is good at keeping things on the front burner. Take 'voodoo economics' as an example."

Advisory Resources

With the West Wing office and access to the President's paper loop, Bush was able to secure many of the same advisory resources that Mondale received. Bush had plenty of time to develop his working relationships in the postelection transition and had as much energy as any of his recent colleagues, excluding Humphrey. With a full complement of policy advisers and his own experience in foreign affairs, Bush had fair levels of information on the policy issues, the scheduling of meetings, and his potential opposition. With James Baker at the top of the Reagan staff system, Bush had full access to internal information. He also became the second Vice-President to receive the President's Daily Briefing in national security. As a Bush aide argued:

> It is certainly true that Bush is involved. I never fail to give praise to the Mondale people about it. Reagan and Bush picked up on the same agreement as Carter and Mondale. West Wing office, the President's schedule, all the paper. Every day we get the President's schedule and Bush picks the meetings he wants to attend. His scheduling person gets together with Reagan's and they work things out. Bush spends the major part of every day with Reagan. The most the Vice-President can hope to be is a senior adviser to the President, and that is exactly what George Bush is.

However, though Bush did have experience in foreign affairs, his political career had consisted of short-term, not long-term, assignments. He had served as ambassador to the UN, CIA director, and envoy to China, but all three positions had averaged just over a year. He served two terms in the House of Representatives, but had less than eight years of total government experience. Moreover, unlike Mondale who had considerable domestic policy expertise, Bush had specialized in foreign affairs. At least in the first two years of the Reagan administration, it was domestic policy that offered the Vice-President the maximum opportunities for influence. With the natural tensions between the National Security Adviser and the State Department, foreign affairs had much higher conflict potential. Bush did gain proximity to the policy process in his first two years. His West Wing office and the weekly one-on-one meetings with Reagan provided the necessary access. Like Mondale, Bush had an open invitation to attend all meetings. Like Mondale, he used that invitation sparingly.

If Bush had a problem with respect to his early advisory resources, it was Reagan's willingness to listen. As James Baker argued: "Everyone knows the President didn't want to pick Bush. . . . There was absolutely no understanding between them of what Bush's role would be" (*Washington Post*, 30 Mar. 1981). Though Reagan and Bush eventually built a working relationship, past campaign rhetoric had to be forgotten. As an observer noted: "Reagan had to forgive a lot to bring Bush into the White House. Bush had made all the normal attacks during the primaries and Reagan had been hurt. Before Bush could become comfortable in his meetings with Reagan, they had to get over any past animosity. That was actually done easier than you would have expected. Reagan is an easy person to get to know. So is Bush." By the end of the first six months, Bush was able to establish a rapport with Reagan. Whether Bush and Reagan became close friends remains in doubt. However, by the end of the first months, Bush had demonstrated his loyalty to the administration.

No event had a greater impact on Reagan's willingness to listen than the assassination attempt. Bush showed extreme caution in avoiding any suggestion that he was taking the reins of government from the wounded President. Instead of helicoptering to the White House south lawn after returning from Texas, Bush landed at the Vice-President's Naval Observatory residence, taking a limo down to the presidential compound. His demonstration of loyalty during that period increased his internal capital, while building Reagan's interest in listening to his advice. As Bush argued at the end of 1981, the key to his advisory role was "the development of a good confidential relationship with the president . . . in an environment where I feel perfectly free to discuss controversial things with him and give him my honest opinion and best judgement" (*Washington Post*, 20 Dec. 1981). When asked whether he had an opportunity to advise Reagan on Alexander Haig's 1981 China trip, Bush answered yes. "Well, who I talk to about what, again, is privileged. But I do feel that I know something about it and I've had plenty of opportunity to discuss my views with the President and the Secretary and others on that question. . . . The system works. You see people enough. The personal relations are good enough. . . . If I feel strongly about something, I get a chance to say it" (*National Journal*, 20 June 1981).

Influence

Bush's performance after the assassination attempt raised his stock inside the administration. As a Reagan aide noted: "Bush handled that period very gracefully. He never went into the Oval Office, never gave one hint that he was usurping the President. He won a lot of points among the conservatives, especially those who had opposed him in Detroit." Bush had built his internal capital by campaigning hard for the Reagan-Bush ticket in 1980. Like Mondale's, Bush's internal capital increased over the first year. However, Bush came under increasing fire as Reagan's economic program failed to produce immediate results. As conservatives searched for a scapegoat inside the administration, Bush was an attractive target. Like Rockefeller, Bush stood to the left of Reagan, who, in turn, stood to the left of his most intense party criticism. Moreover, once conservatives learned that James Baker was arguing for a reduction in the third year of Reagan's supply-side tax cut, criticism focused on the Bush-Baker connection. As Baker and Bush learned, however, regardless of the intensity of internal advice for a reduction of the tax cut, Reagan was not persuadable on the issue. Though Reagan was persuadable on the size and distribution of spending cuts in his second year, he was fully committed to the tax cut. Yet, as evidence of their influence, the fiscal moderates did gain Reagan's temporary support for a ninety-day delay in the date of the third-year cut, and eventually won a $99 billion tax increase.

Because of the restrictive nature of Reagan's policy agenda, Bush did not have as many opportunities for influence in his first two years as Mondale. The Reagan domestic agenda was drafted under David Stockman's supervision and moved quickly to Congress. As one observer said: "Bush was trying to prove his loyalty then. It wasn't a time for him to go to the mat with Stockman. Furthermore, I'm not sure he disagreed with that much in the budget. He didn't like the size of the tax cut, but it wasn't that hard to swallow." Bush did have more of an impact on Reagan's foreign policy agenda, arguing for movement toward a resumption of strategic arms talks. According to most observers, Bush decided very early to pursue a strategy of defense rather than offense. Because Reagan's policy agenda was limited to a very small number of proposals, Bush had few opportunities for offense.

Bush's influence strategy in the first two years focused on two basic approaches. First, Bush avoided any assignments that would place him in between other players. As a congressional observer argued: "Bush could have been most helpful in foreign affairs, but was afraid to intervene between the three prima donnas: Haig, William Casey, and Allen. Where the President needs the most help, Bush was the most frightened to intervene. He would have been cut to ribbons." The foreign policy vacuum was eventually filled when Allen resigned and was replaced by William Clark. As Bush argued:

> You see, I don't have any line authority except one or two things. I'm a statutory member of the National Security Council, so I have some responsibility there, but not the decision-making responsibility. There's obviously only one vote on the old NSC, and that's the President's. . . . I've got the Task Force on Regula-

tory Relief, which is probably the closest to where I have a line thing. . . . I did have fairly much of an activist role, you might say, in coordinating or helping pull things together on Atlanta. But that was because the President was very concerned and I just said, kind of, well maybe I can help on it (*National Journal*, 20 June 1981).

Second, Bush followed Mondale's advice to be discreet. As Bush noted: "You know, in the Vice-President's role, sometimes it is better to quietly express your differences to the President rather than to command attention at the Cabinet meeting or an NSC meeting. It is a question of style, because you don't want to be putting the President on the spot or make him choose between the Vice President and two Cabinet officers" (*National Journal*, 20 June 1981). Bush was willing to use Baker for hidden-hand influence, but refused to take visible positions on major policies. As one administration ally noted: "I don't have any doubt that George has a large influence in the counsels of the Reagan administration, but it is not a public process as far as he is concerned and his caution and circumspection are entirely appropriate when there are so many right-wing types yearning to isolate him from their hero."

Bush's major influence problem rested on the low level of internal capital at the point when the Reagan agenda was set. Among recent Presidents, Reagan was remarkably fast in forming his policy agenda. Unlike Carter, who took close to six months to move his first-year program to Congress (see Light, 1982a), Reagan's program had arrived in March. Moreover, because Reagan's agenda included only two major items in 1981 — the budget and tax cut — Bush had only limited opportunities to begin with. Unlike Carter, who sent a full legislative slate to Congress, Reagan decided to focus on two priorities. Though Reagan added to his agenda in 1981 and 1982, announcing a Caribbean Basin Initiative and support for Constitutional amendments to balance the budget and permit voluntary school prayer, Bush had few chances for offensive influence. Thus, Bush's major obstacles to influence did not come from resources or strategies, but from the absence of opportunities.

There are two lessons from this brief review of the Bush Vice-Presidency. First, the vice-presidential advisory role has continued into the Reagan administration. Though the role is now less than ten years old, it is established as part of the White House policy process. It is still difficult to conclude that these precedents have become merely habit. However, with each successive Vice-Presidency, it is harder for Presidents to retake the West Wing office or cut the staff budgets. Second, influence remains conditioned by factors that evolve with each new administration. Though the advisory role has become institutionalized, influence is never guaranteed.

Each Vice-President—indeed, each adviser—must fashion an influence strategy to fit unique circumstances. The strategies and opportunities that applied to the Carter White House changed with the Reagan administration. Vice-Presidents can minimize the traps in these shifting sands by entering office with persuasive skills and certain strategies, but they must be able to adapt to the natural life cycles of a presidential term.

THE VICE-PRESIDENT'S ROLE

The problem for Bush or any senior adviser is how to balance the benefits and costs of giving advice. Can the Vice-President disagree with the President? If so, when should the disagreement be voiced? How strong should the voice be? As Humphrey learned, disagreement in open forums carries high costs. After expressing his opposition to the bombing of North Vietnam in at least two National Security Council meetings, Humphrey also composed a long memorandum to the President. As Humphrey remembered: "No one ever said, 'You're out and here are the reasons why.' In the brief span of my vice presidency, I had spoken my mind on Vietnam only in the councils of government, yet the President, in addition, apparently thought I had leaked something about the meetings. I had not, but that became irrelevant" (1976, p. 325). As a Ford aide acknowledged in 1974: "If the Vice President is a Charlie McCarthy, he isn't worth a plug nickle. . . . Ford has an independent streak—it's real and unaffected—which serves his interest and the President's, *just as long as he is fundamentally in support of the President*" (in *National Journal*, 10 Aug. 1974). Yet, when Reagan and Ford discussed the Vice-Presidency in 1980, Ford refused the job unless there were written guarantees, perhaps even a Constitutional amendment to formalize an advisory role as deputy President for foreign affairs.

For Vice-Presidents, as for other White House advisers, there are often high risks associated with outright opposition to the President and staff, or open dissatisfaction with policies. Because they have limited capital, Vice-Presidents do not have the option of "exit." They cannot leave their positions as a protest against presidential policy. This is not to suggest that Vice-Presidents cannot disagree. As Mondale remembered, he disagreed with Carter on "some farm price support matters and later on the minimum wage issue. On some budgetary matters, I made it clear I had some differences. In most instances, I must say the way it worked out was one I could fully support" (*National Journal*, 1 Dec. 1979). Rather, Vice-Presidents and other advisers remain dependent on the President for their daily support. As one presidential aide acknowledged: "You're always more successful if your positions agree with the President going in. Presidents can get very tight if you cross them, especially by going outside with your opinions." Yet, by not going public, Vice-Presidents and other advisers deprive the public of a full and open debate of the issues. Perhaps Humphrey should have made his arguments in public. Since Johnson already suspected Humphrey of disloyalty, why not take the issue outside the White House?

We inevitably return to the question of influence strategies. Should an adviser remain quiet on one issue to preserve some level of influence for the future? Should an adviser go public on issues of national importance? How might an adviser weigh the significance of one issue versus another? For most Vice-Presidents and White House aides, the choice usually falls to the preservation of influence for the future. Whether or not Humphrey deceived himself, at least one aide suggested that the Vice-President believed he could win at some later point in the term. "Humphrey thought that Johnson would turn to him sooner or later, that he'd realize the mistake after a period of time. Eventually, he did come to see the need for de-escalation, particularly after Clark Clifford became involved. But Johnson never did come back to Humphrey. He had convinced himself that Humphrey was not trustworthy and that was it. Humphrey would have been more effective in the Senate." Yet, Humphrey's problem was not in his willingness to voice his opposition to the bombing decision, but in Johnson's unwillingness to listen. The value of dissent rests on the President's willingness to listen, not the Vice-President's ability to talk. Though Vice-Presidents can adapt to changing circumstances, the ultimate problem always rests with the President's belief and style. If voters do not elect a President who will listen to his chosen people, no amount of vice-presidential maneuvering will matter.

PRESIDENT MONDALE/PRESIDENT BUSH?

At the start of Mondale's long run for the 1984 Democratic nomination, he made frequent reference to his days as Vice-President. In a typical quote, Mondale told one reporter: "I learned in a way I could not have learned any other way, my sense of confidence and my ability to be President, to shape a government, where the talent is, how the Presidency works, my knowledge of adversaries as well as friends, my experience in international relations, dealing with intelligence problems and defense problems and Congress—all of that has been possible because I was Vice President" (*New Republic,* 4 April 1983). Though Mondale also told of his disagreements with Carter—trying to distance himself from his former administration—he still valued the entry on his political résumé.

Yet, the critical question is whether Vice-Presidents are somehow more qualified to become Presidents on experience alone. Was Mondale's service in the nation's second highest office enough to qualify him for the first? Mondale was certainly correct to emphasize his new-found understanding of the Presidency. He did know more about the issues that flow through the White House. He did know more about the bureaucratic infighting. He did know where the buttons were (unless, of course, Reagan moved them). But did Mondale know any more about what it was like being President? Could anyone know Carter's frustrations and fears? Though Mondale certainly watched as Carter made very difficult decisions—sending a rescue team into Iran, for example—he could not know the pressures of command. He did not make the final decisions.

The problem is not just with Vice-Presidents. The American political system demands a great deal from Presidents. We ask for the toughness to make decisions against the grain of public opinion, the compassion to recognize and treat national needs, the intelligence to analyze complex issues, the wisdom to set priorities among the myriad of problems that arise, and the stamina to last four years in a political pressure cooker. Whether Vice-Presidents, or any politicians for that matter, can prepare for the intensity of the Presidency is doubtful. At most, a candidate can learn as much as possible about the policy issues and organizational pressures beforehand. To that extent, Mondale and Bush were both well-schooled to enter the Presidency. They both gained considerable exposure to the national policy agenda and understood the problems of White House politics. Whether that alone qualified them over potential competitors is again doubtful. Both could start their terms with an advantage over outsiders, particularly governors, but without any magical gift at command decisions. The Vice-Presidency cannot create toughness, compassion, intelligence, wisdom, and stamina where none existed before. Former Vice-Presidents must be cautious in claiming too much on the campaign trail lest we ask just how much the job did to qualify Spiro Agnew for higher office.

Appendix

Organization of the Vice-President's Office

Source: Adapted from *National Journal,* 10 August 1974.

THE PERSONAL ASSISTANT
TO THE VICE-PRESIDENT

THE EXECUTIVE DIRECTOR OF THE
DOMESTIC COUNCIL COMMITTEE
ON THE RIGHT OF PRIVACY

THE PRESS SECRETARY TO THE
VICE-PRESIDENT AS ASSIGNED

THE LEGAL COUNSEL TO THE
VICE-PRESIDENT, AS HIS ATTORNEY

THE ASSISTANT TO THE
PRESIDENT OF THE SENATE IN THE
SENATE

THE MILITARY AIDE TO THE
VICE-PRESIDENT

THE
VICE-PRESIDENT
OF THE
UNITED STATES

THE CHIEF OF STAFF
TO THE VICE-PRESIDENT

THE PERSONAL STAFF OF
THE VICE-PRESIDENT
OVERALL STAFF SUPERVISION

GOVERNMENTAL AND POLITICAL
LIAISON AS ASSIGNED

EDITORIAL OVERSIGHT

THE ASSISTANT TO THE VICE-
PRESIDENT FOR LEGISLATION
AND DOMESTIC AFFAIRS

EXECUTIVE BRANCH
LIAISON

SENATE LIAISON

HOUSE OF
REPRESENTATIVES
LIAISON

STATE AND LOCAL
GOVERNMENTS
LIAISON

THE ASSISTANT TO THE VICE-
PRESIDENT FOR ADMINISTRATION
AND SERVICES

SCHEDULING
AND APPOINTMENTS

ADMINISTRATION

RESEARCH

MEDIA AFFAIRS

NON-GOVERNMENTAL
ORGANIZATIONS

THE ASSISTANT TO THE VICE-
PRESIDENT FOR DEFENSE AND
INTERNATIONAL AFFAIRS

MILITARY ASSISTANTS

LIAISON
WITH THE
STATE DEPARTMENT

VIP TRAVEL

273

References

Adams, C. F., ed. 1850-56. *The Works of John Adams.* 10 Vol. Boston: Little, Brown.

Anderson, M. 1978. *Welfare: The Political Economy of Welfare Reform in the United States.* Palo Alto: Hoover Institution Press.

Barber, J. D. 1971. "The Interplay of Presidential Character and Style." In *A Source Book for the Study of Personality and Politics,* edited by F. I. Greenstein and M. Lerner. Chicago: Markham.

Barkley, A. 1954. *That Reminds Me.* New York: Doubleday.

Bell, G. B., with Ostrow, R. J. 1982. *Taking Care of the Law.* New York: Morrow.

Crenson, M. A. 1971. *The Un-Politics of Air Pollution: A Study of Non-Decisionmaking in the Cities.* Baltimore: Johns Hopkins University Press.

Cronin, T. E. 1975. *The State of the Presidency.* Boston: Little, Brown.

Davis, E. L. 1979. "Legislative Liaison in the Carter Administration," *Political Science Quarterly* 95:287-302.

Ehrlichman, J. 1982. *Witness to Power.* New York: Simon and Schuster.

Evans, R., and Novak, R. 1966. *Lyndon Baines Johnson: The Exercise of Power.* New York: New American Library.

Fallows, J. 1979. "The Passionless Presidency." *Atlantic* 5:33-48.

Fenno, R. F. 1959. *The President's Cabinet.* Cambridge, Mass.: Harvard University Press.

Ford, G. R. 1974. "On the Threshold of the White House." *Atlantic Monthly* 234:63-65.

_____. 1979. *A Time to Heal.* New York: Harper and Row.

George, A. L. 1980. *Presidential Decisionmaking in Foreign Policy.* Boulder, Col.: Westview.

Goldstein, J. K. 1982. *The Modern American Vice Presidency.* Princeton, N. J.: Princeton University Press.

Graham, D. 1974. "The Vice Presidency: From Cigar Store Indian to Crown Prince." *Washington Monthly* 6:41-44.

Greenstein, F. I. 1979. "Eisenhower as an Activist President." *Political Science Quarterly* 94:575-600.

Greider, W. 1981. "The Education of David Stockman." *Atlantic.* 6:27-54.

Hartmann, R. T. 1980. *Palace Politics: An Inside Account of the Ford Years.* New York: McGraw-Hill.

Hinckley, B. 1981. *Outline of American Government.* Englewood Cliffs, N. J.: Prentice-Hall.

Humphrey, H. H. 1976. *The Education of a Public Man.* New York: Doubleday.

──────. 1974. "On the Threshold of the White House." *Atlantic Monthly* 234:65-67.

Kearns, D. 1976. *Lyndon Johnson and the American Dream.* New York: Harper and Row.

Kernell, S. 1978. "Explaining Presidential Popularity." *American Political Science Review* 72:506-22.

──────. 1975. *The Domestic Presidency.* Brunswick, Ohio: Duxbury.

Kessel, J. H. 1975. *The Domestic Presidency.* Boston: Duxbury Press.

──────. 1982. "The Structures of the Carter White House." Paper delivered at the Annual Meetings of the American Political Science Association, Presidency Research Group, Denver, Col.

King, A. 1978. "The American Policy in the Late 1970s." In *The New American Political System,* edited by A. King. Washington: American Enterprise Institute.

Kingdon, J. W. 1983. *Pre-Decision Public Policy Processes.* Boston: Little, Brown, forthcoming.

Lewis, F. 1980. *Mondale: Portrait of an American Politician.* New York: Harper and Row.

Light, P. C. 1982a. "Passing Nonincremental Policy: Presidential Influence in Congress." *Journal of Congress and the Presidency* 9:61-82.

──────. 1982b. *The President's Agenda.* Baltimore: Johns Hopkins University Press.

Miller, M. 1980. *Lyndon: An Oral Biography.* New York: Putnam.

Neustadt, R. E. 1960; 1980. *Presidential Power.* 1st ed.; 3rd ed. New York: John Wiley.

Persico, J. E. 1982. *The Imperial Rockefeller.* New York: Simon and Schuster.

Porter, R. 1980. *Presidential Decision Making: The Economic Policy Board.* New York: Cambridge University Press.

Reichley, A. J. 1981. *Conservatives in an Age of Change.* Washington, D.C.: Brookings Institution.

Rockman, B. A. 1981. "America's Departments of State: Irregular and Regular Syndromes of Policy Making." *American Political Science Review* 75:911-27.

Schattschneider, E. E. 1960. *The Semi-Sovereign People.* New York: Holt, Rinehart and Winston.

Schlesinger, A. M., Jr. 1974. "On the Presidential Succession." *Political Science Quarterly* 89:475-505.

Shogan, R. 1977. *Promises to Keep: Carter's First Hundred Days.* New York: Thomas Crowell.

Shull, S. A. 1979. *Presidential Policy Making.* New Brunswick, Ohio: King's Court.

Sperlich, P. W. 1975. "Bargaining and Overload: An Essay on *Presidential Power.*" In *Perspectives on the Presidency,* edited by A. Wildavsky. Boston: Little, Brown.

Thomas, N. C., and Wolman, H. L. 1969. "Policy Formulation in the Institutionalized Presidency: The Johnson Task Forces." In *The Presidential Advisory System,* edited by T. E. Cronin and S. D. Greenberg. New York: Harper and Row.

Turner, M. 1978. *Finding a Policy Role for the Vice President: The Case of Nelson A. Rockefeller.* Ann Arbor, Mich.: University Microfilms.

Valenti, J. 1975. *A Very Human President.* New York: Norton.

Young, D. 1972. *American Roulette: The History and Dilemma of the Vice Presidency.* 2d ed. New York: Holt, Rinehart and Winston.

Index

The Johns Hopkins University Press

VICE-PRESIDENTIAL POWER

This book was composed in Baskerville Alphatype
by David Lorton from a design by Gerard A. Valerio.
It was printed on 50-lb. Warren's Sebago paper and bound
in Holliston Kingston cloth by the Maple Press Company.